Rick Steves'
FRANCE
BELGIUM & THE NETHERLANDS
1999

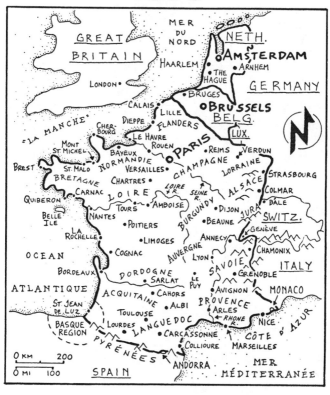

Rick Steves and Steve Smith

John Muir Publications
Santa Fe, New Mexico

Other JMP travel guidebooks by Rick Steves
Rick Steves' Europe Through the Back Door
Europe 101: History and Art for the Traveler (with Gene Openshaw)
Rick Steves' Postcards from Europe
Rick Steves' Mona Winks: Self-Guided Tours of Europe's Top Museums
      (with Gene Openshaw)
Rick Steves' Best of Europe
Rick Steves' Germany, Austria & Switzerland
Rick Steves' Great Britain & Ireland
Rick Steves' Italy
Rick Steves' Russia & the Baltics (with Ian Watson)
Rick Steves' Scandinavia
Rick Steves' Spain & Portugal
Rick Steves' London (with Gene Openshaw)
Rick Steves' Paris (with Gene Openshaw and Steve Smith)
Rick Steves' Phrase Books: German, French, Italian,
      Spanish/Portuguese, and French/Italian/German
Asia Through the Back Door (with Bob Effertz)

Thanks to Steve's wife, Karen Lewis, for her help on covering the cuisine of France.

John Muir Publications, P.O. Box 613, Santa Fe, NM 87504
Copyright © 1999, 1998, 1997, 1996, 1995 by Rick Steves and Steve Smith
Cover copyright © 1999 by John Muir Publications
All rights reserved.

Printed in the United States of America
First printing January 1999

For the latest on Rick's lectures, guidebooks, tours, and public television series, contact Europe Through the Back Door, Box 2009, Edmonds, WA 98020, tel. 425/771-8303, fax 425/771-0833, Web site: www.ricksteves .com, or e-mail: rick@ricksteves.com.

ISSN 1084-4406
ISBN 1-56261-462-2

Europe Through the Back Door Editor Risa Laib
John Muir Publications Editors Krista Lyons-Gould, Jill Metzler,
      Chris Hayhurst
Research in Low Countries Brian Carr Smith
Production Marie J.T. Vigil, Rebecca Cook
Design Linda Braun
Cover Design Janine Lehmann
Maps David C. Hoerlein
Printer Banta Company
Cover Photo Arc d' Triomphe, Paris, France; © Jeff Greenberg/Unicorn
      Stock Photos

Distributed to the book trade by
Publishers Group West
Berkeley, California

CONTENTS

Top Destinations in France, Belgium, and the Netherlands

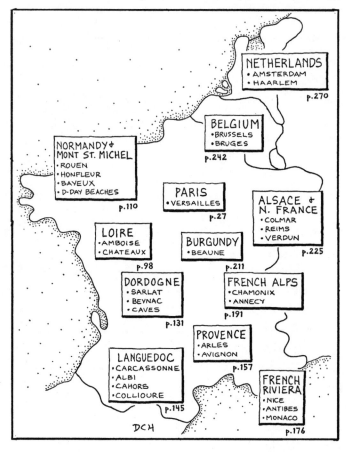

INTRODUCTION

Our compliments. You've made a great choice. France is Europe's most diverse, tasty, and, in many ways, exciting country to explore. And for extra travel thrills, this book takes you north through the best of Belgium and the Netherlands.

France is as big as Texas, with 58 million people and 460 different cheeses. *Diversité* is a French *forté:* this country features three distinct mountain ranges (the Alps, Pyrénées, and Massif Central), remarkably different Atlantic and Mediterranean coastlines, cosmopolitan cities, and sleepy villages. From its Swisslike Alps to its Italianesque Riviera, and from the Spanish Pyrénées to das German Alsace, you can stay in France, feel like you've sampled much of Europe, and never be more than a short stroll from a good *vin rouge*.

Belgium and the Netherlands, called the Low Countries (because nearly half the land is below sea level), are easy to overlook, surrounded by mega-Europe. We've spliced these into our France guide so that your memories can include some Bruges lace, Belgian waffles, a dike hike, and a few Dutch masters. If ever an area was a travel cliché come true, it's the Low Countries.

After years of researching and tour guiding together, Rick Steves has teamed up with Francophile Steve Smith to write this book. Together we give you the region's top destinations and tips on how to use your time and money most efficiently. France, Belgium, and the Netherlands are a many-faceted cultural fondue. Each of our recommended destinations is a dripping forkful (complete with instructions to enjoy the full flavor without burning your tongue).

This book covers the predictable biggies and mixes in a healthy dose of "Back Door" intimacy. Along with the Eiffel Tower, Mont St. Michel, and the French Riviera, you'll take a bike tour of the Loire, marvel at 15,000-year-old cave paintings, and walk the walls of a medieval fortress city. You'll find a *magnifique* castle perch to catch a Dordogne Valley sunset, ride Europe's highest mountain lift, and touch the quiet Romanesque soul of village Burgundy.

Rick Steves' France, Belgium & the Netherlands is a tour guide in your pocket—actually, two tour guides in your pocket. Places covered are balanced to include the most famous cities and intimate villages, from jet-setting beach resorts to the traditional heartland. We've been very selective, including only the most exciting sights. For example, there are *beaucoup* beautiful châteaus surrounding the Loire. We recommend the best three. The best is, of course, only our opinion. But after 25 busy years of travel writing, lecturing, tour guiding, and Francophilia between us, we've developed a sixth sense for what tickles the traveler's fancy.

This Information Is Accurate and Up-to-Date

This book is updated every year. Most publishers of guidebooks that cover a region from top to bottom can afford an update only every two or three years (and even then it's often by letter). Since this book is selective, covering only the places we think make the top month of sightseeing, we can update it each summer. Even with an annual update, things change. But if you're traveling with the current edition of this book, we guarantee you're using the most up-to-date information available. This book will help you have an inexpensive, hassle-free trip. *Use this year's edition.* Saving a few bucks by traveling on old information is not smart. If you're packing an old book, you'll learn the seriousness of your mistake . . . in Europe. Your trip costs at least $10 per waking hour. Your time is valuable. This guidebook saves lots of time.

Planning Your Trip

This book is organized by destinations. Each of these destinations is a mini-vacation on its own, filled with exciting sights and homey, affordable places to stay. For each chapter, you'll find:

Planning Your Time, a suggested schedule with thoughts on how to best use your limited time.

Orientation material, including tourist information, city transportation, and an easy-to-read map designed to make the text clear and your arrival smooth.

Sights with ratings: ▲▲▲—Don't miss; ▲▲—Try hard to see; ▲—Worthwhile if you can make it; No rating—Worth knowing about.

Sleeping and **Eating**, with addresses and phone numbers of our favorite budget hotels and restaurants.

And **Transportation Connections** to nearby destinations by train and route tips for drivers.

The handy Appendix includes a climate chart, campground listings, telephone tips, and French survival phrases.

Browse through this book, choose your favorite destinations, and link them up. You'll travel like a temporary local, getting the absolute most out of every mile, minute, and dollar. You won't waste time on mediocre sights because, unlike other guidebooks, we cover only the best. Since your major financial pitfall is lousy, expensive hotels, we've worked hard to assemble the best accommodations values for each stop. As you travel the route we know and love, we're happy you'll be meeting some of our favorite European people.

Trip Costs

Five components make up your total trip cost: airfare, surface transportation, room and board, sightseeing/entertainment and shopping/miscellany.

Airfare: Don't try to sort through the mess. Find and use a good travel agent. A basic round-trip United States-to-Paris flight costs $700 to $1,100, depending on where you fly from and when. Always consider saving time and money in Europe by flying "open jaws" (into one city and out of another). Flying into Amsterdam and out of Paris costs roughly the same as flying round-trip to Paris. You can get cheaper round-trip flights to London or Amsterdam, but the cost of additional train tickets (to get you back to London or Amsterdam for your flight home) will eliminate most of your savings.

Surface Transportation: For a three-week whirlwind trip of our recommended destinations in France, allow $500 per person for public transportation (trains and key buses), or $650 per person (based on two people sharing) for a three-week car rental, tolls, gas, and insurance. Car rental is cheapest if arranged from the United States. Train passes are normally available only outside of Europe. You may save money by simply buying tickets as you go (see Transportation, below).

Room and Board: You can thrive in France and the Low Countries on $60 a day per person for room and board. With good information, even Paris is affordable. A $60-a-day budget allows $10 for lunch, $15 for dinner, and $35 for lodging (based on two people splitting the cost of a $70 double room that includes breakfast). That's doable. Students and tightwads do it on $40 ($20 per bed, $15–20 for meals and snacks). But budget sleeping and eating require the skills and information covered later in this chapter (and in far more depth in *Rick Steves' Europe Through the Back Door*).

Sightseeing and Entertainment: In big cities, figure $5 to $8 per major sight (Louvre-$8, Anne Frank House-$6), $2 for minor ones (climbing church towers), $10 for guided walks, and $25 for bus tours and splurge experiences (concerts in Paris' Sainte-Chapelle or the Chamonix gondola). An overall average of $15 a day works for most. Don't skimp here. After all, this category directly powers most of the experiences all the other expenses are designed to make possible.

Shopping and Miscellany: Figure $2 per ice-cream cone, coffee, or soft drink. Shopping can vary in cost from nearly nothing to a small fortune. Good budget travelers find that this category has little to do with assembling a trip full of life-long and wonderful memories.

Prices, Times, and Discounts
The prices in this book, as well as the hours and telephone numbers, are accurate as of late 1998. Europe is always changing, and we know you'll understand that this, like any other guidebook, starts to yellow even before it's printed.

In Europe—and in this book—you'll be using the 24-hour

clock. After 12:00 noon, keep going—13:00, 14:00, and so on. For anything over 12, subtract 12 and add p.m. (for example, 14:00 is 2 p.m.).

This book lists spring and fall hours for sightseeing attractions. Off-season, expect generally shorter hours and more lunchtime breaks.

While discounts for sights and transportation are not listed in this book, seniors (60 and over), students (with International Student Identification Cards), and youths (under 18) often get big discounts—but only by asking.

Exchange Rates
We've priced things in this book in the local currency:

5.5 French francs (F) = about $1
33 Belgian francs (BF) = about $1
1 Dutch guilder (f) = about 60 cents

To roughly convert prices into dollars: divide French prices by 5; drop the last zero off Belgian prices and divide by 3; and divide Dutch prices by 2.

When to Go
Late spring and fall are best. Wildflowers proliferate in May and June, while September brings the grape harvest and drier weather. In late October France glistens in fall colors. Europeans vacation in July and August, jamming the Riviera and the Alps (August is worst), leaving the rest of the country reasonably tranquil. And while many French businesses close in August, the traveler hardly notices. Winter travel is OK—you'll find gray, generally mild weather in the south (unless the wind is blowing), cold weather in the north, and rain everywhere. While Holland is a festival of flowers in the spring, the Low Countries have considerably shorter summers and drearier winters than southern France. Sights and tourist-information offices keep shorter hours, and some tourist activities (like English-language castle tours) vanish altogether.

Sightseeing Priorities
Depending on the length of your trip, here are our recommended priorities. The material in this book could keep you wonderfully entertained for a month in France, Belgium, and the Netherlands.

France:

3 days:	Paris and maybe Versailles
5 days, add:	Normandy
7 days, add:	Loire

10 days, add: Dordogne, Carcassonne
14 days, add: Provence, Riviera
18 days, add: Burgundy, Chamonix
21 days, add: Alsace, Champagne

(This includes everything on the following three-week route to match the map on page 7.)

Belgium and the Netherlands: With cheap flights from the United States, minimal culture shock, almost no language barrier, and a super-well-organized tourist trade, the Low Countries are a good place to start a European trip.

     2 days: Amsterdam, Haarlem
3–4 days, add: Bruges
5–6 days, add: Brussels
     7 days, add: Side trips from Amsterdam (e.g., Arnhem)

Whirlwind (Kamikaze) Three-Week Tour of France by Car

Day Plan

1   Fly into Paris, pick up car, visit Giverny and/or Rouen, overnight in Honfleur (save Paris sightseeing for end of trip).

2   9:00–Depart Honfleur, 10:00–Caen WWII Museum, 12:00–Drive to Arromanches for lunch and museum, 15:00–American cemetery, 16:00–Point du Hoc, 17:00–German cemetery, dinner and overnight in Bayeux.

3   9:00–Bayeux tapestry and church, 13:30–Mont St. Michel, 16:00–Drive to Dinan, 17:00–Arrive in Dinan for one Brittany stop, sleep in Dinan.

4   10:00–Depart Dinan and drive to Loire, 14:00–Tour Chambord, 17:00–Arrive in Amboise, sleep in Amboise.

5   8:45–Depart, 9:00–Chenonceaux, 11:30–Cheverny château and lunch, 14:00–Possible stop in Chaumont, back in Amboise for Leonardo's house and free time in town, sleep in Amboise.

6   8:30–Depart, morning stop in Chauvingy, lunch at Mortemart, 13:30–Oradour-sur-Glane, 14:30–Drive to Beynac, 17:30–Wander Beynac, or tour its castle, dinner and overnight in Beynac.

7   9:00–Browse the town and market of Sarlat, 12:00–Font de Gaume tour, 14:00–More caves, castles or canoe extravaganza, dinner and sleep in Beynac.

8   9:00–Depart Beynac, 10:00–Short stop at Cahors bridge, 12:30–Arrive Albi, couscous lunch, 14:00–Tour church and Toulouse-Lautrec Museum, 16:00–Depart for Carcassonne, 18:00–Explore, have dinner, and sleep in Carcassonne.

9   10:30–Depart, 11:00–Lastours castles or Minerve,

15:30–Pont du Gard, 16:30–Drive to Arles, 17:30–Set up for evening in Arles.

10   All day for Arles and Avignon, evening back in Arles.

11   8:30–Depart, 9:00–Les Baux, 11:00–Depart, 12:00–Lunch and wander in Isle sur la Sorgue, 14:00–Luberon hilltown drive, 16:00–Depart for Riviera, 19:00–Arrive Nice or Antibes.

12   Sightsee in Nice and Monaco, sleep in Nice or Antibes.

13   Morning free, 12:00–Drive north, sleep at Clelles.

14   Morning drive north, long stop in Annecy, afternoon arrive in Chamonix. With clear weather do Aiguille du Midi.

15   All day for Alps.

16   9:00–Depart, 12:00–Lunch in Brancion, 14:00–Depart, 15:00–Arrive in Beaune for Hotel Dieu and wine tasting, sleep in Beaune.

17   9:00–Depart for Burgundy village treats or get to Alsace early. Arrive in Colmar after 3.5-hour drive.

18   9:00–Unterlinden Museum, 10:00–Free in town, 14:00–Wine Road villages, evening back in Colmar.

19   8:00–Depart, 12:00–Lunch, tour Verdun battlefield, 15:00–Depart, 16:00–Arrive Reims, church and champagne, 18:00–Turn in car at Reims, picnic dinner celebration on train, 21:00–Collapse in Paris hotel.

20   Sightsee Paris.

21   Sightsee Paris, tour over.

Red Tape and Business Hours

You need a passport but no visa or shots to travel in France, Belgium, and the Netherlands.

You'll find much of rural France closed from 12:00 to 14:00. Lunch is sacred. On Mondays many businesses are closed until 14:00, and often all day. Many small markets, *boulangeries* (bakeries), and the like are open Sunday morning until 12:00. Beware: Many sights stop admitting people 30 to 60 minutes before they close.

PTT (Postal, Telegraph, and Telephone) offices' hours vary, though most are open from 8:00 to 19:00 weekdays and 8:00 to 12:00 Saturday. (Small-town PTTs close for lunch 12:00–14:00.) Stamps are also sold at the *tabac* (tobacco shop).

Banking

Bring your ATM, credit, or debit card, along with traveler's checks in dollars.

The best and easiest way to get cash in French francs is to use the omnipresent French bank machines (always open, lower fees, quick processing); you'll need a four-digit PIN (numbers only, no letters) with your Visa or MasterCard. Some ATM bankcards will work at some banks, though Visa and MasterCard are more reli-

Whirlwind Three-Week Tour of France

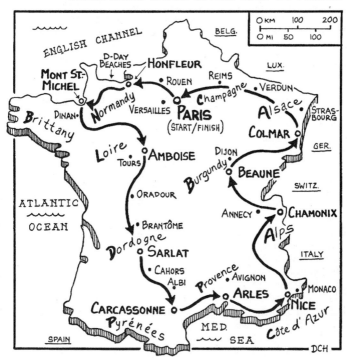

able. Before you go, verify with your bank that your card will
work. Bring two cards; demagnetization seems to be a common
problem. "Cash machine" in French is "*distributeur automatique des
billets*," or *D.A.B.* (day-ah-bay).

Regular banks have the best rates for cashing traveler's
checks. For a large exchange it pays to compare rates and fees.
The Bank of France (Banque de France) offers the best rates but is
generally located only in larger cities. French banking hours vary,
though most are open from 9:00 to 16:30 Tuesday through Friday.
Some branches open Saturday morning, and many close on Monday. Post offices, train stations, and tourist offices usually change
money if you can't get to a bank. Post offices (which take cash or
American Express traveler's checks) give a fair rate, have longer
hours, and charge no fee. Don't be petty about changing traveler's
checks. The greatest avoidable money-changing expense is having
to waste time every few days returning to a bank. Change 10 days'
or two weeks' worth of money, get big bills, stuff them in your
money belt, and travel!

Just like at home, credit (or debit) cards work easily at hotels, restaurants, and shops, but small businesses (like bed-and-breakfasts) accept payment only in local currency. Smart travelers function with hard local cash.

The Language Barrier

You've no doubt heard that the French are "mean and cold and refuse to speak English." This is an out-of-date preconception left over from the de Gaulle days. The French are as friendly as any other people. Parisians are no more disagreeable than New Yorkers. And, without any doubt, the French speak more English than Americans speak French. Be reasonable in your expectations: Waiters are paid to be efficient, not chatty. And small-town French postal clerks are every bit as speedy, cheery, and multilingual as ours are back home.

With an understanding of French culture, you're less likely to misinterpret the French people. The French take great pride in their culture, clinging to their belief in cultural superiority despite the fact that they're no longer a world superpower. Let's face it, it's tough to keep on smiling when you've been crushed by a Big Mac, lashed by Levis, and drowned in instant coffee. To the French, America must seem a lot like Ross Perot in a good mood. The French are cold only if you decide to see them that way. Polite and formal, they respect the fine points of culture. In France, strolling down the street with a big grin on your face is a sign of senility, not friendliness (seriously). The French think that Americans, while friendly, are hesitant to pursue more serious friendships. Recognize sincerity and look for kindness. Give the French the benefit of the doubt.

Communication difficulties in France are exaggerated. To hurdle the language barrier, bring a small English/French dictionary, a phrase book (look for ours), a menu reader, and a good supply of patience. If you learn only five phrases, learn and use these: *bonjour* (good day), *pardon* (pardon me), *s'il vous plaît* (please), *merci* (thank you), and *au revoir* (goodbye). The French place great importance on politeness.

The French are language perfectionists—they take their language (and other languages) seriously. Often they speak more English than they let on. This isn't a tourist-baiting tactic but timidity on their part to speak another language less than fluently. Start any conversation with *"Bonjour, madame/monsieur. Parlez-vous anglais?"* and hope they speak more English than you speak French. In transactions, a small notepad and pen minimize misunderstandings about prices—have vendors write the price down.

In Belgium and the Netherlands, forget the language barrier. Except in smaller untouristy towns, most young or well-educated people speak English (along with other languages). In southern

Belgium, French is foremost; in northern Belgium and the Netherlands it's Dutch, but English is a close second.

Travel Smart

Upon arrival in a new town, lay the groundwork for a smooth departure. Reread this book as you travel, and visit local tourist information offices. Buy a phone card and use it for reservations and confirmations. Enjoy the friendliness of the local people. Ask questions. Most locals are eager to tell you about their town's history and point you in their idea of the right direction. Wear your money belt, pack a pocket-size notepad to organize your thoughts, and see simplicity as a virtue. Those who expect to travel smart, do. Plan ahead for banking, laundry, post office chores, and picnics. Maximize rootedness by minimizing one-night stands. Mix intense and relaxed periods. Every trip (and every traveler) needs at least a few slack days. Pace yourself. Assume you will return.

As you read through this book, note special days (festivals, market days, and days when sights are closed). Sundays have pros and cons, as they do for travelers in the United States (special events and weekly markets, limited hours, shops and banks closed, limited public transportation, no rush hours). Saturdays are virtually weekdays (with most places open until lunchtime). Popular places are even more popular on weekends and inundated on three-day weekends (most common in May).

Tourist Information

The tourist information office is your best first stop in any new city. If you're arriving in town after the office closes, try calling ahead or picking up a map in a neighboring town. In this book we refer to tourist offices as TIs (for Tourist Information). Throughout France and the Low Countries you'll find TIs are usually well-organized and have English-speaking staff. Most will help you find a room by calling hotels (for a small fee) or giving you a complete listing of available bed-and-breakfasts. Towns with much tourism generally have English-speaking guides available for private hire (about $100 for a 90-minute guided town walk).

The French call their TIs by different names. Office de Tourisme and Bureau de Tourisme are used in cities, while Syndicat d'Initiative or Information Touristique are used in small towns. French TIs are often closed from 12:00 to 14:00.

Tourist Offices, U.S. Addresses

Each country's national tourist office in the United States is a wealth of information. Before your trip, request any specific information you may want (such as city maps and schedules of upcoming festivals). The Worldwide Web offers much more information for travelers adept at cyberspace (note Web site info below).

French Tourist Office: 444 Madison Avenue, 16th floor, New York, NY 10022, Web site: www.francetourism.com; 676 North Michigan Avenue, #600, Chicago, IL 60611; 9454 Wilshire Boulevard, #715, Beverly Hills, CA 90212. Their general information number (in Washington, D.C.) is 202/659-7779. For the latest on Paris, log on to www.Pariscope.Fr/.

Belgian National Tourist Office: 780 Third Avenue, #1501, New York, NY 10017, tel. 212/758-8130, fax 212/355-7675, Web site: www.visitbelgium.com. Good country map.

Netherlands National Tourist Office: 225 North Michigan Avenue, #1854, Chicago, IL 60601, tel. 888/GO-HOLLAND (automated) or 312/819-1500 (live), fax 312/819-1740, Web site: www.goholland.com. Great country map.

Recommended Guidebooks

Consider some supplemental travel information, especially if you're traveling beyond our recommended destinations. Considering the improvements they'll make in your $3,000 vacation, $25 or $35 for extra maps and books is money well spent. One simple budget tip can easily save the price of an extra guidebook.

France: Lonely Planet's *France: A Travel Survival Kit* is well-researched and packed with good maps and hotel recommendations for low- to moderate-budget travelers, but is not updated annually (new edition available April '99). The highly opinionated, annually updated *Let's Go: France* (St. Martin's Press) is great for students and vagabonds. The popular skinny green Michelin Guides are dry but informative, especially if you're driving. They're known for their city and sightseeing maps, and for their concise and helpful information on all major sights. English editions, covering most of the regions you'll want to visit, are sold in France for about $12 (or $20 in the United States). Consider our most recent book, *Rick Steves' Paris* (see below). Of the multitude of other guidebooks on France and Paris, many are high on facts and low on opinion, guts, or personality.

Belgium and the Netherlands: For the same reason that this region only appears as an add-on to our France book, the Low Countries seem to fall through the cracks in most travel publishers' catalogs. You'll find skimpy chapters in the big all-Europe books or too much information in the various city or country guidebooks covering the region.

Rick Steves' Books and Videos

Rick Steves' Europe Through the Back Door 1999 (John Muir Publications) gives you budget travel tips on minimizing jet lag, packing light, planning your itinerary, traveling by car or train, finding budget beds without reservations, changing money, avoiding rip-offs, outsmarting thieves, hurdling the language barrier, staying healthy, taking great photographs, using your bidet, and lots more. The book also includes chapters on 37 of Rick's favorite "Back Doors."

Rick Steves' Country Guides are a series of eight guidebooks —including this book—covering Europe; Britain and Ireland; Italy; Spain and Portugal; Germany, Austria, and Switzerland; Scandinavia; and Russia and the Baltics. All but the last two are updated annually and come out in January.

Rick Steves' City Guides, featuring Paris and London, are brand-new for 1999. These easy-to-read guides offer thorough coverage of the best of these grand cities. Enjoy self-guided tours of the top sights with a focus on the great art.

Europe 101: History and Art for the Traveler (cowritten with Gene Openshaw, John Muir Publications, 1996) gives you the story of Europe's people, history, and art. Written for smart people who were sleeping in their history and art classes before they knew they were going to Europe, *101* really helps Europe's sights come alive.

Rick Steves' Mona Winks (also cowritten with Gene Openshaw, John Muir Publications, 1998) gives you fun, easy-to-follow self-guided tours of Europe's top 20 museums, including Amsterdam's Rijksmuseum and Van Gogh Museum, and Paris' Louvre, Orsay Museum, and Palace of Versailles, along with a historic Paris walk.

My rigorously researched *Rick Steves' French Phrase Book* (John Muir Publications, 1999), gives you the words and survival phrases you'll need while traveling in France and much of Belgium.

My television series, *Travels in Europe with Rick Steves*, includes 10 half-hour shows on France, Belgium, and the Netherlands. A new series of 13 shows is planned for 2000 and earlier shows are still airing on both public television and the Travel Channel. They're also available as information-packed videotapes, along with my two-hour slideshow lecture on France (call us at 425/771-8303 for our free newsletter/catalog).

Rick Steves' Postcards from Europe (John Muir Publications, 1999), my new autobiographical book, packs 25 years of travel anecdotes and insights into the ultimate 3,000-mile European adventure. Through my guidebooks, I share my favorite European discoveries with you. *Postcards* introduces you to my favorite European friends.

Maps

The maps in this book, drawn by Dave Hoerlein, are concise and simple. Dave, who is well-traveled in France and the Low Countries, has designed the maps to help you locate recommended places and get to the tourist offices where you'll find more indepth maps (often free) of the cities or regions. For ease of navigation in France, keep in mind that a *rue* is a street, a *place* is a square, and a *pont* is a bridge.

Don't skimp on maps. Excellent Michelin maps are available

throughout France (for 26F, half the U.S. price) at bookstores, newsstands, and gas stations. Train travelers can do fine with Michelin's #989 France map (1:1,000,000). For serious navigation pick up the yellow 1:200,000-scale maps as you travel. Drivers should consider the soft-cover Michelin France atlas (the entire country at 1:200,000, well-organized in a $20 book with an index and maps of major cities). Learn the Michelin key to get the most sightseeing value out of their maps.

Transportation

By Car or Train?
Cars are best for three or more traveling together (especially families with small kids), those packing heavy, and those scouring the countryside. Trains and buses are best for solo travelers, blitz tourists, and city-to-city travelers.

Trains
Train stations are almost always centrally located in cities, making hotel hunting and sightseeing easier. Schedules change by season, weekend, and weekday. Verify train schedules shown in this book.

France's rail system (SNCF) sets the pace in Europe. Its super TGV system has inspired bullet trains throughout the world. The TGV runs at 170 to 220 m.p.h. Its rails are fused into one long continuous track for a faster and smoother ride. The TGV has changed commuting patterns in much of France and put most of the country within day-trip distance of Paris. The Eurostar English Channel tunnel train to Britain and the new Thalys bullet train to Brussels are two more links in the grand European train system of the 21st century.

While Eurailpasses and Europasses work well, those traveling solely within France will save money with a France Railpass (available outside of France only, through your travel agent or Europe Through the Back Door; call us at 425/771-8303 to get our free railpass guide or download it at www.ricksteves.com). For about the cost of a Paris–Avignon–Paris ticket, you can get a railpass that offers three days of travel (within a month) anywhere in France. You can add up to six additional days for the cost of a two-hour ride each. (The Flexi Saver gives two traveling together a 25-percent discount.) Each day of use allows you to take as many trips as you want in a 24-hour period (you could go from Paris to Chartres, see the cathedral, then continue to Avignon, stay a few hours, and end in Nice). Buy second-class tickets in France for shorter trips and spend your valuable railpass days wisely.

If traveling *sans* railpass, inquire about the many point-to-point discount fares possible (youths, those over 60, married couples, families, and others qualify).

Cost of Public Transportation

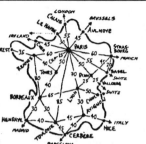

1999 FRANCE FLEXIPASS

	1st class	2nd class
Any 3 days in a month*	$205	$175
France Flexi Companion**	164	140
Any 4 days in 2 months Youth (2nd cl)***	158	

*Extra days $30 (6 max). Kids 4-11: half fare.
**3 days in a month, per person for 2 people traveling together on all journeys (no kids discounts). Extra days $30 (6 max).
***Must be under age 26. Extra days $26 (6 max).

FRANCE RAIL & DRIVE PASS

Any 3 days of rail and 2 days of Avis rental car in a month.

Car category	1st class	2nd class	Extra car day
A-Economy	$204	$187	$50
B-Compact	232	214	75
C-Intermediate	249	232	95
D-Small automatic	247	232	89

Rail & Drive prices are approximate per person, two traveling together. Solo travelers pay about $100 extra, 3rd & 4th members of a group need only buy the equivalent flexi railpass. Extra rail days (6 max) cost $30 per day for first or second class. You can add up to 6 extra car days.

France: The map shows approximate point-to-point one-way 2nd-class rail fares in $US. Add up fares for your itinerary to see whether a railpass will save you money.

Note: For information on ordering France Flexipasses, call us at 425/771-8303; for France Rail & Drive, call your travel agent or Rail Europe at 800/438-7245.

Reservations are generally unnecessary for local trains but are required for any TGV train (generally 20–60F) and for *couchettes* (berths, 100F) on night trains. Even railpass holders need reservations for the TGV trains. To avoid the more expensive reservation fees, avoid traveling at peak times; ask at the station. Validate (*composter*) all train tickets and reservations in the orange machines located before the platforms. (Watch others and imitate.)

Cars, Rail 'n' Drive Passes, and Buses

Car rental is cheapest if arranged in advance through your home-town travel agent. The best rates are weekly with unlimited mileage, or leasing (see below). You can pick up and drop off just about anywhere, any time. Big companies have offices in most cities. Small rental companies can be cheaper but aren't as flexible.

When you drive a rental car you are liable for its replacement value. CDW insurance (Collision-Damage Waiver) gives you the peace of mind that comes with a zero- or low-deductible coverage—for about $15 a day. A few "gold" credit cards provide this coverage for free if you use their card for the rental; quiz your credit-card company on the worst-case scenario. Or consider the $6/day policy offered by Travel Guard in the United States (tel. 800/826-1300).

For a trip of three weeks or more, leasing is a bargain. By

technically buying and then selling back the car, you save lots of money on tax and insurance (CDW is included). Leasing, which you should arrange from the United States, usually requires a 22-day minimum contract, but Europe by Car leases cars in France for as few as 17 days for $400 (U.S. tel. 800/223-1516).

You can rent a car on the spot just about anywhere. In many cases this is a worthwhile splurge. All you need is your American license and money (about 330F, or $60, for a day with 100 km).

In the Netherlands, Campanje rents and sells used VW campers fully loaded for camping through Europe. Rates vary from $500 to $750 per week including tax and insurance. (For a brochure, write P.O. Box 9332, 3506 GH Utrecht, Netherlands; tel. 31/30-244-7070, fax 31/30-242-0981, e-mail: campanje@xs4all.nl). They have a creative program offering short-term, long-term, camping-gear inclusive, rental, and buy/sell-back deals.

Rail 'n' drive passes let you economically mix car and train travel (available outside of France only, from your travel agent.) Generally, big-city connections are best done by train, and rural regions are best scoured with the freewheeling mobility of a car. With a rail 'n' drive pass you get an economic "flexi" railpass and the chance to add on a few "flexi" car days at the cheaper weekly rate rather than the budget-busting daily rate. This allows you to combine rail and drive into one pass—you can take advantage of the high speed and comfort of the TGV trains for longer trips, and rent a car for as little as one day at a time for those regions that are difficult to get around in without a car (like the Loire, the Dordogne, and Provence), all for a very reasonable package price. Within the same country, you can pick a car up in one city and drop it off in another city with no problem.

Another good car/train solution is combining a one-way car rental from Paris to Nice (seeing Normandy, the Loire, the Dordogne, Carcassonne, and Provence), then, if you have more time, returning to Paris with a railpass (via Chamonix, Burgundy, and the Alsace). This allows you to take advantage of weekly car rental rates (for the parts of France most deserving of a car) and France's cheap railpass deals.

Regional buses take over where the trains stop. You can get almost anywhere by rail and bus if you're well organized and patient. Review our bus schedule information and always verify times at the tourist office or bus station, calling ahead when possible. On Sunday regional bus service virtually disappears.

Regional minivan excursions offer organized day tours of regions where bus and train service is virtually useless. For the D-Day beaches, châteaus of the Loire Valley, sightseeing in the Dordogne Valley, and wine tasting in Burgundy, we identify small companies providing this extraordinarily helpful service at reasonable rates.

Standard European Road Signs

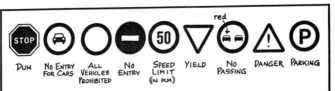

DUH | NO ENTRY FOR CARS | ALL VEHICLES PROHIBITED | NO ENTRY | SPEED LIMIT (IN KM) | YIELD | NO PASSING | DANGER | PARKING

Driving

The hardest thing about driving in France is not stopping at every mouth-watering bakery and *pâtisserie* you pass.

An international driver's license is not necessary. Seat belts are mandatory, and children under age 10 must be in the back seat. Gas is expensive: over $4 per gallon. It's most expensive on autoroutes (you'll save about $4 a tank by filling up at a supermarket).

Go metric. A liter is about a quart, four to a gallon. A kilometer is six-tenths of a mile. I figure kilometers to miles by cutting them in half and adding back 10 percent of the original (120 km: 60 + 12 = 72 miles, 300 km: 150 + 30 = 180 miles).

Four hours of autoroute tolls cost about $20, but the alternative to these super "feeways" is often being marooned in rural traffic. Autoroutes usually save enough time, gas, and nausea to justify the splurge. Mix scenic country-road rambling with high-speed "autorouting."

Roads in France are classified into departmental (D), national (N), and autoroutes (A). D routes (usually yellow lines on maps) are slow and often the most scenic. N routes (usually red lines) are the fastest after autoroutes (orange lines). Green road signs are for national routes; blue are for autoroutes. There are plenty of good facilities, gas stations, and rest stops along most French roads.

Here are a few French road tips: In city centers, traffic merging from the right normally has the right of way (*priorité à droite*). Approach intersections cautiously. When navigating through cities, stow the map and follow the signs to *centre-ville* (downtown), and from there to the tourist information office. When leaving (or just passing through), follow the *Toutes Directions* or *Autres Directions* (meaning anywhere else) signs until you see a sign for your specific destination. Be careful of sluggish tractors on country roads. While the French are eating (12:00–14:00), many sights (and gas stations) are closed, so you can make great time driving. The French drive fast and love to tailgate.

Parking is a headache in the larger cities, and theft is a problem throughout France. Pay to park at well-patrolled lots, or use the parking meters, which are usually free 12:30 to 14:00 and 19:00 to 9:00, and in August. Keep a pile of 1F and 2F coins in your ashtray for parking meters, public restrooms, and Laundromat dryers.

Biking

Throughout France and the Low Countries you'll find areas where public transportation is limited and bicycle touring is an excellent idea. We've listed bike rental shops where appropriate. The TI will always have the best listing. For a good touring bike allow about $14 for a half day and $18 for a full day.

Telephones and Mail

An efficient card-operated system has virtually replaced coin-operated public phones throughout Europe. Each country offers phone cards good for use only in telephones within its borders (though you can use it for international calls). Insert the card in the phone and dial away.

France: Buy a phone card (*une télécarte*) from any post office or train station, or from most newsstands and tobacco shops (*tabac*). There are two denominations of phone cards in France: *Une petite* costs 42F; *une grande* is 98F. When you use the *télécarte* (simply take the phone off the hook, insert the card, and wait for a dial tone) the price of the call (local or international) is automatically deducted. Buy a *télécarte* at the beginning of your trip and use it for hotel reservations, calling tourist information offices, and phoning home. France's newest phone card (KOSMOS) is not inserted into the phone, but allows you to dial from the comfort of your hotel (or anywhere) and charge the call to the card for lower rates than with a *télécarte*. It's simple to use, instructions are provided in English, and the card is sold wherever *télécartes* are sold. And while the per-minute rates are cheaper than a *télécarte*, it's slower to use, so local calls are quicker with a *télécarte* from a phone booth. For short calls back home, the KOSMOS card is also cheaper than your calling card (AT&T, MCI, Sprint; numbers listed in Appendix). Calling-card calls used to be a fine deal until direct-dial rates were cut in half. Now it's cheaper to make your international calls using a European phone card (French or new KOSMOS, Belgian, or Dutch). Definitely avoid using your calling card for calls between European countries; it's far cheaper to call direct.

France has a dial-direct 10-digit telephone system. There are no area codes. To call to or from anywhere in France, including Paris, you dial the 10 numbers directly.

To dial out of France you must start your call with its international code: 00. To call France from another country, start with the international access code of the country you're calling from (00 for most European countries and 011 from the United States), then dial France's country code (33), then drop the initial zero of the 10-digit local number and dial the remaining nine digits. For example, the phone number of one of our favorite hotels in Paris is 01 47 05 49 15. To call it from home, dial 011-33-1 47 05 49 15. For a list of international access codes and country codes, see the Appendix. European time is six/nine hours ahead of the east/west coast of the United States.

Belgium and the Netherlands: Both countries use area codes throughout. For instance, Bruges' area code is 050. To call Bruges long distance from within Belgium, dial 050 then the local number. When calling from another country, drop the first zero in the area code. Calling Bruges from Amsterdam, you'd dial 00 (Netherlands' international access code), 32 (Belgium's country code), 50 (Bruges' area code without the zero), then the local number.

Mail: To arrange for mail delivery, reserve a few hotels along your route in advance and give their addresses to friends, or use American Express Company's mail services (available to anyone who has at least one Amex traveler's check). Allow 10 days for a letter to arrive. Phoning is so easy that we've dispensed with mail stops altogether.

Sleeping

In France and the Low Countries, accommodations are a good value and easy to find. Choose from one- or two-star hotels, bed-and-breakfasts, hostels, and campgrounds. We like places that are clean, small, central, traditional, inexpensive, friendly, and not listed in other guidebooks. Most places we list have at least five of these seven virtues.

Hotels

In this book the price for a double room will normally range from $30 (very simple, toilet and shower down the hall) to $140 (maximum plumbing and more), with most clustering around $60. Rates are higher in Paris and other popular cities. A triple and a double are often the same room, with a small double bed and a sliver single, so a third person sleeps very cheaply. Most hotels have a few singles, triples, and quads. While groups sleep cheap, traveling alone can be expensive—a single room usually costs about the same as a double.

French receptionists are often reluctant to mention the cheaper rooms. Study the room price list posted at the desk. Understand it. You'll save an average of $15 if you get a room with a shower "down the hall" rather than in your room. Ask for a room *sans douche* (without shower) rather than *avec douche* (with shower). A room with a bathtub (*salle de bain*) costs $5 to $10 more than a room with a shower (*douche*). A double bed (*grand lit*) is $5 to $10 cheaper than twins (*deux petits lits*). Hotels have more

Sleep Code

To give maximum information in a minimum of space, we use these codes to describe accommodations listed in this book. Prices listed are per room, not per person.

   S = Single room (or price for one person in a double).

   D = Double or Twin. French double beds can be very small.

   T = Triple (generally a double bed with a single).

   Q = Quad (usually two double beds).

   b = Private bathroom with toilet and shower or tub.

   t = Private toilet only. (The shower is down the hall.)

   s = Private shower or tub only. (The toilet is down the hall.)

   CC = Accepts credit cards (Visa, MasterCard, American Express). If CC isn't mentioned, assume you'll need to pay cash.

   SE = Speaks English. This code is used only when it seems predictable that you'll encounter English-speaking staff.

   NSE = Does not speak English. Used only when it's unlikely you'll encounter English-speaking staff.

   * = French hotel rating system, ranging from zero to four stars.

According to this code, a couple staying at a "Db-275F, CC:V, SE" hotel would pay a total of 275 French francs (or about $50) for a double room with a private bathroom. The hotel accepts Visa or French cash in payment, and the staff speaks English.

rooms with tubs than showers and are inclined to give you a room with a tub (which the French prefer). If you prefer a double bed and a shower, you need to ask for it—and you'll save up to $20. If you'll take twins or a double, ask for a *chambre pour deux* (room for two) to avoid being needlessly turned away.

The French have a simple hotel rating system (zero through four stars) that depends on the amenities offered. We like the one- or two-star hotels and the occasional three-star hotel. More than two stars generally gets you expensive and unnecessary amenities. Unclassified hotels (no stars) can be bargains or depressing dumps. Look before you leap, and lay before you pay. You'll almost always have the option of breakfast at your hotel, which is pleasant and convenient but, at 25F to 50F, often double the price of the corner café. While hotels hope you'll spring for their breakfast, this is optional unless otherwise noted.

In places where demand exceeds supply, many French hotels strongly encourage their peak-season guests to take half-pension; that is, breakfast and either lunch or dinner. By law, they can't require you to take half-pension. While the food is usually good, it limits your ability to shop around. The yellow *logis de France* sign posted at the door indicates a particularly good value.

France is littered with inexpensive, sterile, ultramodern hotels, usually located on cheap land just outside of town. The antiseptically clean Formule 1 chain is most popular. While far from quaint, these can be a fine value (140–220F per room for up to three people).

Rooms are safe. Still, keep cameras and money out of sight. Towels aren't routinely replaced every day; drip-dry and conserve. If that French Lincoln-log pillow isn't your idea of comfort, American-style pillows (and extra blankets) are usually in the closet or available on request. For a pillow, ask for *"un oreiller, s'il vous plaît"* (un oar-ray-yay, see-voo-play).

Making Reservations

It's possible to travel at any time of year without reservations, but given the high stakes, erratic accommodations values, and the quality of the gems we've found for this book, we'd highly recommend calling ahead for rooms several days in advance as you travel.

If you know exactly which dates you need and really want a particular place, reserve a room well in advance before you leave home. This is especially important for Paris, which can be jammed during conventions (May, June, September, and October are worst).

When tourist crowds are down, you might make a habit of calling between 9:00 and 10:00 on the day you plan to arrive, when the hotelier knows who'll be checking out and just which rooms will be available. We've taken great pains to list telephone numbers with long-distance instructions (see Telephones and Mail, above; and the Appendix). Use the telephone and convenient telephone cards. Most hotels listed are accustomed to English-only speakers. A hotel receptionist will trust you and hold a room until 17:00 without a deposit, though some will ask for a credit-card number. *Please honor (or cancel by phone) your reservations.* These family-run businesses lose money if they turn away customers while holding a room for someone who doesn't show up. Long distance is cheap and easy from public phone booths. Don't let these people down—we promised you'd call and cancel if for some reason you won't show up. Don't needlessly confirm rooms through the tourist office; they'll take a commission.

To reserve from home, call, fax, e-mail, or write the hotel. Phone and fax costs are reasonable, e-mail costs are a steal, and simple English is usually fine. To fax, use the form in the Appendix (e-mailers could follow this form as well). If you're writing a letter, add the zip code and confirm the need and method for a deposit. A two-night stay in August would be "2 nights, 16/8/99 to 18/8/99"—European hotel jargon uses your day of departure. You'll often receive a letter back requesting one night's deposit. A credit card will usually be accepted as a deposit, though you may need to send a signed traveler's check or a bank draft in the local currency. If your credit card is the deposit, you can pay with your card or cash when you arrive. If you don't show up you'll be billed for one night. Reconfirm your reservations a day in advance for safety.

Bed-and-Breakfasts

B&Bs offer double the cultural intimacy for less than most hotel rooms. Tourist information offices have listings for each town.

France: *Chambres d'hôte (CH)* are found mainly in the smaller towns and countryside. They are listed by the owner's family name. While some post small *"Chambres"* or *"Chambres d'hôte"* signs in their front windows, many are found only through the local tourist office. Doubles with breakfast cost around 200F (breakfast may or may not be included—ask). This is a great way to get beneath the surface with French locals. While your hosts will rarely speak English, they will almost always be enthusiastic and a delight to share a home with.

Belgium and the Netherlands: B&Bs in the Low Countries are common in well-touristed areas. Hosts are usually English-speaking and interesting conversationalists. Local TIs can book you into a B&B much cheaper than a hotel. B&Bs are more important for budget travelers here than in France.

Hostels

Hostels charge about $14 per bed. Get a hostel card before you go (Hostelling International, tel. 800/444-6111). Travelers of any age are welcome if they don't mind dorm-style accommodations or meeting other travelers. Travelers without a hostel card can generally spend the night for a small extra "one-night membership" fee. Cheap meals are sometimes available, and kitchen facilities are usually provided for do-it-yourselfers. Expect crowds in the summer, snoring, and lots of youth groups in the spring. Family rooms are sometimes available on request, but it's basically boys' dorms and girls' dorms. You usually can't check in before 17:00 and must be out by 10:00. There is often a 23:00 curfew. Official hostels are marked with a triangular sign that shows a house and a tree. In France ask for an *auberge de jeunesse.*

Camping

In Europe camping is more of a social than an environmental experience. It's a great way for American travelers to make European friends. Camping costs about $12 per campsite per night, and almost every destination recommended in this book has a campground within a reasonable walk or bus ride from the town center and train station. A tent and sleeping bag are all you need. Many campgrounds have small grocery stores and washing machines, and some even come with discos and miniature golf. Hot showers are better at campgrounds than at many hotels. Local tourist information offices have camping information. You'll find more detailed information in the *Michelin Camping Guide*, available in most French bookstores; or in the thorough *Guide Officiel Camping/Caravaning (Fédération Française de Camping et de Caravaning)*.

Eating in France

The French eat long and well. Relaxed lunches, three-hour dinners, and endless hours sitting in outdoor cafés are the norm. They have a legislated 35-hour workweek and a self-imposed 36-hour eat-week. The French spend much of their five annual weeks of paid vacation at *la table*. Local cafés, cuisine, and wines become a highlight of any French adventure—sightseeing for your palate. Even if the rest of you is sleeping in cheap hotels, let your tastebuds travel first-class in France. (They can go coach in England.) You can eat well without going broke, but choose carefully: You're just as likely to blow a small fortune on a mediocre meal as you are to dine wonderfully for $15.

Restaurants

You can order *à la carte* like the locals do, or get the no-brainer *menu*, which is a fixed-price meal offering three or four courses— and generally a good value. The fixed-price *menu* gives you your choice of soup, appetizer, or salad; your choice of three or four main courses *(plats)* with vegetables; plus a cheese course and/or a choice of desserts. Service is included, but wine or drinks are generally extra.

In France an *entrée* is the first course and *le plat* is the main course. *Le plat* or *le plat du jour* (plate of the day) is the main course with vegetables (usually 50–70F). For a light, healthy, fast, and inexpensive option in a pricey restaurant, the various salads are 40F to 50F well spent. Soft drinks and beer cost 8F to 20F ($1.50–4), and a bottle or carafe of house wine—which is invariably good enough for Rick, if not always Steve—costs 30F to 70F ($6–14). Service is always included. To get a waiter's attention, simply say, "*S'il vous plaît*" (please).

French Café Culture

French cafés (or *brasseries*) provide reasonable light meals and a refuge from museum and church overload. They are carefully positioned viewpoints from which to watch the river of local life flow by. It's easier for the novice to sit and feel comfortable in a café when you know the system.

Check the price list first. Prices, which must be posted prominently, vary wildly between cafes. Cafés charge different prices for the same drink depending upon where you want to be seated. Prices are posted: *comptoir* (counter/bar) and the more expensive *salle* (seated).

Your waiter probably won't overwhelm you with friendliness. Notice how hard they work. They almost never stop. Cozying up to clients (French or foreign) is probably the last thing on their minds.

The standard menu items are the *Croque Monsieur* (grilled cheese sandwich) and *Croque Madame* (Monsieur with a fried egg on top). The *salade compose* (com-po-zay) is a hearty chef's salad. Sandwiches are least expensive but plain unless you buy them at the *boulangerie* (bakery). To get more than a piece of ham (*jambon*) on a baguette, order a sandwich *jambon-crudite* (crew-dee-tay), which means garnished with lettuce, tomatoes, cucumbers, and so on. Omelettes come lonely on a plate with a basket of bread. The *plat du jour* (daily special) is your fast, hearty 50F-to-60F hot plate. Regardless of what you order, bread is free; to get more, just hold up your bread basket and ask, "*Encore, s'il vous plaît.*"

If you order coffee, here's the lingo:
• *un express* (uh nex-press) = shot of espresso
• *une noisette* (oon nwah-zette) = espresso with a shot of milk
• *café au lait* = coffee with milk. Also called *un grand crème* (uh grahn krem = big) or *un petit crème* (uh puh-tee krem = average)
• *un café longue* (uh kah-fay lone-guh) = cup of coffee, closest to American-style)
• *un décaffine* (uh day-kah-fee-nay) = decaf, and can modify any of the above drinks

Note: By law the waiter must give you a glass of tap water with your coffee if you request it; ask for "*Un verre d'eau*" (uh vayre dough).

House wine at the bar is cheap (5–10F per glass, cheapest by the *pichet*), and the local beer is cheaper on tap (*une pression*) than in the bottle (*bouteille*). While prices include service, tip, and tax, it's polite to round up for a drink or meal well served (e.g., if your bill was 24F, leave 25F).

Breakfast

Petit déjeuner (peh-tee day-zhu-nay) is typically *café au lait* (espresso with hot milk), hot chocolate, or tea; a roll with butter and marmalade; and a croissant. Don't expect much variety for breakfast, but do expect fresh bread and great coffee. While they're available at your hotel (25–50F), breakfasts are cheaper at corner cafés. It's entirely acceptable to buy a croissant or roll at a nearby bakery and eat it with your cup of coffee (no refills) at a café. Some hotels offer a *petit déjeuner buffet* (about 50F) with cereal, yogurt, cheese, fruit, and bread. If the morning egg urge gets the best of you, drop into a café and order *une omelette* or *oeufs sur le plat* (fried eggs). You could also buy or bring plastic bowls and spoons from home, buy a box of French cereal and a small box of milk, and eat in your room before heading out for coffee. We carry fruit and a package of Vache Qui Rit (Laughing Cow) cheese to supplement the morning jelly.

Lunch

For lunch—*déjeuner* (day-zhuh-nay)—we picnic or munch a take-away sandwich from a *boulangerie* (bakery).

French picnics can be first-class affairs and adventures in high cuisine. Be daring. Try the smelly cheeses, ugly pâtés, sissy quiches, and minuscule yogurts. Local shopkeepers are accustomed to selling small quantities of produce. Try the tasty salads to go and ask for *une fourchette en plastique* (a plastic fork).

Gather supplies early; you'll probably visit several small stores to assemble a complete meal, and many close at noon. Look for a *boulangerie*, a *crémerie* (cheeses), a *charcuterie* (deli items, meats, and pâtés), an *épicerie* or *alimentation* (small grocery with veggies, drinks, and so on), and a *pâtisserie* (delicious pastries). Open-air markets (*marchés*) are fun, photogenic, and close about noon (local TIs have details). Local *supermarchés* offer less color and cost, more efficiency, and adequate quality. Department stores often have supermarkets in the basement. On the outskirts of cities you'll find the monster *hypermarchés*. Drop in for a glimpse of hyper-France in action.

If not picnicking, look for food stands and bakeries selling take-out sandwiches and drinks, or *crêperies* or *brasseries* for fast and easy sit-down restaurant food. *Brasseries* are cafés serving basic fare such as omelets, chicken, and fries, as well as simple sandwiches and hearty salads. Look for their *plat du jour* (daily special). Many French restaurants offer good-value three- to five-course *menus* at lunch only. The same *menu* is often 40F more at dinner. Drivers find roadside *frites* trailers selling fries, hot snacks, drinks, and so on. (See Café Culture, above.)

Dinner

For *dîner* (dee-nay) choose restaurants filled with locals, not places with big neon signs boasting, "We Speak English." Consider your hotelier's opinion. If the menu (*la carte*) isn't posted outside, move along. Also look for set-price *menus* and restaurants serving regional specialities. Ask the waiter for help deciphering *la carte*. Go with his or her recommendations and anything *de la maison* (of the house). Galloping gourmets should bring a menu translator (the *Marling Menu Master* is excellent). Remember, if you ask for a *menu*, you'll get a meal (*la carte* is the list of what's cooking); and if you ask for an *entrée*, you'll get a first course (soup, salad, or appetizer). The wines are often listed in a separate *carte des vins*. Tipping (*pourboire*) is unnecessary, though if you enjoyed the service it's polite to leave a few francs. When you're on the road, look for the red and blue *Relais Routier* decal, indicating that the place is recommended by the truckers' union. Restaurants are generally a far better value in the countryside than in Paris.

Drinks

In stores, unrefrigerated soft drinks and beer are one-third the price of cold drinks. Milk and boxed fruit juice are the cheapest drinks. Avoid buying drinks to go at streetside stands; you'll find them far cheaper in a shop. Try to keep a water bottle with you. Water quenches your thirst better and cheaper than anything you'll find in a store or café. We drink tap water throughout France and the Low Countries.

The French often order bottled water with their meal (*eau minérale*; oh mee-nay-rahl). If you'd rather get a free pitcher of tap water, ask for *une carafe d'eau*. Otherwise, you may unwittingly buy bottled water. When ordering a beer at a café or restaurant, ask for *une pression* or *un demi* (draft beer), which is cheaper than bottled. When ordering table wine at a café or restaurant, ask for a pitcher, *un pichet* (pee-shay), again cheaper than a bottle. If all you want is a glass of wine, ask for *un verre de vin*. You could drink away your children's inheritance if you're not careful. The most famous wines are the most expensive, while lesser-known taste-alikes remain a bargain (see our regional suggestions in each chapter). If you like brandy, try a *marc* (regional brandy, e.g., *marc de Bourgogne*) or an Armagnac, cognac's cheaper twin brother. *Pastis*, the standard *apéritif*, is a sweet anise or licorice drink which comes on the rocks with a glass of water. Cut it to taste with lots of water. France's best beer is Alsatian; try Krônenburg or the heavier Pelfort. *Une panache* (pan-a-shay) is a very refreshing French shandy (7-Up and beer). For a fun, bright, nonalcoholic drink, order *un diabolo menthe* (7-Up with mint syrup). The ice cubes melted after the last Yankee tour group left.

Stranger in a Strange Land

We travel all the way to Europe to enjoy differences—to become temporary locals. You'll experience frustrations. Certain truths that we find "God-given" or "self-evident," like cold beer, ice in drinks, bottomless cups of coffee, hot showers, body odor smelling bad, and bigger being better, are suddenly not so true. One of the benefits of travel is the eye-opening realization that there are logical, civil, and even better alternatives. The fact that Americans treat time as a commodity can lead to frustrations when dealing with other cultures. For instance, while an American "spends" or "wastes" time, a French person merely "passes" it. A willingness to go local (and at a local tempo) ensures that you'll enjoy a full dose of European hospitality.

If there is a negative aspect to the European image of Americans, we can appear big, loud, aggressive, impolite, rich, and a bit naive. While Europeans look bemusedly at some of our Yankee excesses—and worriedly at others—they nearly always afford us individual travelers all the warmth we deserve.

Back Door Manners
While updating this book, we heard over and over again that our readers are considerate and fun to have as guests. Thank you for traveling as temporary locals who are sensitive to the culture. It's fun to follow you in our travels.

Tours of France by Rick Steves and Steve Smith
At Europe Through the Back Door, we organize and lead tours covering the highlights of this book. Choose among a 14-day *Feast of the East*, a 14-day *Best of the West*, or the 20-day *Slow Dance with France*. These depart each year from April through October, are limited to 24 people per group, and have two guides and big buses with lots of empty seats. For details call us at 425/771-8303.

Send Me a Postcard, Drop Me a Line
If you enjoy a successful trip with the help of this book and would like to share your discoveries, please fill out and send the survey at the end of this book to us at Europe Through the Back Door, Box 2009, Edmonds, WA 98020. We personally read and value all feedback. Thanks in advance—it helps a lot.

For our latest travel information, tap into our Web site: www.ricksteves.com. My e-mail address is rick@ricksteves.com. Anyone is welcome to request a free issue of our *Back Door* quarterly newsletter.

Judging from all the positive feedback and happy postcards we receive from travelers who have used this book, it's safe to assume you're on your way to a great vacation—independent, inexpensive, and with the finesse of an experienced traveler.

From this point, "we" (your coauthors) will shed our respective egos and become "I."

Thanks, and *bon voyage*!

BACK DOOR TRAVEL PHILOSOPHY
As Taught in *Rick Steves' Europe Through the Back Door*

Travel is intensified living—maximum thrills per minute and one of the last great sources of legal adventure. Travel is freedom. It's recess, and we need it.

Experiencing the real Europe requires catching it by surprise, going casual . . . "Through the Back Door."

Affording travel is a matter of priorities. (Make do with the old car.) You can travel—simply, safely, and comfortably—anywhere in Europe for $60 a day plus transportation costs. In many ways, spending more money only builds a thicker wall between you and what you came to see. Europe is a cultural carnival; time after time you'll find that its best acts are free and the best seats are the cheap ones.

A tight budget forces you to travel close to the ground, meeting and communicating with the people, not relying on service with a purchased smile. Never sacrifice sleep, nutrition, safety, or cleanliness in the name of budget. Simply enjoy the local-style alternatives to expensive hotels and restaurants.

Extroverts have more fun. If your trip is low on magic moments, kick yourself and make things happen. If you don't enjoy a place, maybe you don't know enough about it. Seek the truth. Recognize tourist traps. Give a culture the benefit of your open mind. See things as different but not better or worse. Any culture has much to share.

Of course, travel, like the world, is a series of hills and valleys. Be fanatically positive and militantly optimistic. If something's not to your liking, change your liking. Travel is addicting. It can make you a happier American, as well as a citizen of the world. Our Earth is home to nearly 6 billion equally important people. It's humbling to travel and find that people don't envy Americans. They like us but, with all due respect, they wouldn't trade passports.

Globetrotting destroys ethnocentricity. It helps you understand and appreciate different cultures. Travel changes people. It broadens perspectives and teaches new ways to measure quality of life. Many travelers toss aside their hometown blinders. Their prized souvenirs are the strands of different cultures they decide to knit into their own character. The world is a cultural yarn shop. And Back Door Travelers are weaving the ultimate tapestry. Come on, join in!

PARIS

Paris offers sweeping boulevards, sleepy parks, world-class art galleries, chatty crêpe stands, Napoleon's body, sleek shopping malls, the Eiffel Tower, and people-watching from outdoor cafés. Climb the Notre-Dame and the Eiffel Tower, cruise the Seine and the Champs-Élysées, and master the Louvre and Orsay museums. Save some after-dark energy for one of the world's most romantic cities. Many people fall in love with Paris. Some see the essentials and flee, overwhelmed by the huge city. With the proper approach and a good orientation, you'll fall head over heels for Europe's capital city.

Planning Your Time: Paris in One, Two, or Three Days

Day 1
Morning: Follow "Historic Core of Paris Walk" (see Sights, below) featuring Île de la Cité, Notre-Dame, Latin Quarter, and Sainte-Chapelle.
Afternoon: Tour Louvre Museum.
Evening: Cruise Seine River or take illuminated Paris by Night bus tour.

Day 2
Morning: Métro to Arc de Triomphe and walk down the Champs-Élysées, following the "Champs-Élysées Walk" (below).
Midday: Tour Orsay Museum.
Afternoon: Catch RER from Orsay to Versailles. To avoid crowds, see the park first and the palace late.
Evening: Enjoy Trocadero scene and ride up Eiffel Tower.

Day 3
Morning: Follow "Marais Walk" (below).
Afternoon: Tour Rodin Museum and nearby Les Invalides
(Napoleon's Tomb and Military Museum).
Evening: Explore Montmartre and Sacre Coeur.

Daily Reminder
Monday: Orsay, Rodin Museum, and Versailles are closed; the
Louvre is more crowded because of this. Many small stores don't
open until 14:00. Some restaurants close on Mondays. It's dis-
count night at most cinemas.
Tuesday: The Louvre, L'Orangerie, Marmottan, and most other
national museums are closed today. Versailles and the Orsay can
be jammed.
Wednesday: All museums are open. The weekly *Pariscope* maga-
zine comes out today.
Thursday: All museums are open.
Friday: All museums are open. Afternoon trains and roads leaving
Paris are crowded; TGV reservation fees are much higher.
Saturday: Candlelight visits of Vaux-le-Vicomte (May–October);
otherwise avoid weekend crowds at area châteaus. Paris department stores are busy.
Sunday: Organ concerts at St. Sulpice and possibly at other
churches. Free evening concert at the American Church (18:00).
The fountains run at Versailles. Some museums are two-thirds
price all day (Louvre, Orsay, Cluny, Picasso). The Marais is the
place to window shop and café hop; many of Paris' stores are
closed on Sunday, but as this is the Jewish Quarter, it hops.

Orientation
Paris is split in half by the Seine River, divided into 20
arrondissements (proud and independent governmental jurisdic-
tions), and circled by a ring-road freeway (the *périphérique*).
You'll find Paris easier to negotiate if you know which side of
the river you're on, which *arrondissement* you're in, and which
subway (Métro) stop you're closest to. If you're north of the
river (above on any city map), you're on the Right Bank (*rive
droite*). If you're south of it, you're on the Left Bank (*rive
gauche*).
    Arrondissements are numbered, starting at Notre-Dame
(ground zero) and moving in a clockwise spiral out to the ring
road. The last two digits in a Parisian zip code are the *arrondissement* number, and the notation for the Métro stop is "Mo." In
Parisian jargon, Napoleon's tomb is on *la rive gauche* (the Left
Bank) in the *7ème* (seventh *arrondissement*), zip code 75007, Mo:
Invalides. Paris Métro stops are used as a standard aid in giving
directions, even for those not using the Métro.

Paris Overview

TRAIN STATIONS/ GARES:

① ST-LAZARE TO NORMANDY

② NORD TO LONDON & BRUSSELS VIA EUROSTAR,
   TO N. EUROPE

③ L'EST TO E. FRANCE, S. GERMANY, SWITZERLAND,
   AUSTRIA

④ LYON TO S.E. FRANCE & ITALY

⑤ D'AUSTERLITZ TO S.W. FRANCE, LOIRE & SPAIN

⑥ MONTPARNASSE TO NORMANDY, BRITTANY,
   CHARTRES, TGV TO LOIRE
   & S.W. FRANCE

ARRONDISSEMENTS
(DISTRICTS)

Tourist Information

Avoid the Paris TIs—long lines, short information, and a 5F
charge for maps. This book, the *Pariscope* magazine (described
below), and one of the freebie maps available at any hotel are all
you need. The main TI is at 127 avenue des Champs-Élysées
(daily 9:00–20:00), but the TIs at the Louvre, Eiffel Tower, and
train stations Gare de Lyon and Gare de Montparnasse are handier (daily 8:00–20:00).

The *Pariscope* weekly magazine (or one of its clones, 3F at any
newsstand, explained below) lists museum hours, special art
exhibits, concerts, music festivals, plays, movies, and nightclubs.

For a complete list of museum hours and scheduled English museum tours, pick up the free *Musées, Monuments Historiques, et Expositions* booklet from any museum.

While Paris is littered with free maps, they don't show all the streets. You may want the huge Michelin #10 map of Paris. For an extended stay we prefer the pocket-size and street-indexed *Paris Practique* (40F). For supplemental background on the city, sights, and neighborhoods, you may want to buy an additional guidebook. The *Michelin Green Guide*, which is some-what scholarly, and the more readable *Paris Access Guide* are both well-researched. *Mona Winks*, a guidebook by Rick Steves and Gene Openshaw, is particularly heavy on Paris, with extensive self-guided walking tours of the Louvre, Orsay, Versailles, and the Historic Core of Paris.

There are many English-language bookstores in Paris where you can pick up guidebooks (for nearly double their American price). A few are: Shakespeare and Company (12:00–24:00, lots of used travel books, 37 rue de la Boucherie, across the river from Notre-Dame), W. H. Smith (248 rue de Rivoli), and Brentanos (37 avenue de L'Opéra).

The American Church is a nerve center for the American èmi-grè community and distributes the *Free Voice*, a handy and insightful monthly English-language newspaper, with useful reviews of con-certs, plays, and current events in Paris; and *France—U.S.A. Contacts*, an advertisement paper full of useful information for those looking for work or long-term housing (facing the river between Eiffel and Orsay at 65 quai d'Orsay, Mo: Invalides).

Arrival in Paris

By Train: Paris has six train stations, all connected by Métro and bus, most with banks and TIs, and none that will check bags (blame terrorism). Hop the Métro to your hotel (see Getting Around Paris, below).

Paris' train stations serve many different destinations. The Gare de l'Est handles the east, the Gare du Nord and Gare St. Lazare serve northern and central Europe, the Gare d'Austerlitz and Gare du Lyon cover southern Europe, and the Gare Mont-parnasse handles western France and TGV service to France's southwest. (Any train station can give you the schedule informa-tion you need, make reservations, and sell tickets for any desti-nation.) Buying tickets is handier from a SNCF neighborhood office (e.g.: Louvre, Orsay, Versailles, airports) or at your neigh-borhood travel agency, and it's worth their small fee (SNCF signs in their window indicate they sell train tickets).

By Plane: For detailed information on getting from Paris' airports to downtown Paris (and vice versa), see Transportation Connections at the end of this chapter.

Helpful Hints
Theft Alert: Use your money belt, and never carry a wallet in your back pocket or a purse over your shoulder. Thieves thrive in tourist areas, subway stations, and on the Métro.

Museums: Most museums offer reduced prices and shorter hours on Sunday. Many begin closing rooms 45 minutes before the actual closing time. For the fewest crowds, visit very early, at lunch, or very late. The best Impressionist art museums are the Orsay, Marmottan, and L'Orangerie (each described below). Most museums have slightly shorter hours October through March. French holidays can really mess up your sightseeing plans (Jan. 1, May 1, May 8, July 14, Nov. 1, Nov. 11, and Dec. 25). See Daily Reminder, above, for other "closed" days.

Paris Museum Pass: In Paris there are two classes of sight-seers: those with a museum pass and those without. Serious sight-seers save time (less time in lines) and money by getting this pass. Sold at museums, main Métro stations, and tourist offices, it pays for itself in two admissions and gets you into sights with no lining up (one day-80F, three consecutive days-160F, five consecutive days-240F). Included sights (and admission prices without the pass) you're likely to visit: Louvre (45F), Orsay (39F), Sainte-Chapelle (32F), Arc de Triomphe (35F), Army Museum and Napoleon's Tomb (37F), Carnavalet Museum (35F), Conciergerie (28F), Sewer Tour (32F), Cluny Museum (30F), Notre-Dame towers (30F) and crypt (32F), L'Orangerie (30F), Picasso Museum (30F), Rodin Museum (28F), and the elevator to the top of the Grand Arche de La Defense (40F). Outside Paris, the pass covers the Palace of Versailles (45F), its Grand Trianon (25F), and Château Chantilly (35F). Notable sights not covered: Marmottan Museum, Eiffel Tower, Montparnasse Tower, the ladies of Pigalle, and Disneyland Paris. Tally it up—but remember, an advantage of the pass is that you skip to the front of the line—saving hours of waiting in the summer (though everyone must pass through the slow-moving metal detector lines at a few sights). And with the pass, you'll pop painlessly into sights that you're walking by (even for a few minutes) that might otherwise not be worth the expense (e.g., Notre-Dame crypt, Cluny Museum, Conciergerie, Victor Hugo's House). The free museum and monuments directory that comes with your pass lists the latest hours, phone numbers, and specifics on what kids pay. The cut-off age for free entry varies from 5 to 18. Most major, serious art museums let young people up to age 18 in for free. If buying a pass at a museum with a long line, skip to the front and find the sales window.

Local Guides: Arnaud Servignat (tel. 01 42 57 03 35, fax 01 42 62 68 62, e-mail: arnoud.saigon@wanadoo.fr) and Marianne Siegler (tel. 01 42 52 32 51) are licensed local guides who freelance for individuals and families ($150/4 hrs, $250/day).

Telephone Cards: Pick up the essential France *tèlécarte* at any *tabac* (tobacco shop), post office, or tourist office (*une petite carte* is 42F; *une grande* is 98F). Smart travelers check things by telephone. Most public phones use these cards.

Useful Telephone Numbers: American Hospital, 01 46 41 25 25; American pharmacy, 01 47 42 49 40 (Mo: Opéra); Police, 17; United States Embassy, 01 43 12 22 22; Paris and France directory assistance, 12; AT&T operator, 0800 99 00 11; MCI, 0800 99 00 19; Sprint, 0800 99 00 87. (See Appendix for additional numbers.)

Toilets: Carry small change for pay toilets, or walk into any outdoor café like you own the place and find the toilet in the back. Remember, the toilets in museums are free and generally the best you'll find. Modern super-sanitary street booths provide both relief and a memory.

Getting Around Paris

By Métro: Europe's best subway is divided into two systems—the Métro (puddle-jumping everywhere in Paris) and the RER (which makes giant speedy leaps around town and connects suburban destinations). You'll be using the Métro for most of your trips.

In Paris you're never more than a 10-minute walk from a Métro station. One ticket takes you anywhere in the system with unlimited transfers. Save 40 percent by buying a *carnet* (car-nay) of 10 tickets for 48F at any Métro station (a single ticket is 8F). Métro tickets work on city buses, though one ticket cannot be used as a transfer between subway and bus.

The Mobilis ticket (30F) allows unlimited travel for a single day on all bus and Métro lines. If you're staying longer, the *Carte d'Orange* pass gives you free run of the bus and Métro system for one week (75F and a photo, ask for the *Carte d'Orange Coupon Vert*) or a month (254F, ask for the *Carte d'Orange Coupon Orange*). These pass prices cover only central Paris; you can pay more for passes covering regional destinations (e.g., Versailles). The weekly pass begins Monday and ends Sunday, and the monthly pass begins the first day of the month and ends the last day of that month, so mid-week or mid-month purchases are generally not worthwhile. All passes can be purchased at any Métro station (most have photo booths).

To get to your destination, determine which "Mo." stop is closest to it and which line or lines will get you there. The lines have numbers, but they're best known by their direction or end-of-the-line stop. (For example, the La Defense/Château de Vincennes line runs between La Defense in the west and Vincennes in the east.)

Once in the Métro station, you'll see blue-and-white signs directing you to the train going in your direction (e.g., direction: La Defense). Insert your ticket in the automatic turnstile, pass

Paris

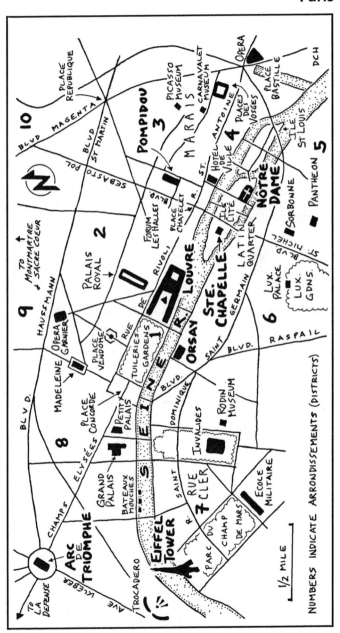

through, then reclaim and keep your ticket until you exit the system (fare inspectors accept no excuses from anyone). Transfers are free and can be made wherever lines cross. When you transfer, look for the orange *correspondence* (connections) signs when you exit your first train, then follow the proper direction sign.

Before you *sortie* (exit), check the helpful *plan du quartier* (map of the neighborhood) to get your bearings, locate your destination, and decide which *sortie* you want. At stops with several *sorties*, you can save lots of walking by choosing the best exit.

Thieves thrive in the Métro. Be on guard. A pocket picked as you pass through a turnstile leaves you on the wrong side and the thief strolling away. Any jostle or commotion (especially when boarding or leaving trains) is likely the sign of a thief or team of thieves in action. Paris is most dangerous late at night.

Paris has a huge homeless population and over 12-percent unemployment; expect a warm Métro welcome by panhandlers, musicians, and those selling magazines produced by the homeless community.

By RER: The RER (*Réseau Express Régionale*, ehr-uh-ehr) suburban train system (thick lines on your subway map identified by letters A, B, C, and so on) works like the Métro but is much

Tips for the Métro and RER

Key Words
direction (dee-rek-see-ohn): direction
correspondance (kor-res-pohn-dahns): transfer
sortie (sor-tee): exit
carnet (kar-nay): cheap set of 10 tickets
Pardon, madame/monsieur (par-dohn, mah-dahm/mes-yur): Excuse me, lady/bud.
Je descend (juh day-sahn): I'm getting off.
Donnez-moi mon porte-monnaie!: Give me back my wallet!

Etiquette
• When waiting at the platform, get out of the way of those exiting their train. Board only once everyone is off.
• Avoid using the hinged seats when the car is jammed; they take up valuable standing space.
• When in a crowded train, try not to block the exit. If you're blocking the door when the train stops, step out of the car and to the side, let others off, then get back on.
• Don't talk loudly in the cars. Listen to how quietly Parisians can communicate and follow their lead.
• On escalators, stand on the right, pass on the left.

speedier because it makes only a few stops within the city. One Métro ticket is all you need for RER rides within Paris. You can transfer between the Métro and RER systems with the same ticket. Unlike the Métro, you need to insert your ticket in a turnstile to exit the RER system. To travel outside the city (to Versailles or the airport, for example) you'll need to buy a separate, more expensive ticket at the station window before boarding, and make sure your stop is served by checking the signs over the train platform (not all trains serve all stops).

By City Bus: The trickier bus system is worth figuring out. Métro tickets are good on both bus and Métro, though you can't use the same ticket to transfer between the two systems. One ticket gets you anywhere in central Paris, but if you leave the city center (shown as section 1 on the diagram on board the bus), you must validate a second ticket. While the Métro shuts down at about 00:30, some buses continue much later. Schedules are posted at bus stops. Handy bus-system maps are available in any Métro station (*plan des autobus*) and are provided in your *Paris Pratique* map book if you invest.

Big system maps, posted at each bus and Métro stop, display the routes. Individual route diagrams show the exact route of the lines serving that stop. Major stops are painted on the side of each bus. Enter through the front doors. Punch your Métro ticket in the machine behind the driver, or pay the higher cash fare. Get off the bus using the rear door. Even if you're not certain you've figured it out, do some joyriding (outside of rush hour). Lines #24, #63, and #69 are Paris' most scenic routes and make a great introduction to the city. Bus #69 is particularly handy, running between the Eiffel Tower, the recommended hotels around rue Cler, the Orsay Gallery, the Louvre, the Marais/Bastille area (more recommended hotels), and Père Lachaise Cemetery. The most handy bus routes are listed for each hotel area recommended (below).

By Taxi: Parisian taxis are almost reasonable. A 10-minute ride costs about 50F (versus about 5F to get anywhere in town on the Métro). You can try waving one down, but it's easier to ask for the nearest taxi stand ("oo ay la tet de stah-see-oh taxi") or ask your hotel to call for you. Higher rates are charged from 22:00 to 6:30, all day Sunday, and to the airport. If you call from your hotel the meter starts as soon as the call is received. Taxis are tough to find on Friday and Saturday night, especially after the Métro closes (around 00:30).

By Foot: Be careful out there! Parisian drivers are notorious for ignoring pedestrians. Never assume you have the right of way, even in a crosswalk. When crossing a street, keep your pace constant and don't stop suddenly. Parisian drivers carefully calculate your speed and will miss you, providing you don't alter your route or pace.

Organized Tours of Paris

Bus Tours: Paris Vision offers handy bus tours of Paris, day and night (advertised in hotel lobbies); their "Illuminated Paris" tour is explained in Entertainment, below. Paris also has a "hop-on, hop-off" bus service called **Open Deck Tours** that connects all the major sights and includes a running commentary; you can get off at a site, explore, and catch a later bus (170F, buy from driver, good for two days, 2 buses per hour). You'll see these bright yellow topless double-decker buses all over town.

Boat Tours: Several companies offer one-hour boat cruises on the Seine. The **Bateaux-Mouches** boats depart every 30 minutes (from 10:00–23:00, best at night) from the pont de l'Alma, the pont Neuf, and Eiffel Tower (40F, 20F for children under age 14, tel. 01 42 25 96 10). Offered from June–September only, the **Bateau-Bus** is a river bus that connects five stops along the river: Eiffel Tower, Orsay, Louvre, Notre-Dame, and place de la Concorde (60F, 30F for youth, departures every 45 minutes from about 10:00–19:00; pick up a brochure at any TI).

Walking Tours: Use the walking tours described in this book and be your own guide. Or, consider Paris Walking Tours, which offers a daily walk for 60F. Choose from architecture, Montmartre, Hemingway's Paris, Medieval Paris, French Revolution, museum tours (admission extra), and more (tel. 01 48 09 21 40, fax 01 42 43 75 51, Web site: http://ourworld.compuserve. com/homepages/pariswalking).

Sights—The "Historic Core of Paris" Walk

(This information is distilled from the Historic Paris Walk chapter in *Rick Steves' Mona Winks*, by Gene Openshaw and Rick Steves.) Allow four hours for this self-guided tour hours, including sightseeing. Start where the city did—on the Île de la Cité, facing the Notre-Dame and following the dotted line on the "Core of Paris" map. To get to the Notre-Dame, ride the Métro to Cité, Hôtel de Ville, or St. Michel, and walk to the big square facing the . . .

▲▲**Notre-Dame Cathedral**—The 700-year-old cathedral is packed with history and tourists. Study its sculpture (Notre-Dame's forte) and windows, take in a Mass, eavesdrop on guides, and walk all around the outside. (Free, daily 8:00–18:45; treasury-15F, daily 9:30–17:30. Ask about the free English tours, normally Wednesday and Thursday at noon and Saturday at 14:30.) Sunday Masses are at 8:00, 8:45, 10:00, 11:30, 12:30, and 18:30. Climb to the top for a great gargoyle's-eye view of the city; you get 400 steps for only 30F (entrance on outside, north tower open 9:30–17:30, closed at lunch and earlier off-season). There are clean 2.70F toilets in front of the church near Charlemagne's statue.

The **Cathedral facade** is worth a close look. The church is

Core of Paris

dedicated to "Our Lady" (Notre-Dame). Mary is center stage—cradling Jesus, surrounded by the halo of the rose window. Adam is on the left, and Eve is on the right.

Below Mary and above the arches is a row of 28 statues known as the Kings of Judah. During the French Revolution, these Biblical kings were mistaken for the hated French kings. The citizens stormed the church, crying, "Off with their heads!" All were decapitated but have since been recapitated.

Speaking of decapitation, look at the carving above the doorway on the left. The man with his head in his hands is St. Denis. Back when there was a Roman temple on this spot, Christianity began making converts. The fourth-century bishop of Roman Paris, Denis, was beheaded. But these early Christians were hard to keep down. The man who would become St. Denis got up, tucked his head under his arm, and headed north until he found just the right place to meet his maker: Montmartre, which means "mountain of the martyr." The Parisians were convinced of this miracle, Christianity gained ground, and a church soon replaced the pagan temple.

Medieval art was OK if it embellished the house of God and

told Bible stories. For a fine example, move to the base of the central column (at the foot of Mary, about where the head of St. Denis could spit if he was real good). Working around from the left, find God telling a barely created Eve, "Have fun but no apples." Next, the sexiest serpent I've ever seen makes apples *à la mode*. Finally, Adam and Eve, now ashamed of their nakedness, are expelled by an angel. This is a tiny example in a church covered with meaning.

Now move to the right and study the carving above the central portal. It's the end of the world, and Christ sits on the throne of Judgment (just under the arches, holding his hands up). Below him an angel and a demon weigh souls in the balance. The "good" stand to the left, looking up to heaven. The "bad" ones to the right are chained up and led off to . . . Versailles on a Tuesday. The "ugly" ones must be the crazy sculpted demons to the right, at the base of the arch.

Wander through the interior. You'll be routed around the ambulatory, much as medieval pilgrims would have been. Don't miss the rose windows filling each of the transepts. Back outside, walk around the church through the park on the riverside for a close look at the flying buttresses.

The neo-Gothic 90-meter spire is a product of the 1860 reconstruction. Around its base are apostles and evangelists (the green men) as well as Viollet-le-Duc, the architect in charge of the work. Notice how the apostles look outward, blessing the city, while the architect (at top, seen from behind the church) looks up, admiring his spire.

The archaeological **crypt** is a worthwhile 15-minute stop with your museum pass (enter 100 yards in front of church, 32F, 50F with Notre-Dame's tower, daily 10:00–18:00, closes at 16:30 October–April). You'll see Roman ruins, trace the street plan of the medieval village, and see diagrams of how the earliest Paris grew and grew, all thoughtfully explained in English.

If you're hungry near Notre-Dame, the only grocery store on the Île de la Cité is tucked away at 16 rue Chanoinesse, one block north of the church (9:00–13:30 and 16:00–20:30, closed Sunday). Nearby Île St. Louis has inexpensive *crêperies* and grocery stores open daily on its main drag. Plan a picnic for the quiet bench-filled park immediately behind the church (public WC).

Behind the Notre-Dame, squeeze through the tourist buses, cross the street, and enter the iron gate into the park at the tip of the island. Look for the stairs and head down.

▲▲**Deportation Memorial (Mémorial de la Déportation)**— This memorial to the 200,000 French victims of the Nazi concentration camps draws you into their experience. As you descend the steps, the city around you disappears. Surrounded by walls, you have become a prisoner. Your only freedom is your view of the sky and the tantalizing glimpse of the river below.

Enter the single-file chamber ahead. Inside, the circular plaque in the floor reads, "They descended into the mouth of the earth and they did not return." A hallway stretches in front of you, lined with 200,000 lighted crystals, one for each French citizen that died. Flickering at the far end is the eternal flame of hope. The tomb of the unknown deportee lies at your feet. Above, the inscription reads, "Dedicated to the living memory of the 200,000 French deportees sleeping in the night and the fog, exterminated in the Nazi concentration camps."

Above the exit as you leave is the message you'll find at all Nazi sights: "Forgive but never forget." (Free, daily 8:30–21:45, weekends and holidays from 9:00, sometimes closes 12:00–14:00, shorter hours off-season, east tip of the island near Île St. Louis, behind Notre-Dame, Mo: Cité.)

Île St. Louis—Back on street level, look across the river to the Île St. Louis. If the Île de la Cité is a tug laden with the history of Paris, it's towing this classy little residential dinghy laden only with boutiques, famous sorbet shops, and characteristic restaurants (see Eating in Paris, below). This island wasn't developed until much later (18th century). What was a swampy mess is now harmonious Parisian architecture. The pedestrian bridge, Pont Saint Louis, connects the two islands leading right to rue Saint Louis en l'Île. This spine of the island is lined with interesting shops. A short stroll takes you to the famous Bertillon ice-cream parlour (#31). Loop back to the pedestrian bridge along the parklike quays (walk north to the river and turn left). This riverside walk is about as peaceful and romantic as Paris gets.

Before walking to the opposite end of the Île de la Cité, loop through the Latin Quarter (as indicated on the map). From the Deportation Memorial cross the bridge onto the Left Bank and enjoy the riverside view of the Notre-Dame and window shop among the green book stalls, browsing through used books, vintage posters, and souvenirs. At the little park and church (over the bridge from the front of Notre-Dame), venture inland a few blocks, basically arcing through the Latin Quarter and returning to the island two bridges down at place St. Michel.

▲Latin Quarter—This area, which gets its name from the language used here when it was an exclusive medieval university district, lies between the Luxembourg Gardens and the Seine, centering around the Sorbonne University and boulevards St. Germain and St. Michel. This is the core of the Left Bank—it's crowded with international eateries, far-out bookshops, street singers, and jazz clubs. For colorful wandering and café-sitting, afternoons and evenings are best (Mo: St. Michel).

Along rue Saint-Severin you can still see the shadow of the medieval sewer system. (The street slopes into a central channel of bricks.) In the days before plumbing and toilets, when people still went to the river or neighborhood wells for their water, "flushing" meant throwing it out the window. Certain times of day were flushing times. Maids on the fourth floor would holler "*Garde de l'eau!*" ("Look out for the water!") and heave it into the streets, where it would eventually be washed down into the Seine.

The **Cluny Museum** (also known by its new name: Musée National du Moyen Age), a treasure trove of medieval art, fills the old Roman baths, offering close-up looks at stained glass, Notre-Dame carvings, fine goldsmithing and jewelry, and rooms of tapestries—the best of which is the exquisite *Lady with the Unicorn*. In five panels, a delicate-as-medieval-can-be noble lady introduces a delighted unicorn to the senses of taste, hearing, sight, smell, and touch (30F, Wednesday–Monday 9:15–17:45, closed Tuesday, 6 place Paul-Painlevé near the corner of boulevards St. Michel and St. Germain, tel. 01 53 73 78 00, Mo: Cluny).

Place St. Michel (facing the St. Michel bridge) is the traditional core of the Left Bank's artsy, liberal, hippie, Bohemian district of poets, philosophers, winos, and tourists. In less commercial times, place St. Michel was a gathering point for the city's malcontents and misfits. Here, in 1871, the citizens took the streets from the government troops, set up barricades *Les Miz*–style, and established the Paris Commune. In World War II the locals rose up against their Nazi oppressors (read the plaques by the St. Michael fountain). And in the spring of 1968, a time of social upheaval all over the world, young students—battling riot batons and tear gas—took over the square and demanded change.

From place St. Michel, look across the river and find the spire of Sainte-Chapelle church and its weathervane angel (below). Cross the river on the Pont St. Michel and continue along boulevard du Palais. On your left you'll see the high-security doorway to Sainte-Chapelle. But first, carry on another 30 meters and turn right at a wide pedestrian street, the rue de Lutece.

Cité "Métropolitain" Stop—Of the 141 original turn-of-the-century subway entrances, this is one of 17 survivors now preserved as a national art treasure. The curvy, plant-like ironwork is a textbook example of Art Nouveau, the style that rebelled against the erector-set squareness of the Industrial Age (e.g., Mr. Eiffel's tower).

The flower market right here on place Louis Lepine is a pleasant detour. On Sundays this square chirps with a busy bird market. And across the way is the Prefecture de Police, where Inspector Clouseau of *Pink Panther* fame used to work, and where the local resistance fighters took the first building from the Nazis in August 1944, leading to the Allied liberation of Paris a week later.

Pause here to admire the view. Sainte-Chapelle is a pearl in an ugly architectural oyster, part of a complex of buildings that includes the Palace of Justice (to the right of Sainte-Chapelle, behind the fancy gates). Return to the entrance of Sainte-Chapelle. You'll need to pass through a metal detector to get in. Free toilets are ahead, on the left. The line into the church may be long. (Museum card holders can go directly in; pick up the excellent English info sheet.) Enter the humble ground floor. . . .

▲▲▲**Sainte-Chapelle**—The triumph of Gothic church architecture is a cathedral of glass like no other. It was speedily built from 1242 to 1248 for St. Louis IX (France's only canonized king) to house the supposed Crown of Thorns. Its architectural harmony is due to the fact that it was completed under the direction of one architect in only six years—unheard of in Gothic times. (Notre-Dame took more than 200 years to build.)

The design clearly shows an Old Regime approach to worship. The basement was for staff and other common folk. Royal Christians worshiped upstairs. The ground-floor paint job, a 19th-century restoration, is a reasonably accurate copy of the original.

Climb the spiral staircase to the *Chapelle Haute*. Fill the place with choral music, crank up the sunshine, face the top of the altar, and really believe that the Crown of Thorns was there, and this becomes one awesome space.

"Let there be light." In the Bible, it's clear: Light is divine. Light shining through stained glass was a symbol of God's grace shining down to earth. Gothic architects used their new technology to turn dark stone buildings into lanterns of light. The glory of Gothic shines brighter here than in any other church.

There are 15 separate panels of stained glass (6,500 square feet—two-thirds of it 13th-century original), with more than 1,100 different scenes, mostly from the Bible. In medieval times, scenes like these helped teach Bible stories to the illiterate.

The altar was raised up high to better display the relic—the Crown of Thorns—around which this chapel was built. The supposed Crown cost King Louis three times as much as this church. Today it is kept in the Notre-Dame Treasury and shown only on Good Friday.

Louis' little private viewing window is in the wall to the right of the altar. Louis, both saintly and shy, liked to go to church without dealing with the rigors of public royal life. Here he could worship still dressed in his jammies.

Lay your camera on the ground and shoot the ceiling. Those pure and simple ribs growing out of the slender columns are the essence of Gothic.

Books in the gift shop explain the stained glass in English. There are concerts (120F) almost every summer evening. (32F, daily 9:30–18:00, off-season 10:00–17:00, call 01 48 01 91 35 for concert information, Mo: Cité.)

Palais du Justice—Back outside, as you walk around the church exterior, look down and notice how much Paris has risen in the

800 years since Sainte-Chapelle was built. You're in a huge complex of buildings that has housed the local government since ancient Roman times. It was the site of the original Gothic palace of the early kings of France. The only surviving medieval parts are the Sainte-Chapelle church and the Conciergerie prison.

Most of the site is now covered by the giant Palais de Justice, home of France's supreme court (built in 1776). *"Liberté, Egalité, Fraternité"* over the doors is a reminder that this was also the headquarters of the revolutionary government.

Now pass through the big iron gate to the noisy boulevard du Palais and turn left (toward the Right Bank). On the corner is the site of the oldest public clock (1334) in the city. While the present clock is said to be Baroque, it somehow still manages to keep accurate time.

Turn left onto Quai de l'Horloge and walk along the river. The round medieval tower just ahead marks the entrance to the Conciergerie. Pop in to visit the courtyard and lobby (free). Step past the serious-looking guard into the courtyard.

Conciergerie—The Conciergerie, a former prison, is a gloomy place. Kings used it to torture and execute failed assassins. The leaders of the Revolution put it to similar good use. The tower next to the entrance, called "the babbler," was named for the painful sounds that leaked from it.

Look at the stark lettering above the doorways. This was a no-nonsense revolutionary time. Everything, even lettering, was subjected to the test of reason. No frills or we chop 'em off.

Step inside; the lobby, with an English-language history display, is free. Marie-Antoinette was imprisoned here. During a busy eight-month period in the Revolution, she was one of 2,600 prisoners kept here on their way to the guillotine. The interior, with its huge vaulted and pillared rooms, echoes with history but is pretty barren (28F, daily 9:30–18:30, 10:00–17:00 in winter, good English descriptions). You can see Marie-Antoinette's cell, housing a collection of her mementoes. In another room, a list of those made "a foot shorter at the top" by the "national razor" includes ex-King Louis XVI, Charlotte Corday (who murdered Marat in his bathtub), and the chief revolutionary who got a taste of his own medicine, Maximilien Robespierre.

Back outside, wink at the flak-vested guard, fake right, and turn left. Listen for babbles, and continue your walk along the river. Across the river you can see the rooftop observatory—flags flapping—of the Samaritaine Department store, where this walk will end. At the first corner, veer left past France's supreme court building and into a sleepy triangular square called place Dauphine. Marvel at how such quaintness could be lodged in the midst of such greatness as you walk through the park to the end of the island. At the equestrian statue of Henry IV, turn right onto the bridge and take refuge in one of the nooks on the Eiffel Tower side.

Pont Neuf—This "new bridge" is now Paris' oldest. Built during Henry IV's reign (around 1600), its 12 arches span the widest part of the river. The fine view includes the park on the tip of the island (note Seine tour boats), the Orsay Gallery, and the Louvre. These turrets were originally for vendors and street entertainers. In the days of Henry IV, who originated the promise of "a chicken in every pot," this would have been a lively scene.

Directly over the river, the first building you'll hit on the Right Bank is the venerable old department store, Samaritaine.

▲**Samaritaine Department Store Viewpoint**—Enter the store and go to the rooftop. Ride the glass elevator from near the Pont Neuf entrance to the ninth floor (you'll be greeted by a W.C., check out the sink). Pass the 10th-floor *terrasse* for the 11th-floor *panorama* (tight spiral staircase; watch your head). Quiz yourself. Working counterclockwise, find: the Eiffel Tower, Invalides/Napoleon's Tomb, Montparnasse Tower, Henry IV statue on the tip of the island, Sorbonne University, the dome of the Panthéon, Sainte-Chapelle, Notre-Dame, Hôtel de Ville (city hall), Pompidou Center, Sacré-Coeur, Opéra, and Louvre. The Champs-Élysées leads to the Arc de Triomphe. Shadowing that—even bigger, while two times as distant—is the Grand Arche la Defense. You'll find light, reasonably priced, and incredibly scenic meals on the breezy terrace, and a super-market in the basement. (Rooftop view is free, daily 9:30–19:00, tel. 01 40 41 20 20. Mo: Pont Neuf.)

Sights—Paris' Museums near the Tuileries Gardens

The newly renovated Tuileries gardens was once private property of kings and queens. Paris' grandest public park links these museums:

▲▲▲**Louvre**—This is Europe's oldest, biggest, greatest, and maybe most-crowded museum. There is no grander entry than through the pyramid, but metal detectors create a long line at times. To avoid the line, either use the nearby entrance over the Richelieu wing (facing the pyramid with your back to the Tuileries Garden, go to your left, which is north; under the arches you'll find the Richelieu entrance and escalator down), or enter the Louvre directly from the Métro stop "Palais Royale Musée de Louvre." Signs to "Musée du Louvre" put you in a slick underground shopping mall that connects with the Pyramid. (Don't get off at the "Louvre Rivoli" Métro stop, which is farther away.)

Pick up the free *Louvre Handbook in English* at the information desk under the pyramid as you enter. Don't try to cover the museum thoroughly. The 90-minute English-language tours, which leave six times daily except Sunday, boil this overwhelming museum down to

Louvre Area

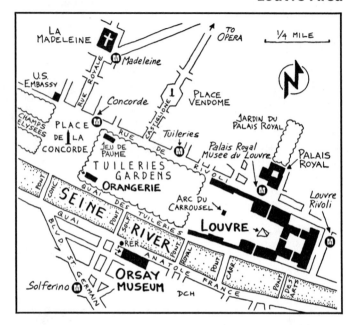

size (33F, tour tel. 01 40 20 52 09, Web site: www. louvre.fr). Clever new 30F digital audio tours (after ticket booths, at top of stairs) give you a receiver and a directory of about 130 masterpieces, allowing you to dial a (rather dull) commentary on included works as you stumble upon them. Rick Steves' and Gene Openshaw's museum guidebook, *Rick Steves' Mona Winks* (buy in the United States), includes a self-guided tour of the Louvre.

If you can't get a guide, start in the Denon wing and visit these highlights, in this order: Michelangelo's *Slaves*, Ancient Greek and Roman (Parthenon frieze, *Venus de Milo*, Pompeii mosaics, Etruscan sarcophagi, Roman portrait busts, Nike of Samothrace); Apollo Gallery (jewels); French and Italian paintings in the Grande Galerie (a quarter-mile long and worth the hike); the *Mona Lisa* and her Italian Renaissance roommates; the nearby neoclassical collection (*Coronation of Napoleon*); and the Romantic collection, with works by Delacroix (*Liberty at the Barricades*—see your 100F note) and Géricault (*Raft of the Medusa*).

Cost: 45F, 26F after 15:00 and on Sunday, those under 18 enter free. Tickets good all day. Reentry allowed.

Hours: Wednesday through Monday 9:00 to 18:00, closed Tuesday, all wings open Wednesday until 21:45, Richelieu Wing (only) open until 22:00 on Monday. Galleries start closing 30 minutes early. Closed January 1, Easter, May 1, November 1, and Christmas Day. Crowds are worst on Sunday, Monday, Wednesday, and mornings. Save money and avoid crowds by visiting in the afternoon. (You can enter the pyramid for free until 21:30. Go in at night and see it glow.) Tel. 01 40 20 53 17 or 01 40 20 51 51 for recorded information.

The newly-renovated Richelieu wing and the underground shopping mall extension add the finishing touches to Le Grand Louvre Project (that started in 1989 with the pyramid entrance). To explore this most recent extension of the Louvre, enter through the pyramid then walk toward the inverted pyramid and uncover a post office, a handy TI and SNCF office, glittering boutiques and a dizzying assortment of good-value eateries (up the escalator), and the Palais-Royal Métro entrance. Stairs at the far end take you right into the Tuileries Gardens, a perfect antidote to the stuffy, crowded rooms of the Louvre.

▲L'Orangerie—This small, quiet, and often-overlooked museum houses Monet's waterlilies, many famous Renoirs, and a scattering of other great Impressionist works. The round rooms of waterlilies are two of the most enjoyable rooms in Paris (30F, Wednesday–Monday 9:45–17:15, closed Tuesday, in Tuileries Gardens near the place de la Concorde, Mo: Concorde, tel. 01 42 97 48 16).

Jeu de Paume—This one-time home to the Impressionist art collection (now located in the Musée d'Orsay) hosts rotating exhibits of top contemporary artists (38F, Tuesday 12:00–21:30, Wednesday–Friday 12:00–19:00, weekends 10:00–19:00, closed Monday; on place de la Concorde, just inside the Tuileries Gardens on the rue de Rivoli side; Mo: Concorde).

▲▲▲Orsay Museum—Paris' 19th-century art museum (actually, art from 1848–1914) includes Europe's greatest collection of Impressionist works. The museum is housed in a former train station (Gare d'Orsay) across the river and 10 minutes downstream from the Louvre. (The RER-C train line zips you right to "Musée d'Orsay"; the Métro stop "Solferino" is three blocks south of the Orsay.)

Start on the ground floor. The "pretty" conservative establishment art is on the right. Then cross left into the brutally truthful and, at that time, very shocking art of the realist rebels and Manet. Then ride the escalators at the far end (detouring at the top for a grand museum view) to the series of Impressionist rooms (Monet, Renoir, Dégas, et al). Don't miss the Grand Ballroom (room 52, *Arts et Decors de la IIIème République*) and Art Nouveau on the mezzanine level.

Cost: 39F, 27F for the young and old, under 18 free, tickets good all day. The booth near the entrance gives free floor plans in English. English-language tours usually run daily except Sunday at 11:30, cost 38F, take 90 minutes, and are also available on audiotape.

City museum passes are sold in the basement; if there's a long line you can skip it by buying one there, but you can't skip the metal detector line into the museum. Tel. 01 40 49 48 48.

Hours: Tuesday, Wednesday, Friday, Saturday 10:00 to 18:00, Thursday 10:00 to 21:45, Sunday 9:00 to 18:00, closed Monday. Museum opens at 9:00 June 20 through September 20. Last entrance is 45 minutes before closing. Galleries start closing 30 minutes early. The Orsay is very crowded Tuesdays, when the Louvre is closed.

Sights—Southwest Paris: The Eiffel Tower Neighborhood

▲▲▲Eiffel Tower—It's crowded and expensive but worth the trouble. Go early (arrive by 9:30) or late in the day (after 18:00) to avoid most crowds; weekends are worst. Pilier Nord (the north pillar) has the biggest elevator and, therefore, the fastest moving line.

It's 1,000 feet tall (six inches taller in hot weather), covers 2.5 acres, and requires 50 tons of paint. The Tower's 7,000 tons of metal are spread out so well at the base that it's no heavier per square inch than a linebacker on tiptoes. Visitors to Paris may find *Mona Lisa* to be less than expected, but the Eiffel Tower rarely disappoints, even in an era of skyscrapers.

Built a hundred years after the French Revolution (and in the midst of an industrial one), the Tower served no function but to impress. Gustave Eiffel won an architectural contest at the 1889 Centennial world's fair by beating out such rival proposals as a giant guillotine. To a generation hooked on technology, the Tower was the marvel of the age, a symbol of progress and of man's ingenuity. To others it was a cloned-sheep monstrosity. The writer Maupassant routinely ate lunch in the tower just so he wouldn't have to look at it.

Delicate and graceful when seen from afar, it's massive—even a bit scary—from close up. You don't appreciate the size until you walk toward it—like a mountain, it seems so close but takes forever to reach. There are three observation platforms, at 200, 400 and 900 feet. The higher you go the more you pay. Each requires a separate elevator (and a line), so plan on at least 90 minutes if you want to go to the top and back. The view from the 400-foot-high second level is plenty. Begin at the first floor, read the informative signs (in English) describing the major monuments, see the entertaining free movie on the history of the tower, and consider a drink overlooking all of Paris at the café or at the reasonable restaurant Altitude 95 (decent 100F meals until 20:00, and Paris' best view bar). Take the elevator to the second floor for even greater views. As you ascend through the metal beams, imagine being a worker, perched high above nothing, riveting this giant erector set together.

On top you can see all of Paris, aided by a panorama guide. On a good day you can see 40 miles. It costs 20F to go to the first

Eiffel Tower to Invalides

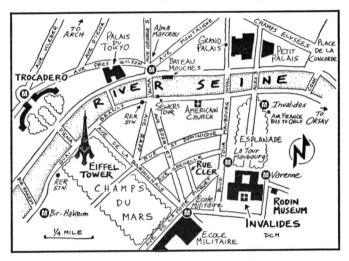

level, 40F to the second, and 57F to go all the way for the 1,000-foot view (not included with museum pass). On a budget? You can climb the stairs to the second level for only 12F (summers daily 9:00–24:00, off-season 9:30–23:00, tel. 01 44 11 23 23, Mo: Trocadero, RER: Champs de Mars).

The best places from which to view the tower are Trocadero square (a 10-minute walk north, across the river) and the long, grassy fields of the Champ-du-Mars (to the south). After about 21:00 the gendarmes look the other way as Parisians stretch out or picnic on the grass. However impressive it may be by day, it's an awesome thing to see at twilight, when the tower becomes engorged with light, and virile Paris lies back and lets night be on top.

For another great view, especially at night, enjoy the tower (and the wild in-line skating scene) by approaching via the Trocadero Métro stop. The big J-number panal clicks down the days (j for *jour*) until the new millenium.

▲**Paris Sewer Tour (Egouts)**—This quick and easy visit takes you along a few hundred yards of underground water tunnel lined with interesting displays, well-described in English, explaining the evolution of the world's longest sewer system. (If you lined up Paris' sewers they would reach beyond Istanbul.) Don't miss the slide show, the fine W.C.s just beyond the gift shop, and the occasional tours in English (32F, 11:00–17:00, closed Thursday and Friday, where the Pont de l'Alma hits the Left Bank, tel. 01 47 05 10 29).

▲▲**Les Invalides: Napoleon's Tomb and Army Museum**—
The emperor lies majestically dead inside several coffins under a

grand dome—a goose-bumping pilgrimage for historians.
Napoleon is surrounded by the tombs of other French war heroes
and Europe's greatest military museum in the Hôtel des Invalides.
Follow signs to the "crypt," where you'll find Roman Empire–style
reliefs listing the accomplishments of Napoleon's administration.
The restored dome glitters with 26 pounds of gold (37F, daily
10:00–18:00, off-season 17:00, tel. 01 44 42 37 67, Métros: La
Tour Maubourg or Varennes).

▲▲**Rodin Museum**—This user-friendly museum is filled with
passionate works by the greatest sculptor since Michelangelo.
See *The Kiss*, *The Thinker*, *The Gates of Hell*, and many more.
Don't miss the room full of work by Rodin's student and mistress, Camille Claudel. (28F, 18F on Sunday; 5F for gardens
only, which may be Paris' best deal as many works are well-
displayed in the beautiful gardens; 9:30–17:45, closed Monday
and at 17:00 off-season, 77 rue de Varennes, tel. 01 44 18 61 10,
Mo: Varennes, near Napoleon's Tomb.) There's a good self-
serve cafeteria as well as idyllic picnic spots in the family-
friendly back garden.

▲▲**Marmottan**—In this private, intimate, less-visited museum
you'll find more than 100 paintings by Claude Monet (thanks to
his son Michel), including the *Impressions of a Sunrise* painting that
gave the movement its start—and name (40F, 10:00–17:30, closed
Monday, no museum pass, 2 rue Louis Boilly, Mo: La Muette, follow the museum signs six blocks through a park to the museum,
tel. 01 42 24 07 02). Combine this fine museum with a stroll down
one of Paris' most pleasant shopping streets, the rue de Passy
(from la Muette Mo. stop).

Sights—Southeast Paris: The Latin Quarter

▲**Latin Quarter**—This Left Bank neighborhood just opposite the
Notre-Dame is the Latin Quarter. (For more information and a
walking tour, see "Historic Core of Paris" walk above.) This was a
center of Roman Paris. But its touristic fame relates to the Latin
Quarter's intriguing artsy, bohemian character. This was perhaps
Europe's leading university district in the middle ages—home,
since the 13th century, to the prestigious Sorbonne University.
Back then, Latin was the language of higher education. And, since
students here came from all over Europe, Latin served as their linguistic common denominator. Locals referred to the quarter by its
language: Latin. In modern times this was the center of Paris' café
culture. The neighborhood's main boulevards (St. Michel and St.
Germain) are lined with cafés—once the haunts of great poets and
philosophers, but now the hang-out of tired tourists. While still
youthful and artsy, the area has become a tourist ghetto filled with
cheap North African eateries.

St. Germain des Prés—A church was first built on this site in

A.D. 452. The church you see today was constructed in 1163. The area around the church hops at night with fire-eaters, mimes, and scads of artists (Mo: St. Germain-des-Prés).

▲**St. Sulpice Organ Concert**—For pipe-organ enthusiasts, this is a delight. The Grand-Orgue at St. Sulpice has a rich history, with a line of 12 world-class organists (including Widor and Dupre) going back 300 years. Marcel Dupre started the tradition of opening the loft to visitors after the 10:30 service on Sundays. Daniel Roth continues to welcome guests in three langueages while playing five keyboards at once. The 10:30 Sunday Mass is followed by a 20-minute recital at 11:40. If you're lucky, at 12:00 the small unmarked door will open (left of entry as you face the rear) and allow visitors to scamper like sixteenth notes up spiral stairs to a world of 6,000 pipes, where they can watch the master perform the next Mass, friends warming his bench, and a committee scrambling to pull and push the 110 stops (Mo: St. Sulpice or Mabillon).

▲**Luxembourg Gardens**—Paris' most beautiful, interesting, and enjoyable garden/park/recreational area is a great place to watch Parisians at rest and play. Bring your kids to the playground or afternoon puppet shows (*guignols*). Challenge the card and chess players to a game (near the tennis courts) or find a free chair near the main pond and take a breather. Notice any pigeons? A poor Ernest Hemingway used to hand-hunt (read: strangle) them here. The grand neoclassical-domed **Panthéon** (now a mausoleum housing the tombs of several great Frenchmen) is a block away and is only worth entering if you have a museum pass. The park is open until dusk (Mo: Odéon). If you enjoy the Luxembourg Gardens and want to see more, visit the more elegant Parc Monceau (Mo: Monceau) and the colorful Jardin des Plantes (Mo: Jussieu).

▲**Montparnasse Tower**—This 59-floor superscraper—it's cheaper and easier to get to the top than it is to that of the Eiffel Tower—offers one of Paris' best views, since the Eiffel Tower is in it and the Montparnasse tower isn't. Buy the photo guide to the city, then go to the rooftop and orient yourself (42F, daily in summer 9:30–23:00, off-season 10:00–22:00, disappointing after dark, entrance on rue l'Arrivé, Mo: Montparnasse). This is efficient when combined with a day trip to Chartres, which begins at the Montparnasse train station.

Sights—Northwest Paris: Champs-Élysées and Arc de Triomphe to La Defense
▲▲**Place de la Concorde and the Champs-Élysées**—This famous boulevard is Paris' backbone and greatest concentration of traffic. All of France seems to converge on the place de la Concorde, the city's largest square. It was here that the guillotine took the lives of thousands—including King Louis XVI. Back then it was called the place de la Revolution.

Catherine de Medici wanted a place to drive her carriage, so she started draining the swamp that would become the Champs-Élysées. Napoleon put on the final touches, and it's been the place to be seen ever since. The Tour de France bicycle race ends here, as do all parades (French or foe) of any significance. While the boulevard has become a bit hamburgerized, a walk here is a must. Take the Métro to the Arc de Triomphe (Mo: Étoile) and saunter down the Champs-Élysées (Métro stops every few blocks: FDR, George V, and Étoile).

▲▲▲**Arc de Triomphe**—Napoleon had the magnificent Arc de Triomphe commissioned to commemorate his victory at the Battle of Austerlitz. There's no triumphal arch bigger (50 meters high, 40 meters wide). And, with 12 converging boulevards, there's no traffic circle more thrilling to experience—either behind the wheel or on foot (take the underpass). An elevator or a spiral staircase leads to a cute museum about the arch and a grand view from the top, even after dark (35F, Tuesday–Saturday 9:00–23:00, Sunday and Monday 9:30–18:00, tel. 01 43 80 31 31, Mo: Étoile).

▲**Grande Arche de La Defense**—The centerpiece of Paris' ambitious skyscraper complex (La Defense) is the Grande Arche. Built to celebrate the 200th anniversary of the 1789 French Revolution, the place is big—38 floors on more than 200 acres. It holds offices for 30,000 people. Notre-Dame Cathedral could fit under its arch. The La Defense complex is an interesting study in 1960s land-use planning. More than 100,000 workers commute here daily, directing lots of business and development away from downtown and allowing central Paris to retain its more elegant feel. This aspect makes sense to most Parisians, regardless of whatever else they feel about the controversial complex. You'll enjoy city views from the Arche elevator (40F includes a film on its construction and art exhibits, daily 9:00–20:00, off-season 9:00–19:00, tel. 01 49 07 27 57, Métro or RER: La Defense, follow signs to Grande Arche).

Sights—Northeast Paris: Marais Neighborhood and More

To better appreciate this area and connect its sights, take our "Marais Walk," described later in this book.

▲**Picasso Museum (Hôtel Salé)**—This is the world's largest collection of Pablo Picasso's paintings, sculpture, sketches, and ceramics, and includes his personal collection of Impressionist art. It's well-explained in English and worth ▲▲▲ if you're a fan (30F, Wednesday–Monday 9:30–18:00, closed Tuesday, 5 rue Thorigny, tel. 01 42 71 25 21, Mo: St. Paul or Chemin Vert).

▲**Carnavalet Museum**—The tumultuous history of Paris is well-displayed in this converted Marais mansion. Explanations are in French only, but most displays are somewhat self-explanatory.

You'll see paintings of Parisian scenes, French Revolution paraphernalia, old Parisian store signs, a guillotine, a model of 16th-
century Île de la Cité (notice the bridge houses), and rooms full of
15th-century Parisian furniture. The medieval and revolution
rooms are the most interesting (35F, included with museum pass,
Tuesday–Sunday 10:00–17:00, closed Monday, 23 rue de Sévigné,
tel. 01 42 72 21 13, Mo: St. Paul).

Promenade Plantée Park—This three-mile garden walk was
once a train track and is now a joy. It runs from the place de la
Bastille (Mo: Bastille) along Avenue Daumesnil to Saint-Mandé
(Mo: Michel Bizot). Part of the park is elevated and part consists
of just walking along the street till you pick up the next segment.
From the place de la Bastille, take Avenue Daumesnil (past the
opera building) to the intersection with avenue Ledru Rollin, then
walk up the stairs and through the gate (hours vary with season,
open roughly 8:00–20:00).

▲**Père Lachaise Cemetery**—Littered with the tombstones of many
of the city's most illustrious dead, this is your best one-stop look at
the fascinating and romantic world of the "permanent Parisians."
The place is confusing, but maps will direct you to the graves of
Chopin, Molière, and even the American rock star Jim Morrison
(who died in Paris). In section 92, a series of statues memorializing
the war makes the French war experience a bit more real (helpful
10F maps at the flower store near entry, across the street from Métro
stop, closes at dusk, Mo: Père Lachaise or bus #69).

▲**Pompidou Center**—(Closed for renovation until 2000.)
Europe's greatest collection of far-out modern art, the Musée
National d'Art Moderne is housed in this colorfully exoskeletal
building. After so many Madonnas and Children, a piano smashed
to bits and glued to the wall is refreshing. It's a social center with
lots of people, street theater, and activity inside and out—a perpetual
street fair. Ride the escalator for a free city view from the café terrace on top and don't miss the free exhibits on the ground floor
(35F, 24F for the young and old, Monday and Wednesday–Friday
12:00–22:00, weekends and most holidays 10:00–22:00, closed
Tuesday, tel. 01 44 78 12 33, Mo: Rambuteau). Kids of any age
enjoy the fun, colorful fountain (called *Homage to Stravinsky*) next
to the Pompidou Center.

Sights—North Paris: Montmartre
▲**Sacré-Coeur and Montmartre**—This Byzantine-looking
church, while only 130 years old, is impressive. It was built as a
"praise the Lord anyway" gesture, after the French were humili-
ated by the Germans in a brief war in 1871. The church is open
daily until 23:00. One block from the church, the place du Tertre
was the haunt of Toulouse-Lautrec and the original Bohemians.
Today it's mobbed by tourists and unoriginal Bohemians, but still

fun. Wander down the rue Lepic to the two remaining windmills
(once there were 30). Rue des Saules leads to Paris' only vineyard.
Métros: Anvers (one Métro ticket buys your way up the funicular
and avoids the stairs) or the closer but less scenic Abbesses. A taxi
to the top of the hill saves time and sweat.

Pigalle—Paris' red light district, the infamous "Pig Alley," is at
the foot of Butte Montmartre. Ooh la la. More shocking than dangerous. Walk from place Pigalle to place Blanche, teasing desper-
ate barkers and fast-talking temptresses. In bars a 1,000F bottle of
cheap champagne comes with a friend. Stick to the bigger streets,
hang on to your wallet, and exercise good judgment. Cancan can
cost a fortune, as can con artists in topless bars. After dark, countless tour buses line the streets, reminding us that tour guides make
big bucks by bringing their groups to touristic nightclubs like the
famous Moulin Rouge (Mo: Pigalle and Abbesses).

Best Shopping
Forum des Halles is a huge subterranean shopping center. It's
fun, mod, and colorful, but lacks a soul (Mo: Halles). The Gal-
leries Lafayette behind the opera house is your best elegant, Old
World, one-stop Parisian department store/shopping center.
Also, visit the Printemps store and the historic (as well as handy)
Samaritaine department store in several buildings near Pont
Neuf. Ritzy shops surround the Ritz Hotel at place Vendôme
(Mo: Tuileries).

Disappointments de Paris
While Paris can drive you in-Seine with superlatives, here are a
few negatives to help you manage your limited time:

La Madeleine is a big, stark, neoclassical church with a postcard facade and a postbox interior. The famous aristocratic deli
behind the church, Fauchon, is elegant, but so are many others
handier to your hotel.

The old Opéra Garnier has a great Chagall-painted ceiling
but is in a pedestrian-mean area. Don't go to American Express
(behind the Opéra) just to change money. You'll get a better rate
at many other banks.

Paris' Panthéon (nothing like Rome's) is another stark neoclassical edifice filled with mortal remains of great Frenchmen
who mean little to the average American tourist.

The Bastille is Paris' most famous nonsight. The square is
there, but confused tourists look everywhere and can't find the
famous prison of Revolution fame. The building's gone and the
square is good only as a jumping-off point for the "Marais Walk"
(see below) or the Promenade Plantée Park (see Sights—Northeast Paris, above).

The Latin Quarter is a frail shadow of its characteristic self.

It's more Tunisian, Greek, and Woolworth's than old-time Paris. The café life that turned on Hemingway and endeared Boul Miche and Boulevard St. Germain to so many poets is also trampled by modern commercialism.

More Paris Walks

Marais Walk—This walk takes you through one of Paris' most characteristic quarters. When in Paris, the natural inclination is to concentrate only on the big sights. But to experience Paris you need to experience a vital neighborhood. This is a good one, containing more pre-Revolutionary buildings than anywhere else in town.

Ride the Métro to Bastille and follow the dotted path outlined on the Marais map in this chapter. This walk is about three miles long. Allow two hours, and add another hour if you visit the Carnavalet Museum.

At **place de la Bastille** there are more revolutionary images in the Métro station murals than on the square. Exit the Métro following signs to rue Saint Antoine (not the signs to rue Saint Antoine du Faubourg). Ascend onto a noisy square dominated by the bronze *Colonne de Juillet* (July Column). Victims of the revolutions of 1830 and 1848 are buried in a vault 55 meters below this gilded statue of liberty. The actual Bastille, a royal fortress-then-prison that once symbolized old regime tyranny and now symbolizes the Parisian emancipation, is long gone. While only a brick outline of the fortress' round turrets survives (under the traffic where rue Saint Antoine hits the square), the story of the Bastille is indelibly etched on the city's psyche.

For centuries the Bastille was used to defend the city (mostly from its own people). On July 14, 1789, the people of Paris stormed the prison, releasing its seven prisoners and hoping to find arms. They demolished the brick fortress and decorated their pikes with the heads of a few bigwigs. By shedding blood, the leaders of the gang made sure it would be tough to turn back the tides of revolution. Ever since, the French have celebrated July 14th as their independence day—Bastille Day.

The flashy, glassy-grey, and controversial **Opéra-Bastille** dominates (some say overwhelms) the square. Designed by the Canadian architect Carlos Ott, this latest Parisian grand project was opened with great fanfare by François Mitterrand on the 200th Bastille Day, July 14, 1989.

Turn your back to the statue and, passing the Banque de France on your right (good rates, long lines, opposite a fine map of the area on your left), head straight down the busy rue Saint Antoine about four blocks into the Marais.

The **Marais** neighborhood, still filled with pre-Revolutionary

Marais Walk

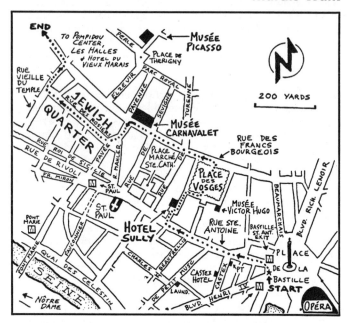

lanes and buildings, is more characteristic than touristy (unlike the Latin Quarter). It's medieval Paris. This is how much of the city looked until, in the mid-1800s, Napoleon III had Baron Hauss-mann blast out the narrow streets to construct broad boulevards (wide enough for the guns and marching ranks of the army, too wide for revolutionary barricades).

Leave rue Saint Antoine at #62 and turn right through two elegant courtyards of **Hôtel de Sully** (62 rue Saint Antoine, open until 19:00, good Marais map on corridor wall). Originally a swamp (*marais*), during the reign of Henry IV it became the hometown of the French aristocracy. In the 17th century, big shots built their private mansions (*hôtels*) like this one—close to Henry's place des Vosges. *Hôtels* that survived the revolution now house museums, libraries, and national institutions. The aristocrats may be gone, but the Marais—which until recently was a dumpy Bohemian quarter—is today a thriving, trendy but real commu-nity, and a joy to explore.

To get to the **place des Vosges** park, continue through the Hôtel de Sully. The small door on the far right corner of the sec-ond courtyard pops you out into one of Paris' finest squares (closes at dusk). Walk to the center, where Louis XIII sits on a horse surrounded by locals enjoying their community park. Children frolic in the sandbox, lovers warm benches, and pigeons guard their fountains, while trees shade this retreat from the glare of the big city. Henry IV built this centerpiece of the Marais in 1605. As hoped, this turned the Marais into Paris' most exclusive neighborhood. **Victor Hugo** lived at #6; you can visit his house (18F, corner closest to the Bastille).

To leave the square, walk behind Louis' horse to the arcade. Follow it left past art galleries and antique shops onto the boutique-filled rue des Francs Bourgeois (the store at #17 sells used silver, often from famous restaurants, by weight). Browse two blocks off the place des Vosges to the corner of rue de Sévigné, where you'll see the Musée Carnavalet (on right).

The **Carnavalet Museum**, focusing on the history of Paris, is housed inside a Marais mansion with classy courtyards and statues (35F, Tuesday–Sunday 10:00–17:00, closed Monday, 23 rue de Sévigné; for more information see Sights—Northeast Paris, above).

To continue the Marais walk, go another block along rue des Francs Bourgeois (peeking through the gate on the right) and turn left at the post office. (The **Picasso Museum**, described more fully in Sights—Northeast Paris, above, is up one block to the right: 30F, Wednesday–Monday 9:30–18:00, closed Tuesday, 5 rue Thorigny.) From rue Pavée, bend right onto rue Rosiers, which runs straight for three blocks through Paris' Jewish Quarter. It's lively every day except Saturday.

The **Jewish Quarter** is lined with colorful shops and kosher eateries. Jo Goldenberg's delicatessen/restaurant (first corner on left, at #7—scene of a terrorist bombing in darker times) is worth poking into. You'll be tempted by kosher pizza and plenty of 20F falafel-to-go (*emporter* = to go) joints. Rue Rosiers dead-ends into rue du Vieille du Temple. Turn right.

Frank Bourgeois is waiting at the corner postcard/print shop. Turn left on rue des Francs Bourgeois. This road leads past the national archives (peek inside the courtyard) and turns into rue Rambuteau.

The pipes and glass of the **Pompidou Center** reintroduce you to our century. Pass that huge building on your left to join the fray in front of the center (also called the Centre Beaubourg). Survey this popular spot from the top of the sloping square. A tubular series of escalators leads up the building (closed for renovation until 2000).

The Pompidou Center follows with gusto the 20th-century architectural axiom "form follows function." To get a more spacious and functional interior, the guts of this exoskeletal building are draped on the outside and color coded: vibrant red for people lifts, cool blue for air-conditioning, eco-green for plumbing, don't-touch-it yellow for electrical stuff, and white for bones. Enjoy the adjacent *Homage to Stravinsky* fountain. Jean Tingley

designed this new-wave fountain as a tribute to the composer. . . .
Every fountain represents one of his hard-to-hum scores.

With your back to the Pompidou Center's escalators, walk
the cobbled pedestrian mall and cross the busy boulevard
Sebastopol to the ivy-covered pavilions of Les Halles. After 800
years as Paris' down-and-dirty central produce market, this was
replaced by a glitzy but soulless modern shopping center in the
late 1970s. The most endearing layer of the mall is its grassy
rooftop park. The fine Gothic Saint Eustache church overlooking
this contemporary scene has a famous 8,000-pipe organ. The Louvre and Notre-Dame are just a short walk away. The mall is served
by Paris' busiest Métro hub (the Chatelet-Les Halles station).

Champs-Élysées Walk—Leaving Paris without strolling the
Champs-Élysées (shan-zay-lee-zay) is like walking out of a great
restaurant before dessert. This is Paris at its most Parisian:
monumental sidewalks, stylish shops, grand cafés, and glimmer-
ing showrooms. The complete walk covers about three miles
and takes three hours. The Arc de Triomphe (open until 22:00,
23:00 in summer) and Champs-Élysées are best at night. Métro
stops are located every three blocks on the Champs-Élysées.

Take the Métro to "Charles de Gaulle Étoile"; follow "access
Arc de Triomphe" signs to the top of the Champs-Élysées and
face the Arc de Triomphe. Underground W.C.s are on the left
side of the Champs-Élysées, while an underground walkway leading to the arch is on its right side.

Begin this walk at the top of the **Arc de Triomphe** (230
steps or elevator—sorry, no discount for walkers; 35F,
Tuesday–Saturday 9:00–23:00, Sunday and Monday 9:30–18:00).
A small museum explains its history; the exhibits are in French,
but there's a good video in English.

Begun in 1806, the arch was intended to honor Napoleon's
soldiers who, despite the fact that they were vastly outnumbered by
the Austrians, scored a remarkable victory at the battle of Austerlitz.
Napoleon died during its construction, but it was finished in time
for his funeral procession—carrying his remains from exile in St.
Helena home to Paris—to pass underneath. Today the Arc de Triomphe is dedicated to the glory of all French armies.

From the rooftop viewpoint, get your bearings with the circular orientation tables. The huge white arch amidst the skyscrapers is the Grande Arche de La Defense (see Sights—Northwest
Paris). French President Mitterand had the arch built as a centerpiece of this mini-Manhattan.

Now look down the Champs-Élysées. Notice the uniform
height and symmetry of the cityscape. The rude Montparnasse
tower (standing like the box the Eiffel Tower came in, at about
two o'clock to your right) served as a wake-up call in the early 70s

Champs-Élysées Walk

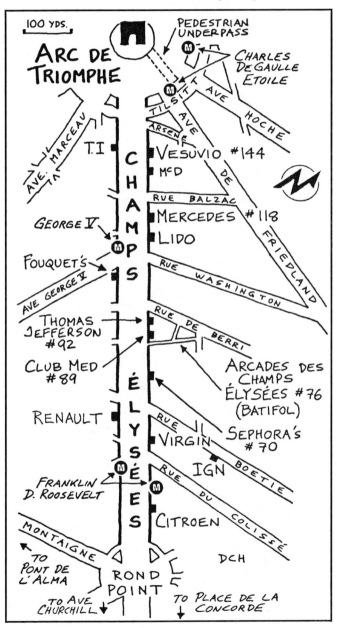

100 YDS.

ARC DE
TRIOMPHE

PEDESTRIAN
UNDERPASS

CHARLES
DE GAULLE
ETOILE

AVE HOCHE

AVE TILSITT

AVE ARSENE

AVE MARCEAU

T.I

VESUVIO #144

McD

RUE BALZAC

MERCEDES #118

LIDO

FRIEDLAND

GEORGE V

FOUQUET'S

AVE GEORGE V

RUE WASHINGTON

THOMAS
JEFFERSON
#92

CLUB MED
#89

RUE DE BERRI

ARCADES DES
CHAMPS
ÉLYSÉES #76
(BATIFOL)

RENAULT

RUE

VIRGIN

SEPHORA'S
#70

IGN

BOETIE

FRANKLIN
D. ROOSEVELT

RUE DU COLISSÉ

CITROEN

DCH

MONTAIGNE

TO
PONT DE
L'ALMA

ROND
POINT

TO AVE
CHURCHILL

TO PLACE DE LA
CONCORDE

CHAMPS ÉLYSÉES

to preserve the building height restriction and strengthen urban design standards.

The 12 boulevards that radiate from the Arc de Triomphe were part of Baron Haussmann's master plan for Paris in the mid-1800s, the creation of a series of major boulevards with monuments (such as the Arc de Triomphe) as centerpieces of the intersections. His plan did not anticipate the automobile—obvious when you watch the traffic scene below. As you gaze down at what appears to be a chaotic traffic mess, watch how smoothly it really functions.

Cars entering the circle have the right of way; those in the circle must yield. Motorcycles are fair game. Pedestrians are used for target practice. Insurance companies split the fault and damages of any Arc de Triomphe accidents 50-50.

Like its Roman ancestors, this arch has served as a parade gateway for triumphal armies and important ceremonies. From 1941 to 1944 a large swastika flew from here. Allied troops marched trimphantly under this arch in August 1944.

Descend the arch and stand on the bronze plaque at the **Tomb of the Unknown Soldier** (from WWI). The flame is re-kindled daily at 18:30, and new flowers are set in place. On the columns you'll see lists of battle victories and officers (with a line under the names of those who died in battle).

Walk over to the arch's massive right column (with your back to the Champs-Élysées) to see its most famous sculpture. The *Departure of the Volunteers*, also called *La Marseillaise*, is a rousing effort to rally the troops by what looks like an ugly reincarnation of Joan of Arc.

Walk out to the traffic circle and look down the Champs-Élysées. Notice that the left sidewalk is more popular with pedes-trians. While the left side is more interesting, cross over at least once for the exhilerating view from the center of the avenue's 10 lanes. The tourist office is immediately on the right at #127. Le Drugstore (next door) has a small grocery store in the back. Cross back under the tunnel to the top of the Champs-Élysées and start your descent. On the first block down, stop by Café Vesuvio (#144, reasonable prices) to enjoy fine views of the arch with its rooftop bristling with tourists.

Next to the Mercedes showroom (#118) is the famous Lido, Paris largest cabaret—check out the photos, video, and prices. These sensational shows pull out every stop for floor customers. Movie-going on the Champs-Élysées is also popular. Check to see if there are films you recognize, then look for the showings (*seances*); if there is a "v.o." next to the time, the film will be in its original version or language.

Now cross the boulevard where the elegant avenue George V (home to several four-star hotels and the Crazy Horse Saloon) spills into the Champs-Élysées. **Fouquet's** café-restaurant (under the orange awning) serves the most expensive shot of espresso I found in Paris (27F), but the setting is great. Since the early 1900s Fouquet's has remained a favorite of French actors and actresses. The welcome mat of golden plaques honors winners of France's Oscar-like film awards, the Cesars.

Cross back to the lively side. At #92, a wall plaque marks the place Thomas Jefferson lived while he was minister to France (1785). Nearby are several arcades. My favorite is the **Arcade des Champs-Élysées** at #76. This refuge of the belle epoque seems out of place. Wander in. A meal at Batifol's gives you a taste of the old Champs-Élysées (climb three steps for the most atmospheric tables; reasonable value; try the *pot au feu*).

Farther down *les Champs*, glide down Sephora's ramp at #74 into a vast hall of hundreds of people squirting perfume samples. Virgin Megastore sells a world of music one block farther down. The Disney and Gap stores are reminders of global ecomomics—the French love these stores as much as Americans. Near the bottom of the Champs-Élysées, Renault and Citroen showrooms glare across the avenue, each offering late-night cafés and restaurants. Renault has a neat little antique car museum.

At the leafy roundabout called **Rondpoint**, the shopping ends and the park begins. The park is always colorful, lined with flowers or seasonal decorations (thousands of pumpkins at Halloween, hundreds of trees at Christmas).

Walk a block past Rondpoint. Look right, down avenue Churchill. You'll see the glass- and steel-domed Grand and Petit Palais exhibition halls, built for the 1900 world's fair. Today these examples of the "can-do" spirit of the turn-of-the-century host a variety of exhibits (details at TI or in *Pariscope*). The **Petit Palais** (left side) houses a permanant collection of 19th-century paintings, including those of Delacroix, Cézanne, Monet, and others. The backside of the Grand Palais is the **Palais de la Découverte**, an extensive hands-on science museum with everything from a planetarium to full-scale dinosaurs. In the distance is the golden dome of **Les Invalides**. Built by Louis XIV as a veteran's hospital for his battle-weary troops, it now houses Napoleon's tomb (see Sights—Southwest Paris, above).

Continue to the **place de la Concorde**, the 21-acre square with the obelisk. The Tuileries Garden is ahead (with the Louvre beyond it), and the Orsay is on the right, across the river.

Walk to the island in the center of the place de la Concorde. During the Revolution this was the place de la Revolution. Over 1,300 heads fell here during the Reign of Terror. The guillotine sat here. A bronze plaque on the Arc de Triomphe side of the obelisk memorializes the place where Louis XVI and Marie Antoinette, among many others, were were made a foot shorter at the top. Three worked the guillotine: One managed the blade, one held the blood bucket, and one caught the head, raising it high to the roaring crowd. The 2,300-year-old **obelisk** of Luxor now forms the centerpiece of the square. It was carted here from Egypt in 1829, a gift to the French King. The gold pictures on the obelisk tell the story of its incredible journey.

Le Crillon, Paris' most exclusive hotel, is one of the twin buildings that guard the entrance to rue Royale (which leads to the Greek-style Basilique de la Madeleine). Eleven years before he lost his head on this square, King Louis XVI met with Benjamin Franklin in this hotel to sign a treaty recognizing the United States as in independent country. (For an affordable splurge, consider high tea at Le Crillon; wear the best clothes you packed, arrive after 15:00, and settle into the royal blue chairs in the *salon du thè*: 45F for a pot of tea or double *café au lait*; 155F for high tea).

The obelisk of place de la Concorde also forms a center point along a line locals call the "royal perspective." From this straight line (Louvre—Obelisk—Arc de Triompe—Grand Arch de la Defense) you can hang a lot of history. The Louvre symbolized the old regime (divine right rule by kings and queens). The obelisk and the place de la Concorde symbolize the peoples' revolution (cutting off the king's head). The Arc de Triomphe calls to mind the triumph of nationalism (victorious armies carrying national flags under the arch). And the huge modern arch in the distance, surrounded by the headquarters of multinational corporations, heralds a future where business entities are more powerful than nations.

The beautiful **Tuileries Gardens** lead through the iron gates to the Louvre. If high tea at Le Crillon isn't your cup of tea, pull up a chair next to the pond or find one of the cafés in the gardens. If you have energy to burn, tour L'Orangerie.

Paris with Children

This city of 3 million is actually kid-friendly. With so much space devoted to parks, squares, and pedestrians, and such a variety of kid-friendly sights, your children can leave Paris wanting to return. While you can take your child to play at the French funplex, you can visit a funplex at home. The art to a successful family trip to Paris is making everyone happy, including the parents. Our family-tested recommendations have this objective in mind. Consider these tips:

•Hotel selection is critical. Stay in a kid-friendly area near a park. The rue Cler neighborhood is ideal.

•Eat dinner early (19:30 at restaurants, earlier at cafés) and you'll miss the romantic crowd. Skip the famous places. Look instead for more relaxed cafés and bistros (or even fast-food restaurants)

where kids can move around without bothering others. Picnic
lunches and dinners work well.
•Follow this book's tips for beating crowds. With kids, standing in
a long line for a museum (that they probably don't even want to
see) adds insult to injury.
•Get your kids in the spirit before you go (e.g., rent or read *The
Hunchback of Notre-Dame* or *The Man in the Iron Mask*).
•The best toy selections are in the large department stores, such as
Galleries Lafayette, Printemps, and Le Bon Marche.
•French marionette shows, called *guignols*, are fun for the entire
family. They take place in several locations in Paris, mostly in the
big parks. See *Pariscope* or *l'Officiel des Spectacles* under "Marionettes" for times and places. The plots, while in French, are easy
to follow. Arrive 20 minutes early for good seats.

Ten Top Kids' Spots in Paris

1. Luxembourg Gardens: This has the most extensive big-toys
play area in Paris with imaginative slides, swings, and jungle gyms
(kids-14F, adults-7.5F, open daily). Kids enjoy the pedal go-carts,
merry-go-round, pony rides, toy sailboats in the main pond, and
big open areas perfect for kicking a ball. Adults and kids enjoy the
terrific puppet shows (*guignols*) held in the afternoons (tel. 01 43
26 46 47, Mo: St. Sulpice, Odéon, or Notre-Dame-des-Champs;
RER: Luxembourg).
2. Jardin des Plantes: These pleasant, colorful botanical gardens
are short on grass, but have a small zoo, a children's maze made of
plants, and several kid-friendly natural science museums. Kids go
bug-eyed at the Insect Museum (Galerie d'Entomologie, kids-10F,
adults-15F, Wednesday–Monday 13:00–17:00) and love the
dinosaur exhibit (Galerie d'Anatomie Comparée et de Paléontolo-
gie, kids-20F, adults-30F, Wednesday–Monday 10:00–17:00;
includes Musée de Mineralogie, featuring precious stones). From
the main riverside entrance on place Valhubert, the museums line
the left side of the park (Mo: Gare d'Austerlitz or Jussieu).
3. Eiffel Tower, Trocadero, and Champs-de-Mars Park: All
ages enjoy the view from Trocadero across the river to the Eiffel
Tower, especially after dark (Mo: Trocadero). Rollerbladers and
skateboarders make Trocadero a Parisian teenage scene, particularly in afternoons and evenings. A ride up the tower is a hit day or
night. See the video on the tower's first floor. The vast Champs-
de-Mars park at the tower offers grassy play areas (bring your own
ball), childrens' big-toys, pony rides, and picnic-perfect benches
(Mo: École Militaire). For more information, see Eiffel Tower
under Sights—Southwest Paris.
4. Notre-Dame, Towers, and Crypt: Paris' famous Gothic
cathedral doesn't have to be dry and dull. Replay Quasimodo's
stunt and climb the tower. Kids love being on such a lofty perch

with an up-close look at a gargoyle. The crypt on the square in front of Notre-Dame is manageable and fun. Kids can push buttons to highlight remains of Roman Paris and leave with a better understanding of how different civilizations build on top of each other. The small but beautiful park along the river and behind Notre-Dame has sandboxes, picnic benches, and space to run (Mo: Cité). For more information on Notre-Dame, see Sights— Historic Core of Paris Walk.

5. Seine River Boat Rides: The Bateaux-Mouches offer one-hour cruises on huge glass boats with departures (every 30 minutes from 10:00–23:00) from the pont de l'Alma, the centrally-located pont Neuf, and from right in front of the Eiffel Tower (20F-under age 14, 40F-adult, tel. 01 42 25 96 10). The Bateau-Bus is a river bus that runs June through September connecting five stops along the river: Eiffel Tower, Orsay, Louvre, Notre-Dame, and place de la Concorde (60F, 30F for kids, departures every 45 minutes from about 10:00-19:00; pick up a brochure at any TI). Use the Bateau-Bus by day and take a twilight cruise on a Bateau-Mouche.

6. Arc de Triomphe, Champs-Élysées, and Palais de la Découverte: Watching the crazy traffic rush around the Arc de Triomphe provides endless entertainment. Then stroll the Champs-Élysées with its car dealerships (particularly Renault's with its antique car museum), Virgin Megastore, Disney Store, and the river of humanity that flows along its broad sidewalks. You can end this walk at the Grand Palais' Palais de la Découverte, a hands-on science musuem for kids (15F-under age 18, 25F-adult, Tuesday–Saturday 9:30–19:00, Sunday 10:00–19:00). For more information, see Champs-Élysées Walk under More Paris Walks.

7. Versailles: This huge complex of palaces, gardens, fountains, and forest is a great Parisian family getaway. Kids even enjoy the 30-minute train ride to Versailles. Rent a bike for the gardens or a rowboat for the canal. Come on Sunday when the fountains are flowing. The *hameau* has barnyard animals nearby. Visit the palace at the end of the day and you can do cartwheels in an empty Hall of Mirrors. For more information, see Versailles, below.

8. The Pompidou Center: The Pompidou Center is closed until 2000, but kids love the wild fountains (Homage to Stravinsky) next door. The big square in front is filled with crazy entertainers (Mo: Rambuteau).

9. The Cité des Sciences in the Parc de la Vilette: Paris' sprawling hands-on Explora science museum has an aquarium, sound and light shows, a flight simulator, and a childrens's playground (25F, Tuesday–Sunday 12:00–20:00, closed Monday). La Geode is a giant spherical movie-screen with films (Mo: Port de la Vilette).

10. La Butte Chaumont Park: Rather than manicured gardens, this is a big park where your kids can explore the hills, lakes, trails, and waterfall. Baron Haussmann designed this converted city dump into a remarkable mix of cafés and outdoor fun (Mo: Buttes-Chaumont).

More Suggestions
•Place des Vosges, with sandboxes and some playground toys, is good for younger children (Mo: Bastille or St. Paul, in Marais neighborhood).
•Palais Royal, with sandboxes, provides an ideal break from the Louvre, across rue du Rivoli. Picnic here in the peaceful gardens (Mo: Palais Royal Musée du Louvre).
•Take a Sewer Tour (see Sights—Southwest Paris).
•Go to a movie on the Champs-Élysées ("v.o." means *version original*; American films have their English soundtracks).
•Bois de Boulogne, Paris' largest park, has lakes, boat rental, and paths ideal for bike riding. Inside this huge park, you'll find a variety of activities for kids, including the Jardins d'Acclimatation with a mini-zoo, mini-golf, pony rides, and bumper cars (12F, Mo: Sablons).

Day Trips: Châteaus near Paris
The region around Paris (the Île de France) is dotted with sumptuous palaces. Paris' booming upper class made this the heartland of European château building in the 16th and 17th centuries. Most of these châteaus were lavish hunting lodges—getaways from the big city. The only thing they defended were noble and royal egos. Consider these two very different châteaus, both ▲▲▲ sights: Versailles (for grandeur) and Vaux-le-Vicomte (for intimacy).

Palace of Versailles
Every king's dream, Versailles was the residence of the French king and the cultural heartbeat of Europe for about 100 years—until the Revolution of 1789 ended the notion that God deputized some people to rule for Him on Earth. Louis XIV spent half a year's income of Europe's richest country turning his dad's hunting lodge into a palace fit for a divine monarch. Louis XV and Louis XVI spent much of the 18th century gilding Louis XIV's lily. In 1837, about 50 years after the royal family was evicted, King Louis Philippe opened the palace as a museum. Europe's next-best palaces are Versailles wannabes.

Information: There's a helpful TI across the street from Versailles' R.G. station (tel. 01 39 50 36 22), two information desks on the approach to the palace, and a very helpful TI at entrance C. The useful brochure, "Versailles Orientation Guide," explains your sightseeing options. Versailles info: tel. 01 30 84 76 18 or 01 30 84 74 00. W.C. and phones are near the main entrance.

Ticket Options: The self-guided one-way palace romp,

Versailles

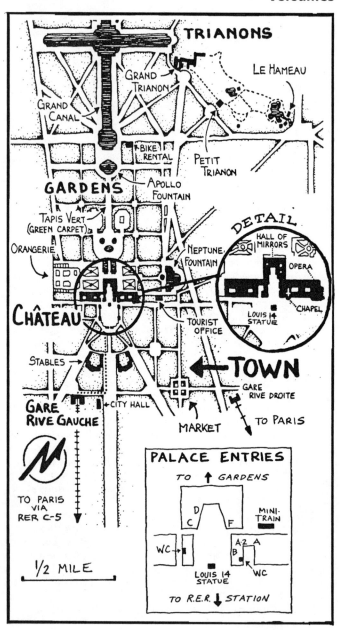

TRIANONS

Le Hameau

Grand Trianon

Grand Canal

Bike Rental

Petit Trianon

Apollo Fountain

GARDENS

Tapis Vert (Green Carpet)

Orangerie

Neptune Fountain

DETAIL

HALL OF MIRRORS

OPERA

CHAPEL

LOUIS 14 STATUE

CHÂTEAU

TOURIST OFFICE

Stables

TOWN

GARE RIVE DROITE

City Hall

TO PARIS

MARKET

Gare Rive Gauche

N

TO PARIS VIA RER C-5

½ MILE

PALACE ENTRIES

TO ↑ GARDENS

D
C   F

MINI-TRAIN

WC →

A-2   A
B

WC

LOUIS 14 STATUE

TO R.E.R. ↓ STATION

including the Hall of Mirrors, costs 45F (35F after 15:30, on Sunday, or for those over 60 or ages 18–25; under 18 free). To supplement this with a guided tour through the other sections, you'll need to pay the 45F base price, then add 25F for a one-hour guided tour, 37F for a 90-minute guided tour, or 30F for a self-guided Walkman-cassette tour. (Tip: If you're waiting for your tour time, have finished a tour, or have a Paris Museum Card, you can go directly into the main palace with no line at the A2 gate and explore the palace on your own.) In the gardens, you can see the Grand and Petit Trianon palaces for 30F total (payable at the site).

Hours: Tuesday through Sunday 9:00 to 18:30, closed Monday; 9:00 to 17:30 October through April; last entry 30 minutes before closing. Versailles is especially crowded Tuesday through Sunday 10:00 to 15:00. To minimize crowds and get a reduced entry ticket, arrive after 15:30. Tour the gardens after the palace closes. The palace is great late. On my last visit, at 18:00, I was the only tourist in the Hall of Mirrors . . . even on a Tuesday.

Time to Allow: Six hours round-trip from Paris (an hour each way in transit, two hours for the palace, two for the grounds).

Self-Guided Tour: For the basic self-guided tour, join the line at entrance A1. Those with a Paris Museum Card are allowed in through entrance A2 without a wait. Enter the palace and take a one-way walk through the state apartments from the "King's Wing," through the magnificent Hall of Mirrors, and out via the "Queen's Wing."

The Hall of Mirrors was the ultimate hall of the day—250 feet long, 17 arched mirrors matching 17 windows with royal garden views, 24 gilded candelabra, eight busts of Roman emperors, and eight classical-style statues (seven of them actually ancient originals). The ceiling is decorated with stories of Louis' triumphs. Imagine this place filled with silk gowns and powdered wigs, lit by thousands of candles. The mirrors—a luxurious rarity at the time— were a reflection of a time when aristocrats felt good about their looks and their fortunes. In another age altogether, this was the room in which the Treaty of Versailles was signed, ending World War I.

Before going downstairs at the end, take a stroll clockwise around the long room filled with the great battles of France murals. If you don't have *Rick Steves' Mona Winks*, the guidebook called *The Châteaux, The Gardens, and Trianon* gives a room-by-room rundown.

Guided Tours: For a guided tour, pay the 45F base-price admission at the same time you pay for your tour (at entrance D). The 60- or 90-minute tours, led by an English-speaking art historian, take you through sections of Versailles not included in the base-price visit. Groups are limited to 30. Of the several tours offered, the 90-minute version covering Louis XV and Louis XVI's apartments and the opera is best. Pay and get your tour appointment at entrance D. Tour times are normally all allotted for the day by 13:00. Tours leave from entrance F.

Walkman Tour: If you're in a hurry, the self-guided Walkman-cassette tour of the king's chamber (25F, entrance C, last entry at 15:00) covers Louis XIV's rooms and is a good option.

Palace Gardens: The gardens offer a world of royal amusements. Outside the palace is the L'Orangerie. Louis, the only one who could grow oranges in Paris, had an orange grove on wheels that could be wheeled in and out of his greenhouses according to the weather. A promenade leads from the palace to the Grand Canal, an artificial lake that, in Louis' day, was a mini-sea with nine ships, including a 32-cannon warship. France's royalty used to float up and down the canal in Venetian gondolas.

While Louis cleverly used palace life at Versailles to "domesticate" his nobility, turning otherwise meddlesome nobles into groveling socialites, all this pomp and ceremony hampered the royal family as well. For an escape from the public life at Versailles, they built more intimate palaces as retreats in their garden. Before the revolution there was plenty of space to retreat—the grounds were enclosed by a 25-mile-long fence.

The beautifully restored **Grand Trianon Palace** is as sumptuous as the main palace but much smaller. With its pastel pink colonnade and more human scale, this is a place you'd like to call home. (See hours and prices below).

The nearby **Petit Trianon**, which has a fine neoclassical exterior with a skippable interior, was Marie Antoinette's favorite residence.

You can almost see princesses bobbing gaily in the branches as you walk through the enchanting forest, past the white marble temple of love (1778) to the queen's fake-peasant **hamlet** (interior not tourable). Palace life really got to Marie Antoinette. Sort of a back-to-basics queen, she retreated further and further from her blue-blooded reality. Her happiest days were at the hamlet, under a bonnet, tending her perfumed sheep and her manicured gardens in a thatch-happy wonderland.

Getting Around the Gardens: It's a 30-minute hike from the palace, down the canal, past the two mini-palaces to the hamlet. You can rent bikes (30F/hr). The pokey tourist train, which costs only 10F, runs between the canal and château (30F, 5/hrly, four stops, you can hop on and off as you like; nearly worthless commentary).

Garden Hours and Admissions: Except for fountain-filled Sundays (below), the gardens are free and open from 7:00 to sunset (as late as 21:30). Grand and Petit Trianon are open May through September Tuesday through Sunday from 10:00 to 18:00, and are closed Monday (off-season 10:00–17:00, Grand Trianon-25F, Petit

Trianon-15F, 30F for both). The park is picnic-perfect. Food is not allowed into the palace, but those with a picnic can check bags (and picnics) at doors A or C. There's a kiosk selling good sandwiches, and there's a decent restaurant on the canal in the gardens.

Fountain Spectacles: Every Sunday, May through October, music fills the king's backyard and the garden's fountains are in full squirt (from 11:15–11:35, and from 15:30–17:00, 25F garden admission on these days only). Louis had his engineers literally reroute a river to fuel these fountains. Even by today's standards they are impressive.

Getting to Versailles: From Paris, take the RER-C train (26F round-trip, 30 min) to "Versailles R.G.," not "Versailles C.H.," which is farther from the palace. Trains, usually named "Vick," leave about five times an hour for the palace. Get off at Versailles Rive Gauche (the end of the line). RER-C trains leave from these RER/Metro stops: "Invalides" (Napoleon's Tomb, Military Museum, Rodin Museum), "Champ de Mars" (Eiffel Tower), "Musée d'Orsay," "St. Michel" (Notre-Dame, Latin Quarter), and "Gare d'Austerlitz." Leaving the station, turn right, then turn left on the major boulevard (10-minute walk). Your Eurailpass is good on the RER trains (show it to get a ticket for the turnstiles; keep this ticket to get out upon arrival). When returning look through the windows past the turnstiles for the departure board. Any train leaving Versailles goes as far as downtown Paris (they're marked "all stations until Austerlitz"). If you're uncertain, confirm with a local by asking, "À Paris?" (To Paris?).

The 100F Paris–Versailles taxi fare is economic for groups of three or four, or for people with more money than time. To cut your park walking by 50 percent, consider having the taxi drop you at the Hamlet (Hameau).

Town of Versailles (zip code: 78000): After the palace closes and the tourists go, the prosperous, wholesome town of Versailles feels a long way from Paris. The central market thrives on Tuesday, Friday, and Saturday until 13:00 (place du Marché; leaving the RER station, turn right and walk 10 minutes). Consider the wisdom of picking up or dropping your rental car in Versailles rather than in Paris. In Versailles, the Hertz and Avis offices are at the Gare des Chantiers (Versailles C.H., served by Paris' Montparnasse station). Versailles makes a fine homebase; see Versailles accommodations under Sleeping, below.

Vaux-le-Vicomte

While Versailles is most travelers' first choice for its sheer historic weight, Vaux-le-Vicomte offers a more lavish interior and a far better sense of 17th-century château life. Sitting in a huge forest with magnificent gardens and no urban sprawl in sight, Vaux-le-Vicomte gave me just a twinge of palace envy.

Vaux-le-Vicomte was the architectural inspiration of Versailles and set the standard for European châteaus to come. The proud owner, Nicolas Fouquet (Louis XIV's finance minister) threw a chateau-warming party. Louis was so jealous that he arrested his host, took his architect (Le Vau), artist (Le Brun), and landscaper (Le Notre), and proceeded with the construction of the bigger and costlier (but not necessarily more splendid) palace of Versailles. Monsieur Fouquet is thought to be Alexandre Dumas' man in *The Man in the Iron Mask*, which was recently filmed here.

Vaux-le-Vicomte is a headache to get to (see below) but a joy to tour. While the gift shop's 25F souvenir booklet has helpful information, the chateau's rooms have English explanations. Start with the fine horse carriages exhibit (*equipages*) in the old stables. Wax figures and an evocative soundtrack get you in the proper mood. Next, stroll like a wide-eyed peasant across the drawbridge and up the front steps into the chateau. You'll notice candles. Over 1,300 flicker for candlelit night visits.

As you wander through Fouquet's dream-home, you'll understand Louis' jealousy. Versailles was a rather simple hunting lodge when this was built. Since Louis confiscated everything, the furniture is not original. It's from other palaces in the area. You'll see cozy bedrooms upstairs, and grand living rooms downstairs, including a billiards room, library, card room, and dining room. The kitchen and wine cellar are in the basement.

Survey the garden from the back steps of the palace. This was the landscaper Le Notre's first claim to fame. This garden set the standards for sculpted French gardens. He integrated ponds, shrubbery, flowers, and trees in a style that would be copied in palaces all over Europe. Take the 30-minute walk (one way) to the Hercules viewpoint, atop the grassy hill way in the distance. Rent golf carts (Club Cars, 80F for 45 minutes) to make the trip easier. Picnics are not allowed.

Hours and Admission: The château is open daily March through October 10:00 to 13:00 and 14:00 to 18:00 (gardens don't close midday), less in winter (tel. 01 64 14 41 90). Steep 56F admission; 30F for gardens only.

The candlelit visits (*visites aux chandelles*) are worth the 75F entry. (20:30–24:00 May–October on Saturdays and holidays except July 14—call to ask about any upcoming holidays; there are many in May. The last train to Paris leaves Melun at about 22:00.)

The fountains run April through October on the second and last Saturday of each month from 15:00 to 18:00. A good indoor/outdoor café-restaurant, offering reasonable prices and good salads, is inside the first courtyard.

Getting to Vaux-le-Vicomte: To reach Vaux-le-Vicomte by car or by a train and taxi combination, head for the city of Melun.

RER trains run to Melun from Paris' Gare du Nord and Chatelet stations. Faster Banlieue trains leave from Paris' Gare de Lyon (43F one-way, 35 min). Taxis make the 10-minute drive from Melun's station to Vaux-le-Vicomte (85F weekdays, 100F evenings and Sundays, taxi phone number posted above taxi stand). Ask a staff person at the château to call a cab for your return, or schedule a pick-up time with your driver. In either direction, split the cab fare with other travelers. Melun's TI is a block from the train station, past the ugly concrete building (Tuesday–Saturday 10:00–12:00 and 14:00 to 18:00, closed Sunday and Monday, 2 avenue Gallieni, tel. 01 64 37 11 31).

Sleeping near Vaux-le-Vicomte: The modern but handy IBIS Hotel is between Melun and the château (Db-300F, less on weekends, tel. 01 60 68 42 45, fax 01 64 09 62 00).

More Day Trips from Paris

▲▲▲**Chartres**—In 1194 a terrible fire destroyed the church at Chartres with the much-venerated veil of Mary. With almost unbelievably good fortune, the monks found the veil miraculously preserved in the ashes. Money poured in for the building of a bigger and better cathedral—decorated with 2,000 carved figures and some of France's best stained glass. The cathedral feels too large for the city because it was designed to accommodate huge crowds of pilgrims. One of those pilgrims, an impressed Napoleon, declared after a visit in 1811: "Chartres is no place for an atheist." Rodin called it "the Acropolis of France." British Francophile Malcolm Miller or his impressive assistant give great "Appreciation of Gothic" tours Monday through Saturday, usually at noon and 14:45 (verify times in advance, no tours off-season, call TI at 02 37 21 50 00). Each 40F tour is different; many people stay for both tours. Just show up at the church (daily 7:00–19:00).

Explore Chartres' pleasant city center and discover the picnic-friendly park behind the cathedral. The helpful TI, next to the cathedral, has a map with a self-guided tour of Chartres (daily 9:30–18:45). Chartres is a one-hour train trip from the Gare Montparnasse (71F one-way, 10/day, last train on Saturday departs at about 19:00). Upon arrival, confirm your return schedule to avoid an unplanned night in Chartres.

▲**Giverny**—Monet spent 43 of his most creative years (1883–1926) here at the Camp David of Impressionism. Monet's gardens and home are split by a busy road. Buy your ticket, walk through the gardens, and take the underpass into the artist's famous lilypad land. The path leads you over the Japanese Bridge, under weeping willows, and past countless scenes that leave artists aching for an easel. For Monet fans, it's strangely nostalgic. Back on the other side, continue your visit with a wander through his more robust and structured garden and his mildly interesting home. The

Paris Day Trips

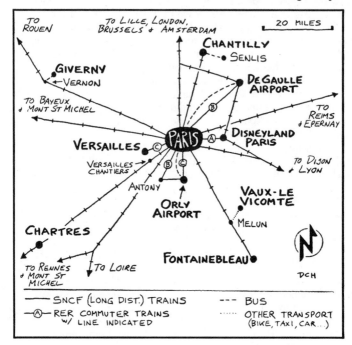

TO ROUEN

TO LILLE, LONDON, BRUSSELS & AMSTERDAM

20 MILES

CHANTILLY
● SENLIS

GIVERNY
←VERNON

DE GAULLE AIRPORT

TO BAYEUX & MONT ST MICHEL

TO REIMS & EPERNAY

B

PARIS

A

DISNEYLAND PARIS

VERSAILLES

C

TO DIJON & LYON

VERSAILLES CHANTIERS

B C

ANTONY

VAUX-LE VICOMTE

ORLY AIRPORT

MELUN

CHARTRES

N

TO RENNES & MONT ST MICHEL

TO LOIRE

FONTAINEBLEAU ●

DCH

———— SNCF (LONG DIST.) TRAINS   --- BUS

—Ⓐ— RER COMMUTER TRAINS W/ LINE INDICATED   ······ OTHER TRANSPORT (BIKE, TAXI, CAR...)

jammed gift shop at the exit is the actual skylit studio where Monet painted his waterlily masterpieces.

While lines may be long and tour groups may trample the flowers, true fans still find magic in those lilypads. Avoid crowds by arriving after 16:00 (35F, 25F for gardens only, April–October Tuesday–Sunday 10:00–18:00, closed Monday and off-season, tel. 02 32 51 28 21). Take the Rouen-bound train from Paris' Gare St. Lazare station to Vernon (about 140F round-trip, long gaps in service, know schedule before you go). To get from the Vernon train station to Monet's garden (four kilometers away), take the Vernon–Giverny bus (5/day, scheduled to meet most trains), hitch, taxi (60F), or rent a bike at the station (55F, busy road). Get return bus times from the ticket office in Giverny or ask them to call a taxi. Big tour companies do a Giverny day trip from Paris for around $60.

The new **American Impressionist Art Museum** (100 yards from Monet's place) is devoted to American artists who followed Claude to Giverny. Giverny had a great influence on American artists of Monet's day. This bright, modern gallery is well-explained in English, has a good little Mary Cassatt section, and

gives Americans a rare chance to see French people appreciating our artists (same price and hours as Monet's home, pleasant café).
▲▲**Disneyland Paris**—Europe's Disneyland is basically a modern remake of California's, with most of the same rides and smiles. The main difference is that Mickey Mouse speaks French (and you can buy wine with your lunch). My kids went ducky. Locals love it. It's worth a day if Paris is handier than Florida or California. If possible, avoid Saturday, Sunday, Wednesday, school holidays, and July and August. The park can get very crowded. When 60,000 have entered, they close the gates (tel. 01 64 74 30 00 for the latest). After dinner, crowds are gone, and you'll walk right onto rides that had a 45-minute wait three hours earlier. Food is fun but expensive. Smuggle in a picnic.

Disney brochures are in every Paris hotel. The RER (40F each way, direct from downtown Paris to Marne-la-Vallee in 30 minutes) drops you right into the park. The last train back into Paris leaves shortly after midnight. (200F for adults, 155F for kids ages 3–11, 25F less in spring and fall. Daily 9:00–23:00 late June–early September and Saturday and Sunday off-season, shoulder-season weekdays 9:00–19:00, off-season 10:00–18:00, tel. 01 60 30 60 30, fax 01 60 30 60 65 for park and hotel reservations.)

To sleep reasonably at the huge Disney complex, try **Hotel Sante Fe** (780F family rooms for two to four people includes breakfast, less off-season; ask for their hotel-and-park package deal). If all this ain't enough, a new Planet Hollywood restaurant opened just outside the park a five-minute walk from the RER stop.

Sleeping in Paris
(5.5F = about $1)
Sleep Code: **S** = Single, **D** = Double/Twin, **T** = Triple, **Q** = Quad, **b** = bathroom, **t** = toilet only, **s** = shower only, **CC** = Credit Card (**V**isa, **M**asterCard, **A**mex), * = French hotel rating system (0–4 stars).

French hotels are rated by stars (indicated in this book by an *). One star is simple, two has most of the comforts, and three is, for this book, plush. Old, characteristic, budget Parisian hotels have always been cramped. Retrofitted with elevators, toilets, and private showers (as most are today), they are even more cramped. Even three-star hotel rooms are small, and generally not worth the extra expense in Paris. Some hotels include the hotel tax (*taxe de sejour*, about 5F per person per day), though most will add this to your bill. Almost every hotel accepts Visa and MasterCard. Fewer take American Express. Two-star hotels are required to have an English-speaking staff. Nearly all hotels listed will have someone who speaks English.

Quad rooms usually have two double beds. Recommended

hotels have an elevator unless otherwise noted. Because rooms with double beds and showers are cheaper than rooms with twin beds and baths, room prices vary within each hotel. To keep things manageable, I've focused on three safe, handy, and colorful neighborhoods (listing good hotels, restaurants, and helpful hints for each).

You can save about 100F by finding the increasingly rare room without a private shower, though some hotels charge for down-the-hall showers. Breakfasts cost 20F to 50F extra. Café or picnic breakfasts are cheaper. Singles (except for the rare closet-type rooms that fit only one twin bed) are simply doubles used by one person. They rent for only a little less than a double.

Conventions clog Paris in September (worst), October, May, and June. Reserve in advance during these months. July and August are no problem. Most hotels accept telephone reservations, require prepayment with a credit-card number, and prefer a faxed follow-up to be sure everything is in order. Get advice for safe parking from your hotel. Meters are free in August. Garages are plentiful (90–140F per day, with special rates through some hotels). Self-serve Laundromats are common; ask your hotelier for the nearest one (*Où est un laverie automatique?*; ooh ay uh lah-vay-ree auto-mah-teek).

Sleeping in the Rue Cler Neighborhood
**(7th arrondissement, Mo: École Militaire,
zip code: 75007)**
Rue Cler, a village-like pedestrian street, is safe, tidy, and makes me feel like I must have been a poodle in a previous life. How such coziness lodged itself between the high-powered government/business district and the expensive Eiffel Tower and Invalides areas, I'll never know. Living here ranks with the top museums as one of the city's great experiences. (But if you're into nightlife, consider one of the other two neighborhoods I list.)

Rue Cler is the glue that holds this pleasant neighborhood together. From rue Cler you can walk to the Eiffel Tower, Les Invalides, the Seine, and the Orsay and Rodin Museums. The first six hotels listed below are within camembert-smelling distance of rue Cler, the others are within a five-minute stroll. Warning: The first two hotels are popular with my readers.

Hôtel Leveque** has been entirely renovated. But, with a helpful staff and a singing maid, it's still cozy. It's a fine value with the best location on the block, comfortable rooms, cable TV, hair dryers, safes, an ice machine, and tasteful decor throughout (Sb-270F, Db-380–450F, Tb-550F, breakfast-35F but free for readers of this book, CC:VMA, 29 rue Cler, tel. 01 47 05 49 15, fax 01 45 50 49 36, Web site: http://interresa.ca/hotel/leveque/fr, e-mail: hotellev@clubinternet.fr). Laurence at the front desk speaks English.

Rue Cler Hotels

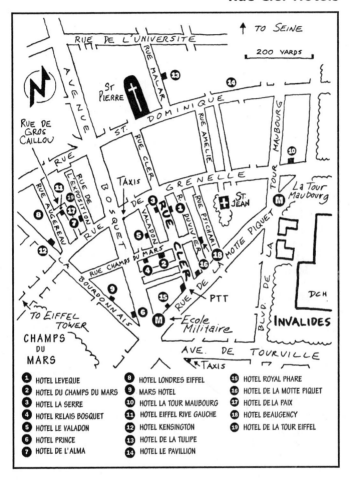

1 HOTEL LEVEQUE	**8** HOTEL LONDRES EIFFEL
2 HOTEL DU CHAMPS DU MARS	**9** MARS HOTEL
3 HOTEL LA SERRE	**10** HOTEL LA TOUR MAUBOURG
4 HOTEL RELAIS BOSQUET	**11** HOTEL EIFFEL RIVE GAUCHE
5 HOTEL LE VALADON	**12** HOTEL KENSINGTON
6 HOTEL PRINCE	**13** HOTEL DE LA TULIPE
7 HOTEL DE L'ALMA	**14** HOTEL LE PAVILLION

15 HOTEL ROYAL PHARE
16 HOTEL DE LA MOTTE PIQUET
17 HOTEL DE LA PAIX
18 HOTEL BEAUGENCY
19 HOTEL DE LA TOUR EIFFEL

Hôtel du Champs de Mars**, with charming, pastel rooms, is an even cosier rue Cler option. The hotel has a Provence-style small-town feel from top to bottom. Rooms are comfortable and a very good value. Single rooms can work as tiny doubles (Db-390–420F, Tb-505F, CC:VMA, cable TV, hair dryers, etc., 30 yards off rue Cler at 7 rue du Champs de Mars, tel. 01 45 51 52 30, fax 01 45 51 64 36, Web site: www: adx.fr/hotel-du-champ-de-mars, e-mail: stg@club-internet.fr, owners Françoise and Stephane SE).

Hôtel la Serre*, across the street from the Hotel Leveque, is a shabby hotel with some renovated rooms, well-worn hallways, no elevator, and a charming location. Request to see your room before you pay; refunds are rarely given (D-270F, Db-390–400F, Tb-520F, cable TV, CC:VM, 24 rue Cler, tel. 01 47 05 52 33, fax 01 40 62 95 66, e-mail: laserre@easynet.fr).

Hôtel Relais Bosquet*** is bright, spacious, and a bit upscale with sharp, comfortable rooms (Db-550–900F, most at 750F, CC:VMA, 19 rue du Champs de Mars, tel. 01 47 05 25 45, fax 01 45 55 08 24, e-mail: Webmaster@relais-bosquet.com). The similar **Hotel Beaugency***** offers similar comfort for less (Db-720F, includes a buffet breakfast, 21 rue Duvivier, tel. 01 47 05 01 63, fax 01 45 51 04 96).

Hôtel Le Valadon**, on a quiet street with a plain lobby and spacious, comfy rooms, has a shy, modern Parisian cuteness and a friendly staff (Db-410–530F, Tb-560F, CC:VM, 16 rue Valadon, tel. 01 47 53 89 85, fax 01 44 18 90 56).

These listings are a five-minute walk west of rue Cler and are listed in order of proximity.

Hotel Prince**, just across avenue Bosquet from École Militaire Métro, has a "we-try-harder" spirit and good-value rooms, many of which overlook a busy street (Db-430–510F, CC:VM, 66 avenue Bosquet, tel. 01 47 05 40 90, fax 01 47 53 06 62 friendly owner Christof SE).

Hôtel de l'Alma*** is a tight and tidy place with 32 delightful look-alike rooms, all of which come with a TV and minibar (Sb-400F, Db-450F, breakfast included, no triples but a kid's bed can be moved in for free, popular with Mexican and Russian groups, CC:VMA, 32 rue de l'Exposition, tel. 01 47 05 45 70, fax 01 45 51 84 47).

Hôtel Eiffel Rive Gauche** is quiet, unassuming, and is being renovated into a fair value (Ds-260F, Db-420–460F, CC:VM, 6 rue du Gros-Caillou, tel. 01 45 51 24 56, fax 01 45 51 11 77).

Hotel Londres Eiffel*** was just renovated with cheerful attention to detail. Its small, cozy rooms are comfortable (and some have Eiffel views), and its friendly owners seem eager to please (Sb-495F, Db-595F, Tb-725F, extra bed-70F, CC:VMA, 1 rue Augerau, tel. 01 45 51 63 02, fax 01 47 05 28 96).

Mars Hôtel** has a richly decorated lobby, spacious—if well-worn—rooms, and a beam-me-up-Maurice coffin-sized elevator. The front rooms look out on the Eiffel Tower (large Sb-320F, Db-380F, Twin/b-480F, CC:VM, 117 avenue de la Bourdonnais, tel. 01 47 05 42 30, fax 01 47 05 45 91).

Hôtel La Tour Maubourg*** is particularly romantic. It lies alone five minutes east of rue Cler, just off the Esplanade des Invalides, and feels like a slightly faded, elegant manor house with spacious Old World rooms. It overlooks a cheery green lawn within sight of Napoleon's tomb (Sb-550–650F, Db-690–850F, suites for up to four-900–1,400F, prices include breakfast with fresh-squeezed juice, prices reduced mid-July–mid-August, CC:VM, at the La Tour

Maubourg Métro stop, 150 rue de Grenelle, tel. 01 47 05 16 16, fax 01 47 05 16 14, e-mail: victor@worldnet.fr).

These places are lesser values but, in this fine area, acceptable last choices: **Hôtel de la Tour Eiffel**** (Sb-330F, Db-380F, Tb-480F, CC:VMA, 17 rue de l'Exposition, tel. 01 47 05 14 75, fax 01 47 53 99 46, Muriel SE); **Hôtel Kensington****, near the Mars Hotel (Sb-315F, Db-400–500F, extra bed-80F, CC:VMA, 79 avenue de La Bourdonnais, tel. 01 47 05 74 00, fax 01 47 05 25 81); **Hôtel de la Tulipe**** (Db-580F, overpriced and wood-beamed with a leafy courtyard, 33 rue Malar, tel. 01 45 51 67 21, fax 01 47 53 96 37); quiet **Hotel le Pavillon** with a small courtyard (Db-460F, family suites-575F, 54 rue St. Dominique, tel. 01 45 51 42 87, fax 01 45 51 32 79); **Hôtel Royal Phare**** (Db-310–410F, facing École Militaire Métro stop, 40 avenue de la Motte Piquet, tel. 01 47 05 57 30, fax 01 45 51 64 41); **Hôtel la Motte Piquet**** (Db-350–440F, duplex suites-730F, CC:VM, 30 avenue de la Motte Piquet, tel. 01 47 05 09 57, fax 01 47 05 74 36); and simple, quiet **Hôtel de la Paix**, run agreeably by English-speaking Noël (S-175F, Ds-310F, Db-345F, Tb-475F, no elevator, 19 rue du Gros-Caillou, tel. 01 45 51 86 17).

Rue Cler Orientation

Become a local at a rue Cler café for breakfast or join the afternoon crowd for une bière pression (a draft beer). On rue Cler you can eat and browse your way through a street full of tart shops, delis, cheeseries, and colorful outdoor produce stalls (see Eating, below). For an after-dinner cruise on the Seine, it's just a short walk to the river and the Bâteaux Mouches.

Your neighborhood TI is at the Eiffel Tower (daily 11:00–18:00 May–September, tel. 01 45 51 22 15). The Métro station (École Militaire) and a post office with phone booths are at the end of rue Cler, on avenue de la Motte Piquet. Taxi stands are on avenue de Tourville at avenue la Motte Piquet (near the Métro stop), and on avenue Bosquet at rue St. Dominique. The Banque Populaire (across from Hôtel Leveque) changes money and has an ATM. Rue St. Dominique is the area's boutique street.

The American Church and College is the community center for Americans living in Paris (65 quai d'Orsay, tel. 01 47 05 07 99). The interdenominational service at 11:00 on Sunday, the coffee hour after church, and the free Sunday concerts (18:00) are a great way to make some friends and get a taste of émigré life in Paris. Stop by and pick up copies of the Free Voice and France–U.S.A. Contacts newspapers for information on housing and employment through the community of 30,000 Americans living in Paris.

Afternoon *boules* (lawn bowling) on the esplanade des

Rue Cler

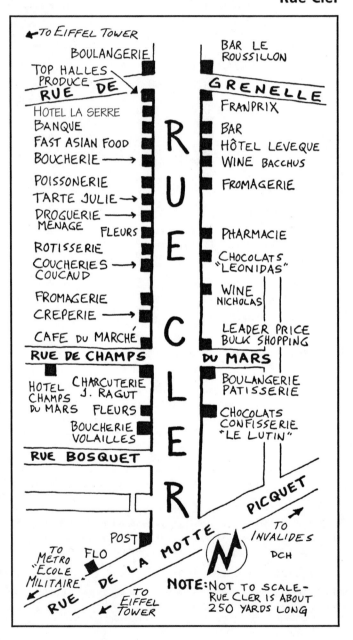

Invalides is a relaxing spectator sport. Look for the dirt area to the upper right as you face the Invalides.

Helpful bus routes: Line 69 runs along rue St. Dominique and serves Les Invalides, Orsay, Louvre, Marais, and Père-Lachaise cemetery. Line 92 runs along avenue Bosquet and serves the Arc de Triomphe and Champs-Élysées in one direction and the Montparnasse tower in the other. Line 49 runs on boulevard La Tour Maubourg and serves St. Lazaire and Gard du Nord stations.

Sleeping in the Marais Neighborhood
(4th arrondissement, Mo: St. Paul or Bastille, zip code: 75004)

Those interested in a more Soho/Greenwich, gentrified, urban-jungle locale would enjoy making the Marais their Parisian home. The Marais is a more happening locale than rue Cler. It's narrow medieval Paris at its finest. Only 15 years ago it was a forgotten Parisian backwater, but now the Marais is one of Paris' most popular residential areas. It's a 15-minute walk to Notre-Dame, Île St. Louis, and the Latin Quarter.

Grand Hôtel Jeanne d'Arc**, a cozy, welcoming place with thoughtfully appointed rooms on a quiet street, is a fine value and a haven for connoisseurs of the Marais (small Db-310F, Db-400–490F, Tb-530F, Qb-590F, extra bed 75F, CC:VM, 3 rue Jarente, Mo: St. Paul, tel. 01 48 87 62 11, fax 01 48 87 37 31). Sixth-floor rooms have a view.

Hotel Bastille Speria*** feels family-run while offering a serious business-type service. Its spacious lobby and 45 rooms are modern, cheery, and pastel; and it's English-language-friendly, from the *Herald Tribunes* in the lobby to the history of the Bastille in the elevator (Sb-525–550F, Db-570–635F, Tb-770F, extra bed-120F, CC:VMA, 1 rue de la Bastille, Mo: Bastille, tel. 01 42 72 04 01, fax 01 42 72 56 38, e-mail: speria@micronet.fr).

Hôtel Castex** is pleasant, clean, cheery, and run by the friendly Perdigao family (Miguel and Vasco). This place is a great value, with comfortable rooms, many stairs, and a great location on a relatively quiet street (Ss-240F, Sb-260–290F, Ds-320–340F, Db-340–360F, Tb-460F, CC:VM, no elevator, 5 rue Castex, just off place de la Bastille and rue Saint Antoine, Mo: Bastille, tel. 01 42 72 31 52, fax 01 42 72 57 91). Reserve by phone and leave your credit-card number. The security code marked on your key opens the front door after hours.

Hôtel de la Place des Vosges**, quasi-classy with a linoleum/antique feel, is ideally located on a quiet street (Sb-350F, Db-450–510F, CC:VMA, 12 rue de Biraque, just off the elegant

Marais Neighborhood

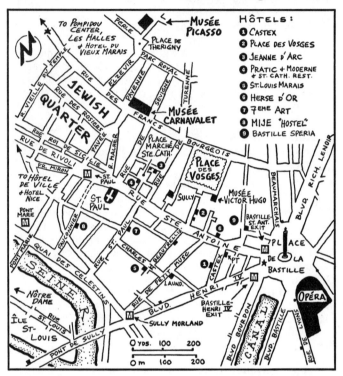

place des Vosges and just as snooty, Mo: St. Paul, tel. 01 42 72 60 46, fax 01 42 72 02 64).

Hotel des Chevaliers***, one block northwest of the place des Vosges, offers pleasant and comfortable rooms with all the comforts from hair dryers to cable TV (Db-630–820F, CC:VMA, skip the overpriced breakfast, 30 rue de Turenne, Mo: St. Paul, tel. 01 42 72 73 47, fax 01 42 72 54 10).

Hotel de la Herse D'Or is dumpy, industrial-strength, three-coats-of-paint simple, with a good location, tortured floor plan, and hard-to-beat prices (S-160F, D-200F, Db-280F, showers 10F, no elevator, 20 rue Saint Antoine, Mo: Bastille, tel. 01 48 87 84 09, fax 01 48 87 94 01).

Hotel Sévigné** provides basic two-star comfort at fair prices with the cheapest breakfast in Paris: 16F (Sb-355F, Db-375F, CC:VM, 2 rue Malher, Mo: Bastille, tel. 01 42 72 76 17, fax 01 42 78 68 26).

Hôtel Pratic* has a slightly Arabic feel in its cramped lobby.

The tidy rooms are simple but not confined, stairs are many, and it's right on a great people-friendly square. Single rooms are bare, tiny, and depressing (S-180F, D-245F, Ds-290F, Db-340F, no elevator, 9 rue d'Ormesson, Mo: St. Paul, tel. 01 48 87 80 47, fax 01 48 87 40 04).

The bare-bones and dumpy **Hôtel Moderne**, next to the Hôtel Pratic, might be better than a youth hostel if you need privacy. The only thing *moderne* about it is the name—which is illegible on the broken sign (D-170F, Ds-190F, Db-220F, 3 rue Caron, Mo: St. Paul, tel. 01 48 87 97 05).

Grand Hotel du Loiret** is a fair value with easy-going management. While it's popular with American students, it's renovating many of its rooms so that they'll no longer be in the student price range (S-190F, Sb-250–350F, D-220F, Db-300–400F, Tb-400F, Qb-500F, CC:VMA, 8 rue des Garcons Mauvais, Mo: Hotel de Ville, tel. 01 48 87 77 00, fax 01 48 04 96 56).

Hôtel de 7ème Art**, a Hollywood-nostalgia place, is run by young, hip Marais types, with average rooms, a full-service café/bar, and Charlie Chaplin murals (Sb-300F, Db-420–490F, a few large double rooms at 670F, CC:VMA, 20 rue St. Paul, Mo: St. Paul, tel. 01 44 54 85 00, fax 01 42 77 69 10).

Hôtel de Nice** is a cozy "Marie Antoinette-does-tie-dye" place with lots of thoughtful touches on the Marais' busy main drag (Sb-380F, Db-480F, Tb-600F, CC:VM, 42 bis rue de Rivoli, Mo: Hotel de Ville, tel. 01 42 78 55 29, fax 01 42 78 36 07). Twin rooms, which cost the same as doubles, are roomier but on the street side (effective double-pane windows).

Hotel de la Bretonniere*** is my favorite splurge in the Marais with elegant decor; tastefully decorated rooms with an antique, open-beam coziness; and an efficient, helpful staff (standard Db-640F, Db with character-790F, elegant Db suites-980F, the standard Db has enough character for me, CC:VMA, between rue du Vielle du Temple and rue des Archives at 22 rue Sainte Croix de la Bretonnerie, Mo: Hotel de Ville, tel. 01 48 87 77 63, fax 01 42 77 26 78, www: HoteldelaBretonnerie.com).

Hotel Caron de Beaumarchais***, renovated into an 18th-century Marais manor house, is charming from the Louis XVI fireplace in the lobby to the period furniture in each room (Db-690–770F, CC:VMA, air-conditioning, 12 rue Vielle du Temple, Mo: Hotel de Ville, tel. 01 42 72 34 12, fax 01 42 72 34 63).

Hotel Rivoli Notre Dame***, another nicely remodeled three-star place with all the comforts, is centrally located in the Marais (Db-660–715F, CC:VMA, 19 rue du Bourg Tibourg, Mo: Hotel de Ville, tel. 01 42 78 47 39, fax 01 40 29 07 00, Web site: www.hotelrivolinotredame.com).

Hotel de Vieux Marais**, tucked away on a quiet street near the Pompidou Center, offers renovated rooms with air-conditioning

(Sb-500F, Db-660–690F, extra bed-100F, CC:VM, just off rue des Archives at 8 rue du Platre, Mo: Hotel de Ville, tel. 01 42 78 47 22, fax 01 42 78 34 32).

MIJE "Youth Hostels": The Maison Internationale de la Jeunesse des Étudiants (MIJE) runs three classy old residences in the Marais for travelers under age 30. Each offers simple, clean, single-sex, mostly four-bed rooms for 126F per bed, including shower and breakfast. Singles cost 200F. Rooms are locked from 12:00 to 15:00 and at 1:00. MIJE Fourcy (cheap dinners, 6 rue de Fourcy, just south of the rue Rivoli), MIJE Fauconnier (11 rue Fauconnier), and the best, MIJE Maubisson (12 rue des Barres), share one telephone number (tel. 01 42 74 23 45) and the same Métro stop (St. Paul). Reservations are accepted at all three hostels.

Marais Orientation

The nearest TIs are in the Louvre and Gare de Lyon (arrival level, open 8:00–20:00, tel. 01 43 43 33 24). The Banque de France changes money; it offers good rates but sometimes long lines (where rue Saint Antoine hits the place de la Bastille, Monday–Friday 9:00–11:45 and 13:30–15:30). Most banks, shops, and other services are on rue Saint Antoine between Métro stops St. Paul and Bastille. You'll find one taxi stand on the north side of Saint Antoine where it meets rue Castex, and another on the south side of Saint Antoine in front of the St. Paul church.

The new Bastille opera house, Promenade Plantée Park, place des Vosges (Paris' oldest square), and the Jewish Quarter (rue des Rosiers) are all nearby. The Marais' main drag, rue Saint Antoine, starts at the Bastille and leads west toward the hopping Beaubourg/Les Halles area. Paris' biggest and best budget department store is BHV, next to the Hôtel de Ville. Marais post offices are on rue Castex and on the corner of rues Pavée and Francs Bourgeois. (See "Bastille/Marais/Beaubourg Walk," above, for more information on this area.)

Helpful bus routes: Line 69 on rue Saint Antoine takes you to the Louvre, Orsay, Rodin, and Invalide museums, and ends at the Eiffel Tower. Line 86 runs down boulevard Henri IV crossing the Île St. Louis and serving the Latin Quarter along boulevard St. Germain. Line 65 serves the Gares Austerlitz, Est, and Nord from the place de la Bastille.

Sleeping in the Contrescarpe Neighborhood
(5th arrondissement, Mo: place Monge, zip code: 75005)
This lively, colorful neighborhood—just over the hill from the Latin Quarter and behind the Panthéon—is walking distance from Notre-Dame, Île de la Cité, Île St. Louis, Luxembourg Gardens, and the grand boulevards St. Germain and St. Michel. The rue Mouffetard and delightfully Parisian place Contrescarpe are the

heart and soul of this area. Rue Mouffetard is a market street by day and touristy restaurant row by night. Fewer tourists sleep here and I find the hotel values consistently better than most other neighborhoods. These hotels are listed in order by proximity to the Seine River.

The low-energy, bare-bones **Hôtel du Commerce** is run by Monsieur Mattuzzi, who must be a pirate gone good (S-130F, D-140F, Ds-150F, Ts-210F, Qs-260F, showers-15F, no elevator, takes no reservations, call at 10:00 and he'll say *"oui"* or *"non,"* 14 rue de La Montagne Ste. Geneviève, Mo: Maubert-Mutualité, tel. 01 43 54 89 69). This 300-year-old place (with vinyl that looks it) is a great rock-bottom deal and as safe as any dive next to a police station can be. In the morning, the landlady will knock and chirp, *"Restez-vous?"* ("Are you staying tonight?")

Hôtel des Grandes Écoles** is as good as a two-star Parisian hotel gets (and better than most three-star hotels). It's idyllic and peaceful, with three buildings protecting a flowering garden courtyard. This romantic place is deservedly popular, so call well in advance (Db-520–670F, Tb-620–770F, Qb-670–870F, 75 rue de Cardinal Lemoine, Mo: Cardinal Lemoine, tel. 01 43 26 79 23, fax 01 43 25 28 15, run by mellow Marie.)

Hôtel Central* is unprententious with a charming location, a steep and slippery castlelike stairway, simple rooms (all with shower, though toilets are down the hall), so-so beds, and plenty of smiles. It's a fine budget value (Ss-165–190F, Ds-240–270F, no elevator, 6 rue Descartes, Mo: Cardinal Lemoine, tel. 01 46 33 57 93).

The hotels listed below lie on or at the bottom of the rue Mouffetard (Mo: Cardinal Lemoine, and often have rooms when others don't.

Hotel Comfort Inn**, with its modern chain-hotel rooms, seems out of place in this nonconformist area, but it's brilliantly located right on the rue Mouffetard, a stone's throw from the place Contrescarpe and the late-night action (Sb-535F, Db-620F, CC:VM, 56 rue Mouffetard, Mo: Cardinal Lemoine, tel. 01 43 36 17 00, fax 01 43 36 25 78).

Y&H Hostel offers a great location, easygoing English-speaking management, and basic but acceptable hostel-like conditions (100F-beds in four-bed rooms, 120F-beds in double rooms, 15F for sheets, rooms closed 11:00–17:00 though reception stays open, reservations must be paid in advance, 80 rue Mouffetard, Mo: Censier-Daubenton, tel. 01 45 35 09 53, fax 01 47 07 22 24).

Hotel de l'Esperance** gives you nearly three stars for the price of two. It's quiet, fluffy, and comfortable, with thoughtfully appointed rooms complete with canopy beds, hair dryers, cable TV, and a flamboyant owner (Sb-380–410F, Db-410–480F, Tb-550F, CC:VM, rue Pascal 15, Mo: Censier-Daubenton, tel. 01 47 07 10 99, fax 01 43 37 56 19).

Hotel Pascal* is a good value with simple, clean rooms, small double beds, and miniscule bathrooms (S-200F, Db-300F, Tb-450F, Qb-600F, funky studio lofts with kitchenettes-450F, 20 rue Pascal, Mo: Censier-Daubeuton, tel. 01 47 07 41 92, fax 01 47 07 43 80, e-mail: hotpascal@mail.opsion.fr).

Hotel de France**, on a busy street, has fine, modern rooms and hardworking, helpful owners (Sb-360F, Db-410–430F, CC:VM, 108 rue Monge, Mo: Censier-Daubenton tel. 01 47 07 19 04, fax 01 43 36 62 34). Its best and quietest rooms are *sur le cour* (on the courtyard).

Hotel Port Royal* is a budget traveler's dream with helpful owners and spotless, comfortable rooms at great prices (S-180–225F, D-225F, Db-335–350F, CC:VM, 8 boulevard de Port Royal, Mo: Gobelins, tel. 01 43 31 70 06, fax 01 43 31 33 67).

Contrescarpe Orientation

The nearest TI is at the Louvre Museum. The post office (PTT) is between rue Mouffetard and rue Monge at 10 rue de l'Épée du Bois. Place Monge hosts a colorful outdoor market on Wednesday, Friday, and Sunday until 13:00. The street market at the bottom of rue Mouffetard bustles daily from 8:00 to 12:00 and 15:30 to 19:00 (five blocks south of Contrescarpe), and the lively place Contrescarpe hops in the afternoon and well after dark.

The flowery Jardin des Plantes park is close by and great for afternoon walks, as are Luxembourg Gardens, which justify the 15-minute walk. The doorway at 49 rue Monge leads to a hidden Roman arena (**Arènes de Lutèce**). Today, *boules* players occupy the stage while couples cuddle on the seats. Walk to the Panthéon, admire it from the outside (it's not worth paying to go in), and go into the wildly beautiful St. Étienne-du-Mont church.

Sleeping near Paris, in Versailles

For a laid-back alternative to Paris within easy reach of the big city by RER-C train (5/hrly, 30 min, use Versailles C.H. station), Versailles can be a good overnight stop. Parking is free and easy.

Hôtel Le Cheval Rouge**, built in 1676 as Louis XIV's stables, now houses tourists comfortably. It's a block behind the place du Marche in a quaint corner of town on a large quiet courtyard (Ds-275F, Db-340–390F, extra bed-90F, CC:VMA, 18 rue Andre Chenier, 78000 Versailles, tel. 01 39 50 03 03, fax 01 39 50 61 27).

Ibis Versailles**, a slick business-class place, offers all the comfort with none of the character (Db-390–490F, CC:VMA, across from RER station, 4 avenue du Gen. de Gaulle, tel. 01 39 53 03 30, fax 01 39 50 06 31).

Hotel du Palais, facing the RER station, has cheap and handy beds; get one off the street. It's a pink and funky place, dumpy enough to lack stars but proud enough to put candy on the

Contrescarpe Hotels

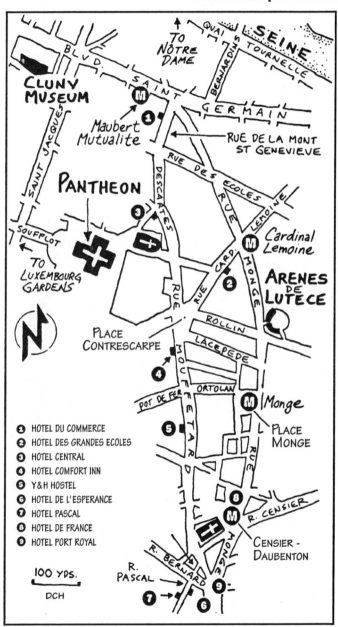

1 HOTEL DU COMMERCE
2 HOTEL DES GRANDES ECOLES
3 HOTEL CENTRAL
4 HOTEL COMFORT INN
5 Y&H HOSTEL
6 HOTEL DE L'ESPERANCE
7 HOTEL PASCAL
8 HOTEL DE FRANCE
9 HOTEL PORT ROYAL

100 YDS.

DCH

beds (D-170F, Ds-220F, Db-250F, 30F per additional person, miles of stairs, 6 place Lyautey, tel. 01 39 50 39 29, fax 01 39 50 80 41).

Hotel d'Angleterre** is a peaceful, well-worn old place near the palace (Db-300–350F, extra bed-60F, CC:VM, first-floor rooms are best, 2 rue de Fontenay, tel. 01 39 51 43 50, fax 01 39 51 45 63).

Eating in Paris

Paris is France's wine and cuisine melting pot. While it lacks a style of its own, it draws from the best of France. Paris could hold a gourmet's Olympics—and import nothing.

Picnic or go to bakeries for quick take-out lunches, or stop at a café for a lunch salad or *plat du jour*, but linger longer over dinner. You can eat well, restaurant-style, for 100F to 140F. Your hotel can also recommend nearby restaurants in the 60F to 100F range. Remember, cafés and simple small restaurants are happy to serve a *plat du jour* (garnished plate of the day, about 60F) or a chef-like salad (35–50F) day or night. Famous places are often overpriced, overcrowded, and overrated. Find a quiet neighborhood and wander, or follow a local recommendation. Restaurants open for dinner around 19:00. Small local favorites get crowded after 21:00.

Cafeterias and Picnics

Many Parisian department stores have huge supermarkets hiding in the basement and top-floor cafeterias offering not really cheap but low-risk, low-stress, what-you-see-is-what-you-get meals. For picnics, you'll find handy little groceries (*épiceries*) and delis (*charcuteries*) all over town but rarely near famous sights. Good picnic fixings include roasted chicken, drinkable yogurt, fresh bakery goods, melons, and exotic pâtés and cheeses. Great take-out deli-type foods like gourmet salads and quiches abound. Boulangeries make good, cheap mini-quiches and sandwiches. While wine is taboo in public places in the United States, it's *pas de problème* in France. The budget eating tips in this book's introduction will save piles of francs in Paris.

Good Picnic Spots: The pedestrian bridge, Pont des Arts, with unmatched views and plentiful benches; and the park under the Eiffel Tower are my favorite dinner-picnic places. Bring your own dinner feast and watch the riverboats or the Eiffel Tower light up the city for you. The Palais Royal (across the street from the Louvre) is a good spot for a peaceful and royal picnic. Also try the little triangular Henry IV Park on the west tip of the Île de la Cité, people-watching at the Pompidou Center, the elegant place des Vosges (closes at dusk) in the Marais neighborhood, the gardens at the Rodin Museum, and Luxembourg Gardens.

Restaurants

The Parisian eating scene is kept at a rolling boil. Entire books (and lives) are dedicated to the subject. If you are traveling outside of Paris, save your splurges for the countryside, where you'll enjoy better cooking for less money. I've listed places that conveniently fit a busy sightseeing schedule and places near recommended hotels. If you'd like to visit a district specifically to eat, consider the many romantic restaurants that line the cozy Île St. Louis' main street and the colorful, touristic-but-fun string of eateries along rue Mouffetard behind the Panthéon.

Eating in the Rue Cler Neighborhood

Restaurants: The rue Cler neighborhood isn't famous for its restaurants. That's why I eat here. Several small family-run places serve great dinner *menus* for 100F and *plats du jour* for 60 to 80F.

Café du Marché, with the best seats, coffee, and prices on rue Cler, serves hearty salads and great 60F *plats du jour* for lunch or dinner. Arrive before 19:30 or wait at the bar. A chalkboard listing the plates of the day—each a meal—will momentarily be hung in front of you (at the corner of rue Cler and rue Champs du Mars).

Leo le Lion has been run by Mimi for 20 years and must be the friendliest place in the neighborhood. A warm, charming souvenir of old Paris, it's popular with locals. The 105F *menu* comes with a first course that could feed two for an entire meal (but no splitting), and a fully garnished main course (closed Sunday, 23 rue Duvivier, tel. 01 45 51 41 77).

Vegetarians will appreciate the Mediterranean cuisine at **7ème Sud**, though the restaurant can be smoky (at the corner of rue de Grenelle and rue Duvivier).

Thoumieux, the neighborhood's classy, traditional Parisian *brasserie*, is deservedly popular (82F and 160F *menus*, complete á la carte, 79 rue St. Dominique, tel. 01 47 05 49 75).

For a special dinner, survey the handful of fine places that line rue de l'Exposition (between rue St. Dominique and rue de Grenelle): **Restaurant La Serre**, at #29, has fun ambience (*plats* 50–70F, daily from 19:00, often a wait after 21:00, good onion soup and duck specialties, tel. 01 45 55 20 96, Marie-Alice and Philippe SE). Across the street at #28, **Le P'tit Troquet** is popular with locals and ideal for a last-night splurge—allow 150F per person for dinner (closed Sunday and Monday, tel. 01 47 05 80 39). The quieter **La Maison de Cosima** at #20 offers a refined, creative French cuisine and excellent 100F and 150F *menus* that include a vegetarian option (closed Sunday, tel. 01 45 51 37 71, run by friendly Helene). The softly-lit tables and red velvet chairs of **Auberge du Champ de Mars** at #18 draw a romantic crowd in search of a good value (100F *menu* only, limited wine menu, closed Sunday, tel. 01 45 51 78 08).

Around the corner, just off rue de Grenelle, the friendly and unpretentious **La Varanque** is a good budget bet with 60F *plats* and an 80F *menu* (27 rue Augereau, tel. 01 47 05 51 22).

Ambassade du Sud-Ouest, a wine and food boutique/restaurant, specializes in French Southwest cuisine such as *daubes de canard*–duck meatballs (46 avenue de la Bourdonnais, tel. 01 45 55 59 59). **L'Ami de Jean** is a lively place to sample Basque cuisine (closed Sunday, 27 rue Malar, tel. 01 47 05 86 89).

Picnicking: Rue Cler is a moveable feast that gives "fast food" a good name. The entire street is clogged with connoisseurs of good eating. Only the health-food store goes unnoticed. A festival of food, the street is lined with people whose lives seem to be devoted to their specialty: Stacking polished produce, rotisserie chicken, crêpes, or cheese squares.

For a magical picnic dinner, assemble it in no fewer than six shops on rue Cler and lounge on the best grass in Paris (the police don't mind after dark) with the dogs, Frisbees, a floodlit Eiffel Tower, and a cool breeze in the Parc du Champs de Mars.

The **crêpe stand** next to the Café du Marche does a wonderful top-end dinner crêpe for 25F. An Asian deli, **Traiteur Asie** (across from Hôtel Leveque; another is across from the Hotel de Champs de Mars), has tasty low-stress, low-price take-out treats. Its two tables offer the cheapest place to sit, eat, and enjoy the rue Cler ambience. For quiche, cheese pie, or a pear/chocolate tart, try **Tarte Julie's** (take-out or stools, 28 rue Cler). The elegant **Flo Prestige** *charcuterie* (at École Militaire Métro stop) is open until 23:00 and offers mouthwatering meals to go. **Real McCoy** is a little shop selling American food and sandwiches (194 rue de Grenelle). There's a small late-night grocery on rue de Grenelle at rue de l'Exposition.

The bakery (*boulangerie*) on the corner of rue Cler and rue de Champs de Mars is the place for a fresh baguette, sandwich, tiny quiche, or *pain au chocolat*, but the almond croissants at the *boulangerie* on rue de Grenelle at rue Cler make my day. The bakery at 112 rue St. Dominique is in a league by itself and worth the detour, with classic decor and tables to enjoy your *café au lait* and croissant.

Cafés and Bars: If you want to linger over coffee or a drink at a sidewalk café, try **Café du Marché** (see above), **Petite Brasserie** (opposite #53 rue Cler), or the traditional **La Terasse** café (at École Militaire Métro). **Café La Roussillon**, peopled and decorated belle epoque, also offers a quintessential café experience. Sip a 7F wine at the bar or enjoy the good bistro fare at a table (hearty 50F *plats du jour* and salads, corner of Grenelle and Cler). **Le Sancerre** wine bar/café is wood beam–warm and ideal for a light lunch or dinner (great omelets), or just for a glass of wine after a long day of sightseeing. You'll be served by the owner, whose cheeks are the same color as his wine (open until 21:30, 22 avenue Rapp, tel. 01 45 51 75 91). The almost no-name **Maison**

Altmayer is a hole-in-the-wall place for a drink quietly festooned with reality (9:00–19:30, 6 rue du Gros Caillou, next to Hôtel Eiffel Rive Gauche). Cafés like this originated (and this one still functions) as a place where locals enjoyed a drink while their heating wood, coal, or gas was prepared for delivery.

Nightlife: This sleepy neighborhood is not the place for night-owls, but there are three notable exceptions: **Café du Marché** (above) hops with a Franco-American crowd until about midnight. **O'Brien's Pub** is an upscale and popular Parisian rendition of an Irish pub (77 St. Dominique). **Café Thoumieux** is a new hip, happening place with big-screen sports and a young international crowd (4 rue de la Comete, Mo: Latour Maubourg).

Eating in the Marais Neighborhood

The windows of the Marais are filled with munching sophisticates. The place du Marche Ste. Catherine, a tiny square midway between the St. Paul Métro and place des Vosges, is home to several good places. **Le Marais Ste. Catherine** is a good value (100F *menu*, daily from 19:00, extra seating in their candlelit cellar, 5 rue Caron, tel. 01 42 72 39 94), though many seem willing to pay 30F more for the *menu* at **Le Marche** (2 place Marche Ste. Catherine, tel. 01 4 77 34 88). Just off the square, **l'Auberge de Jarente** offers a well-respected and traditional cuisine (117F *menu*, closed Sunday and Monday, 7 rue Jarente, tel. 01 42 77 49 35).

Dinners beneath the candlelit arches of the place des Vosges are *très* romantic: **Nectarine** at #16 serves fine salads, quiches, and *plats du jour* day and night; while **Ma Bourgogne** is where locals go for a splurge (at the northwest corner, daily, tel. 01 42 78 44 64).

For a fast, cheap change of pace, eat at (or take-out from) the Chinese/Japanese **Delice House**. Two can split 200 grams of chicken curry (or whatever, 26F) and a heaping helping of rice (20F). There's lots of seating, with pitchers of water at the ground-floor tables and a roomier upstairs (81 rue Saint Antoine, open until 21:00).

Near Hôtel Castex, the restaurant **La Poste** and the *crêperie* across the street (13 rue Castex) offer inexpensive, light meals (both closed on Sunday). I like **La Bastoche's** cozy ambience and good 100F *menu* (7 rue Saint Antoine, tel. 01 48 04 74 34). Across the street, **Le Paradis de Fruit** serves organic foods to young locals (on the small square at rues Tournelle and Saint Antoine). Several cafés on the Boulevard Henri IV (**Brasserie Le Reveil** at #29, near rue Castex) offer reasonable *plats du jour* and salads.

Wine lovers shouldn't miss the excellent Burgundy wines and exquisite, though limited *menu* selection at the cozy **Au Bourguignon du Marais** (52 rue Francois Miron, call by 19:00 to reserve, tel. 01 48 87 15 40).

For a worthwhile splurge, try the romantic and traditional **L'Excuse** (185F *menu*, closed Sunday, 14 rue Charles V, call ahead, tel. 01 42 77 98 97). Across the street, **L'Énoteca** has lively and reasonable Italian cuisine in a relaxed, open setting (across from Hôtel du 7ème Art at 20 rue St. Paul, closed Sunday, tel. 01 42 78 91 44).

Vegetarians will appreciate the fine cuisine at **Picolo Teatro** (closed Monday, 6 rue des Ecouffes, tel. 01 42 72 17 79), and at **l'As du Falafel**, which serves the best falafel on the rue Rosier at #34.

Picnicking: Hobos and connoisseurs picnic at the peaceful park at place des Vosges (closes at dusk). Connoisseurs prefer the busy gourmet take-out places all along rue Saint Antoine, such as **Flo Prestige** (open until 23:00, on the tiny square where rue Tournelle and rue Saint Antoine meet). Hobos stretch their francs at the supermarket in the basement of the Monoprix department store (close to place des Vosges on rue Saint Antoine). A few small grocery shops are open until 23:00 on the rue Saint Antoine (near intersection with rue Castex). An open-air market, held Sunday morning, is just off the place de la Bastille on boulevard Richard Lenoir.

For a cheap breakfast, try the tiny *boulangerie/pâtisserie* where the hotels buy their croissants (coffee machine, 3F; 10F baby quiches, 5F *pain au chocolat*, one block off place de la Bastille at corner of rue Saint Antoine and rue de Lesdiguieres).

Cafés and Bars: This hip area is overrun with atmospheric cafés and bars (open generally till 2:00), most of which lie north of rue Saint Antoine and rue Rivoli. Here are a few keys areas to consider for café sitting: along the rue du Vielle du Temple; at the rue de la Croix Bretonnière and the rue Tresor; or on the rue Rosiers for ethnically hip cafés like the **Hamman** cyber-café (4 rue des Rosiers, on the pleasant place du Marche Ste. Catherine). The *trés* local wine bar at **Au Temps des Cerises** is amiably run and a welcoming if smoky place (rue du Petit Musc and rue de Cerisaie, around the corner from the Hôtel Castex).

Nightlife: The streets running north of rue Saint Antoine and Rivoli play host to a lively after-hours scene. Wander rue du Vielle du Temple, rue de la Croix Bretonnière, and rue des Archives. **Le Vieux Comptoir** is tiny, lively and not too hip (just off the place des Vosges at 8 rue Biraque). **La Perla** is trendy with Parisian yuppies in search of the perfect margarita (26 rue Francois Miron). **Auld Alliance**, Paris' only Scottish pub, feels a bit like a frat house in Paris with Scottish barmen (80 rue Francois Miron).

Eating in the Contrescarpe Neighborhood

Rue Mouffetard and rue du Pot-de-Fer are lined with inexpensive, lively, and forgettable restaurants. Study the many *menus*, compare crowds, then dive in. **Le Jardin d'Artemis** is one of the better inexpensive values on the rue Mouffetard at #34 (85F *menu*). **Restaurant l'Epoque**, a fine neighborhood restaurant, has excellent-value *menus* at 68F and 118F (one block off place Contrescarpe at 81 rue Cardinal Lemoine, tel. 01 46 34 15 84). **Restaurant Le Vigneron** is well respected and serves traditional French cuisine (20 rue du Pot-de-Fer); and **Savannah Café**'s creative Mediterranean cuisine attracts a loyal, artsy crowd (27 rue Descartes, tel. 01 43 29 45 77). **Le Jardin des Pâtes** is popular with vegetarians, serving pastas and salads at fair prices (4 rue Lacepede, near Jardins des Plantes, tel. 01 43 31 50 71). **Café Tournebride** serves delicious salads (104 rue Mouffetard).

　　　Cafés: Brasserie La Chope, a classic Parisian *brasserie* right on the place Contrescarpe, is popular until the wee hours. Indoor and outdoor seating is people-watching good. **Café Le Mouffetard** is in the thick of the street-market hustle and bustle (at the corner of rue Mouffetard and rue de l'Arbalete). At **Café de la Mosque** you'll feel like you've been beamed to Morocco in this purely Arab café. Order a mint tea, pour in the sugar, and enjoy the authentic interior and peaceful outdoor terrace (2 rue Daubenton, behind the mosque).

Eating in the Latin Quarter

La Petite Bouclerie is a cozy place with classy family cooking (70F *menu*, closed Monday, 33 rue de la Harpe, center of touristy Latin Quarter, tel. 01 43 54 18 03). The popular **Restaurant Polidor** is an old turn-of-the-century-style place, with great *cuisine bourgeois*, a vigorous local crowd, and a historic toilet. Arrive at 19:00 to get a seat in the restaurant (65F *plat du jour*, 100F *menus*, 41 rue Monsieur le Prince, midway between Odéon and Luxembourg Métro stops, tel. 01 43 26 95 34).

Eating on the Île St. Louis

Cruise the island's main street for a variety of good options from cozy *crêperies* to romantic restaurants. Sample Paris' best sorbet and ice cream at any place advertising *les glaces Berthillon*; the original Berthillon shop is at 31 rue St. Louis en l'Île.

　　　All listings below are on rue St. Louis en l'Île. **Café Med** at #53 serves inexpensive salads and crêpes in a delightful setting. My romantic splurge is **Le Tastevin** (150F and 220F *menus*, #46, tel. 01 43 54 17 31). **La Castafiore** at #51–53 serves fine Italian dishes in a cozy setting (160F *menu*). For crazy, touristy, cellar atmosphere and hearty fun food, feast at **La Taverne du Sergeant Recruiter**. The "Sergeant Recruiter" used to get young Parisians drunk and stuffed here, then sign them into the army. It's all-you-can-eat, including wine and service, for 190F (daily from 19:00, #41, tel. 01 43 54 75 42). There's a near-food-fight clone next door at **Nos Ancêtres Les Gaulois** ("Our Ancestors the Gauls," 190F, daily at 19:00, tel. 01 46 33 66 07).

Eating near the Pompidou Center

The **Mélodine** self-service is right at the Rambuteau Métro stop. **Dame Tartine** overlooks the Homage to Stravinsky fountain, serves a young clientele, and offers excellent, cheap, lively meals. The popular **Café de la Cité** fills one long line of tables with locals enjoying their 44F lunches and 65F dinner specials (22 rue Rambuteau, tel. 01 48 04 30 74).

Elegant Dining on the Seine

La Plage Parisienne is a nearly dress-up riverfront place popular with locals, serving elegant, healthy meals at good prices (Port de Javel-Haut, Mo: Javel, tel. 01 40 59 41 00).

Parisian Entertainment

Paris is most beautiful after dark. Save energy from your day's sightseeing and get out at night. Whether it's a concert at Sainte Chapelle, a boat ride on the Seine, a elevator up the Arc de Triomphe, or a late-night café, experience the city of light lit. The *Pariscope* magazine (3F at any newsstand) offers a complete weekly listing of music, cinema, theater, opera, and other special events— we decipher this useful periodical for you below. The *Free Voice* newspaper, in English, has a monthly review of Paris entertainment (available at any English-language bookstore, French-American establishments, or the American Church at 65 quai d'Orsay, Mo: Invalides, tel. 01 47 05 07 99).

A Tour of Pariscope

The weekly *Pariscope* (3F) or *L'Officiel des Spectacles* (2F) are both cheap and essential if you want to know what's happening. Pick one up and page through it. For a head start, check out *Pariscope's* Web site: www.pariscope.fr.

Each publication begins with culture news. Skip the bulky *Theatres* and *Diners/Spectacles* sections and anything listed as *des environs* (outside of Paris). *Musique* or *Concerts Classiques* follow, listing each day's events (program, location, time, and price). Venues with phone numbers and addresses are listed in an *Adresses des Salles de Concerts* sidebar. Touristic venues (such as Sainte-Chapelle and Église de la Madeleine) are often featured in display ads. *Opéras, Musique Traditionelle, Ballet/Danse,* and *Jazz/Rock* listings follow.

Half of each of these magazines is devoted to Cinema—a Paris forte. After the *Films Nouveaux* section trumpets new releases, the *Films en Exclusivité* pages list all the films playing in town. While a code marks films as *Historique, Karate, Erotisme,* and so on, the key mark for tourists is "v.o." which means *version origi-*

nal (American films have their English soundtracks and French
subtitles). Films are listed alphabetically, with theaters and their
arrondissements at the end of each entry. Later films are listed by
neighborhood (*Salles Paris*) and by genre. To find a showing near
your hotel, simply match the *arrondissement*. (But don't hesitate to
hop on the Métro for the film you want.) *Salles Périphérie* is out in
the suburbs. Film festivals are also listed.

   Pariscope has a small English "Time Out" section listing the
week's events. The *Musées* sections (*Monuments, Jardins, Autres
Curiosites, Promenades, Activites Sportives, Piscines*) give the latest
hours of the sights, gardens, curiosities, boat tours, sports, swimming pools, and so on. *Clubs de Loisirs* are various athletic and
social clubs. Pour les Jeunes is for young people (kids' films, ani-
mations/cartoons, marionettes, circuses, and amusement parks
such as Asterix and Disney). *Conferences* are mostly lectures. For
cancan mischief, look under *Paris la nuit*, cabarets, or the busty
spectacles erotiques.

   Finally, you'll find a TV listing. Paris has four country-wide
stations: TF1, France 2, France 3, and the new Arte station (a
German/French cultural channel). M6 is filled with American
series. Canal Plus (channel 4) is a cable channel that airs an
American news show at 7:00 and an American sports event on
Sunday evening.

Music

Jazz Clubs
With a lively mix of American, French, and international musicians, Paris has been an internationally acclaimed jazz capital since
World War II. You'll pay from 30–130F to enter a jazz club (one
drink may be included; if not, expect to pay 30–60F per drink;
beer is cheapest). See *Pariscope* magazine under *Musique* for listings, and the American Church's *Free Voice* paper for a good
monthly review (in English). Music starts after 22:00 in most of
clubs. Here are good bets:

   Caveau de la Huchette, the handiest characteristic old jazz
club for visitors, fills an ancient Latin Quarter cellar with live jazz
and frenzied dancing every night (60F weekday, 70F weekend
admission, 30F drinks, open 21:30–2:30 or later, closed Monday, 5
rue de la Huchette, tel. 01 43 26 65 05).

   Au Duc des Lombards is one of the most popular and
respected jazz clubs in Paris (42 rue des Lombards, Mo: Chatelet,
20-minute walk from place des Vosges).

   At **Le Cave du Franc Pinot**, enjoy a glass of chardonnay at
the main floor wine bar, then drop downstairs for a cool jazz
scene. (1 quai de Bourbon, centrally located on Île St. Louis, Mo:
Pont Marie, tel. 01 46 33 60 64).

The **American Church** regularly plays host to fine jazz musicians for the best price in Paris (65 quai d'Orsay, Mo: Invalides, RER-C: Pont de l'Alma, tel. 01 47 05 07 99).

Come to **Le Sunset** for more traditional jazz—Dixieland, Big Band—and fewer crowds (near Au Duc des Lombards, 60 rue des Lombards, Mo: Chatelet, tel. 01 40 26 46 60).

All Jazz Club, more expensive than the rest, is a hot club in the heart of the St. Germain area, attracting a more mature crowd in search of recognizable names (7 rue St. Benoit, Mo: St. Germain-des-Près, tel. 01 42 61 53 53).

Classical Concerts

For classical music on any night, consult *Pariscope* magazine; the *Musique* section under *Concerts Classique* lists concerts (free and fee). Look for posters at the churches. Churches that regularly host concerts include St. Sulpice, St. Germain-des-Près, Basilique de Madeleine, St. Eustache, and Sainte Chapelle. It's worth the 90–130F entry for the pleasure of hearing Mozart surrounded by the stained glass of the tiny Sainte Chapelle. Even the Galleries Lafayette department store offers concerts. Many are free (*entrée libre*), such as the Sunday *Atelier* concert sponsored by the American Church (18:00, 65 quai d'Orsay, Mo: Invalides, RER: Pont de l'Alma, tel. 01 47 05 07 99).

Opera

Paris is home to two fine operas. **The Opéra Garnier**, Paris' first opera house, hosts opera and ballet performances. Come here for less expensive tickets and grand Belle Epoque decor (Mo: Opéra, tel. 01 44 73 13 99). The **Opéra de la Bastille** is the massive modern opera house that dominates place de la Bastille. Come here for state-of-the-art special effects and modern interpretations of classic ballets and operas (Mo: Bastille, tel. 01 43 43 96 96). For tickets, either write ahead, call 01 44 73 13 00, or go to the opera ticket offices, open 11:00–18:00.

Bus Tours

Paris Illumination Tours, run by Paris Vision, connects all the great illuminated sights of Paris with a 100-minute bus tour in 12 languages. Double-decker buses have huge windows, but Moulin Rouge customers get the most desirable front seats. You'll stampede on with a United Nations of tourists, get a hand-held audio stick, and listen to a tape-recorded spiel (interesting but occasionally hard to hear). Uninspired as it is, this provides a fine first-night overview of the city at its floodlit scenic best. Left seats are marginally better. Visibility is fine in the rain. You're on the bus entirely except for one five-minute cigarette break at the Eiffel Tower viewpoint (150F-adult, 75F-ages 4 to 11, free-

under 3, second adult pays only 100F on 20:30 tours, departures
at 20:30 nightly all year, and 22:00 April–October only, departs
from Paris Vision office at 214 rue de Rivoli, across street from
Mo: Tuileries). These trips are sold through your hotel
(brochures in lobby) or direct at the address listed above (tel. 01
42 60 30 01, fax 01 42 86 95 36, Web site: www.parisvision.com).

Seine River Cruises

The **Bateaux-Mouches** offer one-hour cruises with departures
(every 30 minutes from 10:00–23:00) from the pont de l'Alma, the
centrally-located pont Neuf, and from right in front of the Eiffel
Tower (40F, 20F-under age 14, tel. 01 42 25 96 10).

Walks

Go for a walk to best appreciate the city of light. Break for ice
cream, pause at a café, and enjoy the sidewalk entertainers as you
join the post-dinner Parisian parade. Take the Champs-Élysées
Walk (see More Paris Walks, above) or consider these:

Trocadero and Eiffel Tower

These monuments glimmer at night. Take the Métro to the Trocadero stop, follow *sortie Tour Eiffel* signs, and join the party on
place de la Trocadero for a magnificent view of the glowing Eiffel
Tower. It's a festival of gawkers, drummers, street acrobats, and
entertainers. Pass the fountains and walk across the river to the
base of the tower, worth the effort even if you don't go up. If you
spring for the elevator, go to the 1st floor (20F) where the view is
best at night and pause for a break at the Altitude 95 restaurant/
bar. For more info, see Eiffel Tower under Sights.

Notre-Dame, Île St. Louis, and the Latin Quarter

From the elegant Île St. Louis to the fire-breathing Latin Quarter,
this evening stroll covers 1.5 miles. Start by strolling the main street
of the tiny island, Île St. Louis. Have dinner at a classy café (see
Eating) or at least an ice-cream cone at Berthillon. Cross the foot
bridge to the neighboring island (Île de la Cite) and take an immediate left across the bridge (pont de l'Archeveque) to the Left Bank.
Turn right (for great views of Notre-Dame) and drop down to the
riverbank. After walking the length of the Notre-Dame along the
riverbank, climb back up to street level and venture into Left Bank.
Here (opposite the cathedral), the tangle of small, people-filled
lanes leads eventually to the big busy boulevard St. Germain (if lost,
ask for that street). At boulevard St. Germain, turn right and head
toward St. Germain-des-Près church. You'll pass mimes, fire-
breathers, musicians, and expensive cafés (see Le Grand Cafés of
Paris). From St. Germain-des-Près, the Métro or city bus (bus 86 to
Marais, 63 to rue Cler) takes you home.

Transportation Connections—Paris

Paris is Europe's transportation hub. You'll find trains and buses (day and night) to most any French or European destination. Paris has six central rail stations, each serving different regions. For train schedule information, call 08 36 35 35 35 (3F/min).

Gare St. Lazare: Serves Upper Normandy. To **Rouen** (15/day, 75 min), **Honfleur** (6/day, 3 hrs, via Lisieux then bus), **Bayeux** (9/day, 2.5 hrs), **Caen** (12/day, 2 hrs).

Gare Montparnasse: Serves Lower Normandy and Brittany, and offers TGV service to the Loire Valley and southwestern France. To **Chartres** (10/day, 1 hr), **Mont St. Michel** (2/day, 4.5 hrs, via Rennes), **Dinan** (7/day, 3 hrs, via Rennes and Dol), **Bordeaux** (14/day, 3.5 hrs), **Toulouse** (7/day, 5 hrs, possible transfer in Bordeaux), **Albi** (6.5 hrs, via Toulouse), **Carcassonne** (6.5 hrs, via Toulouse), **Tours** (14/day, 1 hr).

Gare d'Austerlitz: Provides non-TGV service to the Loire Valley, southwestern France, Spain, and Portugal. To **Amboise** (8/day, 2.5 hrs), **Sarlat** (5/day, 5.5 hrs), **Cahors** (5/day, 7 hrs), **Barcelona** (3/day, 13 hrs), **Madrid** (5/day, 16 hrs), **Lisbon** (1/day, 24 hrs).

Gare du Nord: Serves northern France and several international destinations. To **Brussels** (10/day, 3.5 hrs), **Bruges** (3/day, 2.5 hrs), **Amsterdam** (10/day, 5.5 hrs), **Copenhagen** (3/day, 16 hrs), **Koblenz** on the Rhine (3/day, 7 hrs), **London** via the Eurostar Chunnel (12/day, 3 hrs, Full fare: $219 first class/$149 second class; nonexchangeable Leisure Ticket: $179 first class/$109 second class; call 800/EUROSTAR in the U.S. for more info).

Gare de l'Est: Serves eastern France and points east. To **Colmar** (6/day, 5.5 hrs, transfer in Strasbourg or Mulhouse), **Strasbourg** (10/day, 4.5 hrs), **Reims** (8/day, 2 hrs), **Verdun** (5/day, 3 hrs), **Munich** (4/day, 8.5 hrs), **Vienna** (3/day, 13 hrs), **Zurich** (4/day, 6 hrs).

Gare du Lyon: Offers TGV and regular service to southeastern France, Italy, and other international destinations. To **Beaune** (8/day, 2–3 hrs), **Dijon** (13/day, 90 min), **Chamonix** (3/day, 9 hrs, transfer in Lyon and St. Gervais, one direct and very handy night train), **Annecy** (8/day, 4-7 hrs), **Lyon** (12/day, 2.5 hrs), **Avignon** (10/day, 4 hrs), **Arles** (10/day, 5 hrs), **Nice** (8/day, 7 hrs), **Venice** (5/day, 11 hrs), **Rome** (3/day, 15 hrs), **Bern** (5/day, 5 hrs).

Buses: Long-distance bus lines provide a cheaper, if less comfortable and less flexible, means of transportation to major European cities. The principal bus station in Paris is the Gare Routière du Paris-Gallieni (avenue du General de Gaulle, in suburb of Bagnolet, Mo: Gallieni, tel. 01 49 72 51 51). Eurolines buses depart from here.

Charles de Gaulle Airport

Paris' primary airport has three main terminals (T-1, T-2, and T-9). Those flying to or from the United States will probably use T-1. (Air France uses T-2; charters dominate T-9.) Terminals are connected every few minutes by a free *navette* (bus).

At T-1 you'll find an American Express cash machine, an automatic bill changer (at baggage claim 30), and an exchange window (at baggage claim 18). A bank (with barely acceptable rates) and an ATM machine are near gate 16. At the Meeting Point you'll find the TI, which has free Paris maps and information (open until 23:00); and Relais H, where you can buy a *télécarte* (phone card). Car rental offices are on the arrival level from gates 10 to 22; the SNCF (train) office is at gate 22. For flight information, call 01 48 62 22 80.

Transportation between de Gaulle Airport and Paris: There are three efficient public-transportation routes, taxis, and a couple of airport shuttle services linking the airport's T-1 terminal and central Paris. The free *navette* runs between gate 28 and the **RER Roissy Rail** station, where a train zips you into Paris' subway system in 30 minutes (48F, stops at Gare du Nord, Chatelet, St. Michel, and Luxembourg Gardens). The **Roissy Bus** runs every 15 minutes between gate 30 and the old Paris Opéra (stop is on rue Scribe, in front of American Express), costs 45F (use the automatic ticket machine), and takes 40 minutes, but can be jammed. The **Air France Bus** leaves every 15 minutes from gate 34 and serves the Arc de Triomphe and the Porte Maillot in about 40 minutes for 60F, and the Montparnasse Tower in one hour for 75F (from any of these stops, you can reach your hotel by taxi). For most people the RER Roissy Rail works best. A **taxi** ride with luggage costs about 230F; there is a taxi stand, often with long waits, at gate 16. (The RER Roissy Rail, Roissy Bus, and Air France bus described above serve T-2 as efficiently and economically as T-1.) The Disneyland Express bus departs from Gate 32.

For a stress-free trip between either of Paris' airports and downtown, an **airport shuttle minivan** is ideal for single travelers or families of four or more (costs 120F for one person, 90F per person for two or more, 45F for kids under 12). Reserve from home and they'll meet you at the airport. Paris Shuttle Services (tel. 01 49 62 78 78, fax 01 49 62 78 79, e-mail: pas@magic.fr); or even better, Airport Shuttle (tel. 01 45 38 55 72, fax 01 43 21 35 67, Web site: www.paris-anglo.com/clients/ashuttle.html, e-mail: ashuttle@clubinternet.fr).

Skipping Paris: A new TGV rail station (located at T-2, take *navette* from T-1, gate 26) links this airport with Lille to the north and Lyon, Avignon, Nîmes, Marseille, and Montpellier to the south, without passing through Paris. You can transfer easily from these cities to many other French and European destinations.

Sleeping at or near Charles de Gaulle Airport: Those with early flights can sleep in T-1 at Cocoon (60 "cabins," Sb-250F, Db-300F, CC:VM, tel. 01 48 62 06 16, fax 01 48 62 56 97). Take the elevator down to "boutique level" or walk down from the departure level; it's near the Burger King. You get 16 hours of silence buried under the check-in level with TV and toilet. Hôtel IBIS, at the Roissy Rail station, offers more normal accommodations (Db-420F, CC:VMA, free shuttle bus to either terminal takes two minutes, tel. 01 49 19 19 19, fax 01 49 19 19 21).

Drivers who want to stay near the airport can consider the pleasant city of Senlis, a 15-minute drive. Hostellerie de la Porte Bellon is adequate (Sb-215F, Db-365–420F, CC:VM, 51 rue Bellon, tel. 03 44 53 03 05, fax 03 44 53 29 94).

Orly Airport

Orly has two terminals: Sud and Ouest. International flights arrive at Sud. After exiting baggage claim (near gate H) you'll be greeted by signs directing you to city transportation, car rental, etc. Turn left to enter the main terminal area and you'll find exchange offices with barely acceptable rates, an ATM machine, the ADP (a quasi–tourist office that offers free city maps and basic sightseeing information), and an SNCF French rail desk (sells train tickets and even Eurailpasses). Downstairs is a sandwich bar, bank (lousy rates), newsstand (buy *télécarte* phone card), and post office (great rates for cash or American Express traveler's checks). For flight info on any airline serving Orly, call 01 49 75 15 15.

Transportation Between Paris and Orly Airport: There are four efficient public-transportation routes, taxis, and a couple of airport shuttle services linking Orly and central Paris. The **Air France bus** (outside gate F) runs to Paris' Invalides Métro stop (40F, 4/hrly, 30 min), and is best for those staying in or near the rue Cler neighborhood (from the Invalides terminal, take the Métro two stops to École Militaire to reach recommended hotels). The **Jetbus #285** (outside gate F, 24F, 4/hrly) is the quickest way to the Paris subway, and the best way to the recommended hotels in the Marais and Contrescarpe neighborhoods (take Jetbus to Villejuif Métro stop, buy a carnet of 10 Métro tickets, then take the Métro to the Sully Morland stop for the Marais area or the Cardinal Lemoine stop for the Contrescarpe area). If you're staying elsewhere in Paris, consider the RER; you can reach two different RER lines from Orly. The shuttle bus from Gate H (35F, 4/hrly) takes you to the RER C-2 line at the Port du Rungis/Aeroport d'Orly station (serving Gare d'Austerlitz, St. Michel, Musée d'Orsay, Invalides, and Eiffel Tower); the Orly bus (30F, 4/hrly) takes you to the Denfert-Rochereau RER-B line (serving Luxembourg Gardens, St. Michel, and Gare du Nord). The Orlyval trains are overpriced (57F) and unnecessary to reach central Paris. Allow 150F for a **taxi** into central Paris.

An **airport shuttle minivan** is ideal for single travelers or families of four or more (costs roughly 120F for one person, 90F per person for two or more, 45F for kids under 12). Reserve from home and they'll meet you at the airport. Try Paris Shuttle Services (tel. 01 49 62 78 78, fax 01 49 62 78 79, e-mail: pas@magic.fr); or even better, Airport Shuttle (tel. 01 45 38 55 72, fax 01 43 21 35 67, Web site: www.paris-anglo.com/clients/ashuttle.html, e-mail: ashuttle@clubinternet.fr).

Sleeping near Orly Airport: The only reasonable airport hotel is the IBIS (Db-400F, CC:VMA, tel. 01 46 87 33 50, fax 01 46 87 29 92). The Hilton offers more comfort for a price (Db-660F, tel 01 45 12 45 12, fax 01 45 12 45 00). Both offer free shuttle service to the terminal. If you have a car you'll find a variety of fast-food hotels within a few minutes drive of Orly. Chartres and Versailles are convenient to Orly by car—beware of rush hour on the freeways. Check Versailles hotels under Sleeping, above.

THE LOIRE

Named for France's longest river, the Loire Valley is carpeted with fertile fields, crisscrossed by rivers, and studded with hundreds of chateaus in all shapes and sizes. The medieval castles are here because the Loire was strategically important during the Hundred Years' War. The Renaissance palaces replaced medieval castles when the Loire became fashionable among the Parisian rich and royal during that age.

The valley of a thousand châteaus is also the home to many good wines. As you travel through the Loire, look for "*Dégustation*" (tasting) signs. Inquire at TIs for winery tour and tasting information. Vouvray, several miles west of Amboise, and Chinon, 20 minutes west of Tours, both have many proud and hospitable family wineries.

Planning Your Time

One and a half days is sufficient to sample the best of the Loire châteaus. Amboise is the ideal springboard for a visit to the region's three most interesting ones: Chambord, Chenonceau, and Cheverny. If you have more time, tour Azay le Rideau, Villandry's gardens, and Langeais (using Chinon as a home base).

If arriving by car, try to see one château on your way in (e.g., Chambord if arriving from the north, Langeais from the west, or Azay le Rideau from the south). If arriving by train, go directly to Amboise.

Don't go overboard on château-hopping. Two châteaus, possibly three (if you're a big person), is the recommended daily dosage. Famous châteaus are least crowded early, at lunchtime, and late. Most open around 9:00 and close between 18:00 and 19:00. During the off-season many close from 12:00 to 14:00.

The lazy plan for those with low energy, no car, and no money for a day-long bus tour is to catch the once-per-day Amboise–Chenonceau bus (from near the TI at 10:54, giving you 90 minutes at the château and departing the château at 12:40). Spend the afternoon enjoying Amboise, its château, and Leonardo's place.

Best Day on the Loire (from Amboise by car):

9:00–11:00:	Chenonceau
11:30–14:00:	Cheverny (beware off-season noon closing) and lunch
15:00–16:00:	Chambord or Chaumont
17:00:	Return to Amboise and tour Le Clos Lucé

Getting Around the Loire Valley

By Train: Amboise is well-connected to Tours. The châteaus of Chenonceau, Langeais, Chinon, and Azay le Rideau all have train service from Tours. Check the schedules carefully, as service is sparse on some lines.

By Bike: The cycling options are endless in this region, where the only serious elevation gain is via medieval spiral staircases. Amboise, Blois, and Chinon make the best bike bases. From Amboise it's 45 minutes to Chenonceau and 90 minutes to Chaumont. (Connect Amboise, Chenonceau, and Chaumont with an all-day 60-kilometer pedal; see "Loire Valley" map in this chapter for details.) From Blois by bike to Chambord and Cheverny, it's a full-day 50-kilometer round-trip; call the Blois TI for bike rental information (tel. 02 54 90 41 41). My favorite bike rides are from Chinon to Ussè, Azay le Rideau, Villandry, and/or Langeais (see Chinon, below, for more information).

By Minibus Tour from Amboise: Pascal Accolay runs Acco-Dispo, a small and personal minibus company with excellent all-day château tours from Amboise (160–220F depending on the number of people). English is the primary language. While you'll get a fun and enthusiastic running commentary on the road covering château background as well as the region's contemporary scene, you're on your own at each château covered (you pay the admission fee). Tours depart at about 9:00. Most visit three châteaus (Chenonceau, Chambord, Cheverny), view several others, and return by 18:00. Groups range from two to eight château-hoppers (61 rue Victor-Hugo in Amboise, tours go daily in tourist season, less in winter, free hotel pickups, reserve by tel. 02 47 57 67 13, fax 02 47 23 15 73). If this doesn't work, any Loire TI can explain your minibus options.

By Taxi: A taxi from Amboise to Chenonceau costs about 100F. Your hotel can call one for you. The meter doesn't start until you do.

The Loire Valley

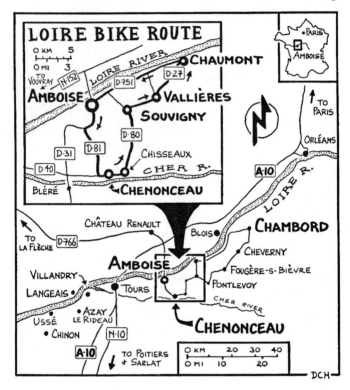

By Rental Car: Amboise has one car rental agency (Garage Jourdan, 105 route de Tours, tel. 02 47 57 17 92, fax 02 47 23 19 51). The smallest Renault goes for about 300F per day (100 km free).

Cuisine Scene—Loire Valley

Here in "the garden of France," anything from the earth is bound to be good. Loire Valley rivers produce fresh trout (*truite*), salmon (*saumon*), and smelt, which is fried (*friture*). *Rilletes*, a stringy pile of whipped pork fat and liver, makes for a cheap, mouthwatering sandwich spread (use lots of mustard and add a *cornichon*—baby pickle). The area's fine goat cheeses include Crottin de Chavignol (*crottin* means horse dung, which is what this cheese, when aged, resembles), Saint-Maure Fermier (soft and creamy), and Selles-sur-Cher (mild). The best and most expensive white wines are the Sancerres and Pouilly-Fumés. Less expensive but still tasty are Tourraine Sauvignons and the sweeter Vouvrays. The better reds come from Chinon and Bourgeuil. For dessert try a mouth-watering *tarte-tatin* (caramel apples on a pastry).

AMBOISE

Straddling the widest part of the Loire, Amboise slumbers in the shadow of its château. Leonardo da Vinci retired here . . . just one more fine idea. With or without a car, Amboise is the ideal small-town home base for exploring the best of château country. A castle has overlooked the Loire from Amboise since Roman times. As the royal residence of François I, the town wielded far more importance than you'd imagine from a lazy walk down the pleasant pedestrian-only commercial zone at the base of the palace.

Amboise (am-bwaz, population: 11,000) covers both sides of the Loire and an island in the middle. The station is on the north side of the river, but everything else of interest is on the south (château) side, including the information-packed TI on the riverbank.

Tourist Information: The TI is on quai du Général de Gaulle in the round building. Their Amboise city map shows restaurants, hotels, and château information, including the time and place of English-language sound-and-light shows, and the rundown on minibus tours of the chateaus. (Open mid-June–September 9:00–20:30, Sunday 10:00–18:00; October–mid-June Monday–Saturday 9:00–12:30 and 15:00–18:00, Sunday 10:00–12:00; tel. 02 47 57 09 28, Web site: www.amboise-valloire.com.) The Michelin green guide to the Loire (sold for 60F—40-percent off the U.S. price—at all tourist shops) provides a good historical and architectural background on the region and each château.

Bike Rental: You can rent a bike at Locacycle (70F per half day, 90F per full day, leave passport for security, daily 9:00–19:00, near the TI at 2 rue Jean-Jacques Rousseau, tel. 02 47 57 00 28), Cycles Richard (on the train-station side of the river, just past the bridge at 2 rue de Nazelles, tel. 02 47 57 01 79), or near the Hotel Le Blason at Cycles Leduc (5 rue Joyeuse, tel. 02 47 57 00 17).

Laundromat: The handy coin-op Lav'centre is a block from the rue Chaptal toward the château on 9 allée du Sergent Turpin (daily 7:00–21:00, 22F to wash, bring four 10F coins to wash and dry a big load, figure 90 minutes; change machine, 2F detergent dispenser). The door locks at 21:00, but if you're already inside you can stay longer.

Arrival in Amboise

By Train: Amboise's train station (tel. 02 47 23 18 23), with a post office and taxi stand, is birds-chirping peaceful. From the station walk down rue de Nazelles five minutes to the bridge that leads you over the Loire and into town. Within three blocks of the station are a recommended hotel, B&B, and bike-rental shop.

Amboise

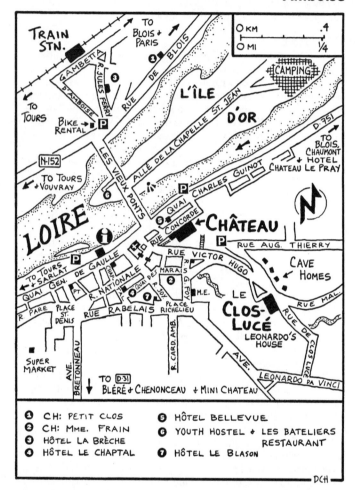

By Car: Drivers simply set their sights on the flag-festooned château capping the hill above downtown Amboise. Most accommodations and restaurants listed in this book cluster just downriver of the château. Street parking near your hotel should be easy.

Sights—Amboise

▲**Château d'Amboise**—This one-time royal residence was used in the Middle Ages to greet royal pilgrims en route from Paris to Spain's Santiago de Compostela. Leonardo da Vinci is said to have designed the château's vaulted spiral staircases. Pick up the fine free English tour flier as you enter. The lacy, petite chapel (first stop) is flamboyant Gothic, with two fireplaces to "comfort the king" and a plaque "evoking the final resting place" of Leonardo. Where he's actually buried no local really seems to know. After a fine town and river view, continue into and through the well-furnished château—which, while much larger in the 15th century, feels plenty big. Your last stop is the horsemen's tower, a brick ramp—climbing 40 meters in five spirals—designed to accommodate a mounted soldier in a hurry (35F, daily 9:00–18:00 April–October, until 19:30 in summer; closes for lunch and at 17:00 in winter, tel. 02 47 57 00 98). The château puts on a sound-and-light spectacle on Wednesday and Saturday evenings in summer.

▲▲**Le Clos Lucé** (luh clo loo-say)—This "House of Light" is the plush palace where Leonardo spent his last three years. France's Renaissance king François I set Leonardo up just so he could enjoy his intellectual company. There's a touching sketch in Leonardo's bedroom of François comforting his genius pal on his deathbed. The house thoughtfully re-creates (with adequate English descriptions) the everyday atmosphere Leonardo enjoyed as he pursued his passions to the very end. Of all the palaces I've seen on the Loire, I'd live here. The ground floor is filled with sketches recording the storm patterns of Leonardo's brain and models of his remarkable inventions (built from his notes by IBM). It's hard to imagine that this Roman candle of creativity died nearly 500 years ago. (39F, daily 9:00–19:00 mid-March–mid-November, otherwise 9:00–18:00, closes at 17:00 in January. Located a pleasant 10-minute walk from downtown Amboise; you'll pass interesting troglodyte homes on your left.)

La Maison Enchantée—Your kids will love you for taking them to this automated doll museum. Push the buttons and watch dolls dance in 25 different settings. (25F, 18F for children, Tuesday–Sunday 10:00–19:00 May–September, otherwise 14:00–17:00 only, closed Monday; 7 rue du General Foy, walk down rue de la Tour from the château, tel. 02 47 23 24 51.)

Mini Château—This new five-acre park on the edge of Amboise shows off all the Loire châteaus in 1:25-scale models, forested with 600 bonzai trees and laced together by a model TGV train (55F, kids ages 4 to 16 pay 37F, open 9:00–19:00 April–September, until 22:00 in summer, closes at 17:00 in winter, tel. 02 47 23 44 44).

Sound-and-Light Shows—Many Loire Valley châteaus (including Amboise's) offer nighttime sound-and-light shows in the summer. They mix colored floodlights, tape-recorded history, and theater in Renaissance château courtyards. Ask if an English version is offered (they can be impressive even in French) and prepare for a late night. The local TI has up-to-date schedules.

Sleeping in Amboise
(5.5F = about $1, zip code: 37400)

Sleep Code: **S** = Single, **D** = Double/Twin, **T** = Triple, **Q** = Quad, **b** = bathroom, **t** = toilet only, **s** = shower only, **CC** = Credit Card (Visa, MasterCard, Amex), **SE** = Speaks English, **NSE** = No English, * = French hotel rating system (0–4 stars).

Amboise is busy in the summer, but there are lots of hotels and *chambres d'hôte* in and around the city. Many hotels require half-pension. The TI has photo albums of local hotels and CHs, and will reserve either. Except for the first hotel and the last CH, all listings are right in the old town center.

Hotels

Hôtel La Brèche** is a refuge of spotless rooms and a peaceful garden café. It's a 10-minute walk from the city center, and 100 meters from the train station. Many rooms overlook the garden. During summer half-pension is required, which gets you a prize-winning dinner for an extra 80F per person (S/D-160F, Sb/Db-260F, Tb-300F, Qb-320F, huge six-bed room-360F, CC:VM, 26 rue Jules Ferry, tel. 02 47 57 00 79, fax 02 47 57 65 49).

Hôtel Le Chaptal** is cheaper and more central. While less idyllic, it's wonderfully frumpy, with birds in the lobby, comfortable rooms (quieter off the street), but marginal beds (Db-210–275F, Tb-260F, Qb-295F, CC:VM, 13 rue de Chaptal, tel. 02 47 57 14 46, fax 02 47 57 67 83, NSE). In summer they request that you dine in their cheery, inexpensive dining room.

Hôtel Belle-Vue*** overlooks the river where the bridge hits the town. It has grand public rooms and effective double-pane windows, so traffic is not a serious problem (Sb-270F, Db-300–340F, Tb-360–420F, Qb-460F, CC:VM, 12 quai Charles-Guinot, tel. 02 47 57 02 26, fax 02 47 30 51 23).

Hotel Le Blason**, with a very friendly though hard-to-find staff, is a half-timbered old building sitting on a square five blocks off the river. It offers small, bright, and modern rooms (Sb-270F, Db-300F, Tb-360F, CC:VMA, TV, telephones, easy parking, 11 place Richelieu, tel. 02 47 23 22 41, fax 02 47 57 56 18, Danielle SE). The well-respected restaurant deserves every one of its plaques.

Hotel de France Cheval Blanc* offers big, clean, simple rooms across from the TI (D-150F, Db-195–245F, T-195F, Tb-245–315F, CC:VM, 6 quai du General de Gaulle, tel. 02 47 57 02 44, fax 02 47 57 69 54). *Rue* (street) rooms have double-pane windows but some traffic noise. *Cour* (courtyard) rooms are quieter.

Bar Hotel de la Tour is a dumpy but clean little place with rickety furniture and springy beds in a great location just under the castle entrance in the old town. For those on a tight budget, this beats the hostel (S-120F, D-175F, twin-190F, T-230F, only sinks in the room, 32 rue Victor-Hugo, tel. 02 47 57 25 04, NSE).

Auberge de Jeunesse is a friendly hostel and a great value (dorm bed-58F, sheets-15F, ideally located on western tip of island, Centre Charles Péguy, tel. 02 47 57 06 36, fax 02 47 23 15 80).

Chambres d'Hôte *in Amboise*

The Amboise TI has a long list of private rooms. In summer, if possible, call a day in advance to reserve a room.

Le Petit Clos, three blocks from the station, rents three cheery cottage-type ground-floor rooms on a quiet picnic-perfect private garden with easy parking (Db-290F, family room takes up to five-500F, includes big farm-fresh breakfast, a block off the river at 7 rue Balzac, tel. 02 47 57 43 52, Madame Roullet NSE).

Katia Frain must be the most engaging person in Amboise. Her comfortable *chambres* are cavernous and bright. Stay here for a complete French experience—you'll dive right into French family life. Get ready for a warm reception (Db-250F, huge Tb-320F, 14 quai des Marais, tel. 02 47 30 46 51, SE).

Sleeping near Amboise

For a taste of château hotel luxury without going broke, try the cozy **Château de Pray***,** only a few minutes upriver from Amboise (toward Chaumont, same side of river as the Amboise château). You'll feel a hint of the original medieval fortified castle behind the Renaissance elegance of this 750-year-old château. This place is very popular with Americans (Db-600–900F, Tb/Qb-900–1,000F, 37400 Amboise, tel. 02 47 57 23 67, fax 02 47 57 32 50). If that seems high, try the elegant *chambre d'hôte* at the **Château de la Huberdière** (Db-400–585F, four miles from Amboise in Nazelles-Negron, zip code: 37530, tel. 02 47 57 39 32, fax 02 47 23 15 79). Or cheaper yet, stay three miles from Amboise in the manor home of **M. Bazinet** (Db-270F, 10 rue de Blois, 37530 Limeray, tel. & fax 02 47 30 09 31). **Auberge Forestière,** with comfortable rooms and friendly owners, is in a forest (Db-300F, allée de Paradis, Forêt d'Amboise, tel. 02 47 57 27 57).

Sleeping in Chenonceaux

If you prefer a quiet village, set up in sleepy little Chenonceau (zip code: 37150). **Hostel du Roy**** is a steal with better rooms in the annex, spotless bargain rooms in the main building, a quiet garden courtyard, and a cozy but average restaurant (S-120F, Sb-220F, D-130F, Db-225–260F, Tb/Qb-260–310F, CC:VMA, 9 rue Dr. Bretonneau, a five-minute walk to the château of Chenonceau, tel. 02 47 23 90 17, fax 02 47 23 89 81).

The best three-star value in France might be at the **Hotel La Roseraie***.** While English-speaking Laurent spoils you, his delightfully decorated, country-elegant rooms will enchant you (Db-280–380F, grand family rooms 480–650F, the best rooms overlook the large gardens, CC:VMA, free parking, heated pool, wood-beamed dining room and bar, located dead center on main drag, tel. 02 47 23 09 09, fax 02 47 23 91 59).

Eating in Amboise

Local reasonable eateries abound in Amboise. **Crêperie L'Ecu** is a fine spot to sample French crêpes (open daily, indoor and outdoor tables, 7 rue Corneille, just off the pedestrian street). Their speedy three-course, 55F *menu* gives you a good salad, dinner crêpe, dessert crêpe, and coffee. **Anne de Bretagne** on the rampe du Chateau also serves good crêpes. In balmy weather try the garden terrace at **La Brèche** (moderately priced restaurant at recommended hotel of same name, 26 rue Jules Ferry, near station). If you're feeling romantic, try **L'Epicerie** (110F *menu*, closed Monday and Tuesday off-season, 46 place Michel DeBre, across from the château, tel. 02 47 57 08 94). **L'Amboiserie** offers fine value and a friendly staff (7 rue Victor Hugo, tel. 02 47 39 50 40). **Les Bateliers** serves elegant meals at fair prices on the island (7 rue Commire, tel. 02 47 30 49 49). **La Closerie** attracts wine lovers—the owner serves a different wine with each course (included in the reasonable *menu*, closed Monday, 2 rue Paul Louis Courier, a 10-minute walk down rue Leonardo da Vinci from Hotel Le Blason, tel. 02 47 23 10 76). For an after-dinner walk, cross the bridge to the island for a floodlit view of the château.

Transportation Connections—Amboise

Twelve 15-minute trains per day link Amboise to the regional train hub of St. Pierre de Corps (suburban Tours). From there you'll find reasonable connections to distant points (including the TGV to Paris–Montparnasse, about hrly, 1 hr). The fastest way to many points, even in the south, is back through Paris.

By train to: Sarlat (2/day, 6 hrs, departures 7:38 and 14:23, transfer at St. Pierre de Corps and Bordeaux-St. Jean), **Mont St. Michel** (2/day, 8 hrs, transfer at St. Pierre de Corps, Paris, Rennes, Pontorson), **Paris** (14/day, 90 minutes, via St. Pierre de Corps/Tours and TGV to Paris' Gare Montparnasse; or by regular train, 8/day, 2 hrs, direct from Amboise to Paris' Gare d'Austerlitz).

The Loire's Top Châteaus

▲▲▲**Chenonceau** (sheh-non-so)—The toast of the Loire, this 15th-century Renaissance palace arches gracefully over the Cher River. One look and you know it was designed by women: The original builder's wife designed the part of the château that parallels the river; Diane de Poitiers, mistress of Henry II, added an arched bridge across the river. She enjoyed her lovely retreat until Henry died (pierced in a jousting tournament) and his vengeful wife, Catherine de Medici, unceremoniously kicked her out (and into the château of Chaumont). Catherine added the three-story structure on Diane's bridge. She died before completing her vision of a matching château on the far side of the river, but not before turning Chenonceau into the local aristocracy's place to see and be seen. This castle marked the border between free and Nazi France in World War II. Dramatic prisoner swaps took place here. Chenonceau is self-tourable (pick up the English translation), with piped-in classical music and glorious gardens (45F, skip the 10F Musée de Cires—wax museum, daily 9:00–19:00 March 16– September 15, early closing off-season, tel. 02 47 23 90 07). There are three trains daily from Tours. To beat the crowds arrive at 8:45. It's a 15-minute walk from the parking lot to the château. The village of Chenonceau welcomes you with a helpful TI, a handy grocery shop, and several cafés.

▲▲▲**Chambord** (sham-bor)—More like a city than a château, this place is huge. Surrounded by a lush park with wild deer and boar, it was originally built as a simple hunting lodge for bored Blois counts. François I, using 1,800 workmen over 15 years, made a few modest additions and created this "weekend retreat." (You'll find his signature salamander everywhere.) Highlights are the huge double-spiral staircase designed by Leonardo da Vinci, second-floor vaulted ceilings, enormous towers on all corners, a pin-cushion roof of spires and chimneys, and a 100-foot lantern supported by flying buttresses. To see what happens when you put 365 fireplaces in your house, wander through the forest of spires on the rooftop (fine views). Only 80 of its 440 rooms are open to the public—and that's plenty. With limited time or energy, skip the ground floor and second floor (rather bare rooms featuring "the hunt") and focus on the first floor, where you'll find the best royal furnishings. The brochure is useless, so consider the 25F self-guided Walkman tour or the free tours given in English one to three times per day; call ahead to get times. (40F, daily 9:30–18:15 April–September, until 19:15 in summer, closes at 17:15 in winter, tel. 02 54 50 40 00.) Chambord's TI, next to the souvenir shops, will show you where to rent bikes (25F/hour, 50F/half-day, 80F/full-day) and has a good list of nearby *chambres d'hôte*. Four daily 40-minute buses connect Chambord with Blois' train station on weekdays (two on Saturday, one on Sunday). To wake up with Chambord out your window, the **Hotel du Grand St-Michel**** comes with Old-World hunting-lodge charm, an elegant dining room (100F *menu*), and a chance to roam the château grounds after the peasants leave (Db-300–450F, extra person-70F, CC:VM, 41250 Chambord, tel. 02 54 20 31 31, fax 02 54 20 36 40).

▲▲**Chaumont-sur-Loire** (show-mon-sur-lwahr)—Chaumont's first priority was defense—you can't even see it from the town below. As you approach the château (an interesting mix of Gothic and Renaissance architecture), veer left along the path for a better view. Originally there was another wing on the riverside, completely encircling the courtyard. Catherine de Medici force-swapped this place for Diane de Poitier's Chenonceau, so you'll see tidbits about both women inside. Don't miss the the royal horse house (*écuries*); they took this hobby seriously. From June to September, enjoy the Festival des Jardins (Garden Festival)—a new display of gorgeous flowers makes this the Loire's best flower-garden stop. There's a guide during summer; otherwise, pick up the English brochure. (32F, 45F during garden festival, daily 9:30–18:00 mid-March–September, 10:00–16:30 during off-season, tel. 02 54 20 98 03.)

▲▲▲**Cheverny** (sheh-vayr-nee)—The most lavish furnishings of all the Loire chateaus decorate this very stately hunting palace. Those who complain that the Loire chateaus have stark and barren interiors missed Cheverny. Today's château was built in 1634. It's been in the same family for nearly seven centuries. Family pride shows in its flawless preservation and intimate feel. The viscount's family still lives on the third floor—you'll see some family photos. Cheverny was spared by the French Revolution, as the owners were popular then, as today, even among the poorer farmers. Barking dogs remind visitors that the viscount still loves to hunt. The kennel (200 yards in front of the château) is especially interesting at dinnertime (17:00), when the 70 hounds are fed. (The dogs—half English foxhound and half French bloodhound or Poitevin—are a hunter's dream come true.) The trophy room next door bristles with 2,000 stag antlers. (33F, pick up the English self-guided tour brochure at the château—not where you buy your ticket, daily 9:15–18:30 June–September 15, otherwise 9:30–12:00 and 14:15–17:00, tel. 02 54 79 96 29.) Cheverny village, in front of the château, has a grocery shop and a few cafés.

▲**Azay le Rideau** (ah-zay luh ree-doh)—Most famous for its romantic reflecting pond setting, Azay le Rideau features glorious gardens and costly imaginaires (60F, self-touring sound-and-light show nightly at about 22:00). The château interior is nothing special. (32F, daily 9:30–18:00, until 19:00 summer, closes from 12:30–14:00 and at 17:30 off-season, tel. 02 47 45 42 04.) If staying the night in the pleasant town of Azay, try the reasonable rooms at the **Hôtel Biencourt** (Ds-210F, Db-270–330F, CC:VM, 7 rue de Balzac, zip code: 37190, tel. 02 47 45 20 75, fax 02 47 45 91 73).

▲▲**Chinon** (shee-non)—This pleasing medieval town hides its ancient cobbles under a historic castle filled with Joan of Arc memories (28F, 9:00–18:00). Don't underestimate this interesting château, especially if you're looking for a stark medieval contrast to those of the lavish hunting-lodge variety.

Chinon makes the best home base for seeing chateaus to the west of Tours (Azay le Rideau, Villandry, Langeais, Ussè). The TI (in the village center at 12 rue Voltaire, tel. 02 47 93 17 85) can tell you about bike rental, *chambres d'hôte*, and wine-tasting. Two good hotels in Chinon are the atmospheric and friendly **Hôtel Jeanne d'Arc*** (Db-180–220F, Tb-220F, 11 rue Voltaire, zip code: 37500, tel. 02 47 93 02 85) and the almost-elegant, less-warmly run **Hôtel Diderot****, with fine rooms in a centrally located 18th-century manor house (Sb-250F, Db-300–350F, CC:VMA, 4 rue Buffon, zip code: 37500, tel. 02 47 93 18 87, fax 02 47 93 37 10). **Les Années 30** is one of many good-value restaurants in town (78 rue Voltaire).

▲▲**Langeais** (lahn-glay)—This epitome of a medieval castle, complete with a moat, drawbridge, lavish defenses, and turrets, is elegantly furnished and has English descriptions in each room. Langeais, which provides a good feudal contrast to the other more playful châteaus, is the area's fourth most interesting castle after Chenonceau, Chambord, and Cheverny. (40F, open daily 9:00–18:30, until 21:00 in summer, closes 12:00–14:00 and at 17:00 November–March, tel. 02 47 96 72 60, frequent train service from Tours.)

▲**Villandry** (vee-lahn-dree)—This otherwise mediocre castle has elaborate geometric gardens and a fine *Four Seasons of Villandry* slide show. Skip the château interior. Come here for the Loire's most complete gardens. Don't miss the overview high above the gardens. (45F, 32F for gardens, daily 9:00–19:00 Easter–September, until 20:00 in summer, closes at 17:00 October–Easter, tel. 02 47 50 02 09.)

Ussè (oos-seh)—This château, famous as the "Sleeping Beauty castle," is worth a quick photo stop for its fairy-tale turrets and gardens, but don't bother touring it. The best view, with reflections and a golden-slipper picnic spot, is from just across the bridge.

NORMANDY

These are lands of lush green rolling hills, apple orchards, dramatic coastlines, half-timbered homes, and thatched roofs. Parisians call Normandy "the 21st *arrondissement*." It's their escape—the nearest beach. The British call this close enough for a weekend away.

Viking Norsemen settled here in the ninth century, giving Normandy its name. William the Conqueror invaded England from Normandy in the 11th century. To see his victory commemorated in a remarkable tapestry, weave Bayeux into your trip. In Rouen, France's all-time inspirational leader, Jeanne d'Arc (Joan of Arc), was convicted of heresy and burned at the stake by the English, against whom she had rallied France during the Hundred Years' War. (For more information, see the Appendix.)

The rugged coast of Normandy harbors tiny fishing villages like little Honfleur, which today has more charm than fish. The cliff-hanger coast, two hours south of Honfleur, was the scene of a WWII battle that changed the course of history. South of the D-Day beaches, on the border of Brittany, is the almost surreal island abbey of Mont St. Michel, rising serene and majestic, oblivious to its tides of tourists.

Planning Your Time
Three Days in Normandy by Car:
Day 1 Depart Paris by 8:15. Be in line at Giverny for the 10:00 opening, afternoon walk in Rouen, evening in Honfleur.
Day 2 9:00–Depart Honfleur, 10:00–Caen Battle of Normandy Museum/Memorial, 13:00–Arromanches for lunch and museum, 15:00–American cemetery, 16:00–Pointe du Hoc Ranger Memorial, 17:00–German cemetery, 18:00–Bayeux or Arromanches hotel.

Normandy

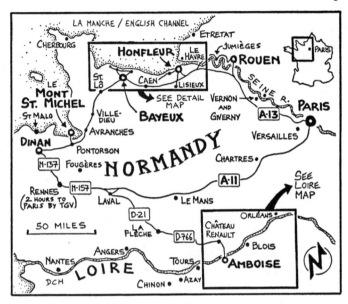

Day 3 Bayeux tapestry in morning, Mont St. Michel in afternoon, overnight in Dinan or (if you're really pushed for time) drive to Loire Valley.

Without a car and without a lot of time, consider skipping Giverny and Honfleur and taking a minivan excursion from Bayeux to the D-Day beaches.

Cuisine Scene—Normandy

Known as the land of the four Cs (Calvados, Camembert, cider, and *crème*), Normandy's cuisine specializes in cream sauces, organ meats (kidneys, sweetbreads, and tripe—the "gizzard salads" are great), and seafood (*fruits de mer*). Dairy products are big here. Local cheeses are Camembert (mild to very strong), Brillat-Savarin (buttery), Livarot (spicy and pungent), Pavé d'Auge (spicy and tangy), and Pont l'Evéque (earthy flavor). Normandy is famous for its powerful Calvados apple brandy, Benedictine brandy (made by local monks), and three kinds of alcoholic apple ciders (*cidre* can be *doux*—sweet, *brut*—dry, or *bouche*—sparkling and the strongest).

ROUEN

This 2,000-year-old city of 100,000 people mixes dazzling Gothic architecture, exquisite half-timbered houses, and contemporary bustle like no other in Europe. A one-time powerhouse, medieval Rouen walked a political tightrope between England and France. It was an English base during the Hundred Years' War. William the Conqueror lived here, and Joan of Arc was burned here.

Tourist Information: The TI, in a fine Renaissance building, faces the cathedral. Pick up their map highlighting an ideal walking tour (open Monday–Saturday 9:00–19:00, Sunday 9:00–13:00 and 14:30–18:00 May–September 15; Monday–Saturday 9:00–18:30, Sunday 10:00–13:00 during off-season, tel. 02 32 08 32 40).

Arrival in Rouen

By Train: Rue Jeanne d'Arc cuts from Rouen's station straight through the town center to the Seine River. Upon arrival, walk down rue Jeanne d'Arc to rue du Gros Horloge, the medieval center's pedestrian mall that connects the Old Market and Jeanne d'Arc church (to the right) with the cathedral and TI (to the left). To go directly to the start of the Rouen walking tour, described below, turn right on rue du Gros Horloge (you'll see the sweeping roof of the modern Église Jeanne d' Arc).

By Car: Follow signs to *centre-ville* and Rive Droite and park along the river (metered) or in the pay lot next to the cathedral.

Sights—Rouen

▲▲**Rouen Walking Tour**—For a good quick dose of Rouen's Gothic and half-timbered wonders, begin at the Jeanne d'Arc church and follow the route described below (most sights close 12:00–14:00). With the town's lacy Gothic skyline and half-timbered building solidly on vertical hold, it's hard to imagine the town devastated by WWII bombs. Its restoration attests to the French commitment to their people-friendly city centers (rather than to suburban sprawl).

The striking half-timbered houses (14th to 19th centuries) that line Rouen's streets remind us that there's more oak than stone in this region. Cantilevered floors were standard until about 1520. These top-heavy designs made sense because city land was limited, property taxes were based on ground-floor square footage, and the cantilevering minimized unsupported spans on upper floors.

Église Jeanne d'Arc—This modern church is a tribute to Jeanne d'Arc. Nineteen-year-old Jeanne was burned at the stake on this square in 1431. The church, completed in 1979, feels Scandinavian inside and out—reminding us again of Normandy's Nordic roots. Pick up an English pamphlet describing the church (closed 12:00–14:00). A W.C. is 30 yards from the church doors. Next door, under a modern roof, is a great outdoor morning market for picnic fixings. It runs until 12:30.

Rue du Gros Horloge—This has been Rouen's main pedestrian

Rouen

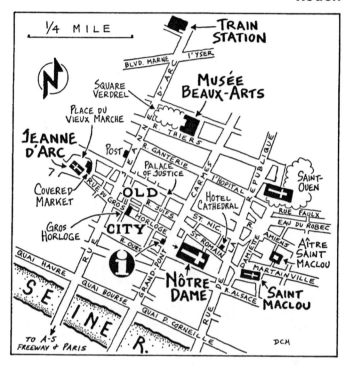

and shopping street since Roman times. It links the Église Jeanne d'Arc and the Cathédrale Notre Dame, and shows off the impressive Renaissance (1528) public clock, le Gros Horloge. Admire the clock and sculpture in the arch from below. The 10F climb to the top is good only for the exercise.

Palace of Justice—Take the first left after the old clock and in a block you'll see the impressive Flamboyant Gothic Palace of Justice (largely restored after WWII bombing, though the western facade remains littered with pockmarks from German guns).

Returning to rue du Gros Horloge, turn left and continue to the . . .

Cathédrale Notre Dame—The exterior is considered one of France's most beautiful, a fine example of the last overripe stage of Gothic architecture called "*flamboyant*"—flamelike. Make a marvel-at-the-Gothic circuit inside, stopping halfway down the nave on the right to see photos showing the severe World War II bomb damage. This is the church Monet painted at various times of day from the apartment he rented for this purpose opposite the cathedral. You can see four of these paintings at the Musée d'Orsay in Paris.

Leave the cathedral via the left (northern) transept, enjoy the Gothic facade behind you, then turn right to rue St. Romain. This fine old medieval lane leads a few blocks to the St. Maclou Church. A plaque on your right (under the ruined Gothic arch) identifies the site of an old chapel where Joan of Arc was sentenced to death—and where she was proclaimed innocent 25 years later. Take a look down rue des Chanoines (next left) for a half-timbered fantasy. Rue St. Romain leads to the . . .

St. Maclou Church—Study the unique bowed facade. Inside, walk to the end of the choir and look back at the stained glass framed by the suspended crucifix.

Leaving the church, turn right and right (giving the boys on the corner a wide berth) and wander past a fine wall of half-timbered buildings fronting rue Martainville. Within a block a passageway on the left leads to . . .

Aître St. Maclou—Wander all the way into this half-timbered courtyard/graveyard/cloister. This was a cemetery for 14th-century plague victims. Notice the ghoulish carvings lurking around you. It's now an art school. Peek in on the young artists.

Return to the center via the half-timbered antique shops of rue Damiette and Rouen's third fine Gothic church, St. Ouen. A thousand-year-old Danish rune stone stands by the church door, reminding locals of their Nordic heritage. From there, rue Hôpital takes you back to rue Jeanne d'Arc and the station.

The town's other sights, such as the **Musée des Beaux Arts** (paintings from all periods, including works by Caravaggio, Rubens, Veronese, Steen, Géricault, Ingres, Delacroix, and the Impressionists), are described in the free TI Rouen map.

Sights—Near Rouen

▲**La Route des Anciennes Abbayes**—The route of the ancient abbeys is punctuated with abbeys, apple trees, Seine River views, and pastoral scenery (follow the D-982 west of Rouen if driving, or inquire about buses at the TI). Monks are the guides at l'Abbaye de St. Wandrille, and Jumièges has Normandy's most romantic ruined abbey. Get details at Rouen's TI.

Sleeping and Eating in Rouen
(5.5F = about $1, zip code: 75000)

Sleep Code: **S** = Single, **D** = Double/Twin, **T** = Triple, **Q** = Quad, **b** = bathroom, **t** = toilet only, **s** = shower only, **CC** = Credit Card (Visa, MasterCard, Amex), **SE** = Speaks English, **NSE** = No English, * = Hotel rating (0–4 stars).

The central **Hôtel de la Cathédrale** has a seductive courtyard and generally good rooms (Sb-255–310F, Db-305–360F, 12 rue St. Romain, tel. 02 35 71 57 95, fax 02 35 70 15 54). Another good value—**Hotel de la Vieille Tour****—is just as central and

more welcoming (D-180F, Db-310F, CC:VM, 42 place Haute
Vieille Tour, tel. 02 35 70 03 27, fax 02 35 98 08 54). Rouen's best
moderately-priced seafood restaurant is **La Mirabelle**, across from
Église Jeanne d'Arc (tel. 02 35 71 58 21), though you'll find many
inexpensive alternatives between St. Maclou and St. Ouen
churches.

Transportation Connections—Rouen

Rouen is well served by trains from Paris, through Amiens to
other points north, and through Caen to other destinations west
and south.

By train to: Paris' Gare St. Lazare (nearly hrly, 75 min),
Bayeux (8/day, 3 hrs, transfer in Caen), **Mont St. Michel**
(6/day, 4 hrs, via Caen and Pontorson; short bus ride from Pontorson to Mont St. Michel), **Honfleur** (6/day, 90 min to Lisieux,
then bus to Honfleur, hrly, 30 min). The *Inter Normandie* buses
(tel. 02 31 44 77 44) to Honfleur are a quicker but less frequent
alternative (2/day, 2 hrs, transfer in Pont Audemer). Inquire at
either TI.

HONFLEUR

Honfleur (ohn-fluer) actually feels as picturesque as it looks. Its
cozy harbor, surrounded by skinny, soaring houses, was a
favorite of 16th-century sailors and 19th-century Impressionists.
Today Honfleur, eclipsed by the gargantuan port of Le Havre
just across the Seine, happily uses its past as a bar stool and sits
on it. All of Honfleur's interesting streets and activities are
packed together within a few minutes' walk of the old port
(Vieux Bassin).

Honfleur is low on sights but high on ambience. (Arriving
in the afternoon and leaving after breakfast is not a bad plan for
drivers.) Snoop around the streets behind place Berthelot and
the Église Ste. Catherine for some of Normandy's oldest half-
timbered homes and interesting art galleries. Honfleur escaped
the bombs of WWII.

Tourist Information: The helpful, English-speaking TI
hides a few blocks just off the Vieux Bassin, on the lower-building
side of the harbor. Pick up their handy town map and any information you need on Normandy (daily Easter–October Monday–
Saturday 9:00–12:30 and 14:00–18:30, no midday closing in summer, Sunday 10:00–13:00; Monday–Saturday 9:00–12:00 and
14:00–17:30, closed Sunday during off-season; place Arthur
Boudin, tel. 02 31 89 23 30).

Arrival in Honfleur

By Bus: The bus station is a five-minute walk north of the old
port (Vieux Bassin). Walk up rue des Fosses and turn right on rue

de la Ville to reach the TI, or continue straight to the old port and hotels.

By Car: Follow *centre-ville* signs, then park as close to the old port (Vieux Bassin) as possible. Parking lots are just north of the old port, though you can probably park very near your hotel. Parking is free from 19:00 to 9:00.

Sights—Honfleur

▲**Église Ste. Catherine**—As you step inside this church your first thought is, "If you could turn it over it would float." This unusual church was built in the 15th century—logically, in this ship-building town—by naval architects. Rough-hewn wood beams give it a feel-good warmth you don't find in stone churches. In the last months of WWII, a bomb fell through the roof but didn't explode. The exterior is a wonderful conglomeration of wood shingle, brick, and half-timbered construction.

The church's bell tower was built across the square to lighten the load on the roof of the wooden church and to minimize fire hazards. (Tower and church open 9:00–12:00 and 14:00–18:00, 9:00–18:30 in summer.) The church is free. There's only one room with a few church artifacts open in the tower—not worth the 10F.

Eugène Boudin Museum—This pleasant museum houses a variety of early Impressionist paintings and Normand costumes (22F, Wednesday–Monday 10:00–12:00 and 14:00–18:00, closed Tuesday, rue de l'Homme de Bois).

Saturday Morning Farmers' Market—The area around the Église Ste. Catherine is transformed into a colorful market each Saturday morning from 9:00 to 12:30.

▲**Normandie Bridge**—The new 2.1-kilometer-long Pont de Normandie is the longest suspension bridge in the world (until a Japanese bridge, which will beat it by 40 meters, is completed). This is a key piece of a super-freeway which, by the year 2000, will link the Atlantic ports from Belgium to Spain. Honfleur's TI has a fine brochure with all the engineering details. You can view the bridge from Honfleur (really impressive when floodlit) or drive over and visit the free Exhibition Hall (under the tollbooth on the Le Havre side, daily 8:00–19:00). The Seine finishes its winding 500-mile journey here. From its source it drops only 1,500 feet. It flows so slowly that in certain places a stiff breeze can send it flowing "upstream."

Sleeping in Honfleur
(5.5F = about $1, zip code: 14600)

Honfleur is busy on weekends, holidays, and in the summer, when many hotels require half-pension. I've listed places which normally don't. English is widely spoken in this town where local merchants post banners saying, "We welcome our liberators."

Honfleur

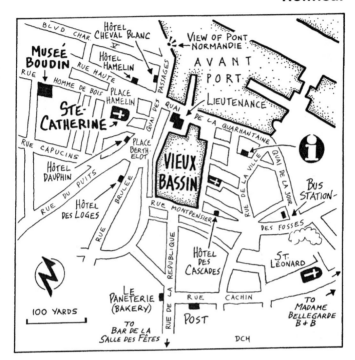

Hôtel Dauphin✶✶ is a solid midrange bet, with a family feel, homey lounge/breakfast room, Escher-esque floorplan, great plumbing, some delightfully funky rooms (many with open beam ceilings), and many just-renovated rooms (Db-350–400F, Tb-460–660F, no elevator, some smoke-free rooms, CC:VMA, a block off the harbor at 10 place Berthelot, tel. 02 31 89 15 53, fax 02 31 89 92, e-mail: hotel.dudauphin@wanadoo.fr).

Hôtel des Loges✶✶, next to the Dauphin, is tranquil and very sharp with many tastefully renovated rooms and pleasant common areas (Db-325–410F, Tb-350F, CC:VM, 18 rue Brûlée, tel. 02 31 89 38 26).

Hôtel des Cascades✶ is comfortable and well-located—a block off the harbor—but has a tangled-fishnet floor plan (Db-200–300F, add 50F for a third person, only 10F for a fourth, dinner required during summer weekends, CC:VM, facing rue Montpensier at 17 place Thiers, tel. 02 31 89 05 83, fax 02 31 89 32 13, Melanie SE).

Hôtel Hamelin✶ is barely basic and half-pension is required. The rooms are small and have showers, but toilets are down the hall (Ss-185–235F, Ds-185–235F, Ts-310F, half-pension is extra but cheap, 16 place Hamelin, tel. & fax 02 31 89 16 25).

Hôtel Le Cheval Blanc*** is a good three-star splurge, with port views from every room (many just remodeled) and the only elevator I saw in town. It's a big, half-timbered place with no restaurant and a professional staff that caters to artists—who can get room discounts (Db-450–1,100F, most at 630F, add 100F per person for triple and quad, prices include breakfast, CC:VMA, quai de Passagers, tel. 02 31 81 65 00, fax 02 31 89 52 80, e-mail: lecheval.blanc@wanadoo.fr).

Hotel LeChat** has faded-elegant rooms in a fine old building with a great setting across from Ste. Catherine church (Db-420–490F, CC:VMA, place Ste. Catherine, tel. 02 31 14 49 49, fax 02 31 89 28 61, e-mail: lechat@mail.cpod.fr).

Chambres d'hôte offer a good option here (the TI has a list), though most are at least one mile from the center of Honfleur. Try the bargain rooms above the very local **Bar de la Salle des Fêtes**, where French is spoken with a smile (Db-170F, place Albert Sorel, a quarter mile out rue de la République, tel. 02 31 89 19 69). **Madame Bellegarde** offers quiet, simple, and comfortable rooms (D-180F, Ts-300F, private shower and toilet down the hall, a 10-minute walk from the tourist office, three blocks uphill from the church St. Leonard in nontouristed Honfleur, 54 rue St. Leonard, look for the sign in window, tel. 02 31 89 06 52).

Eating in Honfleur

Eat seafood. I like the restaurants located along the rue de l'Homme de Bois. Savor a slow meal at **La Tortue** (95F *menu*, 36 rue de l'Homme de Bois, tel. 02 31 89 04 93), or, better yet, enjoy Honfleur's best seafood in the cozy **Au Petit Mareyeur** (120F *menu*, 4 place Hamelin, tel. 02 31 98 84 23 for necessary reservations). **Le Bistro du Port** is also good with a variety of reasonable *menus*. It's near the TI (14 quai de la Quarantaine, tel. 02 31 89 21 84). The classy but intimate **Auberge du Vieux Clocher** will tempt the discerning romantic (160F *menu*, 9 rue de l'Homme de Bois, tel. 02 31 89 12 06, reserve ahead, closed Sunday and Wednesday except in summer). For light meals or a relaxing drink, try the friendly **La Cidrerie**, a cozy cider bar with freshly-made crêpes, calvados, and ambience (26 place Hamelin). The old harbor is ideal for evening picnics, especially as the sun sets. Try the steps in front of the port's bureau (La Lieutenance). **Le Paneterie** is Honfleur's best *boulangerie-pâtisserie* (26 rue de la République).

Transportation Connections—Honfleur

Buses connect Honfleur with Deauville or Lisieux, where you'll catch a train to other points. Train and bus service is usually coordinated.

To: Bayeux (6/day, 2.5 hrs; bus to Caen, then train to Bayeux); **Paris'** Gare St. Lazare (5/day, 3 hrs; bus to Deauville or Lisieux, train to Paris; buses from Honfleur meet most trains).

BAYEUX

Only six miles from the D-Day beaches, Bayeux was the first city liberated after the landing and makes an ideal base for visiting the area's sights. Even without its famous tapestry and proximity to the D-Day beaches, Bayeux would be worth a visit for its pleasant *centre-ville* and imposing cathedral. Navigating in Bayeux is a breeze on foot or by car. Look for the church spires and follow the signs to *centre-ville* or Tapisserie to reach the city center. Saturday is market day in Bayeux.

Tourist Information: Pick up a town map at the friendly TI on the bridge (Pont St. Jean) leading to the pedestrian street rue St. Jean (Monday–Saturday 9:00–12:00 and 14:00–18:00; also open Sunday June–mid-September 10:00–12:00 and 15:00–18:00; tel. 02 31 51 28 28, fax 02 31 51 28 29).

Bayeux History—The Battle of Hastings

The most memorable date of the Middle Ages is probably 1066 because of this pivotal battle. England's King Ethelred was about to die without an heir, and the question was who would succeed him: Harold, an English noble, or William, the Duke of Normandy? Harold was captured during a battle in Normandy. To gain his freedom he promised William that, when the ailing King Ethelred died, he would allow William to ascend the throne. Shortly after that oath was taken, Harold was back in England, Ethelred died, and Harold grabbed the throne. William, known as William the Bastard, invaded England to claim the throne he figured was rightfully his. Harold met him in southern England at the town of Hastings, where their forces fought a fierce 14-hour battle. Harold was killed and his Saxon forces routed. William— now "the Conqueror"—marched on London to claim his throne, becoming King of England as well as Duke of Normandy. (The advent of a Norman king of England muddied the political waters, setting in motion 400 years of conflict between England and France not to be resolved until the end of the Hundred Years' War in 1453.)

The Norman Conquest of England brought England into the European mainstream. The Normans established a strong central English government. They brought with them the Romanesque style of architecture (e.g., the Tower of London and Durham Cathedral) that the English call "Norman." Historians speculate that, had William not succeeded, England would have remained on the fringe of Europe (like Scandinavia), and French culture (and language) would have prevailed in the New World.

Sights—Bayeux

▲▲▲**Bayeux Tapestry**—Actually woolen embroidery on linen cloth, this document—precious to historians—is a 70-meter cartoon telling the story of William the Conqueror's rise from Duke of Normandy to King of England and his victory over Harold at the Battle of Hastings. Long and skinny, it was designed to hang from the nave of Bayeux's cathedral.

Your visit has three parts (explaining the basic story of the battle three times—which was about right for me): First you'll walk through a "mood-setting images on sails" room into a replica of the tapestry with extensive explanations and a room designed to set the cultural scene for the battle. Next, a 15-minute AV show in the cinema gives a relaxing dramatization of the event. Finally you'll get to the real McCoy. It's worth the 5F (have exact change) and the wait for the headphones, which give a top-notch, fast-moving, 20-minute, scene-by-scene narration complete with period music. If you lose your place you'll find subtitles in Latin. Remember, this is a piece of Norman propaganda—the English (the bad guys—referred to as *les goddamns*, after a phrase the French kept hearing them say) are shown with mustaches and long hair; the French (*les* good guys) are clean-cut and clean-shaven (38F, daily 9:00–18:30 March 15–October 15, otherwise 9:00–12:30 and 14:00–18:00, tel. 02 31 92 05 48). When buying your ticket, get the English film showtimes. If you're rushed and the cinema schedule doesn't match yours, skip the film. If you have time, see the film first then exit the way you entered and backtrack to see the replica (don't follow everyone else; cinemagoers pile into the tapestry room with a crowd).

▲**Bayeux Cathedral**—Enjoy the view of the nave from the top of the steps as you enter the church. Historians believe the tapestry originally hung here. Imagine it proudly circling the congregation, draped around the nave from the mini-arches just below the big and bright upper windows of the clerestory. The nave's huge round lower arches are Romanesque (11th century) and decorated with the same zigzag pattern that characterizes this "Norman" art in England. But this nave is much brighter because of the later Gothic windows of the top half of the nave. The finest example of 13th-century "Norman Gothic" is in the choir (the fancy area behind the central altar). For maximum 1066 atmosphere, step into the crypt (below the central altar). Study the frescoed angels and the ornately carved 11th-century capitals decorated with Roman-style acanthus leaves and grey meanies (free, daily 9:00–18:00).

Bayeux Memorial Museum/Battle of Normandy—This museum offers a fine overview of the Battle of Normandy. It features tanks, jeeps, uniforms, and countless informative displays

(31F, daily 9:30–18:30 May–mid-September, closes from
12:30–14:00 during off-season; on the Bayeux's ring road, 20 minutes on foot from the center).

Sleeping in Bayeux
(5.5F = about $1, zip code: 14400)

Hotels are a good value here. **Hôtel Notre Dame***, ideally situated right across from the cathedral, has comfortable rooms with
wall-to-ceiling carpeting and asks that you dine at its elegant but
reasonable restaurant (D-160F, Db-270F, Tb-360F, Qb-465F,
showers 20F if not in room, CC:VMA, 44 rue des Cuisiniers, tel.
02 31 92 87 24, fax 02 31 92 67 11). **Hôtel de Reine Mathilde****,
just one block from the Tapestry, is well run with modern and
very comfortable rooms (Sb-260F, Db-275–295F, Tb-300F, Qb-
400F, CC:VMA, 23 rue Larcher, tel. 02 31 92 08 13, fax 02 31 92
09 93). For three-star comfort stay at the **Hotel Churchill*****,
perfectly located on the pedestrian street, two blocks from the
Tapestry. The place feels British. Its fine rooms with real wood
bed frames overlook a central courtyard (Db-360–460F, easy parking, tel. 02 31 21 31 80, fax 02 31 21 41 66, 14 rue St. Jean). The
most convenient for train travelers is the *trés* local **Hôtel de la
Gare***, sandwiched between the train tracks at the station and a
ring road with simple, spotless rooms and a cat pee odor (S-90F,
D-100F, Db-210F, T-140F, Tb-300F, Q-200–280F, tel. 02 31 92
10 70, fax 02 31 51 95 99).

Sleeping near Bayeux: When driving in this area, I prefer
the rural *chambre d'hôte* option. And it's worth the effort to find
Andre and Madeleine Sebire's wonderful, working farmhouse
with four terrific rooms decorated with family furnishings, a do-
it-yourself common kitchen and living room, and a pleasant garden. Located between Bayeux and Arromanches, it's in the tiny
village of Ryes at the Ferme du Clos Neuf—look for the faded
Chambres signs (Sb-180F, Db-200F, Tb-250F, breakfast
included, zip code: 14400, tel. 02 31 22 32 34, NSE). For more
chambre d'hôte listings, inquire at the Bayeux or Arromanches TI.
Dead-center in Arromanches, the friendly **Pappagall Hotel
d'Arromanches**** is the best value (Db-250F low season, 300F
high season, 2 rue Colonel Rene Michel, 14117 Arromanches,
tel. 02 31 22 36 26, fax 02 31 22 23 29). It sports a cozy bar and
a good, cheery restaurant.

Eating in Bayeux

Bayeux's old city centers around the pedestrian rue St. Jean, which is
lined with *crêperies*, cafés, and the best *charcuterie* in town (salads,
quiches to go) across from the Hotel Churchill. The restaurants at the
Hôtel Notre Dame (95F *menu*, see hotel listing) and **Le Petit Normand** (*menus* start at 80F, 35 rue Larcher) both have fine reputations.

Transportation Connections—Bayeux

By train to: Paris' St. Lazare (12/day, 2.5 hrs), **Mont St. Michel** (3 trains/day, 2 hrs to Pontorson, the nearest train station; to Mont St. Michel from Pontorson, you can either catch a bus—6/day, 15 min; rent a bike at Pontorson's train station; or take a taxi—75F on weekdays or 100F on weekends; tel. 02 33 60 26 89).

By bus to: D-Day Beaches (#76 to American Cemetery and Pointe du Hoc, 4/day; #75 to Arromanches, 4/weekday, 2/Saturday, 0/Sunday; catch bus at Bayeux train station or place St. Patrice in city center, arrive Arromanches at site of artificial harbor. There's one bus per day from Arromanches to the American Cemetery and Pointe du Hoc).

D-DAY BEACHES

Along the 75 miles of Atlantic coast north of Bayeux (from Sainte Marie du Mont to Ouistreham), you'll find museums, monuments, cemeteries, and battle remains left in tribute to the courage of the WWII British, Canadian, and American armies who successfully carried out the largest military operation in history. It was on these beautiful beaches, at the crack of dawn, June 6, 1944, that the Allies finally gained a foothold in France, and Nazi Europe began to crumble.

"The first twenty-four hours of the invasion will be decisive . . . the fate of Germany depends on the outcome . . . for the Allies, as well as Germany, it will be the longest day."

—Field Marshall Erwin Rommel to his aide, April 22, 1944. From *The Longest Day*.

Getting Around the D-Day Beaches

A car is ideal (the TI lists local agencies), though biking is an option for those with time and energy (rent a bike in Bayeux at M. Roue's shop for 80F, boulevard W. Churchill, tel. 02 31 92 27 75). Buses connect Bayeux and Arromanches (see Bayeux Transportation Connections, above) to allow you to see the most impressive D-Day (*Jour J* in French) sights. Consider a minivan tour for an even better look. Several companies offer tours of the D-Day beaches from Bayeux for about 160 to 180F per person (includes Arromanches Museum entry). Jean-Marc Bacon of Normandy Tours (Hôtel de la Gare) does it in a minivan with a friendly personal touch (tel. 02 31 92 10 70, fax 02 31 51 95 99). Bus Fly offers similar minivan tours, as well as day trips to Mont St. Michel for 300F (tel. 02 31 22 00 08). Taxis are another good option; figure 95F from Bayeux to Arromanches and 150F to the American Cemetery. Ask about "waiting rates" (tel. 02 31 92 92 40). Caen's Museum (below) offers informative tours of the beaches.

D-Day Beaches

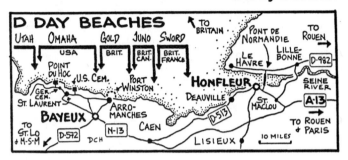

Sights—D-Day Beaches

▲▲▲**Caen's Battle of Normandy Museum**—Caen, the modern capital of lower Normandy, has the best World War II museum in France. Officially named "Memorial for Peace," its intent is to put the Battle of Normandy in a broader context. Your visit has four parts: the lead-up to WWII, the actual Battle of Normandy, the video presentations, and the ongoing fight for peace.

The museum is absolutely brilliant. Begin with a downward spiral stroll tracing—almost psychoanalyzing—the path of Europe from WWI to the rise of fascism to WWII.

The entire lower level gives a thorough look at how WWII was fought—from General de Gaulle's London radio broadcasts to Hitler's early missiles to wartime fashion.

You then see a series of three powerful movies (15 minutes each, for all languages, the cycle starts every 20 minutes—a clock at the end of the lower-level exhibits lets you plan your time). Ninety percent of the incredible D-Day footage is real, with a bit taken from the movie *The Longest Day*.

The memorial then takes you beyond WWII to the Gallery of Nobel Prizes. This is a celebration of the courageous work of people like Andrei Sakharov, Elie Wiesel, and Desmond Tutu, who understand that peace is more than an absence of war.

The finale is a walk through the U.S. Armed Forces Memorial Garden. I was a bit bothered by the mindless laughing of light-hearted children unable to appreciate their blessings. Then I read on the pavement, "From the heart of our land flows the blood of our youth, given to you in the name of freedom." And their laughter made me happy.

Allow 2.5 hours, including an hour for the videos. The memorial is just off the freeway in Caen (exit: Université, follow signs to "Memorial"). By bus, take #17 from Caen's city center and station to the end of the line (every 15 minutes).

Memorial Museum entry: 69F, free for WWII veterans, 20F

for other veterans, free admission and nursery for kids under 10, daily 9:00 to 19:00, until 21:00 from mid-July through mid-August, ticket office closes 1.5 hours before museum (tel. 02 31 06 06 44—as in June 6, 1944, Web site: www.unicaen.fr/memorial). Tickets are 8F less if purchased at Caen's TI on place St. Pierre (daily 9:30–19:00, tel. 02 31 27 14 14).

The museum recently began offering half- and full-day tours of WWII sights and beaches—call to reserve and pay in advance (prices range from 340–480F, CC:VM).

▲▲▲ **Arromanches (Musée du Débarquement)**—The first-ever prefab harbor was created by the British in this town. Churchill's brainchild, it was named Port Winston. Eighteen old ships and 115 huge cement blocks (called Mulberries) were towed across the English Channel and sunk in Arromanches bay to create a seven-mile-long breakwater and harbor for landing 54,000 vehicles and 500,000 troops in six days. You can still see remains of the temporary harbor and visit the beachfront museum where this incredible undertaking is recreated with models, maps, mementos, and two short audiovisual shows—ask for English (34F, daily 9:00–18:30 May–September, off-season 9:30–17:30, closed January, tel. 02 31 22 34 31). Walk to the top of the bluff behind the museum for a fine view and ponder how, from this makeshift harbor, the liberation of Europe commenced. Here you'll find **Arromanches 360**, a new surround theater showing *The Price of Freedom*, a well-produced film that gives you "18 minutes of total emotion" about the Normandy invasion with no narration (22F, two showings per hour, 9:00–18:40 June–August, otherwise 10:00–17:40, closes at 16:40 in winter).

Longues Sur Mer—Several German bunkers, guns intact, are left guarding seaborn attacks on the city of Arromanches. Walk out to the observation post for a territorial view over the Channel (located between Arromanches and Port en Bessin; look for signs).

▲▲▲ **American Cemetery at St. Laurent**—Beautifully situated on a bluff just above Omaha Beach, the 9,400 brilliant white-marble crosses and Stars of David seem to glow in memory of Americans who gave their lives to free Europe on the beaches below. Notice the names and home states inscribed on the crosses. Behind the monument, surrounded by roses, are the names of 1,557 missing or unidentified soldiers. France has given the United States free permanent use of this 172-acre site. It is immaculately maintained by the American Battle Monuments Commission. The trail to the beach below is open from 8:00 to 18:00, until 17:00 during the off-season.

German Military Cemetery—For an opportunity to ponder German losses, drop by this somber, thought-provoking resting place of 21,000 German soldiers. While the American cemetery is the focus of American visitors, visitors here speak in hushed

German. The site is glum, with two graves per simple marker and dark crosses that huddle together in groups of five. It's just south of Point du Hoc (right off N-13 in village of La Cambe, 22 km west of Bayeux; follow signs to Cimitiere Allemand).

▲▲**Pointe du Hoc**—During the D-Day invasion, 225 U.S. Rangers attempted a castle-like siege of the German-occupied cliffs by using grappling hooks and ladders borrowed from London fire departments. Only 90 survived. German bunkers and bomb craters remain as they were found (20 minutes by car west of the American cemetery in St. Laurent, just past Vierville-sur-Mer).

MONT ST. MICHEL

The distant silhouette of this Gothic island-abbey sends the tired sightseer's spirits soaring. Mont St. Michel, which through the ages has been among the top four pilgrimage sites in Christendom, is one of those rare places that looks as enchanting in person as it does in dreams. While it floats like a mirage on the horizon, it does show up on film.

The causeway, built in 1878, stopped the water from flowing around the island. This contributed to the filling in of the bay around Mont St. Michel. Because of this, it is no longer an island. A new bridge is being planned that will let the water circulate and Mont St. Michel become an island again.

Orientation

Mont St. Michel is connected by a two-mile causeway to the mainland and surrounded by a mud flat. Your visit features a one-street village that winds up to the fortified abbey. As you wind up the hill, tourists trample the dreamscape. A ramble on the ramparts offers mud-flat views and an escape from the tourist zone. The only worthwhile entry is the abbey itself, at the summit of the island.

Daytime Mont St. Michel is a touristic gauntlet—worth a stop, but a short one will do. The tourist tide recedes late each afternoon. During non-summer nights, the island is abbey-quiet, and the illumination, beautiful. Poets prefer evenings here. The abbey interior is not an essential visit (and it's open late at night as a sound-and-light show anyway), so arriving late and departing early is a good option.

Tourist Information: The TI (and WC) is to your left as you enter Mont St. Michel's gates. They have handy brochures listing hotels, *chambres d'hôte*, restaurants, English tour times for the abbey, bus schedules, and the tide table (*Horaires des Marées*), essential if you explore outside Mont St. Michel (daily 9:00–19:00 in summer, 9:00–12:30 and 14:00–18:30 during off-season, tel. 02 33 60 14 30).

Tides: The tides here (which rise 50 feet) are the largest and most dangerous in Europe. During a flood tide the ocean rushes in at 12 miles per hour. In medieval times it was faster, rushing in "at the speed of a galloping horse." Even today the undertow can sweep a slow horse away. High tides (*grandes marées*) lap against the tourist office door (where you'll find tide hours posted).

Parking: Remember, very high tides rise to the edge of the causeway—leaving the causeway open but all cars left parked below well under water. Safe parking is available at the foot of Mont St. Michel; you will be instructed where to park under high-tide conditions. There's plenty of parking provided you arrive off-season, or early or late in high season.

Sights—Mont St. Michel

The Village below the Abbey—Mont St. Michel's main street of shops and hotels leads to the abbey. With only 30 full-time residents, the village lives solely for tourists. After the TI, check the tide warnings posted on the wall. Before the drawbridge, on your left, poke through the door of Restaurant Le Mere Poulard, where a virtual theater-kitchen in action shows the colorful making of the traditional omelet. Don't spend 95F for this edible tourist trap. But watch the show as old-time costumed cooks beat omelets, daddy, eight to the bar.

Passing through the old drawbridge, Mont St. Michel welcomes you with the most touristy street this side of Tijuana. You can trudge through this touristic gauntlet uphill past several gimmicky "museums" and human traffic jams to the abbey (all island hotel receptions are located on this street). Or better, to avoid the tourist deluge, climb the first steps after the drawbridge on your right, then turn right or left at the top; the ramparts lead all the way up and up to the abbey in either direction (quieter if you turn right). Public W.C.s charge according to altitude: 1F at the entry to Mont St. Michel, 2F halfway up, and 3F at the abbey entrance.

▲▲**Abbey of Mont St. Michel**—Mont St. Michel has been an important pilgrimage center since A.D. 708, when the Archangel Michael told the bishop of Avranches to "build here and build high." With impressive foresight he reassured the bishop, "If you build it . . . they will come." Today's abbey is built on the remains of a Romanesque church, which was built on the remains of a Carolingian church. Saint Michael, whose gilded statue decorates the top of the spire, was the patron saint of many French kings, making this a favored sight for French royalty through the ages. As you enter, imagine the headaches and hassles the monks ran into while building it. They had to ferry the granite from across the bay (then deeper and without the causeway) and make the same hike you just did—with more luggage.

The visit is a one-way route through fine—but barren— Gothic rooms. You'll explore the impressive church, delicate cloisters, and refectory (where the monks ate in austere silence), then climb down into the dark, damp Romanesque foundations. A highlight is the giant tread-wheel, which six workers would power hamster-style to haul two-ton loads of stones and supplies from the landing below. This was used right up until the 19th century. You'll better appreciate the abbey by renting a Walkman (25F, 35F for two) or by taking a 75-minute English-language tour (free, but tip requested; several tours per day, groups can be large, tour times at TI). For some, the tours make a short story long. Those who go through *sans* tour or Walkman find no English explanations posted—but then, there's not a lot to explain. (40F, daily 9:00–18:30 May 15–September 15, 9:30–17:00 during off-season, ticket office closes one hour earlier, the abbey closes at 16:00 in winter.) Buy your ticket to the abbey, then keep climbing. Tours begin at the view terrace in front of the church. Allow 20 minutes to climb at a relaxed, steady pace from the TI to the abbey. For a free near-abbey visit, hike through the ticket room and gift shop, where you'll find models of the abbey over the ages. From there you can enter the free abbey gardens.

▲▲**Stroll around Mont St. Michel**—To resurrect that Mont St. Michel dreamscape and evade all those tacky tourist stalls, walk out on the mud flats around the island. At low tide it's reasonably dry and a great memory. This can be extremely dangerous, so be sure to double-check the tides. Remember the scene from the Bayeux tapestry where Harold rescues Normans from the quicksand? It happened somewhere in this bay. You may notice entire school groups hiking in from the muddy horizon. Attempting this popular excursion without a local guide is reckless.

▲▲**Evening on Mont St. Michel**—After dark the island is magically floodlit. Views from the ramparts are sublime. Mont St. Michel's latest addition is a somewhat overrated nighttime sound-and-light show, *Les Imaginaires du Mont St. Michel*, inside the abbey. For 60F you can walk through the same rooms visitors see during the day and enjoy an entertaining room-by-room audiovisual show. With flickering fires and Gregorian chant CDs, it's a medieval extravaganza (June–September and holiday weekends, starts after dark and runs very late—ask at TI).

Sleeping on or near Mont St. Michel
(5.5F = about $1, zip code: 50116)

Sleeping on the island, inside the walls, is the best way to experience Mont St. Michel, though you may pay a premium for your hotel bed. On the island, most hotels are impersonal and pad their profits by requiring guests to buy dinner from their restaurant. Skip their outrageously priced breakfasts. Several hotels are closed from November until Easter. To reserve by letter, addresses are simple: name of hotel, 50116 Mont St. Michel, France. Because most visitors only day-trip here, you should be able to find a room at almost any time of the year. You should, however, reserve ahead if possible.

The spotless, cozy, and comfortable rooms offered at the **Restaurant le St. Michel** are the best value on the island (Db-210–310F, no dinner requirements, tel. & fax 02 33 60 14 37). The remaining hotels all offer a token few inexpensive rooms, and many high-priced ones with similar amenities and prices. The rooms at the **Vielle Auberge** are among the best for the price in this crowd, but don't let them talk you into more room than you need (Db-300–500F, Tb-600F, CC:V, tel. 02 33 60 14 34, fax 02 33 70 87 04). You can also try the professionally pleasant **Le Mouton Blanc** (Db-330–400F, Tb/Qb-460–600F, CC:VMA, tel. 02 33 60 14 08, fax 02 33 60 05 62) or the couldn't-care-less **Hôtel Croix Blanche***** (a few fine loft triples, a few superb-view doubles, Sb-390F, Db-450–510F, Tb/Qb-620–900F, CC:VM, tel. 02 33 60 14 04, fax 02 33 48 59 82). The **Hôtel du Guesclin**** offers good, clean rooms at fair prices (Db-320F, a few cheaper rooms available, CC:VM, tel. 02 33 60 14 10, fax 02 33 60 45 81). The more congenial **Hotel les Terrasses Poulard** has several good-value rooms in its main building and too many overpriced rooms in its annex (Db-300–900F, CC:VMA, tel. 02 33 60 14 09 fax 02 33 60 37 31).

Rooms on the nearby mainland are a better budget bet. Among the *chambres d'hôte*, **Madame Brault's La Jacotiere**, with comfortable rooms and views of Mont St. Michel, is a steal (D-200F, in Ardevon, zip code: 50170, tel. 02 33 60 22 92). **Hôtel de la Digue***** is the best and the closest of the hotels on the approach to Mont St. Michel. Spacious, modern, and cushy rooms and a good restaurant with a view of Mont St. Michel make this hard to beat (Db-320–450F, Tb-490F, Qb-520F, CC:VMA, tel. 02 33 60 14 02, fax 02 33 60 37 59).

Eating on Mont St. Michel
Puffy omelets are the island's specialty. Also look for mussels and seafood platters, locally raised lamb (fed on the saltwater grass), and Muscadet wine (dry, cheap, and white). I let Patricia and Phillipe cook for me at the friendly and reasonable **Le St. Michel** (tel. 02 33 60 14 37), across from Hôtel Mouton Blanc.

Transportation Connections—Mont St. Michel
The nearest train station is in Pontorson, 15 minutes away by bus (6/weekday, 2/day weekends). A Pontorson–MSM taxi will cost about 75F, 100F on weekends. You can rent a bike at the Pontorson train station.

To: Bayeux (3 trains/2 hrs, via Pontorson), **Dinan** (6 trains/day, 90 min, via Pontorson), **Amboise** (allow 8 hrs, whether by regular train with transfers in Pontorson, Caen, and Tours; or by

the TGV—transfer in Pontorson, catch TGV at Rennes, catch
TGV at Paris' Montparnasse station, transfer in Tours), **Paris'**
Gare Montparnasse: A bus/train combination is easiest; bus from
Mont St. Michel to Rennes (2/day, 90 min, tel. 02 99 56 76 09),
then TGV to Paris (15/day, 2 hrs). Less convenient is the train
between Pontorson and Rennes (2/day, 4.5 hrs).

Sights near Normandy—Brittany

The Couesenan River marks the border between Normandy and
Brittany. It hits the sea a few hundred meters west of Mont St.
Michel, leaving the island barely in Normandy. The peninsula of
Brittany is rugged, with an isolated interior, a well-discovered
coast, and strong Celtic ties. This region of independent-minded
locals is distinctly different from Normandy.

Dinan

If you have time for only one stop in Brittany, do Dinan. This
delightful city offers Brittany's best-preserved medieval center
(one hour from Mont St. Michel). Dinan feels real and untouristy.

Consider this walk: Start at the TI (9:00–19:00 June–September
30, closes at 18:00 and for lunch in the off-season, 6 rue de l'Horloge, tel. 02 96 39 75 40; the 15F tourist magazine has more information on this self-guided tour). Inspect the nearby lookout tower,
Tour de l'Horloge (15F, good view from the top), then continue
down rue de l'Horloge and turn left into Dinan's historic commercial center, the place des Merciers. The half-timbered arcaded
buildings are Dinan's oldest. They date from that time when property taxes were based on the square footage of your ground floor.
To provide shelter from both the taxes and the rain, owners built
out their first floors. Turn right where the square ends, then rap-
pel down rue Jerzual (for *crêperies*, boutiques, and stiff knees).
Crossing under the medieval gate (Porte Jerzual), turn right and
climb to the only accessible section of the ramparts. Enjoy the
view, then double back down the ramparts. Consider continuing
down to the old port then, to truly feel the pulse of this area, cross
the old bridge, turn right, and follow the river trail 30 minutes to
the pristine little village of Lehon where you'll find a café/*crêperie*.
If your legs disagree, don't descend farther, but jog right after exiting the gate of the ramparts above the Porte Jerzual, then take the
first left uphill to the Jardins Anglais (English Gardens). Survey
Dinan's port and Rance valley. Then peek inside the very Breton
Basilique St. Saveur (bordering the park, English explanation
inside).

Sleeping and Eating in Dinan
(5.5F - about $1, zip code: 22100)

Hôtel de la Duchesse Anne*, warmly run by Giles and Christine, is a salt-of-the-earth budget home base on a large square at the edge of the old town (Sb-175F, Db-250F, 18 place du Guesclin, tel. 02 96 39 09 43, fax 02 96 85 09 76). Even if you're not staying here, drop by the hotel bar and have Giles draw you a *bolee* of *cidre*. For cozy, spotless, and very comfortable rooms, stay in the well-run **Hotel les Grandes Tours** (S-180F, Sb-270F, D-200F, Db-290F, Tb-330F, Qb-450F, CC-VM, 6 rue du Chateau, tel. 02 96 85 16 20, fax 02 96 86 16 04). Nearer the TI, the small and comfortable **Hotel La Tour de l'Horloge**** is another good value (Db-290–310F, 5 rue de la Chaux, tel. 02 96 39 96 92, fax 02 96 85 06 99). For dinner try any of the cozy *crêperies* in the old city. If you're not in the mood for crêpes, try my favorite restaurant, **Le St. Louis**, just around the corner from the Hotel les Grandes Tours. Flames from the fireplace flicker on wood beams and white tablecloths (90F *menu*, great salad bar and desserts, delectable main courses, closed Wednesdays except in summer, 9 rue de Lehon, tel. 02 96 39 89 50).

St. Malo and Fougères

▲**St. Malo**—Come here to experience *the* Breton beach resort. Stroll high up on the very impressive ramparts that circle the entire old city, eat seafood, walk as far out on the beaches as the tides allow, then return to Dinan for the night. An easy day trip, St. Malo is a 45-minute drive or a one-hour bus or train ride from Mont St. Michel or Dinan.

▲**Fougères**—This very Breton city is a delightful stop for drivers traveling between the Loire châteaux and Mont St. Michel. Fougères has one of Europe's largest medieval castles, a fine city center, and a panoramic park viewpoint (from St. Leonard church in Jardin Public). Try one of the café/*crêperies* near the castle, such as the tasty **Crêperie des Remparts**, one block uphill from the castle. (Crêpes are called *gallettes* in Brittany, and are the local fare.) Pick up a city map and castle description in English at the castle entrance. The interior is grass and walls.

DORDOGNE

The Dordogne River Valley is France's version of the Rhine, with an extra splash of beauty. Hundreds of castles dot the Dordogne, a testament to its strategic importance in the Middle Ages. During the Hundred Years' War, this river marked the boundary between Britain and France. The sleepy Dordogne carries more memories now than goods. It's a profoundly French backwater filled with warm, salt-of-the-earth people.

Today Dordogne visitors enjoy rock-sculpted villages, fertile farms surrounding I-could-retire-there cottages, film-gobbling vistas, lazy canoe rides, and a local cuisine worth loosening your belt for. The Dordogne's most thrilling sights are its caves decorated with prehistoric artwork. The cave of Font-de-Gaume has the greatest ancient (15,000-year-old) cave paintings still open to the public.

To explore this beautiful river valley (in the region of Périgord), sleep in Beynac if you have a car and in Sarlat if you don't.

Planning Your Time

You'll need a minimum of a day and a half to explore this magnificent region. Your sightseeing obligations in order of priority are: prehistoric cave art, the Dordogne River Valley and its villages and castles, and the medieval town of Sarlat. The Dordogne riverfront villages offer exciting canoe-trip possibilities and an ideal break from your sightseeing. If possible, call well in advance to reserve a ticket to the cave art at Grotte de Font-de-Gaume.

A good (and exhausting) day might be: Morning and lunch in Sarlat (Wednesday and Saturday are market days), 13:00–Cave tour, 15:00–Two-hour canoe trip, 18:00–Tour Beynac castle with river view, 19:00–Walk back to the goose farm, 20:00–Dine. This plan can also work well with a cave tour as the first or last stop of the day. With part or most of a second day, explore the twisting alleys in Beynac, tour the medieval castle at Castlenaud, and consider visiting Lascaux II caves.

As you drive in or out the day before or after (connecting the Dordogne with the Loire and Carcassonne), break the long drives with stops in Oradour-sur-Glane (to the north) and Cahors/Albi (to the south).

Getting Around the Dordogne

This region is a joy with a car but tough without. Rent a bike or moped, take one of the well-organized minivan tours of the region, hire an all-day taxi service, or get to Beynac and toss your itinerary into the Dordogne.

By Bike or Moped: Bikers find the Dordogne scenic but hilly, with crowded roads. Consider a moped. In Sarlat, rent mopeds (180F per day) or mountain bikes (100F per day) at Peugeot Cycles (36 avenue Thiers, tel. 05 53 28 51 87, fax 05 53 30 23 90). A scenic Dordogne Valley loop ride is described below.

By Train: Train service in this region is limited to important cities and still is sparse. You can train from Sarlat to the caves in Les Eyzies, but service is limited, leaving you all day in Les Eyzies.

By Minivan Tour: Minivan tours of the area are offered by HEP Excursions, a company based in Sarlat (many itineraries to choose from, half day-150F, full day-200F, 280F to Rocamadour, four people minimum, French explanations only, no admissions included, tel. 05 53 28 10 04, fax 05 53 28 18 34). HEP prefers that you reserve through Sarlat's TI (tel. 05 53 31 45 45), though you can contact them directly.

By Taxi: Allo Sarlat Taxi offers customized taxi tours (split the cost with up to six travelers, find partners at your hotel, price varies according to itinerary, tel. 05 53 59 02 43 or 06 08 97 87 37). For taxi service from Sarlat to Beynac or La Roque-Gageac, allow 90F (130F at night); from Sarlat to Les Eyzies allow 150F (230F at night and on Sunday). Allo Taxi Bernard offers similar services (tel. 05 53 59 39 65).

By Car: Ask at the TI about car rentals.

Cuisine Scene—Dordogne River Valley

Gourmets flock to this area for its geese, ducks, and wild mushrooms. The geese produce (involuntarily) the region's famous *foie gras* (they're force-fed, denied exercise, and slaughtered for their livers). *Foie gras* tastes like butter and costs like gold. The duck specialty is *confit de canard* (duck meat preserved in its own fat—sounds terrible but tastes great). *Pommes Sarladaise* are mouthwatering, thinly-sliced potatoes fried in duck fat and commonly served with *confit de canard*. Wild truffles are dirty black mushrooms. Farmers traditionally locate the mushrooms with sniffing pigs, then charge a fortune for them (3,000F per kilo, $250 per pound). Native cheeses are Cabécou (a silver dollar–sized, pungent, nutty-flavored goat cheese) and Echourgnac (made by local Trappist monks). You'll find walnuts (*noix*) in salads, cakes, and liqueurs. Wines to sample are Bergerac (red and white) and Cahors (a full-bodied red). The *vin de noix* is a sweet walnut liqueur.

SARLAT

Sarlat (sar-lah) is a medieval banquet of a town scenically set amidst forested hills. The bustling old city overflows with historical monuments and, in the summer, tourists. Sarlat is just the right size: large enough to have a theater with four screens (as the locals boast) and small enough so that everything is an easy stroll from the town center. One-time capital of Périgord and current capital of *foie gras*, Sarlat has been a haven for writers and artists throughout the centuries and remains so today. Geese hate Sarlat.

Orientation

Like Italy's Siena, Sarlat is a museum city: no blockbuster sights, just a seductive tangle of cobblestone alleys peppered with medieval buildings. Rue de la République slices like an arrow through the circular old town. Sarlat's smaller half has none of the important sights but all the quiet lanes. Get lost.

Tourist Information: The helpful, if overwhelmed, English-speaking TI, in the center on place de la Liberté, has free maps of the city and region, *chambres d'hôte* listings, and the useful *Guide Practique* booklet which includes bus and train schedules; car, bike, and canoe rentals; and so on (9:00–19:00, Sunday 10:00–12:00 and 14:00–18:00 July–September; otherwise Monday–Saturday 9:00–12:00 and 14:00–18:00, tel. 05 53 31 45 45). English-language walking tours are offered June through September and leave from the TI (25F, 90 min, ask TI for times).

Laundromats: Across from the recommended Hôtel Couleverine (daily 6:00–22:00, self-serve or leave and pick up) or at 74 avenue de Selves near the recommended Hotel de Selves.

Sights—Sarlat

▲▲**Stroll through Sarlat**—Start by exploring the musty cathedral. Exit out the right transept. Snoop around through a few quiet courtyards, then turn left, making your way toward the rear of the cathedral. Climb up the steps to that medieval space capsule called the Lanterne des Morts (Lantern of the Dead). Big shots were buried here in the Middle Ages. Exit right (with your back to the Lantern) toward my favorite house in Sarlat. Turn right and climb to the top of this lane for a good look back over Sarlat. Save time to prowl the quiet side of town (the other side of the rue de

Sarlat

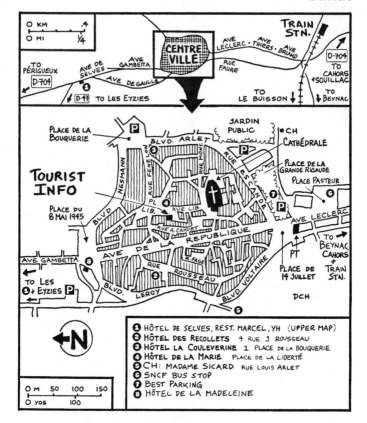

① HÔTEL DE SELVES, REST. MARCEL, YH (UPPER MAP)
② HÔTEL DES RECOLLETS   4 RUE J ROUSSEAU
③ HÔTEL LA COULEVERINE 1 PLACE DE LA BOUQUERIE
④ HÔTEL DE LA MARIE   PLACE DE LA LIBERTÉ
⑤ CH: MADAME SICARD   RUE LOUIS ARLET
⑥ SNCF BUS STOP
⑦ BEST PARKING
⑧ HÔTEL DE LA MADELEINE

la République). If you like *Mayberry RFD*–type museums, try the Chapel of White Penitents on rue Jean-Jacques Rousseau. An automobile museum is just west of the old town (rue Thiers).

▲**Open-Air Markets**—Outdoor markets thrive on Wednesday morning and all day Saturday. Saturday's market seems to swallow the entire town.

Sleeping in Sarlat
(5.5F = about $1, zip code: 24200)

Sleep Code: **S** = Single, **D** = Double/Twin, **T** = Triple, **Q** = Quad, **b** = bathroom, **t** = toilet only, **s** = shower only, **CC** = Credit Card (Visa, MasterCard, Amex), **SE** = Speaks English, **NSE** = No English, * = French hotel rating system (0–4 stars).

Even with its miserable crowds in July and August, Sarlat is the train traveler's best home base. In July and August many hotels require half-pension.

Hôtel des Recollets** offers modern comfort under heavy stone arches, with beautifully renovated rooms on the quiet side of the medieval city (Ds-225F, Db-250–350F, Tb-350F, Qb-400–450F, obligatory breakfast-35F, no half-pension, CC:VM, 4 rue Jean-Jacques Rousseau, tel. 05 53 31 36 00, fax 05 53 30 32 62, Christophe SE).

Hôtel La Couleverine** has hard-to-find management but plenty of medieval character in its well appointed rooms. Families enjoy *les châmbre familles*, particularly the tower room (Db-270–360F, Tb-380F, Qb-420F, CC:VMA, 1 place de la Bouquerie, tel. 05 53 59 27 80, fax 05 53 31 26 83). Half-pension (fine cuisine in an elegant restaurant, about 560F for two) is encouraged at busy periods and in summer.

Hôtel de la Marie** is run haphazardly from the busy café, but has big rooms and is as central as can be (Ds-220F, Db-260–290F, Ts-270–330F, Qb-420F, CC:VM, on place de la Liberté, tel. 05 53 59 05 71, NSE).

Hotel de la Madeleine*** is formal with Old World hotelesque service (Sb-300–375F, Db-350–400F, Tb-415–500F, Qb-480–570F, elevator, CC:VMA, west edge of the old town at 1 place de la Petite Rigaudie, tel. 05 53 59 10 41, fax 05 53 31 03 62, SE, e-mail: hotel.madeleine@wanadoo.fr).

The next four listings are a five-minute walk down Avenue Gambetta from the Hotel de la Madeleine.

Hotel de Selves*** is sleek and modern, with pastel French decor surrounding a swimming pool and quiet garden (Db-450–570F, elevator, satellite TV, all the hotel extras, CC:VMA, west of the old town at 93 avenue de Selves, tel. 05 53 31 50 00, fax 05 53 31 23 52, e-mail: hotel.sarlat@magic.fr). Right across the street, the equally modern but less snazzy **Hotel de Compostelle**** is well run and offers spacious rooms, excellent family suites, and a good value (Db-290–320F, Tb/Qb-450F, 64 avenue de Selves, tel. 05 53 59 08 53, fax 05 53 30 31 65). Just down the street at #50, **Hotel Marcel*** is a souvenir of old Sarlat with a dark, wood-beamed lobby and flowery wallpaper (Db-250–300F, tel. 05 53 59 21 98, fax 05 53 30 27 77). A few blocks farther down avenue Gambetta, the poorly-marked **Auberge de Jeunesse (Hostel)** is a casual and friendly do-it-yourself place (bunks-45F, sheets-16F, opens at 18:00, no curfew, small kitchen, 77 rue de Selves, call ahead for a bed, tel. 05 53 59 47 59 or 05 53 30 21 27).

Chambres d'hôte dot the Dordogne countryside. Several are on the fringe of old Sarlat. The **Sicards** rent two fine rooms—best budget beds in town—on the edge of the old town a five-minute walk from the TI (Sb-170F, Db-180F, Tb-200F, Le Pignol, rue Louis Arlet, tel. 05 53 59 14 28). **Madame Feliu** rents four basic rooms without the homeyness (Db-195–235F, where boulevard Henri hits boulevard Henri Arlet, tel. 05 53 59 03 21).

Eating in Sarlat

Sarlat is packed with moderately priced restaurants, all of which serve local specialties. The inexpensive **Restaurant du Commerce** is popular with locals and smack-dab in the Old City (open daily, 4 rue Alberic Cahuet). Opposite the cathedral, **La Rapiere** offers wood-beam coziness and fine regional cuisine, with *menus* from 85F (daily June–September, off-season closed Sunday, tel. 05 53 59 03 13). On the quieter side, just off rue de la Republique, **Les 4 Saisons** offers a good 85F *menu* (daily June–September, off-season closed Wednesday, 2 Cote de Toulouse).

Transportation Connections—Sarlat

The Sarlat TI has schedules for all modes of transport to and from Sarlat in its handy *Guide Practique*. From Sarlat, Bordeaux–St. Jean is the train travelers' gateway to distant points. Soulliac and Perigueux are the train hubs for points within the region. Sarlat train station: tel. 05 53 59 00 21.

By train to: Bordeaux (4/day, 2.5 hrs; Bordeaux has TGV service going north, south, and east), **Amboise** (2/day, 7 hrs, changing at Bordeaux–St. Jean and Tours), **Cahors**—catch SNCF bus from Sarlat to Souillac (4/day, 45 min), then train to Cahors (8/day, 1 hr), **Carcassonne** or **Albi** (5/day, 6 hrs; for Albi, transfer at Bordeaux–St. Jean; for Carcassonne, probable transfer in Toulouse).

To Beynac: Beynac is accessible only by taxi (90F), though the folks at Hôtel du Château will pick you up at the Sarlat station for no charge (see Sleeping in Beynac, below).

BEYNAC

The cliff-hanging village of Beynac (bay-nak) sees far fewer tourists than its big brother, Sarlat, and feels more welcoming. You'll have the Dordogne River at your doorstep, and a perfectly preserved medieval village winding like a sepia film set from the place where you beach your canoe to the hill-capping castle above. The floodlit village is always open for evening strollers. The **Beynac TI** (daily 9:00–12:30 and 14:30–18:00 July–August, off-season closed Sunday, tel. 05 53 29 43 08), post office, and grocery shop cluster around the village riverside parking lot. Beynac's scenic cafés are on the river below the TI and, high above, near the castle entry.

Sights—Beynac

▲**Château de Beynac**—This cliff-clinging castle soars like a trapeze artist 500 feet straight up above the Dordogne River. During the Hundred Years' War, the castle of Beynac housed the

French, while the British headquarters was across the river at Castelnaud. From the condition of the castles, it appears that France won. The sparsely furnished castle is most interesting for the valley views. From 12:15 to 13:45 you can walk through on your own; otherwise you will be required to tour with a French-speaking guide. Pick up the English translation. (35F, tours 10:00–18:30 except for lunch break, usually starting on the half-hour, in summer last visit is 18:00, open March 15–November 15, tel. 05 53 29 50 40.)

River Cruise Trips—Boats leave regularly from Beynac's parking lot for a mildly interesting but relaxed and scenic view of the Dordogne (35F, one-hour trips daily Easter–October).

Sleeping in Beynac
(5.5F = about $1, zip code: 24220)

Those with a car should sleep in or near Beynac. With hotel pickup services or a taxi, even those without a car may find Beynac worth the trouble. To write any Beynac hotel, simply use the 24220 postal code. The tiny Beynac TI posts a listing of all accommodations with prices and current availability on its door. Leave nothing in your car at night; the riverfront lot is a thief's dream.

The central **Hôtel du Château**** is reasonable and comfortable, although rooms on the river are loud. Charming Patricia (NSE) and *le boss* Phillipe (a *leetle* SE) will welcome you and feed you very well (Db-230–300F, extra person pays 60F, CC:VM, free pickup at the Sarlat train station upon request, tel. 05 53 29 50 13, fax 05 53 28 53 05, e-mail: HotelduChateau@Perigord.com). Right next door is the less personal **Hostellerie Malleville****. They have quieter, cozier rooms up the street at their **Hotel Pontet** (check in at Hostelerie Malleville, Db-230–300F, CC:VMA, tel. 05 53 29 50 06, fax 05 53 28 28 52). For basic, well-worn rooms with a romantic view of the river, hike up to **Hôtel de la Poste***. It's run by gregarious Madame Montestier and her mother-in-law (NSE). Relaxed cleaning standards, no TVs, no credit cards, fax . . . what's that?, but a cool garden and pleasant sitting room (D-175F, Db-215–245F, Tb/Qb-310F, 50 meters up the pedestrian street toward the castle, tel. 05 53 29 50 22). Right across from the castle atop the village (parking available, no views) hides the **Taverne des Remparts**, with four comfortable rooms and a fine restaurant (Db-250–280F, Tb/Qb-350F, CC:VM, tel. & fax 05 53 29 57 76, SE).

Hotel Bonnet**, on the eastern edge of town, offers Old-World comfort, river views from many rooms (noise can be a problem), a peaceful backyard garden, and a good restaurant (Db-360F, Tb-380F, CC:VMA, tel. 05 53 29 50 01, fax 05 53 29 83 74).

For a *chambre d'hôte*, try **M. Vaucel** (one Db-170F, a block from Hôtel du Château, tel. 05 53 29 50 28).

Sleeping near Beynac

Chambres d'Hôte: Less than two kilometers toward Castelnaud is **M. Rubio** (D-160F, tel. 05 53 29 53 32). Six kilometers from Beynac, in Bezenac, friendly British expats **Doug and Jenny Cree** have three very pleasant rooms with great river views (D-200F, tel. 05 53 50 32 69).

Hotels: If you need a pool, drive two kilometers east from Beynac to Vézac and try the modern **Relais des 5 Châteaux**** (Db-280–310F, good restaurant, CC:VM, tel. 05 53 30 30 72, fax 05 53 31 19 39). For affordable French country living, stay in La Roque-Gageac at the remarkably reasonable **Hôtel Belle Étoile****. It sports classic decor, river views from most rooms, some squishy beds, and a great restaurant (Ds-200F, Db-280–310F, Tb/Qb-350F, no half-pension requirement, zip code: 24250, tel. 05 53 29 51 44, fax 05 53 29 45 63).

Eating in and near Beynac

You'll dine well in air-conditioned comfort at **Hôtel du Château**. If you can manage the hike up to the castle or have a car, **Taverne des Remparts** is also a good value (across from the castle, CC:VM, tel. 05 53 29 57 76). Beynac also offers the Dordogne's dreamy dinner-picnic site. Walk up the hill, pass the château, continue out of the village, then turn right at the cemetery.

In nearby La Roque-Gageac, the restaurant **Hôtel Belle Étoile** serves top regional cuisine in elegant surroundings (*menus* from 110F, reserve ahead, tel. 05 53 29 51 44).

Sights—Dordogne Valley Region

Cro-Magnon Caves—There are three caves in this region with original cave paintings that the tourist can still admire: the top-quality Grotte de Font-de-Gaume (tours in English offered only in summer), the less spectacular but friendly Grottes de Cougnac (tours in English), and the immense Grottes de Peche Merle (some English tours). The latter two are listed under Sights—Southeast of the Dordogne, below.

Les Eyzies—The town of Les Eyzies-de-Tayac is the touristic hub of this cluster of historic caves, castles, and rivers. Except for its interesting museum of prehistory (35F, Wednesday–Monday 9:30–12:00 and 14:0–18:00, closed Tuesday and November–March at 17:00) next to the big statue of Mr. Cro-Magnon, there's little reason to stop here.

▲▲▲**Grotte de Font-de-Gaume**—Even if you're not a connoisseur of Cro-Magnon art, you'll dig this cave. It's the last cave in Europe with prehistoric (polychrome) painting still open to the public—and its turnstile days are numbered. On a carefully guided and controlled 100-yard walk, you'll see about 20 red and black bison—often in elegant motion—painted with an impressive sensi-

Heart of the Dordogne

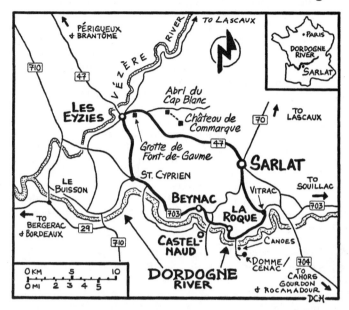

tivity. Your guide—with a laser pointer and great reverence—will trace the faded outline of the bison and explain how, 15,000 years ago, cave dwellers used local minerals and the rock's natural contour to give the paintings dimension. The paintings were discovered by the village school teacher in 1901. Now, since heavy-breathing tourist hordes damage the art by raising and lowering the temperature and humidity levels, tickets are limited to 200 a day.

Visits are by appointment only. Reserve in advance by phone; your hotel can make the call. Summertime spots are booked two weeks in advance. Even during the off-season, when you can generally just show up and get in, it's smart to call ahead and get a time. Request an English tour (usually summers only). Even in French you'll find it interesting, but ask for the English translation brochure and read through the books in the gift shop before you go. (34F, Thursday–Tuesday 9:00–12:00 and 14:00–18:00, closed Wednesday and at 17:00 November–February, no photography or large bags, tel. 05 53 06 90 80.) Drivers or bikers who can't get a spot here can try the caves at Rouffignac (engravings and paintings of mammoths, 10 miles north of Les Eyzies, tel. 05 53 05 41 71). Drivers can also aim for the more remote Grotte de Peche Merle, an hour east of Cahors (see below, Sights—Southeast of the Dordogne).

▲**Abri du Cap-Blanc**—In this prehistoric cave sculpture, early artists used the rock's natural contours to add dimension to their engraving. Look for places where the artists smoothed or roughed the surfaces to add depth. In this single stone room, your French-speaking guide will spend 30 minutes explaining 14,000-year-old carvings. Impressive as these carvings are, their subtle majesty bypasses some. Tours (French only) leave on the half-hour. No lines. (30F, Wednesday–Monday 9:30–19:00 in summer, off-season 10:00–12:00 and 14:00–18:00, closed on Tuesday and November–April, tel. 05 53 29 21 74.)

Château de Commarque and Château de Laussel—These castles' heydays passed 400 years ago with the Hundred Years' War. You can see (and reach) the Château de Commarque from Abri du Cap-Blanc. A 20- to 30-minute hike from here down an ummarked, unmaintained, and often marshy path takes you past Laussel Castle (privately owned) and right to the orange, crumbled walls of Commarque. It's not "officially" open to the public, but it's worth the scratches and soaked feet to get here.

Sights—Along the Dordogne River

▲▲▲**Dordogne Valley Scenic Loop Ride or Drive**—The most scenic stretch of the Dordogne lies between Carsac and Beynac. From Sarlat, follow signs toward Cahors and Carsac, then veer right to the Église de Carsac (wander into this tiny Romanesque church if its open). From Carsac, follow the river via Montfort, La Roque-Gageac, and Beynac. The town of Domme, above in the distance, while impressively situated, is overrun. For bikers, the total round-trip distance from Sarlat is about 45 kilometers (28 miles). Less ambitious bikers will find the 30-kilometer (18-mile) loop ride from Sarlat to La Roque-Gageac to Beynac and back to Sarlat sufficient.

Foie Gras **in the Making**—You can witness (evenings only) the force-feeding of geese (*la gavage*), but beware: You are expected to buy. Between Sarlat and Les Eyzies-de-Tayac you'll pass a small farm with a faded sign on the barn, a small roadside stand, and a flock of fat geese. The Lacombes, who run the place, speak only French and are as gentle with tourists as they are with their geese. Belly up to the stand and, with your mouth wide open, ask about *la gavage* (usually evenings after 18:00). Friendlier Madame Gauthier's farm, which also offers a peek at the *gavage*, is just down the road from the Château de Beynac (park right there or walk 10 minutes from the château away from the river; you'll see the signs; demonstrations 18:00–19:30, tel. 05 53 29 51 45).

▲▲**Castelnaud**—Château de Beynac's crumbling rival looks a little less mighty, but the inside packs a medieval punch. Several rooms display weaponry and artifacts from the Hundred Years'

War. The courtyard comes with a 46-meter-deep well (drop a pebble) and an entertaining video showing the catapults, which litter the grounds, in action. The rampart views are unbeatable, and the siege tools outside the walls are thought-provoking. Borrow the English explanations from the ticket lady for the room-by-room story. (34F, daily 10:00–19:00 May–June, 9:30–20:00 during summer, otherwise 10:00–18:00; from the car park it's a steep hike through a pleasant peasant village; tel. 05 53 31 30 00.) You can stop here halfway through your canoe trip, or take a one-hour hike from Beynac along a difficult-to-follow riverside path (it hugs the river as it passes though camp-grounds and farms).

▲▲▲**Dordogne Canoe Trips**—For a refreshing break from the car or train, explore the riverside castles and villages of the Dor-dogne by rented canoe. Several outfits rent plastic two-person canoes (and one-person kayaks) and will pick them up at an agreed-upon spot. If Beynac is home, make sure the outfit you use allows you to get out in Beynac. For 130F, two can paddle the best two-hour stretch from Cénac to Beynac (shuttle included, call ahead to arrange if you don't have a car, in summer usual pickup time in Beynac is 9:00). In Cénac, look for **Dordogne Randonées** (coming from Sarlat or Beynac, take the first left after crossing the bridge to Cénac, tel. 05 53 28 22 01). Those with less time can float an hour from La Roque-Gageac to Beynac with Canoe-Dordogne (tel. 05 53 29 38 92). Or, you could float all day from Vitrac to Beynac (Safaraid, Vitrac, tel. 05 65 30 74 47, or ask at local TIs). While you need to be in good shape for the longer trips, it's OK if you're a complete novice—the only white water you'll encounter will be your partner frothing at the views. You'll get a life vest and, for a few extra francs, a watertight bucket to store whatever you want to keep dry. Simply beach your boat wherever you want to take a break. The best two stops are the village of La Roque-Gageac and the castle at Castelnaud. This works well for those staying at Beynac and lacking wheels; if you call them they'll pick you up.

▲**La Roque-Gageac**—La Roque (the rock), as the locals call this village, is sculpted into the cliffs rising from the Dordogne River. As you walk along the main street, look for the markers showing the water levels of three floods, and ask someone about the occasional rock avalanches from above. La Roque was once a thriving port, exporting Limousin oak to Bordeaux for making wine barrels. Find the old ramp leading down to the river. Wan-der up the narrow tangle of back streets that seem to disappear into the cliffs. For a splurge, have a romantic dinner; better yet, sleep at **Hôtel Belle Étoile** (Db-280–310F, call to reserve, tel. 05 53 29 51 44). Popular La Roque is best early, at night, or during the off-season. Canoes can be rented near the small TI booth on the river (tel. 05 53 29 38 92).

Sights—North of the Dordogne

▲▲**Lascaux**—The region's most vivid and famous cave paintings are at Lascaux, 30 minutes north of Sarlat. In the interest of preservation, these caves are closed to tourists. But the adjacent Lascaux II copy caves are impressive in everything but authenticity. At Lascaux II, the reindeer, horses, and bulls of Lascaux I are painstakingly reproduced by top artists using the same dyes, tools, and techniques as their predecessors did 15,000 years ago. Anyone into caveman art will appreciate the thoughtful explanations. It's worth working your schedule around English tour times. (Call ahead for English tour times, five times daily in the summer, on demand in off-season; 50F; daily 9:30–19:00 July–August, otherwise Tuesday–Sunday 10:00–12:00 and 14:00–17:30; 2.5 kilometers south of Montignac; in July and August tickets are sold only at the Montignac TI, tel. 05 53 51 95 03.)

▲▲▲**Oradour-sur-Glane**—Located two hours north of Sarlat and 25 kilometers west of Limoges, this is one of the most powerful sights in France. French schoolchildren know this town well. Most make a pilgrimage here. "La Ville Martyr," as it is known, was machine-gunned and burned on June 10, 1944, by Nazi troops. They were either seeking revenge for the killing of one of their officers (by French resistance fighters in a neighboring village), or simply terrorizing the populace in preparation for the upcoming Allied invasion (this was four days after D-Day). With cool German attention to detail, the Nazis methodically rounded up the entire population of 642 townspeople. The women and children were herded into the town church, where they were tear-gassed and machine-gunned. Plaques mark the place where the town's men were grouped and executed. The town was then set on fire, its victims left under a blanket of ashes.

Today the ghost town, left untouched for 50 years, greets every pilgrim who enters with only one English word: Remember. Hushed visitors walk the length of Oradour's main street past gutted, charred buildings in the shade of lush trees to the underground memorial on the market square (rusted toys, broken crucifixes, town mementos under glass). Visit the cemetery where most lives ended on June 10, 1944, and finish with the church with its bullet-pocked altar (free, daily, long hours, 10F English booklet in the shop at either entrance).

Seven daily buses connect Limoges' train station with Oradour in 20 minutes. With a car and extra time, visit the lovely, untouristed village of Mortemart (15 minutes northwest of Oradour on D-675), where you'll find a few cafés; a cute château (good picnic benches behind); and **Hotel Relais****, which offers five comfortable rooms over a superb restaurant (Sb-280F, Db-280F, Tb-300F, CC:VM, *menus* from 95F, across from medieval market hall on main road, 87330 Mortemart, tel. 05 55 68 12 09).

The Dordogne Region

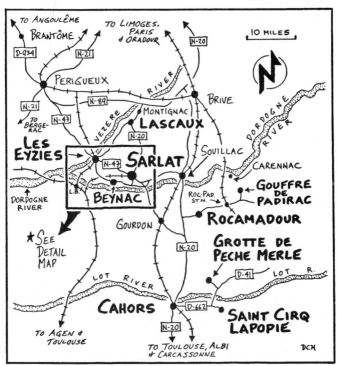

Sights—Southeast of the Dordogne

▲**Rocamadour**—Ninety minutes east of Sarlat, this would be a three-star town if its spectacular setting and medieval charm weren't trampled by daily hordes of tourists and pilgrims. Still, it's a remarkable place, worth a look if you can arrive early or, better, come late and spend the night. **Hotel Sainte Marie****, ideally situated in the Cité Medievale, is comfortable enough and a welcoming place (D-180F, Db-260F , tel. 05 65 33 63 07, fax 05 65 33 69 08.) Trains (via Brive-la-Gaillarde) will leave you five kilometers from the village (taxi, rent a bike from the station, hitch, or hike); a better option may be HEP Excursions' minivan tours from Sarlat (see Getting Around the Dordogne, above).

▲▲**Gouffre de Padirac**—Ten kilometers from Rocamadour is a fascinating cave (lots of stalagmites but no cave art). Follow the 90-minute French-language tour through this huge system of caverns. You'll ride elevators, hike along a buried stream, and even take a subterranean boat ride (47F, daily 9:00–12:00 and 14:00–18:00

April–October only, longer hours in summer, crowds and delays in summer, day trips are organized from Rocamadour, TI tel. 01 65 33 47 17). The nearest train station is in Rocamadour.

Rocamadour and Gouffre de Padirac go together well. Idyllic little Carennac, a good home base for both, has two fine hotel values: the simple, friendly **Hotel des Touristes*** (Db-210F, tel. & fax 05 65 10 94 31); or the more upscale **Hotel Fenelon**** (Db-260–340F, CC:VM, pool, tel. 05 65 10 96 46, fax 05 65 10 94 86).

Lot River and Cahors—Were it not for the Dordogne, the Lot River Valley might be considered France's most beautiful. The prehistoric cave paintings at the Grottes of Peche Merle and Cougnac, the medieval bridge at Cahors (Pont Valentré), and the rocktop village of St. Cirq Lapopie are each remarkable sights, within a half-hour of each other and within a 1.5-hour drive of Sarlat. These sights are worthwhile for drivers connecting the Dordogne (Sarlat) with Albi or Carcassonne, or as a long day trip from Sarlat. Without a car, skip 'em.

▲**Grotte de Cougnac**—Thirty kilometers south of Sarlat, near Gourdon in Payrignac, this far less touristed cave offers a more intimate look at Cro-Magnon cave art and stalagmites (32F; daily 9:00–18:00 in summer, otherwise 9:30–11:00 and 14:00–17:00; 70-minute tours, some in English; call to reserve, tel. 05 65 41 47 54).

▲▲**Pont Valentré at Cahors**—One of Europe's finest medieval monuments, this three-towered, fortified bridge was built in 1308 to keep the English out of Cahors. It worked. Poke around and learn the reason for the devil on the center tower. The steep trail on the non-city side leads up to great views (keep climbing, avoid branch trails, be careful if trail is wet). Just past the city-side end of the bridge is *Le Cedre*, a wine shop/café/souvenir stand, where you can taste Cahors' well-respected black wine and *foie gras* (the duck is cheaper than the goose and just as tasty).

▲▲▲**Grotte de Peche Merle**—About 30 minutes east of Cahors lies this relatively obscure cave with prehistoric paintings rivaling the better-known ones at the Grotte de Font-de-Gaume. The cave is filled with stalactites and stalagmites, and you can even see a Cro-Magnon footprint preserved in the mud. Call to reserve a time. If you arrive early, start at the museum with a film subtitled in English, then descend to the caves. If you can't join an English tour ask for the English translation booklet (46F, 38F during off-season; daily 9:30–12:00 and 14:00–18:00 Easter–October, closes earlier off-season; tel. 05 65 31 27 05, fax 05 65 31 20 47).

▲**St. Cirq Lapopie**—Soaring high above the Lot River, this is one of southern France's most spectacularly situated hill towns. Be careful of summer crowds. Wander the rambling footpaths and stay for lunch. You'll find ideal picnic perches and several reasonable restaurants. Sleep at the **Auberge du Sombral**** (Db-300–400F, good 100F *menu*, CC:VM, tel. 05 65 31 26 08, fax 05 65 30 26 37).

LANGUEDOC

From the 10th to the 13th centuries, this powerful, open-minded, and independent region ruled an area reaching from the Rhône River to the Pyrénées. The Albigensian (Cathar) Crusades started here in 1208, which ultimately led to Languedoc's demise and incorporation into the state of France. The word *languedoc* comes from the language its people spoke at that time: *Langue d'oc* ("language of Oc," *Oc* for the way they said "yes") was the dialect of southern France, as opposed to *langue d'oil*, the dialect of northern France (where *oil*, later to become *oui*, was the way of saying "yes"). As Languedoc's power faded, so did its language.

The Moors, Charlemagne, and the Spanish called this home at various times. You'll see, hear, and feel the strong Spanish influence on this dry, hilly region. We're lumping Albi in with the Languedoc region, though it's no longer a part of what locals think of as true Languedoc.

Planning Your Time

Key sights in this region are Albi, Carcassonne, Minerve, the Cathar castle ruins, and Collioure. Albi makes a good day or overnight stop between the Dordogne region and Carcassonne. Plan your arrival at Carcassonne carefully: Arrive late in the afternoon, spend the night, and leave by noon the next day, and you'll miss the day-trippers. Collioure is your Mediterranean beach town vacation-from-your-vacation. You'll need wheels of your own and a good map to find the Cathar castle ruins and Minerve. If driving, the most exciting Cathar castles—Peyrepertuse and Queribus—work well as stops between Carcassonne and Collioure. No matter what method of transport you use, Languedoc is a logical stop between the Dordogne and Provence, or on the way to Barcelona, which is just over the border.

Languedoc

Getting Around Languedoc

Albi, Carcassonne, and Collioure are a snap by train, but a car is essential for seeing the remote sights in this area. You can rent a car near the train stations in Albi or Carcassonne or in downtown Collioure. Buy the local Michelin map #83. The roads can be tiny and the traffic very slow.

Cuisine Scene—Languedoc

Hearty peasant cooking and full-bodied red wines are Languedoc's tasty trademarks. Be adventurous—treat your tase buds as well. Cassoulet, an old Roman concoction of goose, duck, pork, mutton, sausage, and white beans, is the main-course specialty. You'll also see cargolade, a stew of snail, lamb, and sausage. Local cheeses are Roquefort and Pelardon (a nutty-tasting goat cheese). Corbières, Minervois, and Côtes du Roussillon are the area's good-value red wines. The locals distill a fine brandy, Armagnac, that tastes just like cognac and costs less.

The Cathars

The Cathars, a heretical group of Christians based in Languedoc from the 11th through the 13th centuries, saw life as a battle between good (the spiritual) and bad (the material). They considered material things evil and of the devil. While others called them "Cathars" (from the Greek word for "pure") or "Albigenses" (for their main city, Albi), they called themselves simply "friends of God."

Cathars focused on the teachings of St. John and recognized only baptism as a sacrament. Because they believed in reincarnation, they were vegetarians.

Travelers encounter the Cathars in their Languedoc sightseeing because of the Albigensian Crusades (1209–1240s). The king of France wanted to consolidate his grip on southern France. The pope needed to make a strong point that the only acceptable Christianity was Roman-style. Both found self-serving reasons to wage a genocidal war against these people—who never amounted to more than 10 percent of the local population and who coexisted happily with their non-Cathar neighbors. After a terrible generation of torture and mass burnings, the Cathars were wiped out. The last Cathar was burnt in 1321.

Today tourists find haunting castle ruins (once Cathar strongholds) high in the Pyrénées, and eat hearty *salade Cathar.*

ALBI

Those coming to see the basilica and the Toulouse-Lautrec Museum will be pleasantly surprised by Albi's enchanting city center. The Albigensian Crusades were born here, as was Toulouse-Lautrec. The visitor's Albi (TI, Toulouse-Lautrec Museum, and cobbled pedestrian zone) clusters around its fortress basilica. Consider spending a night.

Tourist Information: Albi's information-packed TI is between the basilica and the Toulouse-Lautrec Museum (Monday–Saturday 9:00–19:30, Sunday 10:30–12:30 and 15:30–18:30 July–August; Monday–Saturday 9:00–12:00 and 14:00–18:00, Sunday 10:30–12:30 and 15:30–17:30 September–June; tel. 05 63 49 48 80).

Arrival in Albi

By Train: Take a left onto avenue Marechal Joffre, then another left on avenue General de Gaulle, then follow signs to *cathédrale* and to Albi's old city.

By Car: Follow signs to *centre-ville* and *cathédrale* and park in front of the cathedral.

Sights—Albi

Pick up a map of the city center at the TI (get the purple *circuit poupre* walking tour in English) and follow its suggested walking tour, reading the English information posted at key points along the way. On this walk you'll see:

▲▲▲**Basilique Ste. Cécile**—This 13th-century fortress/basilica was the nail in the Albigensian coffin. Both the imposing exterior and the stunning interior of this cathedral drive home the message of the Catholic (read "universal") Church. The extravagant porch seems like an afterthought. Inside, be prepared for an explosion of colors and geometric shapes and a vivid *Last Judgment*. Even with the gaping hole that was cut from it to make room for a newer pipe organ, the *Last Judgment* makes its point in a way that would stick with any medieval worshiper (8:30–19:00 June 1–September 30, otherwise closes 12:00–14:00 and at 17:45). The choir is worth the small admission, and the S*on et Lumière Spectacle*, offered in summer, is worth staying up for (30F, 22:00, ask at the TI).

▲▲**Musée Toulouse-Lautrec**—The Palais de la Berbie (once the fortified home of the archbishop) has the world's best collection of Lautrec's paintings, posters, and sketches. The artist, crippled from youth and therefore on the fringe of society, had an affinity for people who didn't quite fit in. He painted the dregs of Parisian society because that was his world. His famous Parisian nightlife posters are here. The top floor houses a skipable collection of contemporary art (25F, daily 10:00–12:00 and 14:00–18:00 April–May; 9:00–12:00 and 14:00–18:00 June–September; Wednesday–Monday 10:00–12:00 and 14:00–17:00 October–March; tel. 05 63 49 48 70). Even if you decide against this museum, walk underneath it to the palace's gardens for the great views.

Église St. Salvy and Clôitre—This is an OK church with fine cloisters. Delicate arches surround an enclosed courtyard, providing a peaceful interlude from the maniacal shoppers that fill the pedestrian streets (open all day).

Market Hall—This quiet Art Nouveau market is good for picnic-gathering and people-watching (open daily except Monday until 13:00, two blocks from the basilica).

Sleeping and Eating in Albi
(5.5F = about $1 zip code: 8100)
Sleep Code: **S** = Single, **D** = Double/Twin, **T** = Triple, **Q** = Quad, **b** = bathroom, **t** = toilet only, **s** = shower only, **CC** = Credit Card (Visa, MasterCard, Amex), **SE** = Speaks English, **NSE** = No English, ***** = French hotel rating system (0–4 stars).

Hôtel St. Clair**, offering steep stairs and elegant rooms, is decorated with a loving touch (Db-240–300F, Tb-350–420F, CC:VM, 20-minute walk from the station, two blocks from the cathedral in the pedestrian zone on rue St. Clair, easy parking, tel. 05 63 54 25 66, fax 05 63 47 27 58). **Le Vieil Alby Hotel****, located in the heart of Albi's pedestrian area, offers an excellent restaurant and fine rooms with all the comforts in a pleasant atmosphere (Sb-250F, Db-250–300F, Tb-330F, 40F garage, 25 rue Toulouse Lautrec, tel. 05 63 54 14 69, fax 05 63 54 96 75). Albi's **hostel** is cheap, clean, and basic (hostel card mandatory, check-in from 18:00–21:00, 13 rue de la République, tel. 05 63 54 53 65).

Albi is filled with inexpensive restaurants. Rue Toulouse-Lautrec (two blocks from the Hotel St. Clair) is home to many good places: For exceptional couscous in a "Little Morocco," try **Le Marrakesh** at #11 (hearty, even splitable 60F couscous, closed Monday and in July and August). **Le Vieil Alby** at #25 is one of Albi's more respected restaurants.

Just off place Vigan, the locally popular and cheap **Lou Sicret** is filled with atmosphere and local specialties . . . such as pig's feet (through the small passage at #1 rue Trimbal).

Transportation Connections—Albi
By train to: Toulouse (12/day, 75 min; no trains 14:00–17:00 from Toulouse, or 18:45–21:00 from Albi), **Carcassonne** (12/day, 2.5 hrs, transfer in Toulouse).

CARCASSONNE
Medieval Carcassonne is a 13th-century world of towers, turrets, and cobblestone alleys. It's a walled city and Camelot's castle rolled into one, frosted with too many day-tripping tourists. At 10:00 the salespeople stand at the doors of their main-street shops, their gauntlet of tacky temptations poised and ready for their daily ration of customers. But an empty Carcassonne rattles in the early morning or late-afternoon breeze. Enjoy the town early or late. Spend the night.

Twelve hundred years ago Charlemagne stood before this fortress/town with his troops, besieging it for several years. A cunning townsperson named Madame Carcas saved La Cité. Just as food was running out, she fed the last bits of grain to the last pig and tossed him over the wall. Splat. Charlemagne's bored and frustrated forces, amazed that the town still had enough food to throw fat party pigs over the wall, decided they would never succeed in starving the people out. They ended the siege and the city was saved. Madame Carcas *sonned* (sounded) the long-awaited victory bells, and La Cité had a name, "Carcas-sonne."

From Rick's journal on his first visit to Carcassonne: "Before me lives Carcassonne, the perfect medieval city. Like a fish that everyone thought was extinct, somehow Europe's great-est Romanesque fortress city has survived the centuries. I was supposed to be gone yesterday, but here I sit imprisoned by choice—curled in a cranny on top of the wall. The wind blows away the sounds of today, and my imagination 'medievals' me.

The moat is one foot over and 100 feet down. Small plants and moss upholster my throne."

Orientation

Contemporary Carcassonne is neatly divided into two cities: the magnificent Cité (medieval city) and the lively *ville basse* (modern downtown).

Tourist Information: Carcassonne has two TIs, one in the Cité and one in the *ville basse*. The handy Cité TI is just to your right as you enter the main gate called Narbonnaise (daily 9:00–19:00 July–September, otherwise 9:00–13:00 and 14:00–18:00). The *ville basse* TI is on the place Gambetta, near the huge French flags, at 15 boulevard Camille Pelletan (Monday–Saturday 9:00–12:15 and 14:00–18:30, closed Sunday, tel. 04 68 10 24 30 or 04 68 25 68 81). Pick up the map of La Cité with English explanations, get English tour times for Château Comtal, and ask about festivals.

Arrival in Carcassonne

By Train: The train station is located in the *ville basse*. Bus #4 connects the station with La Cité except on Sunday and during winter months (2/hrly, about 6F, pay driver, in the winter take bus #2 or #8 to place Gambetta, as close as you can get). Or you can walk 30 minutes across the Canal du Midi, across the traffic circle, and up the pedestrian street to the heart of the *ville basse*. From there a left on the rue de Verdun takes you to place Gambetta and across the Pont Vieux to La Cité. Figure 55F for a taxi to La Cité from the train station.

By Car: Following signs to La Cité, you'll come to a large parking lot (20F) and a drawbridge (Porte Narbonnaise) at the walled city's entrance. If staying inside the walls, show your reservation and you can park free in the outside lot and drive into the city after 18:00. Theft is common—leave nothing in your car overnight.

Sights—Carcassonne

▲▲▲**Medieval Wall Walk**—La Cité is a medieval fortress first constructed during the time of the Roman Empire. It was completely reconstructed in 1844 as part of a program to restore France's important monuments. Walk the entire outer wall (no charge, in town, follow signs to *lices*). The higher inner walls are mostly inaccessible, except for those in Château Comtal. Savor every step and view.

▲**Carcassonne Terre d'Histoire**—A busy medieval fair fills up most of August (Aug. 5–23 in 1999). Don't miss the jousting tournament (*spectacle équestre*), usually at 18:00.

▲▲▲**Walk to Pont Vieux**—For the best view back onto the floodlit city, hike down to the old bridge. As you exit the

Carcassonne

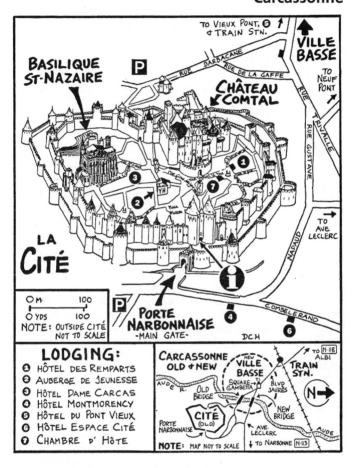

O M   100
O YDS   100
NOTE: OUTSIDE CITÉ NOT TO SCALE

PORTE NARBONNAISE -MAIN GATE-

LODGING:
❶ HÔTEL DES REMPARTS
❷ AUBERGE DE JEUNESSE
❸ HÔTEL DAME CARCAS
❹ HÔTEL MONTMORENCY
❺ HÔTEL DU PONT VIEUX
❻ HÔTEL ESPACE CITÉ
❼ CHAMBRE D' HÔTE

CARCASSONNE OLD & NEW
NOTE: MAP NOT TO SCALE

Narbonnaise Gate, go left on rue Nadaud to rue Gustave, then turn left onto rue Trivalle. Ask, "*Où est le Pont Vieux*?" (oo ay la pohn vee-uh). Return via the back door entry to La Cité near the Basilique St. Nazaire.

▲**Basilique St. Nazaire**—Enter this church and slowly walk down the aisle. Enjoy the colors of the 14th-century stained glass sparkling all around you and find the delicately vaulted Gothic ceiling behind the altar. This is one of the best examples of Gothic architecture in southern France.

Château Comtal—Carcassonne's third layer of defense was originally built in 1125, but was completely redesigned in later reconstructions. Peek into the inner courtyard and admire the towers, but skip the French tour (no English translation) and ask about English tours (free with admission, generally two to four times per day May–September, 32F, daily 9:00–19:00 June–September, 9:30–12:30 and 14:00–18:00 during off-season).

Wine Cooperative—In the tower next to La Cité TI you can sample a fine selection of local wines under Gothic arches. You are expected to buy a bottle if you taste, but it's cheap.

Exposition Torture—You'll have even more sympathy for the Cathars after touring Carcassonne's torture chamber, worth a look only if you've got the time and money to burn (40F, children-20F, daily 10:00–20:00 June–November, 9 rue St. Jean, to the right of the main drag as you enter La Cité, ticket gets you free entry to "The Middle Ages in La Cité.").

"The Middle Ages in La Cité"—This is another entrepreneurial "museum," with five rooms of costumes trying to re-create life in old Carcassonne (40F, children-20F, free with ticket from "Exposition Torture," daily 10:00–18:00, decent English explanations). It's worthwhile only for kids.

Canal du Midi—Completed in 1681, this sleepy 150-mile canal connects France's Mediterranean and Atlantic coasts. Before railways, the Canal du Midi was jammed with commercial traffic. Today it's busy with pleasure craft. Look for the slow-moving hotel barges strewn with tanned, well-fed, and well-watered vacationers. The towpath that spans the length of the canal makes for ideal biking. The canal runs right in front of the train station in Carcassonne.

Sleeping in Carcassonne
(5.5F = about $1, zip code: 11000)

Sleeping in Carcassonne's La Cité
Ideally, sleep in La Cité. Three hotels (**Hôtel de la Cité** is a four-star budget-breaker) and a great hostel offer rooms inside the walls. The obligatory half-pension doesn't seem to exist in Carcassonne, and except for the mid-July to mid-August peak of high season, there are plenty of rooms.

Hôtel des Remparts**, right by the castle, has a 12th-century staircase leading to modern rooms with saggy beds (Db-300–330F, Tb-480F, parking-25F, CC:VM, 5 place de Grands-Puits, tel. 04 68 71 27 72, fax 04 68 72 73 26, grumpy, unpredictable management, Christian and son Jean-Pierre SE a little, Jeanine NSE).

The *chambre d'hôte* across from the Hôtel des Remparts (inquire in the Brocante shop) rents two huge apartment-like rooms that could sleep five, with kitchenette and private *terasse* (Db/Tb-290F, 360F family deals, stocked fridge and self-serve breakfast included, tel. & fax 04 68 25 16 67).

The **Auberge de Jeunesse** (youth hostel) is clean and well-run, with an outdoor garden courtyard, self-service kitchen, TV room, bar, video games, and a welcoming ambience. If you ever wanted to bunk down in a hostel, do it here. Only July is tight. Nonmembers pay 20F extra (70F per bed with breakfast, 15F for a sheet, two doubles, a few quads, otherwise six to a room, open all day, closes at 1:00, rue de Vicomte Trencavel, tel. 04 68 25 23 16, fax 04 68 71 14 84).

Best Western's **Hotel Le Donjon***** offers small but well-appointed rooms at inflated prices, a comfortable lobby, and a great location inside the walls (Sb-325–400F, Db-400–500F, Tb-410–580F, CC:VMA, tel. 04 68 71 08 80, fax 04 68 25 06 60, e-mail: hotel.donjon.best.western@wanadoo.fr).

Sleeping near La Cité

Hôtel Montmorency**, 100 yards away from La Cité's drawbridge, is a Santa Fe–style place sporting a pool with a fortress view (Sb-220F, Db with shower-260–300F, Db with tub-350–450F, Tb-500F, Qb-500F, free parking, CC:VMA, 2 rue Camille St. Saens, tel. 04 68 25 19 92, fax 04 68 25 43 15, SE).

Just down from the Hotel Montmorency, the modern and predictable **Hotel Clarine***** is a good three-star value for drivers, with small but comfortable rooms and a pool (Db-320–470F, air-conditioning, CC:VMA, 15 rue Montee Combeleran, tel. 04 68 47 16 31, fax 04 68 47 33 53).

Hôtel Espace Cité**, just downhill from Hotel Clarine, is sterile and modern but a good two-star value for drivers (Db-300F, Tb-350F, Qb-400F, small rooms, CC:VMA, 132 rue Trivalle, tel. 04 68 25 24 24, fax 04 68 25 17 17).

Hôtel du Pont Vieux** is a 10-minute walk from La Cité. This Old World hotel offers spacious rooms around a garden courtyard, 30F garage parking, and a third-floor three-person suite (#19) that opens out onto a private terrace with a five-star view of La Cité (Db-250–320F, Tb-400F, Qb-400F, CC:VM, 32 rue Trivalle, tel. 04 68 25 24 99, fax 04 68 47 62 71).

Train travelers will appreciate the spotless, dirt-cheap **Hôtel Astoria*** (S-100F, D-120F, Db-175F, Ts-180–200F, Qs-240F, near the station at 18 rue Tourtel, tel. 04 68 25 31 38, fax 04 68 71 34 14, SE).

Sleeping near Carcassonne in Caunes-Minervois

If competing tourists make you ancy, sleep 15 minutes from Carcassonne in the unspoiled wine village of Caunes-Minervois (zip code: 11600). These two great places sit side by side in the heart of the village. Ex-pat Americans Tony and Lois Link take care of your every need at **L'Ancienne Boulangerie** (Db-250F, tel. 04 68 78 01 32). **Hotel d'Alibert****, a wonderful Old World place, is run by Frederic with relaxed panache (large Db-250F, Tb-300F, tel. 04 68 78 00 54). Don't skip a meal in his terrific restaurant (*menus* from 75F).

Eating in La Cité
Other than the touristy joints lining the main drag, prices and quality seem about the same everywhere. Dine with Jacques Brel at **L'Auberge du Grand Puits** (70F for a hearty *salade Cathar* and *cassoulet* with dessert, next to Hôtel des Remparts, tel. 04 68 71 27 88). For good *cassoulet*, try **La Table Ronde** (80F *menu*, 30 rue du Plô, tel. 04 68 47 38 21). For a bit more money, enjoy the fine regional cuisine in an elegant setting at **l'Ecu d'Or** (*menus* from 120F, tel. 04 68 25 49 03), across from the Hôtel Donjon. True gourmets enjoy a splurge at the country-posh **Auberge du Pont Levi** (off the main parking lot just outside the walls, tel. 04 68 25 55 23).

Picnics can be gathered at the small *alimentation* on the main drag (generally open until 20:30). For your beggar's banquet, picnic on the city walls. For fast, cheap, hot food, look for places on the main drag with quiche and pizza to go.

Transportation Connections—Carcassonne
By train to: Sarlat (5/day, 6 hrs, transfer at Bordeaux's St. Jean station), **Arles** (8/day, 3 hrs, a few are direct, but most require a transfer in Narbonne), **Nice** (6.5 hrs, several direct, or transfer in Narbonne and Marseille), **Paris'** Gare Montparnasse (6.5 hrs by TGV via Toulouse; additional transfer possible in Bordeaux), **Toulouse** (hrly, 1 hr), **Barcelona** (3/day, 5 hrs, transfer in Narbonne and Port Bou, the border town).

COLLIOURE
Collioure, while surrounded by unappealing resorts, is blessed with an ideal climate and a romantic setting. By Mediterranean standards this seaside village should be overrun—it has everything. Like an ice-cream shop, Collioure offers 31 flavors of pastel houses and six petite scooped-out beaches sprinkled lightly with beach-goers. This sweet scene, capped by a winking lighthouse, sits under a once-mighty castle in the shade of the Pyrénées.

Come here to unwind and do nothing. Even with its crowds of French vacationers in peak season, Collioure is what many are looking for when heading to the Riviera—a sunny, peaceful vacation from their vacation.

Tourist Information: The TI is at place du 18 Juin (Monday–Saturday 9:00–19:00 and Sunday 10:00–12:00 and 15:00–18:00 in summer only, weekdays 9:30–12:00 and 14:00–18:00 rest of the year, tel. 04 68 82 15 47).

Car Rental: Try the Garage Renault (tel. 04 68 82 08 34).

Sights—Collioure

Check your ambition at the station. Slow down, enjoy a slow coffee at a beachfront café, snuggle into the sand, and lose yourself in the old city's narrow, hilly streets. The 800-year-old **Château Royal** (great ramparts, fine views, and a mildly interesting exhibit on the local history) and waterfront church **Notre Dame des Anges** are worth a look. Consider a **Promenade sur Mer** motorboat excursion (one or three hours, the longer trip is better, boats depart from the breakwater near the château).

Sleeping and Eating in Collioure
(5.5 F = about $1, zip code: 66190)

Stay in the old city, tucked behind the castle. You'll find several *chambres d'hôte* (the TI has a list), such as the clean and comfortable rooms at Monsieur *et* Madame Peroneille's **Chambres** (Db-260F, Tb-360F, Qb-410F, thin walls, 20 rue Pasteur, tel. 04 68 82 15 31, fax 04 68 82 35 94). The Spanish-feeling **Hôtel Templiers** has an easygoing staff and rents creatively decorated rooms (some with views) with wall-to-wall art (Db-335–410F, 12 avenue l'Amiraute, tel. 04 68 98 31 10, fax 04 68 98 01 24). **Hôtel Triton**, just off the main drag across from the old city, but still on the bay, offers just-remodeled rooms at fair rates (Ds-190F, Db-300F, verify prices first, rue Jean Bart, tel. 04 68 98 39 39, fax 04 68 82 11 32). Collioure's best splurge is the Mediterranean-elegant **Casa Pairal*****, with delightful rooms surrounding a garden courtyard—and all the comforts (Db-390–750F, impasse Palmiers, tel. 04 68 82 05 81, fax 04 68 82 52 10). **Le Petit Jardin** has good food (18 rue Vauban, off l'Amiraute).

Transportation Connections—Collioure

By train to: Carcassonne (10/day, 2 hrs, via Narbonne), **Paris** (1/day direct to Gare d'Austerlitz, 10 hrs; or, even better, transfer at Narbonne and Toulouse to TGV and zip into Gare Montparnasse), **Barcelona** (5/day, 3 hrs), **Avignon/Arles** (12/day, 3 hrs, transfer in Perpignan).

Sights—Languedoc

These sights are worth a visit only if you're driving.

▲▲▲**Chateaus of Hautes Corbières**—Two hours south of Carcassonne, toward the boring little country of Andorra, in the scenic foothills of the Pyrénées, lies a series of surreal, mountain-capping castle ruins. The Maginot Line of the 13th century, these sky-high castles were strategically located between France and the Spanish kingdom of Roussillon. As you can see by flipping through the picture books in Carcassonne tourist shops, these castles' crumpled ruins are an impressive contrast to the restored walls of Carcassonne. Bring a good map (lots of tiny roads) and sturdy walking shoes.

The most spectacular is the château of **Peyrepertuse.** The ruins seem to grow right out of a narrow splinter of cliff. The views are sensational—you can almost reach out and touch Spain. Let your imagination soar, but watch your step as you try to reconstruct this eagle's nest (20F, 10:00–sunset all year, tel. 04 68 45 40 55).

Nearby, **Queribus** (20F) is also impressive and is famous as the last Cathar castle to fall. It was left useless when the border between France and Spain was moved (in 1659) farther south into the high Pyrénées.

▲**Châteaus of Lastours**—Ten miles north of Carcassonne (forget public transportation), these five side-by-side ruined hilltop castles offer drivers the most accessible look at the region's Cathar castles and an ideal picnic site. From Carcassonne follow signs to Conques, then Lastours. In Lastours follow signs to the Bellevedere for a panorama overlooking the five castles. The small fee also allows you to hike up to the castles (park back down the hill). It's steep but worthwhile if it's not too hot.

▲**Minerve**—A one-time Cathar hideout, Minerve is remarkably situated in the middle of a deep canyon that provided a natural defense. Strong as it was, it didn't keep out the pope's army. The entire village was destroyed and all residents killed during the Albigensian Crusades. An interesting path leads down to the river and around the village. There are two pleasant cafés, one hotel, an interesting museum of prehistory—and not much more—in Minerve.

Minerve, between Carcassonne and Beziers, is 15 kilometers east of Olonzac (40 minutes by car from Carcassonne). It makes an ideal stop between Provence and Carcassonne. In the mood for wine-tasting? The friendly (and French-only) Remaurys offer an excellent selection and a beautiful setting in which to sample the local product. Just over the hill from Minerve, toward Carcassonne and past Azillanet, you'll see the signs to the **Domaine de Pech d'Andre** (tel. 04 68 91 22 66).

Sleeping and eating in Minerve: If you're tired of competing with tourists, stay here and melt into southern France. Sleep and eat at the friendly and cozy **Relais Chantovent** (Sb-180F, Db-225–260F, Tb-260F, Qb-290F, ask for the new rooms, zip code: 34210, tel. 04 68 91 14 18, fax 04 68 91 81 99). People travel great distances to dine at their moderately-priced restaurant (closed Sunday and Monday), so reserve early.

PROVENCE

This magnificent region is shaped like a wedge of quiche. From its sunburnt crust fanning out along the Mediterranean coast from Nîmes to Nice, it stretches north along the Rhône Valley to Orange. The Romans were here in force and left many ruins—some of the best anywhere. Seven popes; great artists such as van Gogh, Cézanne, and Picasso; and author Peter Mayle all enjoyed their years in Provence. Provence offers a splendid recipe of arid climate (but brutal winds known as the mistral), captivating cities, exciting hill towns, and remarkably varied landscapes.

Wander through the ghost town of ancient Les Baux and under France's greatest Roman ruin, the Pont du Gard. Spend your starry, starry nights where van Gogh did, in Arles. Explore its Roman past, then find the linger-longer squares and café corners that inspired Vincent. Some may prefer Avignon's more elegant feel and softer edge as a home base. Youthful but classy Avignon bustles in the shadow of its brooding popes' palace. It's a short hop from Arles or Avignon into the splendid scenery and villages of the Côtes du Rhône and Luberon regions that make Provence so popular today.

Planning Your Time

Make Arles or Avignon your base (Italophiles prefer Arles, while poodles pick Avignon) and, if driving, consider basing in Isle sur la Sorgue. Avignon (well-connected to Arles by train) is the regional transportation hub for destinations north of Arles: Pont du Gard, Uzès, Orange, and Isle sur la Sorgue. You'll want a full day for sightseeing in Arles (ideally on a Wednesday or Saturday, when the morning market rages), a half day for Avignon, and a day or

Provence

two for the villages and sights in the countryside. To best feel the endearing pulse of Provence, get out of the city and spend a night in a Provençale village (as described below).

Provence Market Days

Provençal market days offer France's most colorful and tantalizing outdoor shopping. Here's a list to help plan your excursions.

Monday: Cadenet (near Vaison la Romaine), Cavaillon
Tuesday: Avignon, Tarascon, Gordes, Vaison la Romaine, Beaumes de Venise
Wednesday: Arles, Avignon, St. Remy, Violes (near Vaison la Romaine)
Thursday: Carianne (near Vaison la Romaine), Nyons, Orange, Avignon, Beaucaire, Vacqueyras, Isle sur la Sorgue
Friday: Remoulins (Pont du Gard), Carpentras, Bonnieux, Visan, Châteauneuf-du-Pape
Saturday: Arles, Avignon, Oppède, Valreas
Sunday: Avignon, Isle sur la Sorgue, Uzès, Coustelet, Beaucaire

Getting Around Provence

The yellow Michelin map to this region is essential for drivers.
Public transit is fairly good: frequent trains link Avignon, Arles,
and Nîmes; Les Baux is accessible by bus from Arles; and the Pont
du Gard and Uzès are accessible by bus from Avignon. The TIs in
Arles and Avignon have information on bus excursions to regional
sights that are hard to reach *sans* car (95F half-day, 150F all-day).
While a tour of the villages of Luberon is worthwhile only by car,
Isle sur la Sorgue is an easy hop by train from Avignon, and several villages of the Luberon can be reached by bus.

Cuisine Scene—Provence

The almost extravagant use of garlic, olive oil, herbs, and tomatoes
makes Provence's cuisine France's liveliest. To sample it, order
anything *à la Provençale*. Among the area's spicy specialties are
ratatouille (a thick mixture of vegetables in an herb-flavored
tomato sauce), *brandade* (a salt cod, garlic, and cream mousse), aioli
(a garlicky mayonnaise often served atop fresh vegetables), *tapenade*
(a sauce of puréed olives, anchovies, tuna, and herbs), *soupe au pis-
tou* (vegetable soup with basil, garlic, and cheese), and *soupe à l'ail*
(garlic soup). Look also for *riz Camarguaise* (rice from the Camargue) and *taureau* (bull meat). Banon (wrapped in chestnut leaves)
and Picodon (nutty taste) are the native cheeses. Provence also
produces some of France's great wines at relatively reasonable
prices. Look for Gigondas, Sablet, Côte du Rhône, and Côte de
Provence. If you like rosé, try the Tavel. This is the place to
splurge for a bottle of Châteauneuf-du-Pape.

ARLES

By helping Julius Caesar defeat Marseille, Arles earned the imperial nod and was made an important port city. With the first bridge
over the Rhône, Arles was a key stop on the Roman road from
Italy to Spain, the Via Domitia. After reigning as a political center
of the early Christian church (the seat of an archbishop for centuries) and thriving as a trading city on and off until the 18th century, Arles all but disappeared from the map. Van Gogh settled
here a hundred years ago but left only memories. American
bombers destroyed much of Arles in World War II, but today
Arles thrives again. Today this compact city is alive with great
Roman ruins, some fine early-Christian art, an eclectic assortment
of museums, made-for-ice-cream pedestrian zones, squares that
play hide-and-seek with visitors, and too many cars. Arles is a fine
springboard for Provence explorations.

Tourist Information: Arles has two TIs. The one at the
train station is relaxed and easy by car (Monday–Saturday
9:00–13:00 and 14:00–18:00, closed Sunday). The main TI on
esplanade Charles de Gaulle is a high-powered mega-information

site (Monday–Saturday 9:00–19:00, Sunday 9:00–13:00 April 1–
September 30; closed 12:00–14:00 and at 18:00 off-season; tel. 04
90 18 41 20). Pick up the free *Arles et Vincent Van Gogh* and the
Guide Touristique 1999, and ask about bullfights and bus excursions
to regional sights.

Supermarket: Place Lamartine has a big handy Monoprix
supermarket/department store (Monday–Saturday 8:30–19:25,
closed Sunday).

Banks: Several banks change money on place de la
République, across from St. Trophime.

Laundry: A Laundromat is at 12 rue Portagnel (Monday–
Saturday 8:00–12:00 and 14:00–19:00). Another, nearby on 6 rue
Cavalarie (near place Voltaire, daily 7:00–21:00, later once you're
in), has a confusing central command panel: 20F for wash (push
machine number on top row), 10F for 25 minutes of dryer (push
dryer number on third row five times slowly), 2F for flakes (button
#11). Dine at the recommended La Giraudiere restaurant, one
block away, while you clean.

Arrival in Arles

By Train and Bus: Both stations sit side by side on the river, a
10-minute walk from the city center. To reach the old town, walk
to the river and turn left.

By Car: Follow signs to *centre-ville*, then be on the lookout
for signs to the *gare SNCF* (the train station; go there for the TI).
You'll come to a huge roundabout (place Lamartine) with a
Monoprix department store to the right. There is parking on the
left, along the base of the wall. Pay attention to no-parking signs
on Wednesday and Saturday until 13:00—they mean it. Theft is a
problem; park at your hotel if possible. Take everything out of
your car for safety. From place Lamartine, walk into the city
through the two stumpy towers.

Getting Around Arles

Arles faces the Mediterranean more than Paris. Its spaghetti
streetplan disorients the first-time visitor. Landmarks hide in the
medieval tangle of narrow, winding streets. Everything is decep-
tively close. While Arles sits on the Rhône, it completely ignores
the river. The elevated riverside walk does provide a direct route
to the excellent ancient history museum and an easy return to the
station. Hotels have free city maps, but Arles works best if you
simply follow the numerous street-corner signs pointing you
toward the sights and hotels of the town center. Racing cars seem
to enjoy Arles' medieval lanes, turning sidewalks into tightropes
and pedestrians into leaping targets.

By Minibus: The free "Starlette" shuttle minibus, which cir-
cles the town's major sights twice an hour, is worthwhile only to

get to or from the distant ancient history museum, though I prefer the 20-minute walk along the river (just wave at the driver and hop in; Monday–Saturday 7:30–19:30, never on Sunday).

By Bike and Car: The Peugeot store rents bikes (15 rue du Pont, tel. 04 90 96 03 77) as does the newsstand next to the main TI (tel. 04 90 96 44 20). You can rent cars at Avis (at the train station, tel. 04 90 96 82 42) and Europcar (downtown at 15 boulevard Victor Hugo, tel. 04 90 93 23 24).

By Taxi: Arles' taxis charge a minimum flat 50F fee. Nothing in town is worth a taxi ride (figure 100F to Les Baux).

Sights—Arles

Arles' *Global Billet* covers all the sights (55F, sold at each sight). Otherwise, it's 15F per sight and museum (35F for the ancient history museum). While any sight is worth a few minutes of your time, many aren't worth the individual admission. For the small price of a *Global Billet*, the city is yours. (All sights except the Arlatan folk museum are open June 1–September 15 9:00–19:00; April, May, and September 16–30 9:00–12:30 and 14:00–19:00; otherwise 10:00–12:30 and 14:00–17:30; closed one hour earlier in winter.) See the Musée Arlatan listing, below, for its hours. The excellent and free *Arles et Vincent Van Gogh* brochure (available at the TI) takes you on several interesting walks through Arles using pavement markers as guides; by far the most interesting walk follows the footsteps of Vincent van Gogh.

▲▲**Place du Forum**—This café-crammed square, while always lively, is best at night. Named for the Roman Forum that stood here, only two columns from a second-century temple survive. They are incorporated into the wall of the Hotel Nord Pinus. (After a few drinks at the Café van Gogh, the corner of that hotel actually starts to look phallic.) Van Gogh hung out here under these same plane trees. In fact, his *Starry Starry Night* was painted from this square. The bistros on the square, while no place for a fine dinner, put together a good salad, and when you sprinkle in the ambience, that's 45F well spent. The guy on the pedestal is Frederic Mistral; in 1904 he received the Nobel Prize for literature. He used his prize money to preserve and display the folk identity of Provence at a time when France was rapidly centralizing. (He founded the Arlatan museum—see below.)

▲▲**Wednesday and Saturday Markets**—On these days until around noon, Arles' ring road (boulevard Emile Combes on Wednesday, boulevard Lices on Saturday) erupts into an outdoor market of fish, flowers, produce, and you-name-it. Join in, buy flowers, try the olives, sample some wine, and slap a pickpocket. On the first Wednesday of the month it's a grand flea market.

▲▲▲**Ancient History Museum (Musée de L'Arles Antique)**—The sights of Roman Arles make maximum sense if you start your

Arles

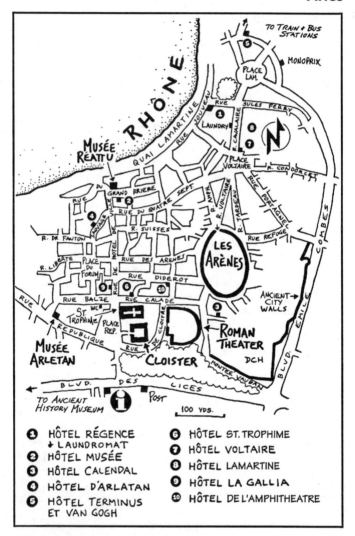

❶	HÔTEL RÉGENCE + LAUNDROMAT	❻	HÔTEL ST. TROPHIME
❷	HÔTEL MUSÉE	❼	HÔTEL VOLTAIRE
❸	HÔTEL CALENDAL	❽	HÔTEL LAMARTINE
❹	HÔTEL D'ARLATAN	❾	HÔTEL LA GALLIA
❺	HÔTEL TERMINUS ET VAN GOGH	❿	HÔTEL DE L'AMPHITHEATRE

visit in this superb, air-conditioned museum. Models and original sculpture (with the help of the free English handout) re-create the Roman city of Arles, making workaday life and culture easier to imagine. Notice what a radical improvement the Roman buildings were over the simple mud-brick homes of pre-Roman peoples.

Models of Arles' arena even illustrate the movable stadium cover, good for shade and rain. While virtually nothing is left of Arles' chariot racecourse, the model shows how it must have rivaled Rome's Circus Maximus. Jewelry, fine metal and glass artifacts, and fine mosaic floors make it clear that Roman Arles was a city of art and culture. The finale is an impressive row of pagan and early Christian sarcophagi (second to fifth centuries). In the early days of the Church, Jesus was often portrayed beardless and as the good shepherd—with a lamb over his shoulder.

Built at the site of the chariot racecourse, this museum is a 20-minute walk from Arles along the river. Turn left at the river and follow it to the big modern building just past the new bridge—or ride the free Starlette shuttle bus. (35F, daily 9:00–19:00 April–September, otherwise Wednesday–Monday 10:00–18:00 and closed Tuesday, tel. 04 90 18 88 88.)

▲▲**Roman Arena (Amphithéâtre)**—Nearly 2,000 years ago, gladiators fought wild animals here to the delight of 20,000 screaming fans—cruel. Today matadors fight wild bulls to the delight of local fans—still cruel. While the ancient third row of arches is long gone, three towers survive from medieval times, when the arena was used as a fortress. In the 1800s it corralled 200 humble homes and functioned as a town within the town. Today modern gladiators fight bulls, and if you don't mind the gore, it's an exciting show. Climb the tower. Walk through the inner corridors of this 440-by-350-foot oval and notice the similarity to 20th-century stadium floor plans.

▲▲**Bullfights (Courses Camarguaise)**—Occupy the same seats fans have been sitting in for 1,900 years, and take in one of Arles' most memorable treats—a bullfight *à la Provençale*. Three classes of bullfights take place here. The *course protection* is for aspiring matadors; it's a daring dodge-bull game of scraping hair off the angry bull's nose for prize money offered by local businesses (no blood). The *trophée de l'avenir* is the next class, with amateur matadors. The *trophée des as excellence* is the real thing *à la* Spain: outfits, swords, spikes, and the whole gory shebang (tickets 30–50F; Saturday, Sunday, and holidays April–early October; skip the "rodeo" spectacle; tel. 04 90 96 03 70 or ask at TI). There are nearby village bullfights in small wooden bullrings nearly every weekend (TI has schedule).

Classical Theater (Théâtre Antique)—Precious little survives from this Roman theater, which served as a handy town quarry throughout the Middle Ages. Two lonely Corinthian columns look from the stage out over the audience. The 10,000 mostly modern seats are still used for local concerts and festivals. Take a stroll backstage through broken bits of Rome.

▲▲**St. Trophime Cloisters and Church**—This church, named after a third-century bishop of Arles, sports the finest Romanesque west portal (main doorway) I've seen anywhere.

But first enjoy the place de la République. Sit on the steps opposite the church. The Egyptian obelisk used to be the centerpiece of Arles' Roman Circus. Watch the peasants—pilgrims, locals, buskers—nothing new about this scene. Like a Roman triumphal arch, the church trumpets the promise of Judgment Day. The tympanum is filled with Christian symbolism. Christ sits in majesty surrounded by symbols of the four evangelists (Matthew—the winged man, Mark—the winged lion, Luke—the ox, and John—the eagle). The 12 apostles are lined up below Jesus. Move up closer. This is it. Some are saved and others aren't. Notice the condemned—a chain gang on the right bunny-hopping over the fires of hell. For them the tune trumpeted by the three angels on the very top isn't a happy one. Ride the exquisite detail back to a simpler age. In an illiterate medieval world long before the vivid images of our Technicolor age, this message was a neon billboard over this town's everything square. A chart just inside the church (on the right) helps explain the carvings. On the right side of the nave, a fourth-century early-Christian sarcophagus is used as an altar.

The adjacent cloisters are the best in Provence (15F, enter from the square, 20 meters to the right of the church). Enjoy the sculpted capitals of the rounded Romanesque columns (12th century) and the pointed Gothic columns (14th century). The second floor offers only a view of the cloisters from above.

Musée Réattu—Highlights of this mildly interesting museum are a fun collection of 70 Picasso drawings (some two-sided, and all done in a flurry of creativity) and a room of Henri Rousseau's Camargue watercolors.

▲**Musée Arlatan**—This cluttered folklore museum, given to Arles by Monsieur Mistral, is filled with interesting odds and ends of Provence life. The employees wear the native costumes. It's like a failed turn-of-the-century garage sale: You'll find shoes, hats, wigs, old photos, bread cupboards, and the beetle-dragon monster. If you're into folklore, this museum is for you (daily 9:00–12:00 and 14:00–19:00 April–September, otherwise closes at 17:00).

Fondation Van Gogh—A two-star sight for his fans, this small gallery features works by several well-known contemporary artists who pay homage to Vincent through their thought-provoking interpretations of his art (30F, daily 10:00–19:00 April 1–September 30, otherwise 10:00–12:30 and 14:00–17:00; facing the Roman arena at #24).

Sleeping in Arles
(5.5F = about $1, zip code: 13200)
Sleep Code: **S** = Single, **D** = Double/Twin, **T** = Triple, **Q** = Quad, **b** = bathroom, **t** = toilet only, **s** = shower only, **CC** = Credit Card (**V**isa, **M**asterCard, **A**mex), **SE** = Speaks English, **NSE** = No English, * = French hotel rating system (0–4 stars).

Hôtel Régence** sits right on the river with immaculate and comfortable rooms, good beds, and easy access to the train station and safe parking. Helpful and gentle Sylvie speaks English (one Ds-150–180F, Db-200–280F, Tb-250–335F, Qb-330F; choose river view or quiet, air-conditioned courtyard rooms; CC:VM, 5 rue Marius Jouveau—from place Lamartine turn right immediately after passing through the towers; tel. 04 90 96 39 85, fax 04 90 96 67 64).

Hotel de l'Amphitheatre** is small, friendly, and *très* cozy with thoughtfully decorated and air-conditioned rooms and a pleasant atrium breakfast room. It's located one block from the arena on a relatively quiet street (Db-290–350F, Tb-420F, 25F garage, CC:VMA, 5 rue Diderot, tel. 04 90 96 10 30, fax 04 90 93 98 69, SE).

Hôtel du Musée** is a quiet, delightful manor house hideaway with air-conditioned rooms and a terrific courtyard terrace. Its friendly owners, M. and Mme. Dubreuil, speak some English (Sb-220F, Db-280–320F, Tb-350–400F, Qb-450F, parking-40F, mostly air-conditioned rooms, CC:VMA, 11 rue de la Grande Prieure, follow signs to Musée Réattu, tel. 04 90 93 88 88, fax 04 90 49 98 15).

Hôtel Calendal** is *très Provençale*, with a tranquil outdoor garden, smartly decorated rooms, and three-star ambience for the price of two (Db-260–460F, Tb-380–470F, Qb-490F, garage-50F, air-conditioned rooms with strong beds and modern bathrooms, CC:VMA, located above the arena at 22 place Pomme, tel. 04 90 96 11 89, fax 04 90 96 05 84, SE).

Hôtel d'Arlatan***, one of France's more affordable classy hotels, comes with a beautiful lobby, courtyard terrace, and air-conditioned, antique-filled rooms. In the lobby of this 15th-century building, a glass floor looks down into Roman ruins (Db-460–800F, Db/suites-1,000–1,400F, garage-70F, elevator, very central, CC:VMA, a block off the place du Forum at 26 rue du Sauvage, tel. 04 90 93 56 66, fax 04 90 49 68 45, e-mail: info@hotel-arlatan.fr, SE).

Hotel Terminus et Van Gogh* has bright, cheery rooms facing a busy square at the gate of the old town a block from the train station. English-speaking Joelle proudly posts photos and pictures showing that her building is in the painting of van Gogh's house, which was bombed in WWII (D-145F with no shower available, Ds-180F, Db-220F, CC:VM, 5 place Lamartine, tel. & fax 04 90 96 12 32).

Hotel St. Trophime** is another fine, very central place with a grand entry, large rooms, and helpful owners (Sb-210F, Db-290–320F, CC:VM, 16 rue de la Calade, near the place de la Republique, tel. 04 90 96 88 38, fax 04 90 96 92 19).

Starving artists can afford these two clean but spartan places: **Hôtel Voltaire*** rents 12 dumpy rooms with great balconies overlooking a caffeine-stained square a block below the arena (D-120–130F, Ds-140F, add 40F per person for three or four, CC:VM, 1 place Voltaire, tel. 04 90 96 13 58). **Hôtel La Gallia** is another sleepable cheapie (Ds-125–145F, above a friendly café, 22 rue de l'Hôtel de Ville, tel. 04 90 96 00 63).

Sleeping near Arles in Fontvielle

Many drivers prefer setting up in the peaceful village of Fontvielle, just 10 minutes from Arles and Les Baux. For weekly rentals at a farmhouse just outside Arles, contact English-speaking Sylvie at the **Domaine de la Foret**. She offers several comfortable two-bedroom apartments with a family-friendly feel (nightly/450F, weekly in summer-2,500F, weekly off-season-2,000F, D-82 route de L'Agueduc, 13990 Fontvielle, tel. 04 90 54 70 25, fax 04 90 54 60 50).

Eating in Arles

On place du Forum the **Le Bistro Arlesien**, **Le Pub** (good 45F *salade niçoise*), and **L'Estaminet** serve basic food with great atmosphere. **L'Olivier** offers exquisite *Provençale* cuisine (150F *menu*, near the Hotel du Musee, 1 bis rue Reattu, reserve ahead, tel. 04 90 49 64 88). For fine, reasonably priced regional cooking, head to the relaxed and friendly **La Giraudiere** (closed Tuesday, 85F *menu*, 55 rue Condorcet on place Voltaire, tel. 04 90 93 27 52). Vegetarians love **La Vitamine**'s salads and pastas (closed weekends, just below place du Forum on 16 rue Dr. Fanton, tel. 04 90 93 77 36). Almost next door, **La Paillotte** specializes in tradional *Provençale* cuisine (90F *menu*, 28 rue Dr. Fanton). **Le Criquet** is cheap, fun, and good, one block from Hôtel Calendal at 12 Porte de Laure.

Transportation Connections—Arles

By bus to: Les Baux (4/day, 30 min; departs Arles' bus station and #16 boulevard Clemenceau in downtown Arles). Service is reduced November through March and on Sunday and holidays (tel. 04 90 49 38 01).

By train to: Paris (two direct TGVs, 4.5 hrs; otherwise, transfer in Avignon, 8/day, 5.5 hrs), **Avignon** (8/day, 20 min, check for afternoon gaps), **Carcassonne** (8/day, 3 hrs, usually with painless transfer in Narbonne), **Beaune** (3/day, 5 hrs, transfer in Lyon), **Nice** (8/day, 3 hrs, likely transfer in Marseille), **Barcelona** (3/day, 7 hrs, at least one transfer), **Italy** (3/day, via Marseille and Nice; from Arles it's 5 hrs to Ventimiglia on the border, 9 hrs to the Cinque Terre, 9 hrs to Milan, 11 hrs to Florence, 13 hrs to Venice or Rome). Train info: tel. 04 90 96 43 94.

AVIGNON

Famous for its nursery rhyme, medieval bridge, and brooding Palace of the Popes, contemporary Avignon bustles and prospers behind its walls. During the 68 years (1309–1377) that Avignon played Franco Vaticano, it grew from an irrelevant speck on the map to the thriving city it still is. Today this city combines a young, hip student population with a white-collar, sophisticated city feel. Street mimes play to crowds enjoying Avignon's slick cafés and chic boutiques. If you're here any time in July, save evening time for Avignon's rollicking theater festival and reserve your hotel early. The streets throng with jugglers, skits, and singing, as visitors from around the world converge on Avignon.

The cours Jean Jaurés (which turns into the rue de la République) leads from the train station to place de l'Horloge and the Palace of the Popes, forming Avignon's spine. Climb to the parc de Rochers des Doms for a fine view, enjoy the people scene on place de l'Horloge, and meander the back streets. Avignon's shopping district fills the pedestrian streets where rue de la République meets the place de l'Horloge. Walk across the Pont Daladier (bridge) for a great view back on Avignon and the Rhône River.

Tourist Information: The main TI is between the train station and the old town at 41 cours Jean Juarés (Monday–Friday 9:00–18:00, Saturday 9:00–12:00 and 14:00–17:00, tel. 04 90 82 65 11, e-mail: information@avignon.fr), while a smaller branch is just inside the city wall at the entrance to Pont St. Bénezet (same hours as main TI). They have regional bus and train schedules and information on Isle sur la Sorgue and the wine villages north of Avignon and the Luberon.

Arrival in Avignon
By Train: In front of the bus or train station, the main drag—the cours Jean Juarés that becomes rue de la République—leads into the old city center (20-minute walk, TI on right in a few blocks).

By Car: Drivers enter Avignon following *centre-ville* signs. Park along the wall close to the Pont St. Bénezet (ruined old bridge) and use that TI. Hotels have advice for smart overnight parking.

Sights—Avignon
▲**Palace of the Popes (Palais des Papes)**—In 1309 a French pope was elected (Pope Clement V). At the urging of the French king, His Holiness decided he'd had enough of unholy Italy. So he loaded up his carts and moved out of the chaos north to Avignon for a steady rule under a friendly, supportive king. The Catholic Church literally bought Avignon, then a two-bit town, and popes resided here until 1403. From 1378 on, there were twin popes, one in Rome and one in Avignon, causing a split in the Catholic Church that wasn't fully resolved until 1417.

The pope's palace is two distinct buildings, one old and one older. Along with lots of big, barren rooms, you'll see brilliant frescoes, enormous tapestries, and remarkable floor tiles. While scheduling your day around the English tour times (several per day) can be a hassle, guided tours can be worthwhile. (49F, includes a guided tour or a self-guided Walkman tour, occasional supplements for special exhibits, daily 9:00–19:00 April–November 1, until 20:00 summer, off-season 9:00–12:45 and 14:00–18:00, ticket office closes one hour earlier, tours in English twice daily March–October, call 04 90 27 50 74 to confirm.)

▲Musée du Petit Palais—This palace superbly displays collections of 14th- and 15th-century Italian painting and sculpture. Since the Catholic Church was the patron of the arts in those days, all 350 paintings deal with Christian themes. Visiting this museum before going to the Palace of the Popes gives you a sense of art and life during the Avignon papacy. Notice the improvement in perspective in the later paintings (30F, Wednesday–Monday 9:30–18:00 in summer, otherwise 9:30–12:00 and 14:00–18:00, closed Tuesday).

▲Parc de Rochers des Doms and Pont St. Bénezet—Hike above the Palace of the Popes for a panoramic view over Avignon and the Rhône valley. At the far end drop down a few steps for a good view of the Pont St. Bénezet. This is the famous "sur le Pont d'Avignon," whose construction and location were inspired by a shepherd's religious vision. Imagine a 22-arch, 3,000-foot-long bridge extending across two rivers to that lonely Tower of Philippe the Fair (the bridge's former tollgate on the distant side). The island the bridge spanned is now filled with campgrounds. You can pay 15F to walk along a section of the ramparts and do your own jig on the bridge (good view), but it's best appreciated from where you are. The castle on the right, the St. André Fortress, was once another island in the Rhône. Cross Daladier Bridge for the best view of the old bridge and Avignon's skyline.

Sleeping in Avignon
(5.5F = about $1, zip code: 84000)
The cozy and almost elegant **Hôtel Blauvac**** is in the pedestrian zone on 11 rue de La Bancasse (Db-335–410F, Tb/Qb-400–500F, CC:VMA, one block off rue de la République, tel. 04 90 86 34 11, fax 04 90 86 27 41). Right on the loud rue de la République at #17, the bright and cheery **Hotel Danelli**** offers modern and comfortable rooms in shiny surroundings at Parisian prices (Db-425F, Tb-460F, CC:VM, tel. 04 90 86 46 82, fax 04 90 27 09 24). **Hotel Medieval**** is good, central, and reasonable (Db-240–340F, 15 rue Petite Saunerie, tel. 04 90 86 11 06, fax 04 90 82 08 64). The clean, compact, and friendly **Hôtel Mignon*** is simpler, but a good value (Ss-150F, Db-220F, Tb-250F, 12 rue Joseph Vernet, tel. 04 90 82 17 30, fax 04 90 85 78 46). **Hôtel Splendid*** rents

firm beds near the station, on the small park near the TI (Ss-140–190F, Ds-170–220F, 17 rue Agricol Perdiguier, tel. 04 90 86 14 46, fax 04 90 85 38 55). Across the street at #17, **Hotel du Parc*** is another good value (Ds-140–170F, Db-180F, tel. 04 90 82 71 55, fax 04 90 85 64 86). For reliable, ultramodern comfort and a great location, try one of two **Hotel Mercures***** (Db-400–650F). One is just inside the walls near the Pont St. Bénezet (Quartier de la Balance, tel. 04 90 85 91 23, fax 04 90 85 32 40); the other is near the Palace of the Popes (Cité des Papes, 1 rue Jean Vilar, tel. 04 90 86 22 45, fax 04 90 27 39 21).

Transportation Connections—Avignon
By train to: Arles (8/day, 20 min), **Orange** (hrly, 15 min), **Nîmes** (hrly, 21 min), **Nice** (10/day, 4 hrs; a few direct, but most require transfer in Marseille), **Carcassonne** (10/day, 3 hrs, possible transfer in Narbonne), **Paris'** Gare de Lyon (10 TGVs/day, 4 hrs), **Barcelona** (2/day, 5 hrs, possible transfer in Narbonne; direct night train is convenient).

Bus service to **Pont du Gard** and **Uzès** (3/day, 1 hr) can leave you stranded for hours. Consider visiting the Pont du Gard, then continuing on to Uzès or Nîmes (both merit exploration) and returning to Avignon from there (trains run hourly from Nîmes to Avignon). Make sure you're waiting for the bus on the right side of the road at the Pont du Gard (ask at the small inn: "Nîmes? Uzès? Avignon? *Par ici?*"). The Avignon TI has all schedules. Service is reduced or nonexistent on Sunday and holidays. The bus station (tel. 04 90 82 07 35) is adjacent to the train station (tel. 08 36 35 35 35).

Sights—Provence
▲▲▲**Les Baux**—This rock-top ghost town is worth visiting for the lunar landscape alone. In summer, arrive by 9:00 or after 17:00 to avoid the crowds. A 12th-century regional powerhouse with 6,000 fierce residents, Les Baux was razed in 1632 by a paranoid Louis XIII, afraid of these trouble-making upstarts. What remains are a reconstructed "live city" of tourist shops and snack stands, and the "dead city" ruins carved into, out of, and on top of a 600-foot-high rock. Spend most of your time in the dead city—it's most dramatic and enjoyable in the morning or early-evening light. Don't miss the slide show on van Gogh, Gaugin, and Cézanne in the small chapel near the entry. Spend some time in the small museum as you enter (good exhibits) and pick up the English explanations before exploring the dead city. In the tourist-trampled live city, you'll find artsy shops, several interesting Renaissance homes, and a fine exhibit of paintings by Yves Brayer (20F), who spent his final years here. (Entrance to the dead city costs 35F; fee includes entry to all the town's sights; 9:00–19:00

Easter–October, until 20:00 in summer, otherwise 9:30–17:00; pick up the excellent brochure, *A Sense of Place*, at the TI, tel. 04 90 54 34 39.) To best experience the bauxite rock quarries and enjoy a great view of Les Baux, drive or hike one kilometer up D-27 and sample wines with atmosphere at the **Caves de Sarragnan** (tel. 04 90 54 33 58).

If tempted to spend the night, try the enchanting **Hotel Reine Jeanne****, 50 yards on your right after the main entry (Db-270–330F, great family suite-520F, ask for the *chambres avec terasse*, *menus* from 110F, CC:VM, 13520 Les Baux, tel. 04 90 54 32 06, fax 04 90 54 32 33). **Le Mas de L'Esparou** is a three-star *chambre d'hôte* with five rooms and a swimming pool one mile from Les Baux (Db-380F, route de St. Rémy de Provence, 13520 Les Baux, tel. 04 90 54 41 32).

Four daily buses serve Les Baux from Arles' train station, and two daily buses (summers only) leave from Avignon. Les Baux is 15 kilometers northeast of Arles, just past Fontvielle.

St. Rémy—This *très Provençale* town is a scenic ride just over the hill from Les Baux. Here you'll find the crumbled ruins of **Glanum**, a once-thriving Roman city located at the crossroads of two ancient trade routes between Italy and Spain, and the mental ward where Vincent van Gogh was sent after cutting off his ear. Glanum is just outside St. Rémy, on the road to Les Baux (D-5). Walk to the gate and peek in to get a feel for its scale. The ruins are worth the effort if you have the time and haven't been to Pompeii or Ephesus (33F, daily 9:00–12:00 and 14:00–19:00 April–September, otherwise 9:30–12:00 and 14:00–17:00). Across the street, opposite the entrance, is a Roman arch and tower. The arch marked the entry into Glanum. The tower is a memorial to the grandsons of Emperor Augustus, located there to remind folks of them when entering or leaving Glanum.

Across the street from Glanum is the still-functioning mental hospital that housed van Gogh (Clinique St. Paul). Wander into the small chapel and intimate cloisters. Vincent's favorite walks outside the hospital are clearly signposted. If St. Rémy charms you into a longer visit, sleep just outside town at the tranquil **Canto Cigalo** (Db-280–340F, chemin Canto Cigalo, tel. 04 90 92 14 28, fax 04 90 92 24 48). Wednesday is market day in St. Rémy.

▲▲▲**Pont du Gard**—One of Europe's great treats, this remarkably well-preserved Roman aqueduct was built before the time of Christ. It was the missing link of a 35-mile canal that, by dropping one foot for every 300, supplied 44 million gallons of water to Nîmes daily. While the top is now closed to daredevils, just walking under it is a marvel. Study it up close—there's no mortar, just expertly cut stones. Signs direct you to "panaromas" above the bridge on either side. The best view of the aqueduct is from the cool of the river below, floating flat on your back—bring a swimsuit and sandals for the rocks (always open and free). Consider renting a canoe from Collas to Remoulins (two-hour trip, 175F per two-person canoe; shuttle included to bus stop, car park, or Remoulins; Collas Canoes, tel. 04 66 22 85 54). Buses run from Nîmes, Uzès, or Avignon. Combine Uzès and the Pont du Gard for an ideal day excursion from Avignon. By car, the Pont du Gard is an easy 30-minute drive due west of Avignon (follow signs to Nîmes) and 45 minutes northwest of Arles (via Tarascon). Park on the *rive gauche* side (you'll see signs).

Uzès—An intriguing, less-trampled town near the Pont du Gard, Uzès is best seen slowly on foot, with a long coffee break in its mellow main square, the place aux Herbes (not so mellow during the colorful Sunday morning market). Check out the Tour Fenestrelle and the Duché de Uzès. Uzès is a short hop west (by bus) of the Pont du Gard and is well-served from Nîmes (9/day) and Avignon (3/day).

The Camargue—This is one of the few truly "wild areas" of France, where pink flamingos, wild bulls, and the famous white horses wander freely amid rice fields and lagoons. Skip it. The Camargue's biggest town is Aigue Mortes. That means "dead town," and it should stay that way.

▲▲Orange—This most northern town in Provence is notable for its Roman arch and theater. Its 60-foot-tall Roman arch (from 25 B.C.) shows off Julius Caesar's defeat of the Gauls in 49 B.C. Its best-preserved Roman theater in existence still seats 10,000. Of particular interest is its 120-foot-high stage wall, the likes of which you'll see nowhere else (34F, daily 9:00–18:30 April–early October, 9:00–12:00 and 13:30–17:00 in winter; ticket includes entrance to the city museum across the street, which has more Roman art; Orange TI tel. 04 90 34 70 88). Trains run hourly between Avignon and Orange (15 min ride; bus #2 takes you the mile from the Orange station to the old town center). From Orange drivers can tour the adjacent wine region, described below.

Villages of the Côtes du Rhône: A Loop Trip for Wine Lovers

If you have a car (or a bike, best rented in Vaison la Romaine—ideal riding from here) and a fondness for fine wine or beautiful countryside, take a loop trip through Provence's finest wine country. If possible, spend a night in one of the villages listed below. From Avignon, head to Carpentras, then connect the Côte du Rhône wine villages of Vaqueryas, Gigondas, Rasteau, Sablet, Vaison la Romaine, and adorable, if over-restored, Seguret (figure on a 100-kilometer round-trip from Avignon). This is a hospitable and relaxed wine-tasting region, with generous samples and little pressure to buy. Near Rasteau village, at Le Domaine des Girasols, friendly Francoise (SE) will take your palate on a tour of some of the area's best wine. It's well-marked and worth a stop, and while you aren't pressured to buy, their wine is a good value.

If you have extra time, consider exploring the little-traveled Dromme region just north of Vaison La Romaine. It's laced with vineyards (producing less expensive yet fine wines), lavender fields (blooms late June to mid-July), and postcard-perfect villages. From Vaison take the loop north to Visan, Valreas, Taulignan, and Nyons, then back to Vaison. Each of these villages is a detour waiting to happen. Picturesque Nyons is France's olive capital and a pleasant place to stroll, particularly on Thursday mornings (market day).

Sleeping and Eating in the Wine Country

Gigondas: Ideally, have lunch in the trendy town of Gigondas at the outdoor restaurant on the small town square. It's in the very comfortable **Hostellerie les Florets*****. Consider sleeping here, too (Db-410F, remarkable restaurant, *menus* from 120F, 84190 Gigondas, tel. 04 90 65 85 01, fax 04 90 65 83 80).

Sablet: The nearby wine village of Sablet, which makes a good base for budget travelers, is chock-full of *chambres d'hôte* (try **Madame Fert's Chambres**, Db-300F, breakfast included, follow the signs, tel. & fax 04 90 46 94 77).

Vaison la Romaine: If you're *sans* car or need a larger town, stay in Vaison la Romaine, where you get two villages for the price of one. Vaison's "modern" lower city is like a mini-Arles with impressive Roman ruins and a *très Provençale* pedestrian street; the medieval hill town (Ville-Haute) overlooks the lower city from across the river with meandering cobbled lanes, art galleries, tranquil cafés, and a ruined castle. The excellent **TI** is in the lower city across from the Roman ruins and the main parking lot at place de Chanoine Sautel (tel. 04 90 36 02 11). **Hotel Burrhus**** is easily the best value in the lower city, and is right in the thick of things on the raucous place Montfort (ask for a room off the square if you want to sleep, Db-320F, tel. 04 90 36 00 11, fax 04 90 36 39 05). The Ville-Haute offers Vaison's quieter and more costly accommodations. You'll sleep and dine like royalty at **Hotel Beffroi***** (Db-470–660F, rue de l'Eveche, tel. 04 90 36 04 71, fax 04 90 36 24 78). **La Bartavelle** is the place to savor a slow meal in the lower town (145F *menu*, 12 place sus-Auze). The Ville-Haute has a crêperie and pizzeria with fair prices. Surrounded by vineyards just outside town, **Château Taulignan**'s *chambres d'hôte* offer a dreamy setting from which to contemplate this beautiful region (Db-450–550F, 84110 St. Marcellin, tel. 04 90 28 71 16, fax 04 90 28 75 84).

The best view in Provence might well be from the **Restaurant Le Panorama** (98F *menu*, or simple *á la carte*, in tiny Le Crestet, a five-minute drive from Vaison la Romaine, call ahead, tel. 04 90 28 86 62).

NOT QUITE A YEAR IN PROVENCE—THE HILL TOWNS OF LUBERON

The Luberon region, stretching 30 miles along a ridge of rugged hills east of Avignon, hides some of France's most appealing hill towns. Bonnieux, Lacoste, Oppède le Vieux, Roussillon, and the very-discovered (and overpriced) Gordes, to mention a few, are quintessential Provençal hill towns.

Those intrigued by Peter Mayle's *A Year in Provence* will enjoy a day joyriding through the region. Mayle's bestselling book describes the ruddy local culture from an Englishman's perspective, as he buys an old home, fixes it up, and adopts the region as his new home.

The Luberon terrain in general (much of which is a French regional natural park) is as appealing as its hill towns. Gnarled vineyards and wind-sculpted trees separate tidy stone structures from abandoned buildings—little more than rock piles—that seem to challenge city slickers to fix them up.

The wind is an integral part of life here. The infamous mistral, finishing its long ride in from Siberia, hits like a hammer—hard enough, it's said, to blow the ears off a donkey. Throughout the region you'll see houses designed with windowless walls facing the mistral. Walking from village to village is a popular pastime here—local TIs have trail information.

Planning Your Time

To enjoy the windblown ambience of the Luberon, plan a leisurely day trip visiting three or four of the characteristic towns. While the area is tough without a car, Isle sur la Sorgue is handy to Avignon by train and offers a fine introduction to this sunny slice of France. An overnight here gives a fine taste of the region's appeal. To reach the hilltowns like Roussillon by bus you must go to Apt, then taxi. By car, town-hop for a day side-tripping from Arles or as a detour en route to the French Riviera. Of course, tumbling in for an hour from the car park, you'll be just another splash-in-the-pan camera-toting Provence fan. Spend a night and you'll feel more a part of the scene. By car, get on the N-100 toward Apt, east of Avignon. Veer left onto the D-2, where you'll see signs to Gordes. Roussillon is signed from Gordes.

Isle sur la Sorgue

This sturdy market town, literally "island on the Sorgue River," sits within a split in its happy little river. (Do not confuse it with the plain town of Sorgue.) Isle sur la Sorgue erupts into a market frenzy with hearty crafts and local produce each Sunday and Thursday. With clear water babbling under flower box–decorated pedestrian bridges and its old-time carousel always spinning, Isle sur la Sorge invites exploration. Navigate by mossy water wheels

which, while still turning, power only memories of the town's
wool and silk industries. The 12th-century church with a festive
Baroque interior seems too big for its town. Next to it is the
antique green **Café de France**—the place to sip a *pastis* with locals
and ponder the action on place de la Liberté. The shady riverside
park one kilometer upstream is popular in the summer. Isle sur la
Sorgue is dead on Mondays.

The helpful **TI** next to the cathedral has information on
handy Avignon train connections (8/day, 20 min) and a line on
rooms in private homes (9:00–12:30 and 14:00–18:00, closed Sunday afternoon and Monday, tel. 04 90 38 04 78).

**Sleeping in Isle sur la Sorgue (zip code: 84800): Hotel
Restaurant La Guelardiere****, while at a busy intersection, has
OK rooms away from the street that open on to a garden courtyard, and an artsy, reasonable restaurant (Db-300F, 1 rue de
l'Apt, tel. 04 90 38 10 52, fax 04 90 20 83 70). **Hotel les
Nevons**** is two blocks from the center and, while ugly from
the outside, it seems to do everything right within, with large,
comfortable, and air-conditioned rooms (a few family suites), a
roof-top pool, and eager-to-please owners (Sb-265F, Db-
285–300F, Tb-360F, Qb-460F, easy free parking, 205 Chemin
des Nevons, tel. 04 90 20 72 00, fax 04 90 38 31 20). If push
comes to shove, **Hotel Bar Restaurant Grill Le Bassin***,
which sits on the river on the upstream tip of the "island," provides a basic, cheery blue and pink home (Ds-200F, Db-240F,
Tb-290F, CC:VM, avenue du General de Gaulle, tel. 04 90 38
03 16, fax 04 90 38 40 83). The tiny **La Saladelle** offers rooms
for a three-day minimum, or one night if reserved the day of
arrival. It's half-pension only, but a good value at 180F per person (33 rue Carnot, tel. 04 90 20 68 59).

Roussillon

With all the trendy charm of Santa Fe on a hilltop, a stop here
will cost you at least a roll of film (and 15F for parking). Climb
a few minutes from either car park, past the picture-perfect
square and under the church, to the summit of the town (signs
to *castum*), where a dramatic view complete with a howling mistral and an interesting *table d'orientation* await. Then, back under
the church, see how local (or artsy) you can look over a cup of
coffee on what must be the most scenic village square in the
Luberon. On the south end of town, beyond the upper parking
lot, a brilliant ochre canyon (10F)—formerly a quarry—stands
ready for those who wish they were in Bryce Canyon. You could
paint the entire town without ever leaving the red and orange
corner of your palette. Many do.

Sleeping in or near Roussillon (zip code: 84220): The **TI**
(tel. 04 90 05 60 25) across from the David restaurant posts a list

of hotels and *chambres d'hôte*. Just below the charm, near the north side lower parking, is the ideal and comfortable **Hôtel Reves d'Ocres**** with helpful owners (Db-350F, Tb-450F, Qb-480F, air-conditioning, CC:VM, tel. 04 90 05 60 50, fax 04 90 05 79 74). **Madame Cherel** rents spotless rooms with firm mattresses (D-200F, inquire at her restaurant, 70 yards north of the PTT just below the village, tel. 04 90 05 68 47). Cherel is well-traveled, speaks English, is a wealth of regional travel tips, and rents mountain bikes (100F/day).

Mas Garrigon*** takes elaborate care of upscale travelers in a beautiful setting with a pool, fine rooms, and an elegant restaurant where they kindly request that you have dinner (Db-670–850F, 300F *menu*, CC:VMA, one mile below Roussillon, tel. 04 90 05 63 22, fax 04 90 05 70 01).

Gordes and Oppède le Vieux

Gordes—This is the most touristy and trendy town in the Luberon. Parisian big shots love it. Once a virtual ghost town of derelict buildings, it's now completely fixed up and filled by people who live in a world without callouses. See it from a distance.

Oppède le Vieux—This is a windy barnacle of a town, with a few boutiques and a dusty main square at the base of a short, ankle-twisting climb to an evocative ruined church and castle. The Luberon views justify the effort. This way-off-the-beaten path, fixer-upper of a village must be how Gordes looked before it became chic. It's ideal for those looking to vanish in Provence. The cozy **Restaurant L'Oppidum** rents two classy rooms (Db-300F, place de la Croix, tel. 04 90 76 74 01 or 04 90 76 84 15, NSE).

THE FRENCH RIVIERA

A hundred years ago, celebrities from London to Moscow flocked here to escape the drab, dreary weather at home. The belle époque is now the tourist *époque*, as this most sought after fun-in-the-sun destination now caters to more than Europe's aristocracy. Some of the Continent's most stunning scenery and intriguing museums lie along this strip of land—and so do millions of sun-worshiping tourists.

Nice is this region's capital and your best home base. Nearby Antibes has a cozy old town center and fine beaches, Monte Carlo welcomes all with open cash registers, and the hill towns offer a breezy and photogenic alternative to the beach scene. Evenings on the Riviera, a.k.a. the Côte d'Azur, were made for the promenade.

Planning Your Time

Nice is the logical base of operation for most, with excellent public transportation to most regional sights, world-class museums, plenty of hotels in all price ranges, and a marvelous beachfront promenade. But Antibes or Villefranche offer sandy beaches and a small-town warmth that lures many their way. I've focused my accommodations listings on these three cities. If you choose Nice, remember that it's France's fifth-biggest city.

Once situated, spend a full day in Nice, then consider half-day trips to Monaco, Antibes, and St. Paul/Vence—in that order.

Getting Around the Riviera

Getting around the Côte d'Azur by train or bus is easy. Nice is perfectly located for exploring the Riviera. Like prostitutes on bar stools, the resort towns of the Riviera await your visit. Monaco,

The French Riviera

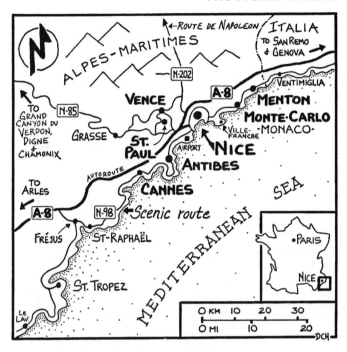

Eze, Villefranche, Antibes, and Cannes are all a 15- to 60-minute bus or train ride apart from each other.

While rail travelers have a tough time breaking away from the tracks, bus service can be cheaper and more frequent and scenic—plus it often drops you closer to where you want to be. At Nice's efficient bus station (*gare routière*, on boulevard J. Jaures—see map of Nice), competing companies vie for your business, offering free return trips (keep your ticket). Get schedules and prices at the helpful information desk in the bus station (sample fares from Nice: to Villefranche-8.5F, 4/hrly, Monaco-20F, 3/hrly, tel. 04 93 85 61 81).

Cuisine Scene—Côte d'Azur

The Côte d'Azur (technically a part of Provence) gives Provence's cuisine a Mediterranean flair. The local specialties are *bouillabaisse* (the spicy seafood stew-soup that seems worth the cost only for those with a seafood fetish), *bourride* (a creamy fish soup thickened with aioli—a garlic sauce), and *salade niçoise* (nee-swaz; a tasty tomato, potato, olive, anchovy, and tuna salad). You'll also find these tasty bread treats: *pissaladière* (bread dough topped with onions, olives, and anchovies), *fougasse* (a spindly, lacelike bread), *socca* (a thin chickpea crêpe), and *pan bagna* (a bread shell stuffed with tomatoes, anchovies, olives, onions, and tuna). Bellet is the local wine, both red and white, and is served chilled.

NICE

Nice is a melting pot of thousands of tanning tourists and 340,000 already-tanned residents. Here you'll see the chicest of the chic, the cheapest of the cheap, and everyone else in this strange scramble to be where the European land hits the water. Nice's spectacular mountain-to-Mediterranean scenery, its thriving Old City, eternally entertaining seafront promenade, and superb museums make settling into this city a joy. Nice is nice—but hot and jammed in July and August.

Take only a piece of Nice and leave the rest to the residents. Outside of a few museums, everything you want is within a small area—near the Old City and along the seafront.

Orientation

Tourist Information: Nice has four helpful TIs (inside the airport; next to the the train station; on the RN-7 as you drive into town, on the right just after the airport; and downtown at 5 Promenade des Anglais). All are open daily from 8:00 to 19:00, until 20:00 in summer (tel. 04 93 87 07 07 or 04 93 87 60 60). Pick up the excellent free Nice map (which lists all the sights and hours), the museums booklet, and the extensive *Practical Guide to Nice*. TIs make hotel reservations for a small fee.

Arrival in Nice

By Train: Nice has one main station with luggage lockers (Nice-Ville) where all trains stop and you get off. Avoid the suburban station (Gare Riquier). To reach my recommended hotels, turn left out of the station, then right on avenue Jean Médecin. To get to the beach and the promenade des Anglais from the station, take bus #12 (catch it across the street from the station). To get to the Old City and the bus station (*gare routière*), catch bus #5 from avenue Jean Médecin (one block left out of the station). The TI is next door to the left as you exit; Avis car rental is to the right.

By Car: For some of the Riviera's best scenery, follow the coast road between Cannes and Fréjus. Use the roadside TI just past the airport and park at the lot at Nice Étoile on avenue Jean Médecin (about 80F/day). Most Nice street parking is metered and garages cost from 60 to 90F per day.

By Plane: Nice's mellow and TI-equipped airport (tel. 04 93 21 30 30) is right on the Mediterranean, a quick 20 to 30 minutes from the city center by bus (three/hr to the bus station, 26F) or taxi (150F). The TI and international flights use terminal 1; domestic flights use terminal 2.

Helpful Hints

Self-serve Laundromats abound in Nice; ask your hotelier and guard your load. Mahfoud runs the friendliest laundry in Europe at 12 rue des Suisses (two blocks west of avenue Jean Médecin, next to the cathedral).

The American Express office faces the beach at 11 promenade des Anglais (tel. 04 93 16 53 53). For new and used English-language books and guidebooks, try The Cat's Whiskers (closed Sunday, 26 rue Lamartine, near the Hôtel Star). Cycles Arnaud rents mountain bikes (100F/day, 4 place Grimaldi, just off avenue Jean Médecin, tel. 04 93 87 88 55).

Sights—Nice

▲▲**Promenade des Anglais**—There's something for everyone along this seafront circus. Watch the Europeans at play, admire the azure Mediterranean, anchor yourself in a blue chair, and prop your feet up on the made-to-order guardrail. Join the evening parade of tans along the promenade. Start at the pink-domed Hotel Negresco and, like the belle époque English aristocrats for whom the promenade was built, stroll to the Old City and Castle Hill.

Hotel Negresco, Nice's finest hotel and a historic monument, offers the city's most costly beds and a free "museum" interior (reasonable attire is necessary to enter). March through the lobby into the exquisite Salon Royal. The tsar's chandelier hangs from an Eiffel-built dome. Read the explanation, stroll the circle, and, on your way out, pop into the Salon Louis XIV.

The next block toward the castle is filled with a lush public park and the Masséna Museum. The TI is just beyond that. Get down to the beach.

Beaches—The beaches of Nice are where the jet set lays on rocks. After settling into the smooth pebbles, you can play beach volleyball, ping-pong, or *boules*; rent paddleboats, Jet Skis, or Windsurfers; explore ways to use your zoom lens as a telescope; or snooze on comfy beach beds with end tables. Before you head off in search of sandy beaches, try it on the rocks.

▲▲**Old City (Vieux Nice)**—This thriving Old City is characteristic Nice in the buff. Here Italian and French flavors mix to create a spicy Mediterranean dressing. The 20th century has driven old Nice into a triangle of spindly streets filling a corner between the castle hill and beach. A broad park-lined boulevard seals it off. The streets, while straight, are anything but predictable. Stealth pigeons fly under tall, pastel, domestic cliffs while tattoo shops show their work. Laundry flaps and tattered squares say "sit."

Nice

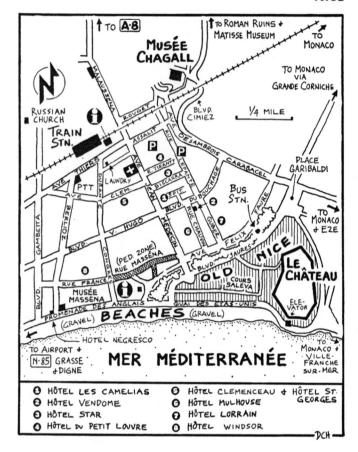

● HÔTEL LES CAMELIAS	⑤ HÔTEL CLEMENCEAU & HÔTEL ST.
● HÔTEL VENDOME	⑥ HÔTEL MULHOUSE
● HÔTEL STAR	⑦ HÔTEL LORRAIN
● HÔTEL DU PETIT LOUVRE	⑧ HÔTEL WINDSOR

—DCH—

Cours Saleya, a long broad square, collects people and produce like a trough between all this and the sea. Restaurant tables tangle with market stalls here. The daily flower and fish market becomes a flea market on Monday.

Castle Hill—Climb this saddle horn for the otherwise flat city center only for exercise or the view. Walk up rue Rossetti or catch the elevator from the beach side. The 360-degree view of Nice, the Alps foothills, and the Mediterranean is a decent reward. You'll find a waterfall, tacky souvenirs, playground, and cemetery, but no castle on Castle Hill.

Shopping Streets—The pedestrian street rue Masséna is packed with tourists, run-of-the-mill cafés, and boutiques. Window-shop

the expensive boutiques and sift through the international crowds.
▲▲▲**Musée National Marc Chagall**—Even if you're suspicious
of modern art, this museum—with the largest collection of Chagall's work anywhere—is a delight. After WWII Chagall returned
from the United States to settle in Vence, a hill town above Nice.
Between 1954 and 1967 he painted a cycle of 17 large murals
designed for and donated to this museum. These paintings,
inspired by the books of Genesis, Exodus, and the Song of Songs,
make up the "nave," or core, of what Chagall called the "House of
Brotherhood."

Each painting is a lighter-than-air collage of images drawing
from Chagall's Russian-folk-village youth, his Jewish heritage,
Biblical themes, and his feeling that he existed somewhere between
heaven and earth. He felt the Bible was a synonym for nature, and
color and Biblical themes were key ingredients for understanding
God's love for His creation. Chagall's brilliant blues and reds celebrate nature, as do his spiritual and folk themes. Notice the focus
on couples. To Chagall, humans loving each other mirrored God's
love of creation.

Don't miss the stained-glass windows of the auditorium,
early family photos of the artist, and a room full of Chagall lith-
ographs. The small 10F-guidebook begins with a philosophical
introduction by Chagall himself. (30F, Wednesday–Monday
10:00–18:00 July 1–September 30, 10:00–17:00 off-season,
closed Tuesday, 30F English tours often available on request,
tel. 04 93 53 87 20.) From the train station turn left along
avenue Thiers and walk about eight blocks (the museum is signposted) or take bus #15 to "Chagall." There's a taxi rank at the
museum (50F to the beach). It's a pleasant 20-minute walk from
here to the Matisse Museum.

Nice City Museum (Musée Masséna)—The city-history museum,
housed in a beautiful mansion, is packed with historical—but
forgettable—paraphernalia (25F, Tuesday–Sunday 10:00–12:00 and
14:00–18:00 May–September; 10:00–12:00 and 14:00–17:00 off-
season, closed Monday; in a fine garden facing the beach next to
Hotel Negresco at 65 rue de France, tel. 04 93 88 11 34).

Modern Art Museum—This ultramodern museum features a fine
collection of art from the 1960s and 1970s (25F, Wednesday–
Monday 11:00–18:00, Friday evening until 22:00, closed Tuesday,
on the promenade des Arts near the bus station).

▲**Russian Cathedral**—Even if you've been to Russia, this Russian
Orthodox church, which claims to be the finest outside Russia, is
interesting. Its one-room interior is filled with icons and candles.
Tsar Nicholas II gave his aristocratic countryfolk—who wintered
on the Riviera—this church in 1912. (A few years later, Russian
comrades who didn't winter on the Riviera shot him.) Here in the
land of olives and anchovies, these proud onion domes seem odd.

But so did, I imagine, those old Russians. (12F, daily 9:00–12:00 and 14:30–18:00, services Saturday at 18:00, Sunday at 10:00, no shorts, 10-minute walk behind the station at 17 boulevard du Tsarevitch, tel. 04 93 96 88 02.)

▲**Matisse Museum**—This is a three-star sight for his fans. The art is beautifully displayed in this newly-renovated showpiece, representing the largest collection of Matisse paintings. Personally, I don't get Matisse. (25F, Wednesday–Monday 10:00–18:00 April–September, otherwise 10:00–17:00, closed Tuesday; take bus #15, #17, #22 to the Arènes stop, or hike 45 minutes to 164 avenue des Arènes de Cimiez, tel. 04 93 81 08 08.)

Nightlife—Nice's bars play host to a lively late-night scene with jazz and rock 'n' roll. Most activity focuses on Old Nice, near the place Rossetti. If you're out very late, avoid walking alone. Plan on a cover charge or expensive drinks.

Sleeping in Nice
(5.5F = about $1, zip code: 06000)
Sleep Code: **S** = Single, **D** = Double/Twin, **T** = Triple, **Q** = Quad, **b** = bathroom, **t** = toilet only, **s** = shower only, **CC** = Credit Card (**V**isa, **M**asterCard, **A**mex), **SE** = Speaks English, **NSE** = No English, * = Hotel rating (0–4 stars).

Don't look for charm in Nice. Go for modern and clean with a central location. Reserve early for summer visits. Prices go down from October to April. There are few hotels in the Old City, and the hotels near the station are overrun, overpriced, and loud. I sleep halfway between the Old City (Vieux Nice) and the train station, near avenue Jean Médecin. From the train station, turn left out of the onto avenue Thiers, then right onto avenue Jean Médecin. Drivers can park under the Nice Étoile shopping center (at avenue J. Médecin and boulevard Dubouchage/Victor Hugo), midway between the Old City, train station, bus station, and seafront.

Hôtel Star** is immaculate in every way, comfortable, and a great value. It's ideally located a few blocks east of avenue Jean Médecin, and warmly run by Françoise and Georges, who practically trip over themselves trying to be helpful (Sb-180–200F, Db-250–320F, Tb-320–390F, CC:VMA, fine beds, beach towels, no elevator, 14 rue Biscarra, tel. 04 93 85 19 03, fax 04 93 13 04 23, SE).

Hôtel du Petit Louvre* has art-festooned walls, light-hearted owners, and close-to-clean rooms (Ds-205F, Db-230F, Tb-250–285F, CC:VM, elevator, 10 rue Emma Tiranty, tel. 04 93 80 15 54, fax 04 93 62 45 08).

Hôtel Clemenceau** comes with spacious, comfortable rooms and a very friendly owner, Madame Lasserre (D-150–165F, Db-200–310F, Tb-250–360F, Qb-400–520F, plus 50F for a kitchenette, CC:VM, one block west of avenue Jean Médecin, 3 avenue Clemenceau, tel. 04 93 88 61 19, fax 04 93 16 88 96, daughter Marianne SE).

Hotel St. Georges**, a block away, is bigger, more modern, and less personal, but still a good value with a peaceful garden and generally spacious rooms (Db-320F, Tb-430F, CC:VM, 7 avenue Clemenceau, tel. 04 93 88 79 21, fax 04 93 16 22 85).

For a taste of faded belle époque, pink pastels, and high ceilings, waltz into **Hotel Vendome*****, well-located in an old manor house with off-street parking. Some rooms are just average, but the best have balconies—request *avec balcon*—ideally rooms 105, 102, or any on the fifth floor (Sb-365–465F, Db-460–570F, Tb-480–650F, Qb-550–750F in loft room, 26 rue Pastorelli, tel. 04 93 62 00 77, fax 04 93 13 40 78).

Hôtel Lorrain* rents clean, inexpensive rooms with kitchenettes, and is conveniently located near the bus station and Old Nice (S-160F, Ds-180F, Db-220–260F, Tb-280F, CC:VM, 6 rue Gubernatis, push the top buzzer to release the door, tel. 04 93 85 42 90, fax 04 93 85 55 54). This simple hotel may request longer stays in the high season and a two-night minimum off-season. Likeable Patricia Scoffier tries her best to speak English.

Hôtel Windsor*** is a pleasant garden retreat with artfully designed rooms and a swimming pool (Sb-425–525F, Db-550–700F, elevator, sauna-60F, free gym, rooms over the garden are worth the higher price, CC:VMA, one block east of the Musée Masséna and five blocks from the sea, 11 rue Dalpozzo, tel. 04 93 88 59 35, fax 04 93 88 94 57, e-mail: windsor @webstore.fr).

Hôtel les Camelias** reminds me of the Old World places I stayed in as a kid traveling with my parents. An ideally located dark and floral place burrowed in a garden, it has simple rooms and a loyal clientele who give the TV lounge a retirement home-after-dinner feeling. Some basic rooms have balconies—*chambre avec balcon* (S-180F, Ss-220F, Sb-300F, Db-360–400F, Tb-400–450F, includes breakfast, parking-30F, elevator, CC:VM, 3 rue Spitaleri, tel. 04 93 62 15 54, fax 04 93 80 42 96. Formal Madame Vimont and her son Jean Claude SE). Guests here will gum their 70F four-course dinner—simple, hearty, and stressless.

Hôtel Mulhouse*** offers the best location of my listings and is being entirely renovated by its new, amiable British owners. They promise a polished product (estimated price: Db-500F, elevator, CC:VMA, 9 rue de Chauvain, tel. 04 93 92 36 69, fax 04 93 13 96 80).

Hotel Mercure-Massena***, a few blocks from place Massena, offers all the comforts (for a price) including air-conditioned rooms and a parking garage (Db-600–850F, CC:VMA, 58 rue Giofreddo, tel. 04 93 85 49 25, fax 04 93 62 43 27, SE).

Sleeping near Nice in Villefranche-sur-Mer
(5.5F = about $1, zip code: 06230)

For small-town atmosphere, nearby Villefranche-sur-Mer is an upscale, mini-Nice. Villefranche (between Nice and Monte Carlo, with frequent 15-minute bus and train service to both) is quieter and more exotic. Narrow, cobbled streets tumble into the mellow waterfront, a scenic walkway below the castle leads to the hidden port, and luxury yachts glisten in the harbor. Even if you're sleeping elsewhere, consider a beachfront dinner or an ice cream–licking village stroll. The first two hotels listed are the fanciest in this entire chapter. Beyond the requisite castle, yachts, and boutiques, Villefranche has the unique rue Obscure. The TI is in the small park called Jardin François Binon, just below the main intersection on boulevard Princess Grace (daily 8:30–12:30 and 14:00–19:00, closed earlier and on Sundays October–March, tel. 04 93 01 73 68). The bus stops above the TI, near all listed hotels. The train station is a 20-minute walk or 40F taxi ride away.

If your idea of sightseeing is to enjoy the view from your hotel's dining room or pool, stay at the friendly and family-run **Hôtel La Flore***** (Db-420–680F, Tb-820F, Qb-920F, less November–March, no half-pension required but a fine restaurant, smartly designed family rooms, elevator, private pool, CC:VMA, high above the harbor with great views, a block from the TI on boulevard Princess Grace de Monaco, tel. 04 93 76 30 30, fax 04 93 76 99 99, e-mail: Hotel-La-Flore@wanadoo.fr, SE). Sea views and balconies are worth the extra cost.

Hotel Welcome*** is buried in the heart of the Old City, right on the water, with most rooms overlooking the harbor. You'll pay top dollar for all the comforts in a formal hotel that seems to do everything right and couldn't be better located (Db-560–950F, extra person 200F, breakfast included, 1 quai Courbet, tel. 04 93 76 27 62, fax 04 93 76 27 66, e-mail: welcome @riviera.fr, SE). The rooms at both Hôtel La Flore and Hotel Welcome, while different in cost, are about the same in comfort. La Flore is on a road; Welcome is on the harbor.

The tight and hotelesque **Hôtel Provençal**** offers fine views from well-worn rooms with a pool (Db-310–470F, Tb-490–560F, Qb-560–650F, CC:VMA, a block from the TI at 4 avenue Maréchal Joffre, tel. 04 93 01 71 42, fax 04 93 76 96 00, e-mail: provencale@riviera.fr).

Hôtel la Darse** is tucked behind the castle away from other hotels, right on the water in Villefranche's Port de la Darse, with quiet, simple, but sleepable rooms, and dark linoleum floors. Ask for a slightly higher-priced bay-side room with a balcony for a million-dollar view (Db-260–370F, extra person-60F, tel. 04 93 01 72 54, fax 04 93 01 84 37).

At **Le Home**, Madame Repellin-Villard rents the town's best budget beds in 10 simple rooms around a cheery garden with a welcoming terrace. From the main road near the TI, walk between the cafés Riche and Regence, then climb the steps and turn left (Db-210F, avenue de Grande Bretagne, tel. 04 93 76 79 88).

Eating in Nice

Nice's Old City overflows with cheap, moderate, and expensive restaurants, pizza stands, and taverns.

Charcuterie Julien is a good deli that sells an impressive array of local dishes by the weight. Buy 200 grams plopped into a plastic carton to go (open 11:00–19:30, closed Wednesday, rue de la Poissonnerie, at the Castle Hill end of cours Saleya). For maximum ambience at fair prices on the Cours Saleya, **Spaghetissimo** serves good Italian and French dishes (1 Cours Saleya). On the same side of the Cours Saleya, locally popular **La Cambuse** serves more traditional cuisine. The **Nissa Socca** café offers the best cheap Italian cuisine in town in a lively atmosphere (a block off the place Rossini on the rue Reparate). Come early.

Rue Droite has Nice's best concentration of pizza stands and local eateries. Check out **Acchiardo's** (#37) for the fish soup. Stop by **Le four à bois** bakery (#38) and watch them make *fougasse*.

Near most hotels recommended in this book: **L'Authentic** offers good pastas and seafood in a relaxed setting. Prices range from 55F for the daily special to 80F *menus* (18 rue Biscarra, tel. 04 93 62 48 88). Just below place Massena, **Lou Nissart** serves excellent regional specialities to appreciative locals (moderate, across place Masséna at 1 rue de l'Opéra, tel. 04 93 85 34 49).

Transportation Connections—Nice

By train to: Arles (10/day, 3 hrs, transfer in Marseille), **Dijon** (8/day, 8 hrs, most are direct), **Chamonix** (there are direct trains around 9:00 and a night train at about 21:30), **Grenoble** (consider the scenic little trains that run fron Nice to Grenoble; see Travel Notes for La Route de Napoleon at the end of this chapter), **Florence** (2/day, 8 hrs, transfer in Pisa and/or Genoa, morning departures), **Paris'** Gare de Lyon (7 TGVs/day, 7 hrs, night train available), **Barcelona** (4/day, 10 hrs, direct night train or day trips with at least one transfer). Train info: tel. 04 36 35 35 35.

ANTIBES

For sandy beaches, an enjoyable old town, and a fine Picasso collection, visit Antibes. A quick 20 minutes from Nice by train, Antibes' glamorous port glistens below its fortifications with luxurious yachts and colorful fishing boats. Boat lovers are welcome to browse. This compact town's attractions lie near the port within the Old City walls (and atop the ruins of the fourth-century B.C. Greek city of Antipolis). The festive Old City is charming in a sandy-sophisticated way. The daily market (Marche Provençal) under a 19th-century canopy brings out the locals (behind the Picasso Museum on cours Masséna, daily until 13:00 except on off-season Mondays). Place Audiberti becomes a flea market on Thursday and Saturday (7:00–18:00).

Tourist Information: The sultry Maison de Tourisme has an interesting "Discovering Old Antibes" brochure (Monday–Saturday 9:00–20:00, Sunday 9:00–13:00, off-season lunch breaks, downtown at 11 place de Gaulle, tel. 04 92 90 53 00). The Nice TI has Antibes maps; plan ahead.

Arrival in Antibes

By Train: From the train station, the port is straight ahead, and the Old City center (and TI) is a five-minute veer to the right down avenue Soleau. The Nice–Antibes train (20 minutes, 21F) beats the Nice–Antibes bus (one hour, 25F). Train info: tel. 04 93 99 50 50.

By Bus: The bus station is a block from the TI on place Guynemer.

By Car: Park near the Old City walls on the port.

Sights—Antibes

▲▲**Musée Picasso**—Sitting serenely where the Old City meets the sea (look for signs from the Old City) in the Château Grimaldi, this museum offers a remarkable collection of Picasso's work—paintings, sketches, and ceramics. Picasso, who lived and worked here in 1946, said if you want to see work from his "Antibes period," you'll have to do it in Antibes. You'll understand why Picasso liked working here. Several photos of the artist make this already intimate museum more so. In his famous *Joie de Vivre* (the museum's highlight), there's a new love in Picasso's life, and he's feelin' groovy (30F, Tuesday–Sunday 10:00–18:00 June–September, closed Monday and off-season from 12:00–14:00, tel. 04 92 90 54 20).

Beaches—The best beaches stretch between Antibes' port and the Cap d'Antibes. The main beaches (near the Cap d'Antibes) are jammed on weekends and in the summer, though the smaller *plage de la Gravette* at the port remains relatively calm in any season.

Sleeping in Antibes
(5.5F = about $1, zip code: 06600)

Relais du Postillon** offers good rooms on a central square with accordion bathrooms and helpful owners who take more pride in their well-respected restaurant (*menus* from 145F, Db-250–400F, extra bed-60F, elevator, CC:VM, 8 rue Championnet, tel. 04 93 34 20 77, fax 04 93 34 61 24, SE).

Hotel Le Cameo** is a big, rambling, refreshingly unaggressive old place. It faces a characteristic square above a bar filled with smoky locals. The public areas are dark and disorienting, but its nine *bon petit* rooms are almost huggable (Ss-230F, Ds-280F, Db-350F, Ts-350F, Tb-400F, 5 place Nationale, tel. 04 93 34 24 17, fax 04 93 34 35 80, NSE).

Auberge Provençale*, on the same square, has seven fine rooms, inattentive management, and a popular restaurant (reception in the restaurant, Sb-250–400F, Db-300–450F, Tb-350–500F, Qb-550F, CC:VMA, 61 place Nationale, tel. 04 93 34 13 24, fax 04 93 34 89 88). Their loft room, named Celine, is huge. It comes with a royal canopy bed, a dramatic open-timbered ceiling, and, if it's available, costs no more than the other rooms.

Hotel Mediterranee** is Old World simple with quiet rooms around a garden courtyard and louder rooms on the street (Sb-260F, Db-310–350F, Tb-390F, Qb-430F, CC:VM, 6 avenue Maréchal Reille, tel. 04 93 34 14 84, fax 04 93 34 43 31, NSE).

Hôtel Ponteil's** gregarious owners offer bungalow-style rooms in and around a breezy manor house, with free and safe private parking, a garden terrace, quick beach access, and a friendly family feel (S-250F, D-240–310F, Db-420–470F, bunky family deals, breakfast is included in room prices, a costly but home-cooked half-pension is required June–September, CC:VM, 11 impasse Jean-Mesnier, tel. 04 93 34 67 92, fax 04 93 34 49 47). A long walk from the train station near the beach on the far side of town, this hotel is best for drivers.

MONACO

Still dazzling despite overdevelopment and crass commercialization, Monaco will disappoint those who look for something below the surface. This two-square-kilometer country is a tax haven for its tiny full-time population. The **TI** is near the casino (Monday–Saturday 9:00–19:00, Sunday 9:00–12:00, 2 boulevard des Moulins, tel. 00-377/92 16 61 66). To call Monaco from France, dial 00, Monaco's country code (377), then the eight-digit number. Within Monaco simply dial the eight-digit number.

Monaco (the principality) is best understood when separated into its two key areas: Monaco Ville, the old city housing Prince Rainier's palace; and Monte Carlo, the area around the casino. The harbor divides the two. A short bus ride (every 10 minutes, 9F, 20F for four tickets) or a 30-minute uphill walk links each area to the bus and train stations. Frequent buses also connect Monaco Ville and the casino.

Start with a look at Monaco Ville for a *magnifique* view (particularly at night) over the harbor and the casino. If you arrive in the morning you can watch the charming changing of the guard (11:55), wander over to the beautiful **Cathédrale de Monaco**, where Princess Grace is buried, and picnic in the immaculate and scenic gardens overlooking the blue Mediterranean. (Pick up a *pan bagna* sandwich in the old city.)

The nearby and costly **Musée de l'Océanographique** (Cousteau Aquarium, 60F, CC:VM) is the largest of its kind. It can be jammed and disappoints some, though aquarium lovers leave impressed. The *Monte Carlo Story* film gives an interesting account in English of this city's history, mostly about Prince Rainier's family (40F, in the parking garage next to the aquarium, take the escalator down to the elevator, then another escalator down one more level).

Leave Monaco Ville and ride the shuttle bus or stroll the harborfront up to the **casino**. Count the counts and Rolls Royces in front of the Hôtel de Paris. Strut inside the lavish casino (opens at 12:00)—anyone can get as far as the one-armed bandits, but only adults (21 and older) can pay the 50F- or 100F-charge to enter the private game rooms and rub shoulders with high rollers (some rooms open at 15:00, others at 21:00). Entrance is free to all games in the new, plebeian American–style Loews Casino, adjacent to the main casino. If you must spend the night, try **Hôtel de France** (moderately priced, 6 rue de la Turbie, near train station, tel. 00-377/93 30 24 64).

You can get to Monaco by train or bus. From Nice it's 20 minutes by train or slower and cheaper by bus (20F, round-trip with same company). Tell the driver you want the place d'Armes stop—Monaco's old city and palace.

MORE FRENCH RIVIERA TOWNS

Menton—Just a few minutes by train (8/day) from Monte Carlo or 40 minutes from Nice, beautiful Menton is a relatively quiet and relaxing spa/beach town (TI tel. 04 93 57 57 00).

Cannes—Its sister city is Beverly Hills, but its beaches and the beachfront promenade are beautiful.

St. Paul-de-Vence and Vence—If you prefer hill towns to beaches, head for St. Paul and Vence (the same bus from Nice's bus station serves both towns, 20F one way, two/hr, 45 min). Unless you go early, you'll escape only some of the heat and none of the crowds. **St. Paul** is part cozy medieval hill town and part local artist shopping mall. It's charmingly artsy but gets swamped with tour buses. Meander into St. Paul's quieter streets and wander far to enjoy the panoramic views (TI tel. 04 93 32 86 95).

The prestigious, far-out, and high-priced **Fondation Maeght** art gallery is a steep, uphill, 10-minute walk from St. Paul. If ever modern art could appeal to you, it would be here. Its world-class contemporary art collection is arranged between pleasant gardens and well-lit rooms (45F, daily 10:00–19:00 July–September, 10:00–12:30 and 14:30–18:00 October–June, tel. 04 93 32 81 63).

The enjoyable hill town of Vence (10 minutes from St. Paul

by bus) disperses St. Paul's crowds over a larger and more engaging city. Vence bubbles with workaday and tourist activity. Catch the daily market (ends at 12:30), and don't miss the small church with its Chagall mosaic and moving Chapelle St. Sacrament. The Vence TI is on place du Grand Jardin (tel. 04 93 58 06 38). Matisse's much-raved-about **Chapelle du Rosaire** (one mile from Vence toward St. Jeannet; taxi or walk) may disappoint all but Matisse fans, for whom this is a necessary pilgrimage. The yellow-, blue-, and green-filtered sunlight does a cheery dance in stark contrast to the gloomy tile sketches (donation, open only Tuesday and Thursday 10:00–11:30 and 14:30–17:30; during the summer the chapel is also open on Wednesday and Friday afternoon and on Saturday from 10:00–11:30 and 14:30–17:30; closed November–December 15; tel. 04 93 58 03 26).

Travel Notes on Connecting Nice and the Alps—*La Route de Napoleon*

By Train: Leave the tourists far behind and take the scenic train-bus-train combination (free with railpass) that runs between Grenoble and Nice through canyons, along white-water rivers, between snow-capped peaks, and through many tempting villages. From Nice start with the little Chemins de Fer de Provence train to Digne (4/day, 3 hrs, Chemins de Fer de Provence departs from a different train station about half a mile from Nice's main station, 4 rue Alfred Binet, tel. 04 93 82 10 17). In Digne catch the bus (free with railpass) to Veynes (6/day, 90 min), and in Veynes catch the most scenic two-car train to Grenoble (5/day, 2 hrs). From Grenoble connections are available to many destinations. Spend the night in one of the tiny villages en route; Clelles (hotel listed below), Sisteron, Entrevaux (hotel listed below), Thoranne-Haute, and Barreme are all appealing with small hotels.

By Car: When driving between the Riviera and the Alps, take the scenic route (from south to north follow Digne, Sisteron, and Grenoble). You'll join the route Napoleon followed when returning from his exile. An assortment of pleasant villages with inexpensive hotels and restaurants lie on this route, making an ovenight easy.

After getting bored in his toy Elba empire, Napoleon gathered his entourage, landed on the Riviera, bared his breast, and told his fellow Frenchmen, "Strike me down or follow me." France followed. But just in case, he took the high road, returning to Paris along the route today's holiday-goers call "La Route de Napoleon." (Waterloo followed shortly afterward.)

This scenic road passes several worth-a-stop villages. Idyllic little Entrevaux feels forgotten and still stuck in its medieval shell. Cross the bridge, meet someone friendly, and consider the steep hike up to the citadel (10F). **Hotel Vauban** provides overnight refuge (tel. 04 93 05 42 40, fax 04 93 05 48 38.) Sisteron's

Romanesque church alone makes it worth a quick leg stretch. If a night in this area appeals, stay farther north, surrounded by mountains near the tiny hamlet of Clelles at **Hôtel Ferrat****. This family-run mountain hacienda at the base of Mont Aiguille (which Gibraltar was modeled after) is the place to break this long drive. Enjoy your own *boules* court, a swimming pool, lovely rooms, a fine restaurant, and a warm welcome (Db-280–380F, zip code: 38930, tel. 04 76 34 42 70, fax 04 76 34 47 47)

THE FRENCH ALPS
(ALPES-SAVOIE)

Savoie is the northern and highest tier of the French Alps (the
Alpes-Dauphiné lie to the south). In the 11th century, Savoie was
a powerful region with borders stretching down to the Riviera and
out to the Rhône. Today it is France's mountain sports capital,
with Europe's highest point, Mont Blanc, as its centerpiece.
Savoie, which didn't become part of France until 1860, feels more
Swiss than French.

The scenery is spectacular. Serene yet thriving Annecy is a
picture-perfect blend of natural and man-made beauty. In Chamonix, it's just you and Madame Nature—there's not a museum
or important building in sight. If the weather's right, take
Europe's ultimate cable-car ride to the 12,600-foot Aiguille du
Midi in Chamonix.

Lyon is the southern gateway to the Alps, easily accessible by
train or car. This surprisingly captivating city is easily France's
most interesting major city after Paris. If you need a city fix, linger
in Lyon.

Planning Your Time

Annecy is charming, elegant, and enjoyable for an evening. But if
you've got Alps on your mind, go directly to Chamonix. Here you
can skip along high ridges or stroll the tranquil Arve river valley
paths. You can zip down the mountain on a wheeled bobsled or rent
a mountain bike. Ride the gondolas early (crowds and clouds roll in
later in the morning) and save your afternoons for lower altitudes.
Plan a minimum of two nights and one day in Chamonix. (Note: If
you're driving from here to the Riviera, see "*La Route de Napoleon*"
tips at the end of the previous chapter.) Mega-urban Lyon is
France's best-kept secret. Strategically situated at the foot of the

The French Alps

Alps where the Saone and Rhone Rivers meet, this very manageable big city merits at least two nights and a full day.

Cuisine Scene—Savoie and Lyon

The Savoie offers mountain-country cuisine. Robust and hearty, it shares much with the Swiss. *Fondue savoyarde* (melted Beaufort and Comté cheese and local white wine, sometimes with a dash of cognac), *raclette* (chunks of semi-melted cheese served with potatoes, pickles, sausage, and bread), *tartiflettes* (hearty scalloped potatoes with melted cheese), *poulet de Bresse* (the best chicken in France), *morteau* (smoked pork sausage), *gratin savoyarde* (a potato dish using cream, cheese, and garlic), and freshly-caught fish are the specialties. Local cheeses are Morbier (look for a charcoal streak down the middle), Comté (like Gruyère), Beaufort (aged for two years; hard and strong), Reblochon (mild and creamy), and Tomme de Savoie (semi-hard and mild). Evian water comes from Savoie, as does Chartreuse liqueur. Aprémont and Crépy are two of the area's surprisingly good white wines.

Lyon is French cuisine at its best. Surprisingly affordable, this is an intense palate experience—try the *salad Lyonnais* (croutons, ham, and a poached egg on a bed of lettuce), *andouillettes* (pork sausages), and *quenelles* (a fish mousse wrapped in a pasta shell).

ANNECY

There's something for everyone in this lakefront resort town: mountain views, cobbled lanes, canals, flowers, a chateau, and swimming or boating in the lake. Annecy (ahn-see) is France's answer to Switzerland's Luzern. You may not have the mountains in your lap as in nearby Chamonix, but the distant peaks make a beautiful picture with Annecy's lakefront setting.

Tourist Information: The TI is a few blocks from the old center in the modern Bonlieu shopping center (daily in summer 9:00–18:30, otherwise 9:00–12:00 and 13:45–18:30, 1 rue Jean Jaures, tel. 04 50 45 00 33).

Sights—Annecy

Strolling—Amble along the canals and famous arcaded streets of the delightful old city. Wander by the Palais de l'Île where you'll find the Museum of Annecy (30F). The views from the château alone make it worth the entry price. Luscious ice-cream shops line the pedestrian streets; scout out the impressive display at Glaces l'Arlequin, across from the Hotel du Palais de l'Isle (see Sleeping, below).

Boating—Rent a paddleboat (60F/hour) and tool around the lake or let a one-hour cruise do the work for you (60F, several departures/day, Compagnie des Bateaux du Lac Annecy, tel. 04 50 51 08 40). Or consider a one-way cruise to the quiet village of Talloires (about 30F, 56F round-trip) and return by bus. Schedules and prices are at the TI or at the boat dock right on the lake where the canal meets the old city.

Open-Air Market—A thriving outdoor market occupies most of the old city center on Tuesday, Friday, and Sunday mornings.

Sleeping and Eating in Annecy
(5.5F=about $1, zip code: 74000)

Sleep Code: **S** = Single, **D** = Double/Twin, **T** = Triple, **Q** = Quad, **b** = bathroom, **t** = toilet only, **s** = shower only, **CC** = Credit Card (Visa, MasterCard, Amex), **SE** = Speaks English, **NSE** = No English, * = French hotel rating system (0–4 stars).

Hike (or drive) up to the spotless and just-renovated rooms at the **Hôtel du Château**** and enjoy its view terrace (Sb-250F, Db-290–320F, Tb-330F, Qb-430F, several rooms with views, on the way up to the château at 16 rampe du Château, reserve early in the summer, tel. 04 50 45 27 66, fax 04 50 52 75 26). Right on the canal near the lake, the cozy and noisy **Hôtel de Savoie**** has a few view rooms (S-150F, D-210F, Db-290–360F, Tb-400–430F, Qb-440–490F, CC:VM, place St. François, tel. 04 50 45 15 45, fax 04 50 45 11 99, e-mail: hotel.savoie@dotcom.fr). **Hotel du Palais de l'Isle***** is in the heart of the old city and offers very modern, almost sterile three-star comfort (Db-385–535F, 100F for extra bed, 13 rue Perriere, tel. 04 50 45 86 87, fax 04 50 51 87 15). The American-esque **Hotel Ibis**** is a good last resort, well situated on a modern square in the old city with modern, tight, and tidy rooms (Sb-320F, Db-335–400F, 55F for extra person, CC:VMA, 12 rue de la Gare, tel. 04 50 45 43 21, fax 04 50 52 81 08). Good, basic budget rooms can be found near the Hotel Ibis above the **Auberge du Lyonnais** restaurant right on the canal (S-165F, Sb-265F, D-205F, Db-265–315F, tel. 04 50 51 26 20, fax 04 50 51 05 04).

Restaurant John specializes in tasty regional cusine (10 rue Per-riére, at the foot of rampe du Château, tel. 04 50 51 36 15). **Restaurant Vivaldi** offers reasonably priced Italian food (where the old city meets the lake at 12 Faubourg des Annociades, tel. 04 50 51 08 41). **Le Lilas Rose** is a fine place for fondue (passage de l'Eveche).

Transportation Connections—Annecy
By train to: Chamonix (nearly hrly, 2.5 hrs, transfer in St. Gervais), **Beaune** (6/day, 6.5 hrs, transfer in Lyon), **Nice** (8/day, 10 hrs, transfer in Lyon), **Paris'** Gare de Lyon (6 TGVs/day, 4 hrs).

CHAMONIX
Hemmed in by snow-capped peaks, churning with mountain lifts, and crisscrossed with hikes of all levels of difficulty, the resort of Chamonix is France's best base for Alpine exploration. Chamonix is the largest of several villages at the base of Mont Blanc and is served by several mountain lifts. Chamonix's purpose in life has always been to accommodate those coming here for some of Europe's top Alpine thrills. To the east is the Mont Blanc range; to the west, the Aiguilles Rouges chain.

Planning Your Time
If you have one sunny day, spend it this way: Start with the Aiguille du Midi lift (go as early as you can), take it all the way to Hellbronner (hang around the needle longer if you can't get to Hellbronner), then double back to the Plan de l'Aiguille and hike to Montenvers (Mer de Glace—snow level–permitting), and train (or hike) down from there. If the weather disappoints or the snow line's too low, hike the Petit Balcon Sud trail (near the Le Brévent lift), go to Les Praz, then return through the valley along the Arve River.

Chamonix Town

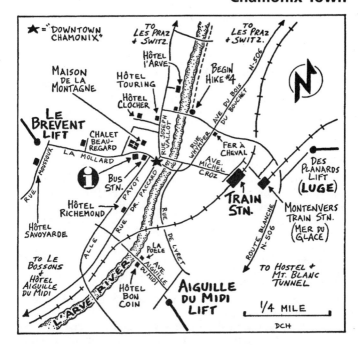

Orientation

The small pedestrian zone is the center of Chamonix, though you'll find most activity along the rue du Docteur Paccard.

Tourist Information: The TI provides hotel and hut reservations, a map of the town and valley (listing restaurants and hotels), and an essential 25F hiking mountain map called "Carte des Sentiers." It's located one block west of rue du Docteur Paccard and the pedestrian zone, on the place de l'Église (daily 8:30–19:30 July–August, 8:30–12:30 and 14:00–19:00 September–June, tel. 04 50 53 00 24, fax 04 50 53 58 90). Ask for the weather forecast.

Laundromats: You'll find one just off rue Joseph Vallot three blocks north of the Hotel Touring at 40 impasse Primaviere (daily 8:00–20:00), and another near the Aiguille du Midi at 174 avenue du Aiguille du Midi (daily 9:00–20:00).

Chamonix Quick History

1786—Mssrs. Balmot and Paccard are the first to climb Mont Blanc
1818—First ascent of Aiguille du Midi
1860—After a visit by Louis Napoleon, the trickle of nature-loving

visitors to Chamonix turns to a gush
1924—First winter Olympics held in Chamonix
1955—Aiguille du Midi *téléphérique* open to tourists
1999—Your visit

Arrival in Chamonix

By Train: Walk straight out of the station and up avenue Michel
Croz. In three blocks you'll hit the center and TI.

By Car: Take the second Chamonix turnoff (coming from
Annecy direction) and park at the huge lot adjacent to the large
traffic circle near the Hôtel Alpina.

Getting Around Chamonix

By Lifts: Gondolas (*téléphériques*) climb mountains all along the
valley, but the best two leave from Chamonix (explained below).
Sightseeing is optimal from the Aiguille du Midi gondola, but hiking is better from the Le Brévent gondola. Those buying tickets at
the hostel, or those over 59, get a 10- to 20-percent reduction on
the area's lifts. Kids ages 4 to 12 ride for half price. While the lift
to Aiguille du Midi stays open year-round, the *télécabines* to the
Panoramic du Mont Blanc in Hellbronner (Italy) close from late
October to June and in bad weather (call the TI to confirm).
Other area lifts close around mid-April through June, and in late
October through December.

By Hiking: For all your options, visit the Office de Haute
Montagne (Office of the High Mountains, a block uphill from the
TI on the third floor of the building marked "Maison de la Montagne"). Review maps and get opinions on the best hikes and up-
to-date weather and trail-condition reports from the English-
speaking staff (daily 8:30–12:00 and 14:30–18:00, tel. 04 50 23 22
08). Remember to bring rain gear, warm clothes, water, sunglasses,
good shoes, and picnic food on your hike.

By Bike: Mountain bikes are rented by the hour and day.
The TI has a brochure proposing the best bike rides. The peaceful
river-valley trail is ideal for bikes and pedestrians. Chamonix
Mountain Bike has good bikes and English-speaking staff (opposite Hôtel Alpina, tel. 04 50 53 54 76).

By Bus or Train: One road and one rail line lace together
the towns and lifts of the valley. Local buses go twice an hour
(from in front of the TI for local destinations).

Sights—Chamonix

▲▲▲**Aiguille du Midi**—This is easily the valley's (and arguably,
Europe's) most spectacular and popular lift. If the weather's clear,
the price doesn't matter. Pile into the *téléphérique* (gondola) and
soar to the tip of a rock needle 12,600 feet above sea level. Chamonix shrinks as trees fly by, soon replaced by whizzing rocks, ice,

Over the Alps—France to Italy

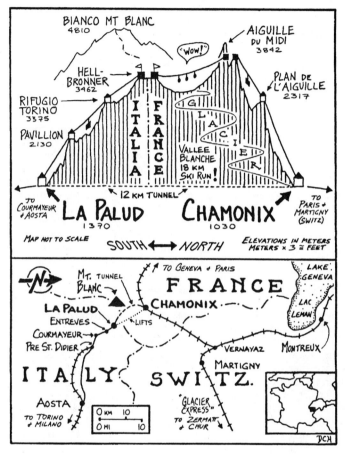

and snow until you reach the top. No matter how sunny it is, it's cold. The air is thin. People are giddy. Fun things can happen at Aiguille du Midi if you're not too winded to join the locals in the halfway-to-heaven tango.

From the top of the lift, cross the bridge and ride the elevator through the rock to the summit of this pinnacle. Missing the elevator is a kind of Alpus-Interruptus I'd rather not experience. The Alps spread before you. In the distance is the bent little Matterhorn (a tall, shady pyramid behind a broader mountain, listed on the observation table in French as "Cervin—4,505 meters"). And looming just over there is Mont Blanc, at 15,781 feet, Europe's highest point. Use the free telescope to spot mountain climbers; over 2,000 climb this mountain each year. Dial English and let the info box take you on a visual tour. Check the temperature next to the elevator.

Explore Europe's tallest lift station. More than 150 meters of tunnels lead to a cafeteria, restaurant, gift shop, and the icicle-covered gateway to the glacial world. This "ice tunnel" is where summer skiers and mountain climbers depart. Just observing is exhilarating. Peek down the icy cliff and ponder the value of an ice axe.

Next, for your own private glacial dream world, get into the little red *télécabine* and head south to the Panoramic du Mont Blanc at Hellbronner Point, the Italian border station. This line stretches five kilometers with no solid pylon. (It's propped by a "suspended pylon," a line stretched between two peaks 400 meters from the Italian end.) In a gondola for four, you'll dangle silently for 40 minutes as you glide over the glacier to Italy. Hang your head out the window; explore every corner of your view. From Hellbronner Point you can continue into Italy (see Connections, below), but there's really no point unless you're traveling that way.

From Aiguille du Midi you can ride all the way back to Chamonix or get off halfway down (Plan de l'Aiguille) and hike three to four hours from 7,500 feet to the valley floor at 3,400 feet. Or better yet, hike the scenic, undulating two-hour trail to Montenvers (the Mer de Glace, 6,000 feet). From there you can hike or ride the train (56F) back into Chamonix.

To beat the clouds and crowds, ride the lifts (up and down) as early as you can. To beat major delays in August, leave by 7:00. If the weather's good, don't dillydally. Lift hours are weather dependent, but generally it runs daily from 7:00 to 17:00 in summer; 8:00 to 16:45 in May, June, and September; and 8:00 to 15:45 in winter. The last *télécabine* departure to Panoramic du Mont Blanc (Hellbronner) is at around 14:00. Summertime travelers can call to reserve up to 10 days in advance (toll-free tel. 08 36 68 00 67; you must retrieve your reservation at the lift station at least 30 minutes before your departure).

Approximate ticket costs for summer (slightly less in off-season) from Chamonix to: Plan de l'Aiguille—82F round-trip (64F one way); Aiguille du Midi—194F round-trip (162F one way, not including parachute); the Panoramic du Mont Blanc at Hellbronner—290F round-trip (220F one way).

Tickets from Aiguille du Midi to Hellbronner/Panoramic du Mont Blanc are sold at the base or on top (96F, or 58F one way). It's L38,000 (about $22, sold there, many currencies accepted) to drop down into Italy. (Yes, you can bring your luggage on board.)

Time to allow: to Aiguille du Midi—20 minutes, two hours round-trip, three to four hours in peak season; Chamonix to Hellbronner: 90 minutes one way, three to four hours round-trip, longer in peak season). Plan on 32 degrees Fahrenheit even on a sunny day. Sunglasses are essential. On busy days, minimize delays by getting your return lift time upon arrival at the top (tel. 04 50 53 30 80).

Mer de Glace—From the little station over the tracks from Chamonix's main train station, a two-car cogwheel train (look for the red trains, 73F round-trip, 56F one way) toots you up to a rapidly moving and very dirty glacier called the Mer de Glace, or Sea of Ice. The glacier—France's largest at six miles long—is interesting, as are its funky ice caves (17F entry) filled with ice sculpture (take the small lift, 13F round-trip to the caves; or a short uphill hike). The view is glorious, but if you've already seen a glacier up close, you might skip this one. One good option is to get off the Chamonix-Aiguille du Midi lift (on the way down) at Plan de l'Aiguille, and hike the pleasant two-hour trail to Montenvers/Mer de Glace. From there you can hike or ride the train into Chamonix.

▲**Luge**—Here's something new for the thrill-seeker in you. You can ride a chairlift up the mountain and scream down a windy, banked concrete slalom course on a wheeled sled. Chamonix has two roughly parallel luge courses. While each course is a kilometer long and about the same speed, one is marked for slower bobsledders and the other for the speed demons. Young or old, hare or tortoise, any fit person can manage a luge. Don't take your hands off your stick. The course is fast and slippery. (34F/one ride, 135F/five rides, 240F/10 rides, splitable with companions, daily 10:00–19:30 July–August, otherwise weekends only from 13:30 until about 18:00; 10-minute walk from the center, just beyond the train station, tel. 04 50 53 08 97.)

▲▲▲**The** *Téléphérique* **to Le Brévent**—While the Aiguille de Midi offers a more spectacular ride, hiking options are better on this lower side of the valley, with views of the Mont Blanc range to the east and the Aiguilles Rouges peaks to the west.

From Chamonix, walk up the road past the TI and keep going to the Le Brévent station. Take the *téléphérique* to Planpraz (55F round-trip, 46F one way, good views and hiking, particularly the two-hour hike along the Grand Balcon Sud to La Flégère lift, see Hike #3, below), then catch the *téléphérique* up to Brévent (great views and hikes, 80F round-trip, 55F one way from Chamonix, daily 8:00–18:00, closed April–mid-June and November).

Chamonix Area Hikes
Four fine hikes give nature lovers of almost any ability in just about any weather a good opportunity to enjoy the valley. You'll find the region's hiking map extremely helpful; pick it up at the TI (25F).

Hike #1: Plan de l'Aiguille to Montenvers (Grand Balcon

Chamonix Valley

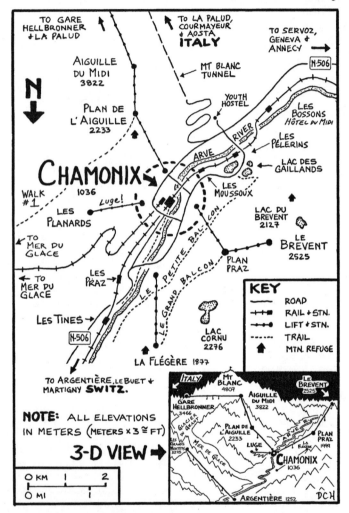

Nord): This is the easiest way to incorporate a two-hour high-country walk into your ride down from the valley's greatest lift and check out a glacier to boot. From Aiguille du Midi, get off halfway down (Plan de l'Aiguille) and hike the scenic up-and-down two-hour trail to Montenvers and the Mer de Glace. From there, hike or ride the train (56F) into Chamonix. Snow covers this trail generally until June.

Hike #2: Chamonix to les Praz (Grand Balcon Sud): For a moderately easy and scenic high-country hike, walk 40 minutes along the Arve River or take the Chamonix bus (five-minute ride, every 30 minutes from the TI) to the tiny village of Les Praz. Ride the lift from Les Praz to La Flégère (43F one way, 56F round-trip), then hike the scenic Grand Balcon Sud two hours back to Chamonix, taking the lift down to Chamonix at Plan Praz (46F one way, 55F-round-trip) or hiking down a very steep trail. Of course, this can be reversed by hiking from Chamonix, taking the Le Brévent lift to Plan Praz, and hiking the Grand Balcon Sud to Les Praz.

Hike #3: Petit Balcon Sud: This hike parallels the Grand Balcon Sud at a lower elevation, and is ideal when snow or poor weather make the Grand Balcon Sud inaccessible. No lifts are required, just firm thighs to climb to the trail. From Chamonix, walk up to Le Brévent lift station, follow the asphalt road to the left of the lift leading uphill. It turns into a dirt road that signs mark as the Petit Balcon Sud trail. Walk north about two hours on the trail to Les Praz village (follow the lift wires leading down to La Flégère lift to reach Les Praz). Return by Chamonix bus or by walking the level Arve River trail (40 minutes); or walk only as far as your legs take you and turn around. This hike works just as well in reverse.

Hike #4: Arve riverbank stroll: For an easy forested-valley stroll, follow the sleepy Arve River out of Chamonix toward Les Praz (the path starts across the river from Chamonix's Hôtel Alpina). Les Praz makes a pleasant destination. Several cafés, restaurants, and a charming village green lend a tranquil air to this alpine hamlet.

Other good hiking destinations: The trail to Lac Blanc (from La Flégère lift in Les Praz) and the trail to La Pierre à Berard refuge (leaves from Le Buet lift) are each ideal, moderate day hikes and offer refuges with overnight accommodations. Get details at the Office de la Haute Montagne.

Sleeping in Chamonix
(5.5F = about $1, zip code: 74400)

Reasonable hotels and dormlike chalets abound. With the helpful TI, you can find budget accommodations anytime. July 20 to August 16 is most difficult, though you may find some last-minute cancellations at the better hotels. Prices tumble off-season.

Hotels

Hôtel de l'Arve** has a slick modern Alpine feel, with fine view rooms right on the Arve River overlooking Mont Blanc, or cheaper rooms without the view (Sb-252–424F, Db-300–462F, extra bed-65F, ask for the few cheaper rooms sans bathroom elevator, across the river from the Olympic complex with a pleasant garden and fireplace lounge, 60 Impasse des Anémones, CC:VMA, tel. 04 50 53 02 31, fax 04 50 53 56 92, friendly Isabelle and Bertrice SE).

Hotel Savoyarde***, a steep but rewarding walk above Chamonix, has good views from the outdoor café tables, elegant chalet ambience, and a fine restaurant. The owner's attention to detail is evident. This is a worthwhile splurge (Db-600–700F, Tb-770–870F, Qb-850–1,000F, CC:VMA, a 15-minute walk above the TI, overlooking Chamonix at 28 rue des Moussoux, tel. 04 50 53 00 77, fax 04 50 55 86 82, e-mail: savoyarde@mail.silicone.fr).

Hôtel de Clocher** is a small family-run place offering eight small but cozy rooms, private parking, a backyard garden, and a smokers' lobby (Sb-265–295F, Db-285–335F, extra beds-50F, CC:VMA, a block to the right of the church as you face it on l'Impasse de l'Androsace, tel. 04 50 53 30 27, fax 04 50 53 73 19).

Hôtel Au Bon Coin** is an Old World place with great views, private balconies, and thin walls in most of its spotless rooms; the cheaper rooms are wood-panel cozy but lack the views (Ds-235F, Db-350–380F, Tb-400F, Qb-450F, closed mid-April–June 30 and October–mid-December, 80 avenue L'Aiguille du Midi, tel. 04 50 53 15 67, fax 04 50 53 51 51, friendly Nadine SE).

The **Boule de Niege*** (snowball) hotel is a fun, simple and central budget option with a backyard view terrace (Ss-160–220F, Ds-205–245F, Ts-285–335F, add 40F for a room with bath, 362 rue Joseph Vallot, tel. 04 50 53 04 48, fax 04 50 55 91 09).

Hôtel Touring**, with basic but cavernous rooms (many with four beds) and a friendly British staff, is ideal for families (Ds-225–275F, Db-285–350F, add 60F for three and 40F more for four, 95 rue Joseph Vallot, tel. 04 50 53 59 18, fax 04 50 53 67 25, e-mail: n.gulliford@aol.com). They also run the nearby **Hotel di Midi**** with a pleasant courtyard café; the Midi often has rooms when other hotels don't (small rooms with view Db-232–320F, same tel. & fax as Hotel Touring).

Chamonix's most classy *chambre d'hôte*, **Chalet Beauregard**, is a friendly and peaceful retreat with a private garden. Five of its seven sharp rooms come with a glorious view balcony (Sb-200F, Db-330–600F, Tb-460–600F, breakfast included, free parking, five-minute walk above the TI toward Le Brévent lift, 182 montée La Mollard, tel. & fax 04 50 55 86 30, Manuel and Laurence SE). **La Girandole** is another fine *chambre d'hôte*, near the Le Brévent lift (Db-320F, includes breakfast, 46 Chemin de la Perserverance, tel. 04 50 53 37 58, fax 04 50 55 81 77).

Hôtel le Chamonix** is tall, old, and skinny with no elevator. Its rooms are clean and simple (some with balconies), above a café, and across from the TI (Db-300–390F, Tb/Qb-400–470F, CC:VM, 58 place de l'Eglise, tel. 04 50 53 11 07, fax 04 50 53 64 78).

Richemond Hôtel** offers Old World alpine elegance, spacious lobbies, overstuffed chairs, a private terrace, serious management, and extraordinary rooms (Sb-300F, Db-365–455F, Tb-510F, Qb-570F, CC:VMA, 228 rue du Docteur Paccard, tel. 04 50 53 08 85, fax 04 50 55 91 69). They're unaccustomed to drop-in guests, so be patient.

Sleeping near Chamonix

If nature beckons or summer crowds heckle, spend the night in one of the valley's overlooked, lower-profile villages. The small village of Les Praz (lay prah), while just up the valley from Chamonix (five minutes by car, 30 minutes on foot), is a world away. The town is home to the Flégère lift, which allows access to the recommended le Grand Balcon Sud and Lac Blanc hikes.

Hotel Rhodendron** sits right on the village green (Db-290–320F, Tb-330–370F, half-pension required in summer, CC:VM, 100 route des Tines, tel. 04 50 53 06 39, fax 04 50 53 55 76). The tranquil, idyllic **La Bagna Auberge-Gîte** is in a beautiful setting. It includes a relaxing patio and common room, and well-maintained rooms at fair prices (70F dorm beds, D-245F, T/Q-320F, 337 route des Gaudenays, tel. 04 50 53 62 90, fax 04 50 53 64 88, e-mail: montblan@cyberaccess.fr).

Three miles away down the valley (toward Annecy), in the village of Les Bossons, is the almost luxurious **Hôtel l'Aiguille du Midi****. The friendly owner offers polished service, gorgeous gardens, a swimming pool, tennis courts, comfortable rooms, and a restaurant where Chamonix locals go for their Sunday meal (Db-280–460F, add 30 percent each for three and four persons, half-pension required in summer, Les Bossons, tel. 04 50 53 00 65, fax 04 50 55 93 69, SE).

Dorm-like Accommodations

For cheaper dorm-like accommodations in a quiet neighborhood a 10-minute walk to Chamonix, try **Les Grands Charmoz**. Seventy-five francs buys a bunk and sheet, showers, and a kitchen. They also have a few clean doubles (200F) with kitchen privileges, as well as apartments upstairs (468 chemin des Cristalliers; turn right out of the station, walk under the bridge and into the Hotel Albert's driveway, veer right, cross the tracks, then turn left; tel. & fax 04 50 53 45 57). The **Chalet Ski Station** also has bunks but no doubles (65F for a bed, reductions on area lifts for clients, next to the Brévent *téléphérique*, a 10-minute hike up from the TI, 6 rue des Moussoux, tel. 04 50 53 20 25).

Chamonix's classy **hostel** was formerly the barracks for the diggers of the Mont Blanc tunnel. Well-run, cheap, and as comfortable as hostels get, it sells substantially discounted lift tickets for the most expensive lifts in the valley. Hostel members are

welcome to drop in and buy these discounted tickets, even if they
sleep elsewhere (76F dorm bed, S-135F, D-210F, 30-minute walk
from the base of the Aiguille du Midi lift or a 15-minute walk from
the Les Pèlerins Station, two kilometers below Chamonix in Les
Pèlerins, daily 8:00–12:00 and 17:00–22:00, tel. 04 50 53 14 52).

Refuges
The French have the perfect answer for hikers who don't want to
pack tents, sleeping bags, stoves, and food: refuges. For about 60F
you can sleep on bunks high in the peaceful mountains. Bring your
own food or let the guardian cook your dinner and breakfast
(80–100F for dinner, 35F for breakfast). The Office de Haute
Montagne in Chamonix can explain your options and make reservations. Some refuges are located an easy walk from a lift station,
and most are open from mid-June to mid-September. Comfort
ranges from very basic to downright luxurious. Try **La Pierre à
Berard** refuge, a beautiful hike from Le Buet (48F per bed, 150F
half-pension, tel. 04 50 54 62 08).

Eating in Chamonix
While Chamonix, like any mountain resort, has its share of bad
food and bad-price restaurants, there are several good values to be
found.
  Bistrot des Sports is a rare souvenir of old Chamonix, with
wood tables, old photos, good food, and smoky locals (50–100F,
182 rue Joseph Vallot, tel. 04 50 53 00 46). **La Bergerie** is where I
go for alpine ambience, fondue, wood-fired raclette, and other
regional dishes (232 avenue Michel Croz, near train station, tel. 04
50 53 45 04). **La Boccalatte** is an excellent value with a large
selection of local specialties (across from the Hotel au Bon Coin at
59 avenue de l'Aiguille du Midi, tel. 04 50 53 52 14).
  If dipping bread into hot, gurgling cheese isn't your idea of
haute cuisine, try **Le Sabot** for crêpes and Italian food on allée
Recteur Payot (above the intersection of avenue Aguille du Midi
and rue du Docteur Paccard). **La Caboulé**, next to the Brévent
téléphérique, is a hip eatery with great omelets and an unbeatable
view from its outdoor tables. **L'Impossible** is a characteristic place
a five-minute walk beyond the Aiguille du Midi lift; it's named for
a local ski champ who could do *"l'impossible"* (100F *menus*, daily in
summer, route des Pelerins, tel. 04 50 53 20 36).
  After dinner, hang out with the local hikers at the **Bar Chou-
cas** (206 rue du Docteur Paccard) or the **Bistrot des Sports** (182
rue Joseph Vallot).
  Picnic assembly: A good *boulangerie* and a vegetable market
are adjacent to the TI. The best grocery is the Codec, below
Hôtel Alpina. The more central Super U is next to Hotel Touring
at #117 (open even Sunday morning), and there's a long-hours

place a block in front of the train station. The park next to the church is picnic-pretty.

Transportation Connections—Chamonix

Bus and train service to Chamonix are surprisingly good. Both the bus and train stations (on the same square) have helpful information desks.

By train to: Annecy (5/day, 2.5 hrs, transfer in St. Gervais), **Beaune** and **Dijon** (3/day, 8 hrs, transfers in St. Gervais and Lyon), **Nice** (5/day, 10 hrs, transfer in St. Gervais and Lyon, night train possible), **Arles** (5/day, 8 hrs, transfer in St. Gervais and Lyon), **Paris'** Gare de Lyon (4/day, 7 hrs, longer at night, transfers in St. Gervais and Annecy; take the handy night train), **Martigny, Switzerland** (2 hrs, a very scenic trip), **Geneva** (3/day, 2.5 hrs, quick transfers in St. Gervais, La Roche-sur-Foron, and Annemasse).

By bus: Buses provide service to destinations not served by train and also to some cities that are served by train, but at a lower cost and higher speed. Get information at the bus station (*gare routière*) in the SNCF station (tel. 04 50 53 01 15).

By bus to: Aosta, Italy (5/day, 90 min; Aosta connects you with the Italian rail system).

Itinerary Options from Chamonix

A Day in French-Speaking Switzerland—There are plenty of tempting Alpine and cultural thrills just an hour or two away in Switzerland. A road and train line sneak you scenically from Chamonix to the Swiss town of Martigny. Remember, while train travelers cross without formalities, drivers are charged the $32 Swiss annual highway tax just to cross the border.

A Little Italy—The remote Valle d'Aosta and its historic capital city of Aosta are a short but costly drive east of Chamonix through the Mont Blanc tunnel, or a spectacular gondola ride over the Mont Blanc range. The side trip is worthwhile if you'd like to taste Italy (spaghetti, gelati, and cappuccino), enjoy the town's great evening ambience, or look at the ancient ruins in Aosta, often called "the Rome of the North."

From Hellbronner (see Aiguille du Midi lift, above), catch the 38,000L lift down to Entreves and take the bus to Aosta (hrly, change in Courmayeur). Those with exceptional social skills can probably talk a gondola mate with a car in Entreves into a ride down the valley. From Aosta, trains or buses will take you to Milan and the rest of Italy, or you can take a bus back to Chamonix under Mont Blanc (5/day, 90 min).

Sleeping in Aosta, Italy (L1,700 = $1, tel. code 0165, zip code: 11100): Hotel Ponte Romano is on the Roman bridge. With a warm woody interior, it's one of Aosta's better hotels (Sb-L90,000, Db-L130,000, Via Ponte Romano 27, tel.

0165/45262, fax 0165/31736). **La Belle Epoque** offers clean and
simple rooms and a grumpy staff (Sb-L40,000–55,000, Db-
L60,000–75,000, Via D'Avise 18, off Via E. Aubert, tel. 0165/262-
276). Cheaper beds are found in a less charming, more industrial
area at the **Barrano** family (S-L30,000, D-L70,000, Via Voison 9,
tel. 0165/43224) and Senora Mancuso's **Albergo Mancuso** (Sb-
L50,000, Db-L60,000, Via Voison 32, tel. 0165/34526).

LYON

Comfortably nestled at the base of the Alps between Burgundy
and Provence, overlooked Lyon is one of France's surprises. After
Paris, Lyon is the most historic and culturally important city in
France. Its strategic location, straddling the Rhône and Saone
Rivers, has made Lyon important since pre-Roman times. On a
three-week tour of France, Lyon merits two nights and a day for
its enchanting old city (Vieux Lyon), fine Roman ruins, fascinating
museums, thriving pedestrian streets, café-lined squares, and
France's undisputedly best cuisine at digestible prices.

Orientation

Lyon is France's second-largest city but inside it feels small.
Most of your sightseeing is near the Saone River and can be
done on foot. If you stick to the sights listed below, you proba-
bly won't need more than the funicular to help you get around.
Your area of focus is from west to east between the hill of
Fourvière and the Rhône River, and from south to north from
Perrache station to the place Terreaux. Place Bellecour is
ground zero.

Lyon's sights are concentrated in three areas: Fourvière hill,
Vieux Lyon, and the Presqu'ile. Start your day on Fourvière hill
(take the funicular near St. Jean Cathedral in Vieux Lyon to
Fourvière) and visit the Gallo-Roman Museum, Roman Theater,
and Basilique Notre Dame before catching the funicular down to
Vieux Lyon. In Vieux Lyon, take the *traboule* walk outlined below,
then finish your day on the Presqu'ile.

Tourist Information: Three well-equipped TIs will quickly
help get you oriented: in Perrache station (Monday–Friday
9:00–13:00 and 14:00–18:00, no midday closing on Saturdays and
in summer); in Vieux Lyon near the funicular on avenue Adolphe-
Max (same hours as Perrache, plus Sunday 10:00–18:00); and in
the middle of place Bellecour (Monday–Friday 9:00–19:00, until
18:00 Saturday and in winter). Pick up the excellent English version map of Lyon with museum hours and descriptions, the map
of Vieux Lyon, the list of open *traboules* (passageways, see below),
and a schedule of events and concerts. Summer concerts in the
Roman Theater and any event in the new opera house keep
Lyon's music scene lively.

Arrival in Lyon

By Train: Two train stations serve Lyon (Perrache and Part-Dieu), most trains stop at both, and through trains connect the two stations every 10 minutes. Both are well served by métro, bus, and taxi. Perrache is more central and within a 20-minute walk of place Bellecour (cross place Carnot and walk straight up rue Victor Hugo). Figure 60 to 80F to taxi from either train station to the hotels listed near place Bellecour.

By Car: The center city is easy to navigate. Follow signs to *centre-ville* and Presqu'ile, then follow the "place Bellecour" signs. Park in the lot under place Bellecour or place des Celestins, or get advice from your hotel.

Sights—Lyon's Fourvière Hill

▲▲▲**Gallo-Roman Museum (Musée de la Civilisation Gallo-romaine)**—Constructed into the hillside with views of the Roman theater, this museum makes Lyon's importance in Roman times clear. Lyon was the military base that Julius Caesar used to conquer Gaul (much of modern-day France). Admire the bronze chariot from the seventh century B.C., then orient yourself with the model of Roman Lyon. As the museum cascades downhill you'll pass Gallo-Roman artifacts that allow you to piece together life in Lyon during the Roman occupation, including 2,000-year-old lead pipes, a speech by Claudius (translated into English), Roman coins, models of Roman theaters complete with moving stage curtains, and haunting funeral masks (20F, daily 9:00–12:00 and 14:00–18:00, helpful English explanations).

Basilique Notre Dame de Fourvière—In the late 1800s the Bishop of Lyon vowed to build a magnificent tribute to God if the Prussians left his city alone (the same reason and vow that built the Sacre Coeur in Paris). The whipped-cream exterior is neo-everything, and the interior screams overdone with mosaics. Don't miss the chapel below or the panoramic views from behind the church.

Sights—Vieux Lyon (Old Lyon)

▲▲**Traboules** (covered passageways)—Lyon is the Florence of France, offering the best concentration of well-preserved Renaissance buildings in the country. From the 16th to the 19th century Lyon was king of Europe's silk industry; at one point it hummed with more than 18,000 looms. The fine buildings of the old center were designed by Italians and paid for by silk profits. Pastel courtyards, beautiful loggias, and delicate arches line the passageways (*traboules*) connecting these buildings. The serpentine *traboules* provided shelter when moving the silk from one stage to the next, and would provide ideal cover for the French resistance in WWII. Several of Lyon's 315 *traboules* are open to the public (press the top button next to the streetfront door to release the door; please respect the residents' peace when wandering through). The TI's map of Vieux Lyon proposes an interesting route connecting some of these most interesting *traboules*: On the Saone River, find the quai Roman Rolland, enter #17, and cross to #9 rue des Trois-Maries. Then find #6 rue des Trois-Maries and cross to #27 rue St. Jean; turn left on St. Jean and take the last *traboule* just before place Neuve-St. Jean (#42), which leads into place Neuve-St. Jean. Now find the rue de Boeuf, go left, then enter Lyon's longest *traboule* at #27 and cross back to rue St. Jean; turn right here to reach the cathedral.

Cathedral of St. Jean—This place reminds me of Italian Gothic—short and squat (Monday–Friday 8:00–12:00 and 14:00–19:30, weekends 14:00–17:00). Inside you'll find a few fine stained-glass windows and a remarkable astrological clock with a performance every hour. Check out the ruins predating the cathedral outside the left transept.

Sights—On Lyon's Presqu'ile

From Perrache station to place des Terreaux, the Presqu'ile is Lyon's shopping spine with thriving pedestrian streets and chic boutiques. Cruise the shops of rue de la Republique and the *bouchons* (characteristic bistros) of the rue Merciere, and relax at a café on place des Terreaux. You'll also find these interesting museums:

▲**Musee des Beaux Arts**—Located in a former abbey, this fine arts museum has an impressive collection ranging from Egyptian antiquities to medieval armor to Impressionist paintings. Still, if you're short on time and going to Paris, it's skippable (25F, Wednesday–Sunday 10:30–18:00, pick up a museum layout on entering, great café-terrace, 20 place des Terreaux, Mo: Hôtel de Ville).

Museums of Fabrics and Decorative Arts (Musées des Tissus et des Arts Decoratifs)—Here you get two museums for the price of one. The beautifully organized Musée des Tissus takes you on a historical tour of Lyon's silk industry. The less engaging Musée des Arts Decoratif is a large manor home decorated with period furniture and art objects (28F covers both musuems, daily 10:00–17:30, 34 rue de la Charite, Mo: Bellecour).

▲▲**Resistance and Deportation Center (Centre d'Histoire de la Resistance et de la Deportation)**—This living tribute to French Resistance members is a must. Located near Vichy, the capital of the French puppet state, Lyon was the center of French resistance from 1942 to 1945. This well-organized museum, once used as a Nazi torture chamber, offers English explanations and multimedia presentations (25F, Wednesday–

Sunday 9:00–17:30, 14 avenue Berthelot, just across the Rhone River from Perrache station).

Sleeping in Lyon
(5.5F = about $1, zip code: 69002)

Hotels in Lyon are a steal compared to Paris. Weekends are discounted. Skip the hotels near Perrache station. All hotels listed below are on the Presqu'ile; the first three are on or very near the delightful place des Celestins (two blocks from place Bellecour, Mo: Bellecour).

Hotel des Artistes***, right on place des Celestins, is plush, comfortable, and central (Sb-330–440F, Db-380–480F, skippable 48F breakfast, CC:VMA, 8 rue Gaspard-Andre, tel. 04 78 42 04 88, fax 04 78 42 93 76, SE).

Hotel du Theatre**, across the small square from Hotel des Artistes, is my romantic choice. All rooms are artsy and different; some are wonderfully funky. Expect friendly owners and plenty of stairs (S-180F, Sb-275–305F, Db-275–345F, 10 rue de Savoie, entrance on the backside of place des Celestins, tel. 04 78 42 33 32, fax 04 72 40 00 61).

Hotel Colbert**, spotless but not homey, provides the necessary comforts (Db-305F, 4 rue des Archers, tel. 04 72 56 08 98, fax 04 72 56 08 65).

Hotel Moderne** is an eager yet average hotel with comfortable rooms (Db-315–335F, halfway between places Bellecour and Terreaux in the heart of the shopping area, 15 rue Dubois, Mo: Cordeliers, tel. 04 78 42 21 83, fax 04 72 41 04 40).

Grand Hotel des Terreaux*** is a good value and Old World–elegant (Sb-355F, Db-400–500F, well-located near Saone River and place Terreaux, 16 rue Lanterne, Mo: Hôtel de Ville, tel. 04 78 27 04 10, fax 04 78 27 97 75).

Eating in Vieux Lyon

With an abundance of excellent restaurants in all price ranges, it's hard to go wrong, unless you order *tripes* (cow intestines). Look instead for these classics: *quenelles* (a fish mousse wrapped in a pasta shell), roasted chicken from Bresse, and *salades Lyonnais* (lettuce, ham, and potatoes).

Bouchons are small bistros evolving from the days when mama would feed the silk workers. I can't imagine a more delightful area to restaurant shop than in Vieux Lyon (look along rue St. Jean and rue de Boeuf) or along the rue Merciere on the Presqu'ile. Here are a few *bouchons* to get you started:

Le Lyonnais is fun, light hearted, and locally popular, with photo-portraits of loyal customers lining the walls (90F *menu*, 1 rue Tramssac, tel. 04 78 37 64 82). **Les Retrouvailles** offers an excellent 120F *menu*, a pleasant dining room, and a terrific overall experience (32 rue de Boeuf). **Le Comptoir de Boeuf** is worth the reservations you'll need to make (80F and 120F *menus*, outdoor terrace, 3 place Neuve-St. Jean, tel. 04 78 82 35). **Aux Trois-Maries** is quieter and more serene, with outdoor tables (105F and 200F *menus*, 1 rue Trois-Marie, tel. 04 78 37 67 28). **L'Amphitryon** is lively, fun, and right in the thick of things (75F and 99F *menus*, 33 rue St. Jean, tel 04 78 37 23 68).

Transportation Connections–Lyon

After Paris, Lyon is France's most important rail hub. The first TGV train built connected Paris and Lyon. Many rail travelers will find this gateway to the Alps, Provence, the Riviera, and Burgundy a convenient stopover. To **Paris** (30/day, 2 hrs), **Dijon** (16/day, 2 hrs), **Beaune** (9/day, 2 hrs), **Avignon** (18/day, 2.5 hrs), **Nice** (20/day, 6 hrs), **Annecy** (8/day, 90 min), **Venice** (4/day, 10 hrs), **Rome** (4/day, 11 hrs), **Florence** (4/day, 10 hrs), **Geneva** (6/day, 2 hrs), **Barcelona** (2/day, 9 hrs).

Drivers: If heading south to Provence, consider a three-hour detour through the spectacular Ardeches Gorges (exit the A-6 autoroute at Privas, then follow Aubenas, Vallon Pont d'Arc, and Pont St. Esprit.) All-day canoe/kayak floats through the gorges are easy to find in Vallon Pont d'Arc.

BURGUNDY

The soft rolling hills of Burgundy gave birth to superior wine, fine cuisine, and sublime countryside crisscrossed with canals and dotted with untouristed hilltowns. Bucolic Burgundy is the transportation funnel for eastern France and makes a convenient stopover for travelers (car or train), with quick access north to Paris or the Alsace, east to the Alps, and south to Provence. Only a small part of Burgundy's land is covered by vineyards, but winemaking is what they do best. The white cows you see everywhere are Charolais. They make France's best beef and end up in *boeuf bourguignon*. The Romanesque churches dotting the countryside owe their origin to the once-powerful influence of the Abbey of Cluny in southern Burgundy.

Planning Your Time
Dijon, the capital of Burgundy, is worth a look, but set up camp in cozier Beaune. It's better located for touring the vineyards and countryside. You'll want two days here—a half day for Dijon, and one day in Beaune and its environs. Trains link Beaune and Dijon with ease. Bikes, buses, and minivan tours get nondrivers into the countryside.

Cuisine Scene—Burgundy
Your taste buds are going to thank you for bringing them here. Considered by many to be France's best, Burgundian cuisine is peasant cooking elevated to an art. Several classic dishes were born here—*escargots bourguignonne* (snails served sizzling hot in garlic butter), *boeuf bourguignon* (beef simmered for hours in red wine with onions and mushrooms), *coq au vin* (chicken stewed in red wine), *oeufs en meurette* (poached eggs on a large crouton in red

Beaune Area

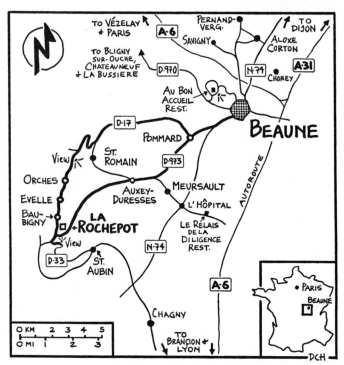

wine)—as were the famous Dijon mustards. Look also for *jambon persillé* (cold ham layered in a garlic-parsley gelatin), *pain d'épices* (spice bread), and *gougère* (light, puffy cheese pastries). Native cheeses are Epoisses and Langres (both mushy and great), and, my favorite, Montrachet (a tasty goat cheese). *Crème de cassis* (a black currant liqueur) is another Burgundian specialty; look for it in desserts and snazzy drinks (try a *kir*).

With Bordeaux, Burgundy is why France is famous for wine. From Chablis to the Beaujolais you'll find it all here—great, fruity reds, dry whites, and crisp rosés. The three key grapes are Chardonnay (dry white wines), Pinot Noir (medium-bodied red wines), and Gamay (light, fruity wines like Beaujolais). Every village produces its own distinctive wine—like Chablis and Meursault; road maps read like fine wine lists. If the wine village has a hyphenated name (most do), the latter half of its name comes from the town's most important vineyard (e.g., Gevery-Chamberin, Ladoix-Serrigny). Look for the "*Dégustation Gratuite*" (free tasting) signs and prepare for serious tasting and steep prices if you're not

careful. For more relaxed tastings head for the hills; the less prestigious *Hautes-Côtes* (upper slopes) produce some terrific and overlooked wines. Look also for village cooperatives, or see my
suggestions for Beaune tastings. The least expensive (but still tasty)
wines are the Bourgogne Aligote (white), Bourgogne Ordinaire
and Passetoutgrain (both red), and those from the Macon, Chalon,
and Beaujolais areas. If you like rosé, try the Marsannay, considered the best rosé in France.

BEAUNE

You'll feel comfortable right away in this polished but fun-loving
wine capital. Here life centers around the production and con-
sumption of the prestigious, expensive Côte d'Or wines. "Côte
d'Or" means "golden hillsides," and they are a spectacle to enjoy
in late October, as the leaves of the vineyards turn colors.

Beaune is a compact, thriving little city (population: 25,000)
with vineyards on its doorstep. Limit your Beaune ramblings to
the town center, contained within its medieval walls and circled by
a one-way ring road. All roads and activities converge on the perfectly French place Carnot.

Tourist Information: The info-packed TI, across the street
from Hôtel Dieu on place de la Halle, has city maps, a room-
finding service, *chambre d'hôte* pamphlets, bus schedules, and
information on minibus wine-tasting tours. (Open daily 9:00–
19:00 April–September, summers until 20:00, closes at 18:00 in
winter; from place Carnot, walk toward the thin spire; tel. 03 80
26 21 30, e-mail: otbeaune@hol.fr.)

Arrival in Beaune

By Train: To reach the city center, walk straight out of the train
station up avenue du Huit (8) Septembre, cross the busy ring road,
and continue up rue du Château.

By Car: Follow *centre-ville* signs to the ring road. Once on
the ring road, turn right at the first signal after the new post office
(rue d'Alsace) and park (free) in the place Madeleine.

Sights—Beaune

▲▲▲**Hôtel Dieu**—The Hundred Years' War and the Black
Death devastated Beaune, leaving more than 90 percent of its population destitute. Nicholas Rolin, Chancellor of Burgundy and a
peasant by birth, had to do something for "his people." So, in
1443, he paid to build this flamboyant Flemish/Gothic charity
hospital. It was completed in only eight years. Tour it on your
own; you'll find (for once) good English explanations; pick up a
tour brochure at the ticket desk. Start in the oldest part of the hospital, the church-like room of the paupers. At busy times there
were twice as many beds filling this room with two patients per

Beaune

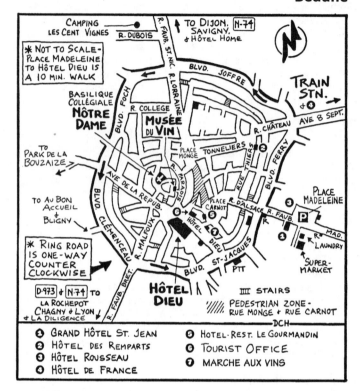

Not to Scale - Place Madeleine to Hôtel Dieu is a 10 min. walk

Ring Road is One-Way Counter Clockwise

D-973 & N-74 to La Rochepot Chagny & Lyon & La Diligence

STAIRS

PEDESTRIAN ZONE - Rue Monge & Rue Carnot

—DCH—

- ❶ Grand Hôtel St. Jean
- ❷ Hôtel des Remparts
- ❸ Hôtel Rousseau
- ❹ Hôtel de France
- ❺ Hotel·Rest. Le Gourmandin
- ❻ Tourist Office
- ❼ Marche Aux Vins

bed! Notice the inverted ship-hull ceiling and sea-monster beams. The extraordinary five-paneled polyptych by Roger Van der Weyden (which you'll see later) was hung behind the altar in the chapel at the end of the room. Next, shuffle though the St. Hughes room (wealthier clients stayed here) and study the images of blood-letting operations. The infirmary (now the hospital museum) is next—how about those medical instruments? Yeow! The nearby pharmacy once provided slug-slime cures for sore throats and cockroach powders for constipation. In the St. Louis wing (where patients replaced winepresses that occupied this space) you'll find Van der Weyden's dramatic *Last Judgment* polyptych, commissioned by Rolin to give the dying something to ponder. Ask the attendant to let the giant roaming monocle give you a closer look. Your visit ends with a look at Flemish tapestries. *The Story of Jacob*, woven by one person in 17 years, is magnificent (32F, daily 9:00–18:30 April–November, otherwise 9:00–11:30 and 14:00–17:30).

▲**Collégiale Notre Dame**—Built in the 12th and 13th centuries, this is a good example of Cluny-style architecture (except for the front porch). Enter to see the 15th-century tapestries (behind the altar, drop in a franc for lights), a variety of stained glass, and what's left of frescoes depicting the life of Lazarus (daily 10:00–12:30 and 13:30-19:00). To find the Musée du Vin from here, walk 30 steps straight out of the cathedral, turn left down a cobbled alley, keep left and enter the courtyard of the Hotel des Ducs, today's Musée du Vin, located in the old residence of the dukes of Burgundy.

Musée du Vin—You don't have to like wine to appreciate this folk-wine museum. The history and culture of Burgundy and wine were fermented in the same bottle. Even if you opt against the museum, wander into the courtyard for a look at the Duke's Palace, antique winepresses (in the barn), and a nifty model of 15th-century Beaune. Inside the museum you'll find a great model of the regions, tools, costumes, and scenes of Burgundian wine history, but no tasting. English explanations are promised in each room for 1999 (25F, ticket good for other Beaune museums, daily 9:30–18:00, closed Tuesday during winter).

Parc de la Bouzaise and vineyards—Walk toward the ring road on avenue de la République, cross it, then follow the stream for three blocks: The park and vineyards are straight ahead. Stroll through the peaceful park then enter the vineyards just beyond, climbing high on dirt paths for the best views.

Wine-Tasting in and near Beaune

Countless opportunities exist (for a price) for you to learn the fine points of Burgundy wine. You'll find many small wine shops that offer free tastings (with the expectation that you'll buy), and several large cellars (caves) that charge an entry fee and allow you to taste from a variety of wines with no expectation to buy. Most caves offer some form of introduction or self-guided tours and are open daily from 9:30 to 11:30 and 14:00 to 17:30. (Also see Minibus Tours, below.)

Start or end your tour with a visit to **Athenaeum**, a bookstore (with many titles in English), wine-bar, and Burgundian wine chamber of commerce all rolled into one (across from Hotel Dieu, next to TI).

▲▲▲**Marché aux Vins**—This is Beaune's wine smorgasbord and the best way to sample its impressive wines. You pay 50F for a traditional wine-tasting cup (you keep it) and get 45 minutes to sip away at Burgundy's beloved. Plunge into the labyrinth of candlelit caves dotted with 18 wine-barrel tables, each offering a new tasting experience. You're on your own. Relax; this is world-class stuff. The $70 reds are upstairs in the chapel, at the end of the tasting. (Hint: Taste better by sneaking in a hunk of bread or crackers.) If you grab an empty wine basket at the beginning and at least pretend you're going to buy, the occasional time checker will leave you alone. (Daily 9:00–12:00 and 14:30–18:30, last entry at 18:00, closes at 17:00 in winter, tel. 03 80 25 08 20.)

More Self-Guided Tours in Beaune—While the Marché aux Vins is the ultimate wine-tasting experience, it can overwhelm some. If you have less time for wine, **Caves des Cordeliers** offers good self-guided tours of its convent premises (with English explanations) and six wines to taste for just 20F (9:00–19:00 in summer, 6 rue de l'Hôtel Dieu, tel. 03 80 24 53 79). **Maison Patriache Père et Fils** also has self-guided tours and Beaune's largest underground cellars, with a selection of 13 different wines to sample (50F, tasting cup included, 7 rue du Collège, tel. 03 80 24 53 78).

Minibus Tours of Vineyards near Beaune—*Wine Safari* minibus wine-tasting tours offer several itineraries (190F, tour #2 is best for beginners, two hours each, departs from TI, call TI for information, tel. 03 80 26 21 30). These tours are well-run, English-speaking, and will get you through the countryside and to the wineries you couldn't get into otherwise. The TI also has a complete list of area vintners for those who want to organize their own routes; remember, you're expected to buy. (Look also under Sights—Beaune Region for ideas for tastings in the less prestigious, more relaxed Hautes-Côtes.

Sleeping in Beaune
(5.5F = about $1, zip code: 21200)
Sleep Code: **S** = Single, **D** = Double/Twin, **T** = Triple, **Q** = Quad, **b** = bathroom, **t** = toilet only, **s** = shower only, **CC** = Credit Card (Visa, MasterCard, Amex), **SE** = Speaks English, **NSE** = No English, * = French hotel rating system (0–4 stars).

Hôtel des Remparts*** offers affordable luxury, with fine rooms in a manor house complete with beamed ceilings, period furniture, a quiet courtyard, and great rooms for families (Db-300–450F, Tb-490–520F, Qb-520–690F, attic rooms are cozy, parking garage-38F, CC:VM; toward the train station from the center, but inside the center city at 48 rue Thiers; tel. 03 80 24 94 94, fax 03 80 24 97 08, SE, e-mail: hotel.des.ramparts @ wanadoo.fr).

Tulip Inn-Athanor*** mixes modern comfort with a touch of old Beaune and is very central (Db-375–540F, most at 450F, Tb/Qb-550–750F, elevator, CC:VMA, 9 avenue de la République, tel. 03 80 24 09 20, fax 03 80 24 09 15, SE, e-mail: Hotel.Athanor @wanadoo.fr).

The three spacious and comfortable rooms sold through the restaurant **Le Gourmandin** are as central as you can get (Db-350F, Tb/Qb-450F, many stairs, 8 place Carnot, tel. 03 80 24 07 88, fax 03 80 22 27 42).

Train travelers will appreciate the **Hôtel de France****, across from the train station (Sb-200F, Db-260–360F, Tb/Qb-350–420F, 35 avenue du 8 Septembre, tel. 03 80 24 10 34, fax 03 80 24 96 78).

Sleeping on Place Madeleine
These hotels are a few blocks from the city center and offer easy parking.

What **Hôtel au Grand St. Jean**** lacks in character, it makes up for with value and location (Db-230F, Tb/Qb-290F, CC:VM, on place Madeleine, tel. 03 80 24 12 22, fax 03 80 24 15 43). Like a sprawling motel with ample and safe parking, it's simple, practical, and, with its helpful, English-speaking owner, M. Neaux, plenty French. Color-blind travelers will love the TV lounge.

Two doors down, **Hotel de la Cloche***** offers two stars for the price of three. It has wicker furniture and a few rough edges, but a fine restaurant (small Db-300F, large Db-380F, a few good family rooms-450–580F, CC:VMA, 40 place Madeleine, tel. 03 80 24 66 33, fax 03 80 24 04 24).

Across the square, the no-frills **Hôtel Rousseau** will make you smile, with cheerful and quirky owners, pet birds, and a pleasant enclosed garden. The cheapest rooms are simple but fine; those with showers are like grandma's, though maintenance can be spotty. (S-125F, Ss-170F, D-175F, Db-300F, Tt-245F, Tb-350F, Q-290F, Qb-350F, includes breakfast, 20F showers down the hall, free private parking, 11 place Madeleine, tel. 03 80 22 13 59).

Sleeping near Beaune
Hotels: **Hôtel Le Home**** is an old vine-covered mansion and Beaune's most elegant two-star hotel value. It's a half mile out of town on the N-74 toward Dijon. The less expensive rooms are just fine, but the rooms on the parking courtyard (400F) come with a nice terrace (Db-330–460F, Tb/Qb-500F, free parking, CC:VM, 138 route de Dijon, tel. 03 80 22 16 43, fax 03 80 24 90 74). Call ahead—it's popular.

Drivers can park below their room window at one of many modern chain hotels on the way into Beaune from the autoroute. The simple, sterile **Villages Hotel*** is dirt cheap (Db/Tb-155F, CC:VM, rue Burgalat, tel. 03 80 24 14 50, fax 03 80 24 14 45). For twice the price, **Hotel IBIS**** offers more comfort, a pool, play area, and reasonable restaurant (Db-305–375F, avenue Charles de Gaulle, tel. 03 80 22 46 75, fax 03 80 22 21 16). The comfortable **Hotel Arcade**** (Db-300F) is closest to the town center, located right at the ring road and avenue Charles de Gaulle, tel. 03 80 22 75 67, fax 03 80 22 77 17).

Chambres d'Hôte: The Côte d'Or has many *chambres d'hôte*; get a pamphlet at the TI. Most can be found only in small wine villages, and many are only a short drive from Beaune. In Magnyle

Villers, the friendly **Dumays** have two attached rooms in a restored farmhouse. They're great for three or more (Ss-185F, Db-225F, Tb-285F, Qb-350F; from Beaune go north on N-74 then west at Ladoix; in Magny look behind the church; tel. 03 80 62 91 16). You'll find many *chambres d'hôtes* in the cliff-dwelling village of Orches, just under La Rochepot (zip code: 21340). **M. Muhlenbaumer** has two good rooms (Db-250F, Tb/Qb suite-450F, Baubigny-Orches, tel. 03 80 21 81 13) and **M. Rocault** has five small, modern rooms (Db-260F, tel. 03 80 21 78 72, fax 03 80 21 85 95).

Sleeping in the Burgundian Countryside
(zip code: 21320)
Those with a car should consider one of these exceptional listings. Each is located about 30 minutes from Beaune and 10 minutes off the A-6 autoroute (toward Paris, exit: Pouilly en Auxois, see also the description of, and directions to Châteauneuf-en-Auxois, under Sights—Beaune Region, below).

Hostellerie du Château**, in Châteauneuf-en-Auxois, offers rooms in two locations: Its main building is a better-value "Hotel," and its annex up the street is called "La Residence." Many rooms in the "Hotel" are half-timbered with views over the château next door; the tiny top-floor double rooms will melt a romantic's heart (Db-280–380F, T/QB-430F. The "Residence" has larger, pricier rooms, but they're very comfortable (D-430F, Tb-480F). The elegant restaurant serves *menus* from 140F (tel. 03 80 49 22 00, fax 03 80 49 21 27).

To sleep floating on a luxury-hotel barge at two-star hotel prices with views up to Chateauneuf's brooding castle, find the canal-front village of Vandenesse en Auxois. Here the *Lady A* barge offers tight yet surprisingly comfortable rooms (Sb-250F, Db-300F, includes breakfast, tel. 03 80 49 26 96, fax 03 80 49 27 00, call way ahead for summer, friendly Lisa SE and cooks dinner upon request—130F includes wine). The *ecluse* (lockhouse) at the bridge offers drinks, snacks, wine tastings, and the excellent-value *chambre d'hôte* of **chez Monique et Pascal** (Sb-200F, Db-250F, Tb-300F, tel. 03 80 49 27 12, fax 03 80 49 26 05).

Ten minutes away in the village of Sainte Sabine, **Hostellerie du Château de Sainte Sabine***** provides a country-elegant retreat (Db-300–750F, most around 480F, the 620F rooms are worth the splurge, two huge duplexes with five beds-1,050F, tel. 03 80 49 22 01, fax 03 80 49 20 01). This château/hotel has elegant public rooms, spacious bedrooms, a pool, and a panoramic view terrace all at fair prices. The equally elegant restaurant seems less loved (*menus* 150–300F).

Eating in Beaune
For a traditional Burgundian setting, I enjoy dining in the wine-cellar atmosphere of **Caveau des Arches** (good 85F *menu*, 10

boulevard Perpreuil, on the ringroad at rue d'Alsace, tel. 03 80 22
10 37). For good steaks, salads, and *oeufs en Meurette*, cross the
ringroad and try **Le Picboeuf** (closed Thursday, 2 rue Faubourg
Madeleine). Almost next door, at #8, step down into the relaxed
ambience and friendly surroundings of **les Caves Madeleine** and
dine surrounded by shelves of wine (good wines by the glass, reasonable *plats du jour* and 89F *menu*). **Le Gourmandin** is a good
value and seems popular with locals (90F *menus*, closed Tuesday, 8
place Carnot). For traditional Burgundian cuisine at digestible
prices, consider **La Grilladine** (75F, 100F, and 129F *menus*, fine
escargots, hot goat-cheese salad, and *oeufs en Meurette*, closed
Monday, 17 rue Maufoux, tel. 03 80 22 22 36). Beaune's best budget restaurant is **Relais de la Madeleine**, run by the entertaining
M. Neaux Problem, pronounced "no problem" (44 place
Madeleine, tel. 03 80 22 07 47).

Beaune's most interesting wine bar is the relaxed **Bistrot
Bourgignon** (excellent but costly wines by the glass, and a good
but limited *menu*; 8 rue Monge, a pedestrian-only street). If you've
had enough wine, drop by **Café Hallebarde** for a grand selection
of draft beer (24 rue d'Alsace). If you're tired of speaking French,
pop into the late-night-lively **Pickwicks Pub** (behind the church
at 2 rue Notre Dame).

Eating near Beaune
My favorite restaurants are outside Beaune. Just five minutes away
is **Le Relais de la Diligence**, where you can dine surrounded by
vineyards and taste the area's best budget Burgundian cuisine with
many *menu* options (inexpensive/moderate, closed Tuesday
evening and Wednesday, take N-74 toward Chagny/Chalon and
make a left at L'Hôpital Meursault on D-23, tel. 03 80 21 21 32).
Au Bon Accueil is relaxed and ideal. On a hill overlooking
Beaune (Montagne de Beaune), it has Burgundy's friendliest wait-
ress (Gina) and waiter (Christophe). Try the *coq au vin*. Leave
Beaune's ring road and take the Bligny-sur-Ouche turnoff. A few
minutes outside Beaune you'll see signs to Au Bon Accueil (tel. 03
80 22 08 80, closed Monday, Tuesday, and Wednesday). If you're
willing to drive 45 minutes, consider a late afternoon and evening
in Châteauneuf-en-Auxois. Several reasonable restaurants line the
little main drag of this sky-high hill town. For more information,
read about Châteauneuf under Sights—Beaune Region, below.

Transportation Connections—Beaune
By train to: Dijon (9/day, 30 min), **Colmar** (5/day, 4.5 hrs, trans-
fers in Dijon and Belfort), **Arles** (7/day, 5 hrs, transfer in Lyon),
Nice (7/day, 8 hrs, transfer in Lyon), **Chamonix** (3/day, 8.5 hrs,
transfers in Lyon and St. Gervais), **Paris'** Gare de Lyon (3
TGVs/day, 2 hrs; otherwise transfer to the TGV in Dijon, 3 hrs).

Getting Around the Beaune Region

By Bus: Transco buses run from Beaune through the vineyards and villages north to Dijon, south to Chalon-sur-Saône, and west to La Rochepot. Ask at the TI for schedules and bus stops, or call for bus information (tel. 03 80 42 11 00).

By Bike: The well-organized, English-speaking, and helpful Bourgogne Randonnées has excellent bikes, bike racks, maps, and good itineraries through the countryside (bike rental 20F/hour, 90F/full day, daily 9:00–12:00 and 13:30–19:00, located near train station at 7 avenue Huit Septembre, tel. 03 80 22 06 03).

Sights—Beaune Region

Bike Routes—Get the local Michelin map and suggestions from Bourgogne Randonnées (see above), then consider the long scenic loop ride through vineyards and over hills to La Rochepot, St. Aubin, the tiny road from Gamay to Puligny, Montrachet, and Meursault, then back to Beaune (all-day, 35 kilometers round-trip). To give your legs a break, ride instead along the D-18 to Savigny-les-Beaune and Pernand Vergelesses. (Check out Savigny's unusual château.)

▲▲Château La Rochepot—Twelve kilometers from Beaune, accessible by car, bike (hilly), or infrequent bus, you'll find this very Burgundian castle rising above the trees. The sign across the drawbridge asks you to knock three times with the ancient knocker, then push the doorbell. (Ask for the English explanations.) This pint-size castle is splendid inside and out. The kitchen will bowl you over. Look for the 15th-century highchair in the dining room. Don't leave the castle without climbing the tower and seeing the Chinese room, singing chants in the resonant chapel, and making ripples in the well. (Can you spit a bull's-eye? It's 72 meters down!) And don't leave La Rochepot without driving, walking, or pedaling up the D-33 a few hundred meters toward St. Aubin (behind the Hôtel Relais du Château) for a romantic view of this classically Burgundian castle. (32F, Wednesday–Monday 10:00–18:00 June–August, closed Tuesday, closes from 11:30–14:00 and at 16:30 in winter, tel. 03 80 21 71 37.)

▲The Hautes-Côtes to Châteauneuf-en-Auxois—This half-day loop trip takes you through untouristed vineyards and pastoral landscapes, along the Burgundy canal, past abbeys, and through medieval villages. It requires a car, the local Michelin map, and navigational patience. From Beaune's ring road head toward Dijon on the N-74. In a few minutes take the Savigny les Beaune turnoff, then connect Pernand Vergelesses with the Hautes-Côtes villages of Echevronne, Magny-les Villiers, Villers la Faye, and Marey-les-Fussey. These wineries in these villages offer stress-free tastings. Remember, you should plan on buying when tasting. (More serious tasters should consider these wineries: Lucien Jacob in Echevronne, tel. 03 80 21 91 50, SE; Domaine Thevenot Le Brun in Marey-les-Fussey, tel. 03 80 62 91 64, NSE; and Marcel Fribourg in Villers la Faye, tel. 03 80 62 91 74, NSE.) Then head west over the Hautes-Côtes to Pont d'Ouche. At Pont d'Ouche go straight and follow the canal toward Châteauneuf en Auxois. In about 10 minutes you'll see a stunning view of Châteauneuf's brooding castle; follow the signs.

Châteauneuf's medieval château towers over the valleys below. The village huddles securely in the shadow of the castle and merits close inspection. Park at the lot in the upper end of the village and stroll down into the village. Don't miss the panoramic viewpoint near the parking lot or the small church at the opposite end of town. Walk into the château's courtyard but skip the interior. Relax at the **Café au Marroniers** on the small square. Four small restaurants in Châteauneuf offer Burgundian cuisine at fair prices. Try **La Grill du Castel** (good-for-a-meal salads, great escargots, fine *boeuf bourguignon*, CC:VM, tel. 03 80 49 26 82) and **L'Oree du Bois Creperie** (friendly owner, many inexpensive dishes and a few *chambre d'hôte* rooms, tel. 03 80 49 25 32). You can sleep in Châteauneuf's one hotel (see listings under More Accommodations, above).

Following the signs behind Châteauneuf, take the tiny roads to La Bussière and wander into its abbey grounds. La Bussière's abbey was founded in the 1200s by Cistercian monks but goes largely unnoticed by most tourists today. Stroll the lovely gardens, check out the refectory (look for the door in the rear of the main building marked *"Accueil"* and enter here), and consider the cheap 90F dinner (includes wine, must call to reserve, tel. 03 80 49 02 29). Ask for the key to the *vieux pressoir* (old press).

To return to Beaune in scenic fashion, go back to Pont d'Ouche, turn left, and head uphill through Bouilland then downhill through Savigny-les Beaune.

▲▲**Brancion and Chapaize**—An hour south of Beaune by car (20 kilometers west of Tournus on the D-14) are two must-see churches that owe their existence and architectural design to the nearby, once-powerful Cluny Abbey. Brancion's nine-building hamlet floats on a hill above Chapaize and offers the purest example of Romanesque architecture I've seen—a 12th-century church (with faint frescoes inside), a cute château (climb the tower for views), and a 15th-century market hall. The Auberge du Vieux Brancion offers fine Burgundian cuisine at fair prices. For a peaceful break, spend a night in one of the Auberge's cozy rooms (D-210F, Db-300F, tel. & fax 03 85 51 03 83). If you're really on vacation, a night here is ideal. One mile downhill from Brancion, Chapaize's beautifully restored church is famous for its 11th-century belfry and its listing interior. Wander around the back for a great view of the belfry and check out the friendly café across the street.

Cluny and Taizé—Twenty kilometers southwest of Brancion lies the historic town of Cluny. The center of a rich and powerful monastic movement in the Middle Ages is today a pleasant town with very sparse and crumbled remains of its once-powerful abbey. For a new trend in monasticism, consider visiting the booming Christian community of Taizé (teh-zay), just north of Cluny. Brother Roger and his community welcome visitors who'd like to spend a few days getting close to God through meditation, singing, and simple living. Call or write first if you plan to stay overnight. There are dorm beds only. (Taizé Community, 71250 Cluny, tel. 03 85 50 14 14.)

DIJON

Beaune may be Burgundy's wine capital, but prosperous and sprawling Dijon is its undisputed economic powerhouse and cultural capital. This is an untouristed and enjoyable city (population: 150,000), offering a main course of half-timbered houses, bustling pedestrian streets, and interesting churches. Allow half a day on your schedule.

Tourist Information: Dijon has two helpful TIs—one between the train station and the city center (daily 9:00–21:00 May–October, otherwise 9:00–13:00 and 14:00–19:00; place Darcy) and another in the pedestrian-street thick of things (Monday–Friday 9:00–12:00 and 13:00–18:00, 34 rue des Forges, tel. 03 80 44 11 44). Pick up the English map (2F) illustrating a walking tour through the nicely restored old town center, and consider the Dijon museum package deal with a self-guided Walkman tour of Dijon (40F, worthwhile only if you have at least a full day for Dijon).

Arrival in Dijon

By Train: Walk straight out of the station and up avenue Marechal Foch. Stop at the main TI then continue to the arch to enter Dijon's center.

By Car: Enter Dijon following signs to *centre-ville*, then follow the blue "P" (parking) for place Darcy and park in the underground structure.

Sights—Dijon

▲▲**Dijon Walking Tour**—You can use the TI's maps and English explanations and follow an extensive walking tour of old Dijon, or save time and focus on the heart of Dijon with an abbreviated walk explained here (still using the TI map and explanations). From the TI (on place Darcy), walk through the arch at the other end of place Darcy and down rue de la Liberté (passing the famous Grey Poupon store on the right in one block, #32) to place Rude, ground zero in Dijon. Veer left down rue François Rude to the market hall (open Tuesday and Friday mornings and all day Saturday). Explore this famous market hall (picnic today?) then return to rue Musette and walk toward the Venetian-like facade of the Église Notre Dame (see description below).

From Notre Dame follow rue de Chouette along the north side of the church, then stop to rub the tiny stone owl for good luck (down about 50 yards on your right). Continue to rue Verrerie, take a left, and admire the antiques. A right on rue Chaudronnerie, another right on rue Lamonnoye, and a left on rue Vaillant lead to Église St. Michel. Admire the jumble of 16th-century Gothic and Renaissance styles and don't miss the free Musée Rude (next to the church) for a great look at Napoleonic (neoclassical) sculpture (you'll come face-to-face with an overpowering study for the Arc de Triomphe). Then double back on rue Vaillant to the Musée des Beaux Arts (entrance is through a courtyard opposite the BNP bank, description below) and peek into the duke's five-chimneyed kitchen in the museum courtyard. The Musée des Beaux Arts occupies part of what was once the Palace of the Dukes of Burgundy. The only interesting vestige that remains is the Tour (tower) Phillipe Bon; you can climb it for fine views over Dijon (escorted trips up the tower leave every 30 minutes from 9:00–17:30, 15F for 320 steps). To find the tower, leave the Musée des Beaux Arts courtyard by passing beneath the arch guarded by two strange stone soldiers, enter another large courtyard, then walk into the doorway under the French flag. Leave the tower (and the dukes' palace) through the doorway leading into the small park. A left on rue des Forges leads to a pleasant pedestrian street with many fine houses (wander into the surprise courtyard at #34) and, eventually, to place Rude and the end of this tour. Celebrate with a refreshment at the Café des Moulin à Vent.

▲**Église de Notre Dame**—Gushing with three tiers of gargoyles (stare straight up before entering), this is a fine example of 13th-century Burgundian design. Notice the clock Jacquemart above the right tower; for 600 years it has rung out the time in three-part harmony. Inside you'll find beautiful 13th-century stained glass and a curious, almost haunting, 11th-century *vierge noir* (black virgin), whose hands and feet were sawed off during the Revolution.

▲▲**Musée des Beaux Arts**—This excellent museum occupies one wing of the once-powerful Palace of the Dukes of Burgundy and has a little something for everyone. Besides its fine collection of European paintings from all periods are the Salle des Gardes (home to two incredibly ornate tombs, climb the stairs to the balcony for the best angle), the sculptures of Carpeaux and Rude near the Salles des Gardes, a 3-D modern art room, and the huge model of the Palais des Ducs de Bourgogne (22F, free on Sunday; Monday and Wednesday–Saturday 10:00–18:00, Sunday 10:00–12:30 and 14:00–18:00, closed Tuesday).

Sleeping in Dijon
(5.5F = about $1, zip code 21000)
Stay at the well-located **Hotel le Jaquemart** (D-180F, Db-280–350F, 32 rue Verrerie, Dijon 21000, tel. 03 80 60 09 60, fax 03 80 60 09 69).

Transportation Connections—Dijon
Dijon is Burgundy's hub, with excellent bus and rail service.

By train to: Colmar (5/day, 4 hrs, transfer in Belfort), **Beaune** (9/day, 30 min), **Paris'** Gare de Lyon (10 TGVs/day, 95 min), **Arles** (5/day, 5 hrs; other departures possible with a transfer in Lyon), **Nice** (8/day, 8 hrs, most are direct), **Chamonix** (3/day, 8 hrs, transfer in Lyon and St. Gervais).

By bus: Buses leave from the train station for villages along the wine route and many Burgundian cities (tel. 03 80 42 11 00).

ALSACE AND NORTHERN FRANCE

The French province of Alsace stands like a flower-child referee between Germany and France. Bounded by the Rhine on the east and the softly rolling Vosges Mountains on the west, this is a lush land of villages, vineyards, ruined castles, and almost naive cheeriness. Wine is the primary industry, topic of conversation, dominant mouthwash, and perfect excuse for countless festivals.

Because of its location, natural wealth, naked vulnerability, and the fact that Germany thinks the mountains are the natural border while France thinks the Rhine is, Alsace has changed hands several times. Having been a political pawn between Germany and France for 1,000 years, Alsace has a hybrid culture—locals who swear do so bilingually, and the local cuisine features sauerkraut and fine wine.

The humbling battlefields of Verdun and the bubbly vigor of Reims in northern France are closer to Paris than the Alsace, and follow logically only if your next destination is Paris.

Planning Your Time
Set up in or near Colmar. Allow most of a day for Colmar, and a full afternoon for the Route du Vin. Wander Colmar's sights until after lunch, then set out for the Route du Vin. Strasbourg has a big, impressive church but is otherwise only a bloated version of Colmar. With limited time, I'd skip it. Reims and Verdun are doable by car as stops between Paris and Colmar—if you're speedy. Train travelers with only one day between Colmar and Paris must choose Reims or Verdun.

Cuisine Scene—Alsace
Alsatian cuisine is a major tourist attraction in itself. You can't miss the German influence—sausages, potatoes, onions, and sauerkraut

Reims, Verdun, and Colmar

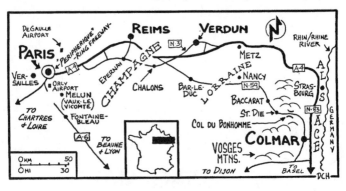

are everywhere. For dinner, look for *choucroute* (sauerkraut and sausage—although it seems a shame to eat it in a fancy restaurant), *baeckeanoffe* (potato, meat, and onion stew), *rosti* (oven-baked potato and cheese dish), fresh trout, and *foie gras*. At lunch or for a lighter dinner, try a *tarte à l'oignon* (like an onion quiche but better) or *tarte flambée* (like a thin-crust pizza with onion and bacon bits). If you're picnicking, buy some smelly Münster cheese. Dessert specialties are *glace Kugelhopf* (a light cake mixed with raisins, almonds, dried fruit, and cherry liqueur) and *tarte Alsacienne* (fruit tart).

Alsatian Wines

Alsatian wines are named for their grapes, unlike in Burgundy or Provence where wines are commonly named after villages, or in Bordeaux where wines are commonly named after châteaus. White wines dominate in the Alsace; the following wines are made entirely of that grape variety: Sylvaner (fairly light, fruity, and inexpensive), Riesling (more robust than Sylvaner but drier than the German style you're probably used to), Gewurztztraminer (spicy with a powerful bouquet; good with pâtés and local cheeses), Muscat (very dry with a distinctive bouquet and taste; best as a before-dinner wine), Tokay/Pinot Gris (more full-bodied than Riesling but fine with many local main courses), Pinot Noir (the local red is overpriced; very light and fruity, and generally served chilled), and the tasty Crèmant d'Alsace (the region's good and inexpensive champagne). You'll also see Eaux-de-Vie, a powerful fruit-flavored brandy; try the *framboise* (raspberry) flavor.

COLMAR

There isn't a straight street in Colmar. Thankfully, it's a lovely town to be lost in. Navigate by the high church steeples and the helpful signs directing visitors to the various sights.

Colmar is a well-pickled old place of 70,000 residents, offering heavyweight sights in a warm small-town package. Historic beauty was usually a poor excuse to be spared the ravages of World War II, but it worked for Colmar. The American and British military were careful not to bomb the half-timbered old burghers' houses, characteristic red- and green-tiled roofs, and cobbled lanes of Alsace's most beautiful city.

Today Colmar thrives with colorful buildings, impressive art treasures, and popular Alsatian cuisine. Schoolgirls park their rickety horse carriages in front of the city hall, ready to give visitors a clip-clop tour of Old Town. Antique shops welcome browsers, and hotel managers run down the sleepy streets to pick up fresh croissants in time for breakfast.

Orientation

For tourists, the town center is place Unterlinden (a 15-minute walk from the train station), where you'll find the TI, a major museum, and a huge and handy Monoprix department store and supermarket (8:30–20:30, closed Sunday). Every city bus starts or finishes on place Unterlinden.

Colmar is most crowded from May through September. The local wine festival rages for 10 days in early August (August 7–16 in 1999), and Sauerkraut Days are celebrated in October (October 9–12 in 1999). Open-air markets bustle next to the Dominican and St. Martin Churches on Thursday and Saturday.

Tourist Information: The TI is next to the Unterlinden Museum on place Unterlinden. Pick up a city map, a Route du Vin map, and *Colmar Actualités*, a booklet with bus schedules. Ask about wine festivals and Colmar's Folklore Tuesdays (with folk dancing at 20:30 every Tuesday mid-May–mid-September on place de l'Ancienne). The TI organizes walking tours of Old Town for 27F and of the Unterlinden Museum for 22F (daily in summer, weekends only in other months), reserves hotel rooms, and has *chambre d'hôte* listings for the region and Colmar (Monday–Saturday 9:00–18:00, Sunday 10:00–14:00 April–October; Monday–Saturday 9:00–12:00 and 14:00-18:00, Sunday 10:00–14:00 November–March; tel. 03 89 20 68 92). There's a public W.C. 20 yards to the left of the TI.

Tours: You can hire a private guide for a walking tour (450F, ask at TI). A minibus tour company, Les Circuits d'Alsace, organizes day trips around the Alsace (tel. 03 89 41 90 88).

Laundromat: The only central Laundromat is near the Maison Jund (see Sleeping, below) at 1 rue Ruest, just off the pedestrian street rue Vauban (usually open daily 8:00–21:00).

Arrival in Colmar

By Train or Bus: To reach Colmar's center city from the bus or train station (they're side by side), walk straight out, turn left on avenue de la République, and keep walking. Allow 15 minutes. Buses 1, 2, and 3 each go from the station to the TI (about 5.60F, pay the driver).

By Car: Follow signs to *centre-ville*. There are several handy pay lots (place Rapp) and a huge free lot at "parking du Musée Unterlinden" (across from Primo 99 hotel).

Self-guided Tour of Colmar's Old Town

The importance of 15th- to 17th-century Colmar is clear as you wander its pedestrian-friendly old center, which is decorated with 45 buildings classified as historic monuments. Back in feudal times, most of Europe was fragmented into chaotic little prince-doms and dukedoms. Merchant-dominated cities, which were natural proponents of the formation of large nation-states, banded together to form "trading leagues." The Hanseatic League was the super-league of northern Europe. Prosperous Colmar was a member of a smaller league of 10 Alsatian cities called the Decapolis (founded 1354). Delegates of this group met in Colmar's Old Custom House.

Start your tour at the **Old Custom's House** (Koifhus). Walk under it and you'll find yourself facing the place de l'Ancienne Douane and a Bertholdi statue—arm raised, à la Statue of Liberty. The place de l'Ancienne Douane is the festive site of outdoor wine-tasting many summer evenings. The soaring half-timbered commotion of higgledy-piggledy rooftops just beyond marks the **Tanners' Quarters**. These 17th- and 18th-century rooftops competed to get space in the sun to dry their freshly tanned hides. Wander down to the end of the rue des Tanneurs, turn right, then take the first left along the stream and you'll come to the old market hall (fish, produce, and other products were brought here by flat-bottomed boat). Cross the canal, turn right, and you'll enter "la Petite Venise" quarter, a bundle of Colmar's most colorful houses lining the small canal. This area is well-lit and even cuter at night.

Double back to the Old Custom House via rue des Écoles. From the Custom House, walk up rue des Marchands (Merchant's Street). Those overhanging roofs you're walking under were a medieval tax-dodge. Since houses were taxed on square footage at street level, owners would expand tax-free up and over the street. In two blocks you'll come face to face with the Pfister House, a richly-decorated merchant's house from 1537 with an external spiral staircase turret and painted walls showing the city folk's taste for Renaissance humanism. The man carved into the side of the building next door (to the left) was a sheet maker; he's shown holding a bar, Colmar's measure of about one meter. (In the Middle Ages it was common for cities to have their own length for a meter.) One more block on the left is the Bartholdi Museum

Colmar

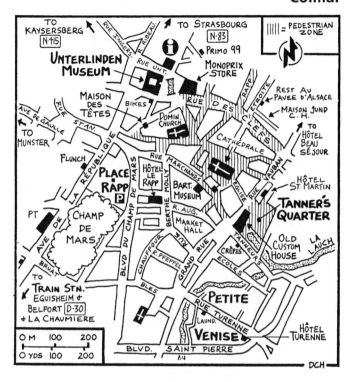

(described below). A passage to the right leads to Colmar's Cathedral St. Martin. Compare this beautiful soaring structure with the typically sober Dominican Church (housing Schongauer's Virgin in the Rosebush, described below), a few blocks toward the TI. The House of Heads on rue des Têtes near the TI is Colmar's other famous merchant's house; it was built in 1609 and is decorated with 105 faces and masks. From here it's a short walk to the TI and the Unterlinden Museum.

Sights—Colmar

▲▲▲Unterlinden Museum—Colmar's touristic claim to fame, this is one of my favorite museums in Europe. Its extensive yet manageable collection ranges from Roman Colmar to medieval wine-making exhibits, and traditional wedding dresses to paintings that give vivid insight into the High Middle Ages.

The highlight of the museum (and, for me, the city) is Grünewald's gripping Isenheim Altarpiece, actually a series of three different paintings on hinges that pivot like shutters (study the little model on the wall, explained in English). Designed to help people in a medieval hospital endure horrible skin diseases (such as St. Anthony's Fire, later called rye ergotism) long before the age of painkillers, it's one of the most powerful paintings ever produced.

Stand medieval in front of the centerpiece and let the agony and suffering of the Crucifixion drag its fingers down your face. The point—Jesus' suffering—is drilled home: the weight of his body bending the crossbar, his elbows pulled from their sockets by the weight of his dead body, his mangled feet, the grief on Mary's face. In hopes that the intended viewers—the hospital's patients—would know that Jesus understands their suffering, he was even painted looking like he, too, had a skin disease. Study the faces and the Christian symbolism.

The three scenes of the painting changed with the seasons of the church year. The happy ending—a psychedelic explosion of Resurrection joy—is the spiritual equivalent of jumping from the dentist's chair directly into a Jacuzzi. The last two panels, showing the meeting of St. Paul the hermit and St. Anthony, are the product of a fertile imagination and the stuff nightmares are made of.

There's more to the museum. Ringing the peaceful cloister is a fine series of medieval church paintings and sculpture and a room filled with old wine presses. Downstairs you'll find Roman and pre-historic artifacts. The upstairs contains local and folk history, with everything from medieval armor to old-time toys (32F, daily 9:00–18:00 April–October, off-season 9:00–12:00 and 14:00–17:00, closed Tuesdays November–March, tel. 03 89 41 89 23).

▲▲**Dominican Church**—Here is another medieval mindblower. In Colmar's Église des Dominicains, you'll find Martin Schongauer's angelically beautiful *Virgin in the Rosebush* (from 1473, but looking like it was painted yesterday) holding court on center-stage. Here, Mary is shown as a welcoming mother. Jesus clings to her, reminding the viewer of the possibility of an intimate rela-tionship with Mary. The Latin on her halo reads: "Pick me also for your child, O very Holy Virgin." Rather than telling a particu-lar Bible story, this is a general scene . . . designed to meet the personal devotional needs of any worshiper. Here, nature is not a backdrop. Mary and Jesus are encircled by it. Schongauer's robins, sparrows, and goldfinches bring extra life to an already impres-sively natural rosebush. The contrast provided by the simple Dominican setting heightens the flamboyance of this late-Gothic masterpiece. Dominican churches were particularly austere, as the 13th-century Catholic Church was combating a wave of heretical movements, such as the Cathars, whose message was a simpler faith (8F, daily Monday–Saturday 10:00–18:00 January–November; daily 10:00–18:00 November–December. This Dominican austerity is

more apparent after a visit to Colmar's fancier—and Franciscan—
St. Martin's cathedral.

Bartholdi Museum—This little museum recalls the life and work
of the local boy who gained fame by sculpting the Statue of
Liberty. Several of his statues grace Colmar's squares (20F,
Wednesday–Monday 10:00–12:00 and 14:00–18:00 March–
December, closed Tuesday and off-season; in the heart of the
Old Town at 30 rue des Marchands).

Sleeping in Colmar
(5.5F = about $1, zip code: 68000)
Sleep Code: **S** = Single, **D** = Double/Twin, **T** = Triple, **Q** = Quad,
b = bathroom, **t** = toilet only, **s** = shower only, **CC** = Credit Card
(Visa, MasterCard, Amex), **SE** = Speaks English, **NSE** = No English, ***** = French hotel rating system (0–4 stars).

Hotels are more expensive here than in other areas of France
and are jammed on weekends in May, June, September, and October.
July and August are busy, but there are always rooms—somewhere.
Should you have trouble finding a room in Colmar, look in a nearby
village where small hotels and bed-and-breakfasts are plentiful, and
see my recommendations for Sleeping in Eguisheim (below).

Maison Jund offers my favorite budget beds in Colmar. This
easygoing B&B is the home of a wine-maker. This ramshackle yet
magnificent half-timbered home feels like a medieval treehouse
soaked in wine and filled with flowers. The simple but comfortable
rooms are spacious and equipped with kitchenettes. Rooms are
generally available only from April to mid-September, with the
cheapest rooms available only in summer (D–170F, Db/Tb-
210–230F, 12 rue de l'Ange, tel. 03 89 41 58 72, fax 03 89 23 15
83). From the Unterlinden Museum walk past the Monoprix and
veer left on the rue des Clefs. This is not a hotel so there is no
real reception, though friendly Myriam (SE) seems to be around,
somewhere, most of the time. You can enjoy a friendly wine-
tasting here without leaving sight of your bedroom door.

Hôtel Turenne** is a fine historic hotel a 10-minute walk from
the city center. It's on a busy street with easy parking, and the rooms
are bright, pastel, and comfortable (Sb-250–385F, Db-270–385F,
Tb-385–600F, garage-20F, CC:VMA, 10 route du Bale, tel. 03 89 41
12 26, fax 03 89 41 27 64, SE). The rooms on the street are cheaper
and noisier. A third of its 85 rooms are nonsmoking.

Hôtel Le Rapp**, with 40 modern and somewhat tight
rooms, a small basement pool, and a sauna, is well located just off
place Rapp and well run (Sb-305–335F, Db-395F, extra person-
80F, nice buffet breakfasts, CC:VMA, 1 rue Berthe-Molley, tel. 03
89 41 62 10, fax 03 89 24 13 58, e-mail: rapp-hot@rmcnet.fr, SE).
Its restaurant serves a classy Alsatian menu with impeccable service
(closed Fridays).

Hotel St. Martin***, next to the Custom's House, is a classy, family-run place right in the old center with a history as a coaching inn going back to 1361. It's small with Old World-yet-modern rooms woven into its antique frame. Half of its 24 rooms are in the annex (*l'annexe*) opposite a peaceful courtyard. While just as comfortable and characteristic, these cheaper rooms have showers instead of tubs, and no elevator or air-conditioning (Sb-295–560F, Db-360–660F, Tb-560–850F, CC:VMA, free public parking nearby, 38 Grand Rue, tel. 03 89 24 11 51, fax 03 89 23 47 78, the Winterstein family SE). For about the same money without a hint of the Old World or a family, you can sleep comfortably and park easily in one of two central and modern **Hotel Mercures***** (Db-550F, a few rooms for disabled people, air-conditioning, CC:VMA), one in Colmar's central park just off place Rapp on 2 avenue de la Marne (tel. 03 89 41 54 54, fax 03 89 23 93 76), the other near the Unterlinden Museum on 5 rue Golbery (tel. 03 89 41 71 71, fax 03 89 23 82 71, SE).

Primo 99**, near the Unterlinden Museum, is a French prefab hotel—a modern, cheap, efficient, bright, nothing-but-the-plastic-and-concrete-basics place to sleep for those to whom ambience is a four-letter word and modernity is next to godliness. It's one of Colmar's best budget deals (S/D/T-160F, Sb-270F, Db-300F, add 50F for a third person, family discounts, friendly staff, garage-30F, CC:VM, 5 rue des Ancêtres, free parking in the big square in front, rooms held for a phone call until 18:30, tel. 03 89 24 22 24, fax 03 89 24 55 96, e-mail: hotel-primo-99@rmcnet.fr, SE). Half the beds have footboards—a problem if you're taller than 6'2".

La Chaumière*, on a big street two blocks from the station (walk straight out of the station and turn left on rue de la République), offers good-value rooms over a real French café. The simple, sleepable rooms surround a courtyard and are much quieter off the street (S-155F, Sb-180F, D-180F, Db-220–240F, Tb-275–330F, CC:VM, 74 avenue de la République, tel. 03 89 41 08 99).

Hôtel Beau Séjour** is upscale and cushy, with a flowery garden and well-respected restaurant (Db-320–520F, Tb-400–550F, Qb-450–650F, private parking for drivers, a 15-minute walk from the center, 27 rue du Ladhof, tel. 03 89 41 37 16, fax 03 89 41 43 07).

The best cheap beds in Colmar are located in a fine mansion at **Maison des Jeunes** (46F in large rooms, sheets-20F, meals-60F; office open 7:00–12:00 and 14:00–23:00; walk straight out of the station, take the second right after the light, 17 rue Schlumberger, tel. 03 89 41 26 87, fax 03 89 23 20 16, SE). The less central **hostel** is open March through October (dorm bed-68F, sheets-25F, breakfast included, cheap meals, midnight curfew, 15-minute walk from station and downtown or take bus #4, 2 rue Pasteur, tel. 03 89 80 57 39, fax 03 89 80 76 16).

Sleeping near Colmar in Eguisheim
(5.5F = about $1, zip code: 68420)
Enchanting Eguisheim is surrounded by vineyards and makes a perfect village base for exploring Colmar and the wine road. It's ideal by car and reasonably accessible by bus (6/day, five minutes from Colmar's train station). There are several hotels and scads of B&Bs. Eguisheim's TI has a complete list of accommodations including over 20 *chambres d'hôte* (daily 9:00–12:00 and 14:00–18:00, 22 Grand Rue, tel. 03 89 23 40 33). See also Sights—The Wine Road, below, for more information on Eguisheim.

Chambres d'Hôte: **Madame Dirringer's** five spacious rooms surround a traditional courtyard (Db-165–185F, breakfast-30F, 11 rue Riesling, tel. 03 89 41 71 87). **Hertz-Meyers** welcomes you with big rooms in a vineyard mansion only 75 yards from the village center (Db-250–270F, Tb-355F, 3 rue Riesling, tel. 03 89 23 67 74). It's hard to imagine a better set-up or location than the comfortable rooms offered by friendly **Monique Freudenreich** (Db-235F, includes breakfast, 4 cour Unterlinden, one block from the TI, tel. & fax 03 89 23 16 44). **Les Bombenger's** modern home has nice views over Eguisheim (D-155F, 3 rue de Trois Pierres, tel. 03 89 23 71 19). The **Stockys** offer comfortable rooms (Db-155–175F, 24 rue de Colmar, tel. 03 89 41 68 04).

Hotels: Eguisheim also has hotels for every taste and budget. The simple, funky, and fun **Auberge de Trois Chateaux** is creaky wood-beamed and unpolished, with sleepable rooms, each with a kitchenette and shower; WCs are down the hall (Ds-180–210F, 26 Grand Rue, tel. 03 89 23 70 61). At the other extreme, the dazzling **Hostellerie du Chateau***** is charmingly located in front of the small château and provides stylish luxury that contemporary art lovers would appreciate. It also has an elegant restaurant (Db-480–550F, 2 rue du Château St. Leon IX, tel. 03 89 23 72 00, fax 03 89 23 68 00). The picturesque **Auberge Alsacienne***** gives three stars for the price of two (Db-280–320F, Tb-390F, 12 Grand Rue, tel. 03 89 41 50 20, fax 03 89 23 89 32). Overlooking the village, the modern yet cozy **Hotel St. Hubert***** offers polished top comfort, an indoor pool and sauna, vineyards out your window, and a free pick-up at Colmar's train station (Db-450–580F, rue des Trois Pierres, tel. 03 89 41 40 50, fax 03 89 41 46 88).

Eating in Colmar
For reasonably priced, good traditional Alsatian cuisine, try **La Maison Rouge** (78F and 95F menus, closed Sunday, 9 rue des Écoles, tel. 03 89 23 53 22). Join the fun in wood-cozy ambience at **Winstub Schwendi**; try one of their robust 50F Swiss *rosti*

plates (facing the Old Custom's House at 3 Grand Rue). **La Taverne** serves fine *tartes flambées* and other regional specialities (closed Sunday, 2 impasse de la Maison Rouge, tel. 03 89 41 70 33). For crêpes and salads with atmosphere, eat at **Crêperie Tom Pouce** (daily, 10 rue des Tanneurs). I also like the crêpes at **Regal Aur** (near Hotel Rapp at 35 Berthe-Molley). For canal-front dining, head into La Petite Venise to the bridge on rue Turenne, where you'll find a pizzeria, a *winstub*/café (both cheap), and a fine but pricey canal-level restaurant, **Les Bateliers**.

Hôtel Restaurant Le Rapp is my dress-up, high-cuisine splurge. I comb my hair, spit out my gum, and savor a slow, elegant meal served with grace and fine Alsatian wine (*menus* start at 95F). Its **Rappstub Bistrot** offers a cheaper *menu* from the same kitchen (60F to 70F plate of the day, great and hearty salads, closed Friday, air-conditioned, 1 rue Berthe-Molley, tel. 03 89 41 62 10, SE).

Salon de Thé Kuhn, just across the photo-perfect bridge in La Petite Venise on place des Six Montagnes Noires, serves good quiche and salads (open until 19:00, closed Monday).

Transportation Connections—Colmar
By train to: Strasbourg (hrly, 50 min), **Reims** (3/day, 5–7 hrs, with probable transfers in Strasbourg, Nancy, and Chalons-sur-Marne or Epernay), **Dijon/Beaune** (5/day to Dijon, 4 hrs, transfer in Besançon; it's another 30 min to Beaune), **Paris'** Gare de l'Est (10/day, 5.5 hrs, transfer in Strasbourg or Mulhouse), **Amboise** (go first to Paris, then catch direct train from Paris' Gare d'Austerlitz; allow all day), **Basel, Switzerland** (8/day, 1 hr), **Karlsruhe, Germany** (3/day, 90 min, via Strasbourg; from Karlsruhe it's 90 min to Frankfurt, 3 hrs to Munich).

The Wine Road (Route du Vin)
Alsace's Route du Vin is an asphalt ribbon tying 90 miles of vineyards, villages, and feudal fortresses into an understandably popular tourist package. The generally dry, sunny climate has made for good wine and happy tourists since Roman days. Colmar and Eguisheim are ideally located for exploring the 30,000 acres of vineyards blanketing the hills from Marlenheim to Thann. If you have only a day, focus on towns within easy striking range of Colmar. Top ones are Eguisheim, Kaysersberg, Riquewihr, and Hunawhir. Get a map of the Route du Vin from any TI.

Throughout Alsace you'll see "Dégustation" signs. *Dégustation* means "come on in and taste," and *gratuit* means "free;" otherwise, there's a small charge. Most towns have wineries that give tours; those in Eguisheim and Riquewihr are good. The modern cooperatives at Bennwhir, Hunawhir, and Ribbeauville, created after the destruction of World War II, provide a good look at a more modern and efficient method of production. Most villages are filled with

Alsace's Wine Road

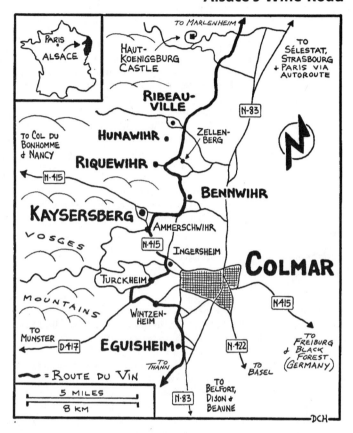

TO MARLENHEIM

PARIS
ALSACE

HAUT-
KOENIGSBURG
CASTLE

TO
SÉLESTAT,
STRASBOURG
+ PARIS VIA
AUTOROUTE

RIBEAU-
VILLE

N-83

ZELLEN-
BERG

TO COL DU
BONHOMME
& NANCY

HUNAWIHR

RIQUEWIHR

N-415

BENNWIHR

KAYSERSBERG

AMMERSCHWIHR

VOSGES

N-415

INGERSHEIM

COLMAR

TURCKHEIM

N-415

MOUNTAINS

WINTZEN-
HEIM

TO
MUNSTER

D-417

EGUISHEIM

N-422

TO
FREIBURG
& BLACK
FOREST
(GERMANY)

TO
THANN

TO
BASEL

= ROUTE DU VIN

5 MILES

8 KM

TO
BELFORT,
DIJON &
BEAUNE

N-83

—DCH—

more personal, small wineries eager to impress you with their wines.
The Colmar TI can give you advice, or even telephone a winery for
you to confirm tour times. You may have to wait for a group and tag
along for a tour and free tasting at the big places. Be sure to try the
local spicy specialty, Gerwurtztraminer. Crèmant, the Alsatian
"champagne," is very good—and much cheaper. The French term
for headache, if you really get "Alsaced," is *mal à la tête*.

Getting Around the Wine Road
Pick up a Michelin regional map before heading out.

By Bus: Public buses connect Colmar's train station with
most of the villages along the Route du Vin. The schedules are
fairly convenient, less so on Sunday (Eguisheim: 6/day, 5 min;

Kaysersberg: hrly, 30 min; Riquewihr, Bennwhir, Hunawhir, and Ribbeauville: 6/day, 30–45 min). Get schedules from the TI, and buy tickets from the driver.

By Bike: The Wine Road's level terrain makes biking a good option. You can rent a bike at Colmar's train station or the Peugeot bike store (60F/5 hrs, 90F/day, leave Visa number for security, Tuesday–Saturday 8:30–12:00 and 14:00–18:00, next to Unterlinden Museum; ask at TI for other bike rental locations). Kaysersberg and Eguisheim are fine biking destinations.

By Car: The easiest approach to the Wine Road is to leave Colmar on the N-83 toward Belfort; you'll soon see signs to Eguisheim—from there you're on your own.

By Foot: A few well-signed walking trails connect Route du Vin villages through the vineyards, and serious walkers can climb to the higher ruined castles of the Vosges Mountains (Eguisheim and Ribbeauville are good bases). Kaysersberg to Riquewihr is a pleasant one- to two-hour walk (use the bus to return). Get more information at a local TI.

Sights—The Wine Road

Eguisheim—Just a few kilometers (a flat and easy bike ride) from Colmar, this flowery scenic little town is ideal for a relaxing lunch and makes a good base for exploring the Alsace (see *Sleeping near Colmar*, above). The **TI** on the street that bisects the town has information on festivals, walks in the vineyards, and hikes into the Vosges (daily 9:00–12:00 and 14:00–18:00, closed Sunday and Monday October–March, 22 Grand Rue, tel. 03 89 23 40 33). Eguisheim is best explored by walking around its narrow circular road (rue des Remparts), then cutting through the middle. Visit the newly-renovated church and one of Eguisheim's countless cozy wineries or the big and modern Wine Cooperative (Wolfberger, Cave Vinicole d'Eguisheim, daily 10:00–12:00 and 14:00–19:00, folklore and tastings in summer on Wednesday 17:00–19:00, 6 Grand Rue, tel. 03 89 22 20 20). If you have a car, follow signs straight up to Les Husseren and Les Châteaux for a pleasant walk to the ruined castle towers and a fine view of the Vosges above and vineyards below.

Kaysersberg—Albert Schweitzer's hometown is cute but feels overrun much of the year. Climb to the castle (under long-term renovation), browse the boutiques, and enjoy the colorful jumble of 15th-century houses and the stork's nest near the fortified town bridge. Drop by Dr. Schweitzer's house (10F, closed 12:00–14:00), check out the church with its impressive 400-year-old altarpiece, taste some wine, and wander into nearby vineyards. Kaysersberg's TI is inside the Hôtel de Ville (tel. 03 89 78 22 78). Walking trails through the vineyards to Riquewihr (1.5–2.5 hours) and other Route du Vin towns are well-marked; walk under the arch (10 yards

to the right of the TI as you face it) and you'll see signs.
Riquewihr—Overly picturesque and tourist-trampled, this little
walled village is crammed with shops, cafés, art galleries, cobblestones,
and flowers. Tastings and tours can be found at Caves Dopff et Irion
(Cour du Château, tel. 03 89 47 92 51, TI tel. 03 89 47 80 80).
Hunawihr—Here's another bit of wine-soaked Alsatian cuteness,
complete with a 16th-century fortified church that today is shared
by Catholics and Protestants (the Catholics are buried next to the
church, the Protestants are buried outside the church wall). Park
below the church at the small lot with picnic tables and follow the
trail up to the church, then loop back through the village. This
cheery, tranquil village is less touristed than its more famous
brothers, with a few *Chambres d'Hôte* and a good wine cooperative.

STRASBOURG
Sitting right on the Rhine River, Strasbourg provides an urban
blend of Franco-Germanic culture, architecture, and ambience.
It's home to the European Parliament and a fascinating *vielle ville*
(old city) of pedestrian streets, canals, and half-timbered homes. If
it's a big-city fix you need, come here.
    Tourist Information: The TI is in front of the train station
(park there). Pick up a city map and walk 15 minutes straight up rue
Marie Kuss to rue Gutenberg to find the old city and cathedral.

Sights—Strasbourg
▲▲**Strasbourg Cathedral**—This uniquely Alsatian cathedral,
with its tall, slender spire, multicolored tile, and red stone roof is
well worth a side trip. Approach the cathedral on foot from place
Gutenberg and rue Mercière. It's particularly stunning in the late-
afternoon light. Don't miss the doomsday pillar, the 15th-century
astronomical clock inside, or the walk up the tower. The view is
worth the struggle (10F, tower open 8:30–18:30). After touring the
cathedral, take a stroll through Strasbourg's enchanting La Petite
France—follow signs from place Gutenberg.

Transportation Connections—Strasbourg
Strasbourg is an easy side trip from Colmar or a stop on the way
to or from Paris.
    By train to: Colmar (hrly, 50 min), **Paris'** Gare de l'Est
(10/day, 4.5 hrs), **Karlsruhe, Germany** (3/day, 50 min), **Basel,
Switzerland** (hrly, 2 hrs).

VERDUN
Little remains in Europe today to remind us of World War I. Ver-
dun provides a fine tribute to the million-plus lives lost in the
World War I battles fought here. While the lunar landscape of
WWI is now forested over, countless craters and trenches are visi-

ble (look into the woods as you drive)—along with millions of undetonated bombs in vast cordoned-off areas. Drive through the eerie moguls that surround the city of Verdun, stopping at melted sugar-cube forts and plaques marking where towns once existed. With two hours and a car, or a full day and a bike, you can see the most impressive sights and appreciate the awesome scale of the battles. The town of Verdun is not your destination but a springboard into the surrounding battlefields.

Tourist Information: The TI is on place Nation (daily 8:30–18:30 May–September, otherwise closed 12:00–14:00 and at 18:00; closes at 17:30 during winter months; tel. 03 29 86 14 18).

Arrival in Verdun

By Train: Walk straight out of the station and down avenue Garibaldi to the town center.

By Car: Follow signs to *centre-ville*, place Nation, and Porte Chatel, and you'll pass the TI just before crossing the river.

Getting Around the Verdun Battlefield

The TI has good maps of the battlefields. French-language minivan tours of the battle sites are available June through September, and leave the TI around 14:00 (occasionally in English—ask). You can rent a bike opposite Verdun's train station at **Cycles Flavenot** (tel. 03 29 86 12 43). To reach the battlefields by car or bike (about 20 miles round-trip), take the D-112 from Verdun (look for signs to Douaumont), then take the D-913 to Douaumont.

The battlefield remains are situated on two sides of the Meuse River; the Rive Droite has more sights. By following signs to Fort Douaumont and the Ossuaire, you'll pass the Musée Fleury.

Sights—Verdun

▲▲**Battlegrounds**—The most compelling sights are the Mémorial-Musée de Fleury, the Ossuaire, and Fort Douaumont. Start with the **Mémorial-Musée de Fleury**, built around an impressive recreation of a battlefield with hard-hitting photos, weapon displays, and a worthwhile 15-minute movie narrated in English with headphones (20F, 9:00–18:00 March–December, closes at 17:00 in winter). The museum is built on the site of a village (Fleury) that was obliterated during the fighting.

Don't miss **l'Ossuaire**, the tomb of the 130,000 French and Germans whose last home was the muddy trenches of Verdun (daily 9:00–18:00 March–early September, otherwise closes 12:00–14:00 and at 17:30). Look through the low windows for a bony memorial to those whose political and military leaders asked them to make the "ultimate sacrifice" for their countries. Enter the monument and experience a humbling and moving tribute. Ponder a war that left half of all the men in France aged 15 to 30

Verdun

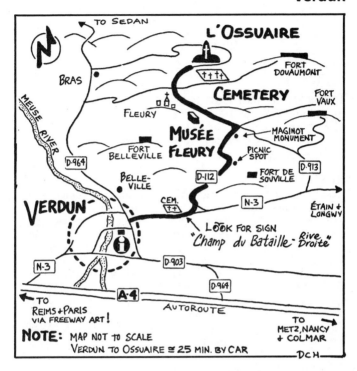

TO SEDAN

L'OSSUAIRE

FORT DOUAUMONT

BRAS

CEMETERY

FORT VAUX

FLEURY

MAGINOT MONUMENT

MUSÉE FLEURY

PICNIC SPOT

FORT BELLEVILLE

D-964

FORT DE SOUVILLE

D-913

BELLE-VILLE

D-112

N-3

ÉTAIN + LONGWY

VERDUN

CEM.

LOOK FOR SIGN "Champ du Bataille - Rive Droite"

N-3

D-903

D-964

A-4

AUTOROUTE

TO REIMS + PARIS VIA FREEWAY ART!

TO METZ, NANCY + COLMAR

NOTE: MAP NOT TO SCALE
VERDUN TO OSSUAIRE ≅ 25 MIN. BY CAR

-DCH-

dead or wounded. See the thought-provoking 20-minute film (16F, theater in basement, ask for English version, closed November–March). You can climb the tower for a territorial view (6F). The little 1F picture boxes in the gift shop are worth a look if you don't visit the Mémorial-Musée de Fleury (turn through all the old photos before the time expires).

Before leaving, walk to the cemetery and listen for the eerie buzz of silence and peace. You can visit the nearby **Tranchée des Baionnettes**, where an entire company of soldiers was buried alive in their trench (many of the soldier's bayonets remained above ground until recently); or, even better, visit the nearby **Fort Douaumont**, a strategic command center for both sides at various times. It's more interesting from the outside than inside (walk on top to appreciate the strategic setting of this fort and notice the round, iron gun emplacements that could rise and revolve). A walk inside (15F) completes the picture, with long damp corridors and a German memorial where 1,600 Germans were killed by a single blast. Halfway between the Ossuaire and Fort Douaumont (on either side of the road) are the best examples of trenches I've found here.

Citadelle Souterraine—This is a disappointing train ride through the tunnels of the French Command in downtown Verdun. While it tries to re-create the Verdun scene, it's not worth your time or money.

Transportation Connections—Verdun

By train to: Colmar (3/day, 5–7hrs, transfers in Chalons-sur-Marne and Strasbourg), **Reims** (4/day, 3 hrs, transfer in Chalons-sur-Marne), **Paris'** Gare de l'Est (5/day, 3 hrs, transfer in Chalons-sur-Marne).

REIMS

Deservedly famous for its cathedral and champagne, contemporary Reims (rhymes with France) is a modern, bustling city with little character. Just 90 minutes from Paris by car or train, it makes a good day trip or handy stop for travelers en route elsewhere. Most sights of interest (champagne caves included) are within a 20-minute walk from the cathedral.

    Tourist Information: The TI is just to the left of the cathedral as you face the front (daily 9:00–19:30 Easter–June, closes earlier off-season, tel. 03 26 77 45 25). Their free city map shows the champagne caves. Ask about guided tours of the cathedral in English (summer only, 90 min), or consider the self-guided Walkman tour available any season.

Arrival in Reims

By Train: Walk out of the station, look up, and follow the cathedral's spire. It's a 15-minute walk.

    By Car: A piece of cake—just follow the *"cathédrale"* signs and park as close to it as possible. You may find parking easier behind the cathedral.

Sights—Reims

▲▲▲**Cathedral**—The cathedral of Reims is a glorious example of Gothic architecture, with the best west portal (inside and outside) anywhere. (Since medieval churches always face east, the end you enter is the west portal.) The coronation place of 800 years for French kings and queens, it houses many old treasures, great medieval stained glass, and a lovely modern set of Marc Chagall stained-glass windows from 1974 on the east end. Joan of Arc led a reluctant Charles VII here to be coronated in 1429; the event rallied the French to finally push the English out of France and end the Hundred Years War. Helpful English explanations are provided along the right aisle (daily 7:30–19:30).

▲**Champagne Tours**—Reims is the capital of the Champagne

region, and while the bubbly stuff's birthplace was closer to Epernay, you can tour a champagne cave right in Reims. All charge for tastings (20–30F, daily, most close 12:00–14:00 and at about 17:00). The **Taittinger Company** does a great job trying to convince you they're the best (walk 10 minutes up rue de Barbatre from the cathedral to 9 place St. Nicaise, tel. 03 26 85 84 33). After seeing their movie (in comfortable theater seats), follow your guide down into some of the three miles of chilly, chalk caves, many of which were dug by ancient Romans. Popping corks signal when the tour's done and the tasting's begun (20F, tour includes a tasting, 9:30–12:00 and 14:30–16:30).

One block beyond Taittinger, on place des Droits de l'Homme, you'll find several other champagne caves. **Piper Heidsieck** offers a remarkable train-ride tour and tasting (35F, 51 boulevard Henri-Vasnier, call first, tel. 03 26 84 43 44).

Champagne purists may want to visit Epernay (26 km away, well-connected to Paris and Reims), where the granddaddy of champagne houses, **Moet Chandon**, offers tours (20F with tasting, tel. 03 26 51 21 00). According to the story, it was near here that, in about 1700, the monk Dom Perignon, after much fiddling with double fermentation, stumbled onto this bubbly treat. On that happy day he ran through the abbey shouting, "Brothers, come quickly . . . I'm drinking stars!"

Sleeping in Reims
(5.5F = about $1, zip code: 51100)
If you need a place to stay, **Grand Hotel de l'Univers**** is conveniently located near the station and a small pedestrian plaza, with easy parking and fair rates (Db-260–320F, 41 boulevard Foch, tel. 03 26 88 68 08, fax 03 26 40 95 61).

Transportation Connections—Reims
By train to: Epernay (8/day, 30 min), **Verdun** (8/day, 3 hrs, transfer in Chalons-sur-Marne), **Paris'** Gare de l'Est (10/day, 90 min), **Colmar** (3/day, 5 hrs, transfer in Vitry and Strasbourg).

BELGIUM

- 12,000 square miles (a little smaller than Maryland)
- 10 million people (830 people per square mile)
- 33 Belgian francs = about $1

Belgium falls through the cracks. Nestled between Germany, France, and Britain, and famous for waffles, sprouts, and endive, it's no wonder many travelers don't even consider a stop here. But many who visit remark that Belgium is one of Europe's best-kept secrets. There are tourists, but not as many as the country's charms merit.

The country is split between the French-speaking Walloons in the south and the Dutch-speaking Flemish people (60 percent of the population) in the north. The capital city, Brussels, while mostly French-speaking, is officially bilingual. There is a small minority of German-speaking people and, because of Belgium's international importance, more than 20 percent of its residents are foreigners.

It is in Belgium that Europe comes together: where Romance languages meet Germanic languages; Catholics meet Protestants; and the Benelux union was established, planting the seed 40 years ago that, today, is sprouting into the unification of Europe. Belgium flies the flag of Europe as vigorously as any place you'll visit.

Bruges and Brussels are the best two first bites of Belgium. Brussels is one of Europe's great cities and the capital of the European Community. Bruges is a wonderfully-preserved medieval gem that expertly nurtures the tourist industry, bringing the town a prosperity it hasn't enjoyed since it helped lead northern Europe out of the Middle Ages 500 years ago.

Belgians brag that they eat as much as the Germans and as well as the French. They are the world's leading beer consumers and among the world's leading carnivores. In Belgium you should never bring chrysanthemums to a wedding. And tweaking little kids on the ear is considered rude.

Ten million Belgians are packed into 12,000 square miles. At 830 people per square mile, it's the second most densely populated country in Europe (after the Netherlands). This population concentration, coupled with a dense and well-lit rail and road system, causes Belgium to actually shine at night when viewed from space, a phenomenon NASA astronauts call the "Belgian Window."

Belgium's rail system is tops, and its various rail deals are worth considering. The second-class Multipass gives groups of three to five people any two trips in Belgium. Three people pay

Belgium and the Netherlands

1,260BF, four pay 1,420BF, and five pay 1,580BF; at least one of the Multipass users must be age 26 or older. People under age 26 can get a Go Pass: 1,420BF for 10 rides anywhere in Belgium. (The one-way fare from Brussels to Bruges is 370BF per person.) Seniors age 60 and up can get any six rides for 1,260BF (second class) or 1,940BF (first class). Anyone traveling on the weekend should ask for the weekend discount (40-percent reduction for one person, 60-percent off for traveling companions).

BRUGES (BRUGGE)

With Renoir canals, pointy gilded architecture, time-tunnel art, and stay-awhile cafés, Bruges is a heavyweight sightseeing destination, as well as a joy. Where else can you ride a bike along a canal, munch mussels, wash them down with the world's best beer, savor heavenly chocolate, and see Flemish Primitives and a Michelangelo, all within 300 yards of a bell tower that rings out "Don't worry, be happy" jingles every 15 minutes? And there's no language barrier.

The town is "Brugge" (broo-gha) in Flemish. It's "Bruges" (broozh) in French and English. Before it was Flemish or French, the name was a Viking word for "wharf" or "embarkment." Right from the start, Bruges was a trading center. By the 14th century Bruges' population was 35,000, in a league with London, and the city was the most important cloth market in northern Europe. By the 16th century the harbor had silted up and the economy had collapsed. In the 19th century a new port, Zeebrugge, brought renewed vitality to the area. Today Bruges prospers mainly because of tourism: it's a uniquely well-preserved Gothic city and a handy gateway to Europe. It's no secret, but even with the crowds it's the kind of city where you don't mind being a tourist.

Planning Your Time

Bruges needs at least two nights and a full, well-organized day. Even non-shoppers enjoy browsing here, and the Belgian love of life makes a hectic itinerary seem a little senseless. With one day, the speedy visitor could do this: 9:30–Climb the belfry, 10:00–Catch the minibus orientation town tour, 11:00–Tour the Burg sights (visit the TI if necessary), 12:15–Walk to the brewery, have lunch, and catch the 13:00 tour, 14:30–Walk through the

Beguinage, 15:00–Tour the Memling Museum (six paintings), 15:45–See the Michelangelo in the church, 16:00–Tour the Groeninge Museum (closes at 17:00). Rent a bike for an evening ride through the quiet backstreets (or take a 900BF half-hour horse-and-buggy tour or catch a canal-boat tour). Lose the tourists and find a dinner. (If this schedule seems insane, skip the belfry and the brewery.)

Orientation (tel. code: 050)

The tourists' Bruges (you'll be sharing it) is contained within a one-kilometer-square canal, or moat. Nearly everything of interest and importance is within a cobbled and convenient swath between the train station and Market Square (a 15-minute walk).

Tourist Information: The main office is on Burg Square (Monday–Friday 9:30–18:30, Saturday and Sunday 10:00–12:00 and 14:00–18:30; off-season closes at 17:00, tel. 050/448-686, public WC in courtyard). The other TI is at the train station office (daily 10:30–13:15 and 14:00-18:30, off-season closes at 17:00 and on Sunday). Both TIs sell a great 25BF all-inclusive Bruges visitors guide with a map and listings of all of the sights and services. The free *Exit* includes a monthly calendar of the many events the town puts on to keep its hordes of tourists entertained. It's entirely in Dutch but almost readable (i.e., *Harmonieconcert*). Skip the TI's "combo" museum ticket. They also have train schedule information and specifics on the various kinds of tours available. Bikers will want the *5X On The Bike Around Bruges* map/guide for 20BF, showing five routes through the countryside.

Cyber Café: An Internet café is at Katelijnestraat 67, halfway between the station and Market Square near Walplein (tel. 050/349-352, e-mail: Kdenys@unicall.be). Wordprocessing and printing are also available: 60BF for 15 minutes.

Laundromat: You'll find it at Gentportstraat 28 (daily 7:00–22:00, English instructions). All the machines use 20BF coins; you'll need about 10 total.

Arrival in Bruges

By Train: From the train, you'll see the square belfry tower on the main square. Upon arrival, stop by the station TI to pick up the Bruges visitors guide (map in centerfold). Most buses (all those marked "CENTRUM") go right to Market Square (40BF ticket, buy from driver, good for an hour). The taxi fare to most hotels is 250BF. It's a 20-minute walk from the station to the center: Cross the busy street and canal in front of the station, head up Oostmeers, and turn right on Steenstraat to reach Market Square. You could rent a bike at the station for the duration of your stay (325BF/day with a 500BF deposit), but other bike rental shops are closer to the center (see below).

By Car: Park at the train station for just 100BF a day and pretend you arrived by train; show your parking receipt on the bus to get a free ride into town. The pricier underground parking garage at t'Zand costs 350BF/day.

Helpful Hints
Change traveler's checks at Best Change (daily 9:00–21:00, until 19:00 in winter, just off Market Square on Steenstraat). The post office is on Market Square near the belfry (Monday–Friday 9:00–19:00, Saturday 9:00–12:00). Shops are open from 9:00 to 18:00, a little later on Friday. Grocery stores are usually closed on Sunday. Market day is Wednesday morning (Market Square) and Saturday morning (t'Zand). On Saturday and Sunday afternoons there is a flea market along Dijver in front of the Groeninge Museum. October through March is off-season (when some museums close on Tuesday). A botanical garden blooms in the center of Astrid Park.

Sights—Bruges
Bruges' sights are listed here in walking order: from Market Square to the Burg, to the cluster of museums around the Church of Our Lady, to the Beguinage (a 10-minute walk from beginning to end). Like Venice, the ultimate sight is the town itself, and the best way to enjoy that is to get lost on the backstreets away from the lace shops and ice-cream stands.

Market Square (Markt)—Ringed by banks, the post office, lots of restaurant terraces, great old gabled buildings, and the belfry, this is the modern heart of the city. Most city buses go from here to the station. Under the belfry are two great Belgian French-fry stands and a quadrilingual Braille description and model of the tower. In its day, a canal went right up to the central square of this formerly great trading center.

▲▲**Belfry (Belfort)**—This bell tower has towered over Market Square since 1300. In 1486 the octagonal lantern was added, making it 88 meters high—that's 366 steps (daily 9:30–17:00, October–March closed 12:30–13:30, ticket window closes 45 minutes before closing times, WC in courtyard). The view is worth the climb and the 100BF. Survey the town. On the horizon you can see the towns along the coast. Just before you reach the top, peek into the carillon room. The 47 bells can be played mechanically with the giant barrel and movable tabs (as they do on each quarter-hour), or with a manual keyboard (as it does for regular concerts) with fists and feet rather than fingers. Be there on the quarter-hour when things ring. It's *bellissimo* at the top of the hour. Carillon concert times are listed at the base of the belfry (usually Wednesday, Saturday, and Sunday 14:15–15:00). With your back to the belfry, turn right on Breidelstraat to get to Burg Square.

Central Bruges

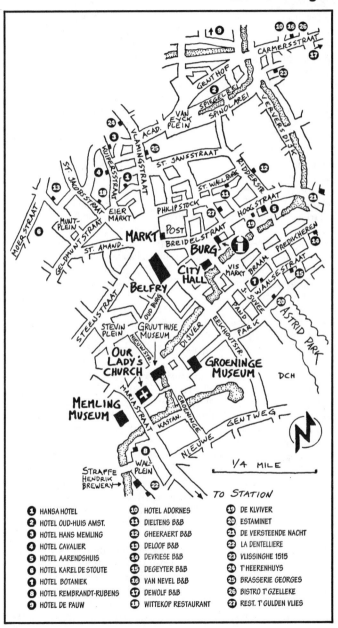

1 HANSA HOTEL
2 HOTEL OUD-HUIS AMST.
3 HOTEL HANS MEMLING
4 HOTEL CAVALIER
5 HOTEL AARENDSHUIS
6 HOTEL KAREL DE STOUTE
7 HOTEL BOTANIEK
8 HOTEL REMBRANDT-RUBENS
9 HOTEL DE PAUW

10 HOTEL ADORNES
11 DIELTENS B&B
12 GHEERAERT B&B
13 DELOOF B&B
14 DEVRIESE B&B
15 DEGEYTER B&B
16 VAN NEVEL B&B
17 DEWOLF B&B
18 WITTEKOP RESTAURANT

19 DE KLUVER
20 ESTAMINET
21 DE VERSTEENDE NACHT
22 LA DENTELLIERE
23 VLISSINGHE 1515
24 T'HEERENHUYS
25 BRASSERIE GEORGES
26 BISTRO T'GZELLEKE
27 REST. T'GULDEN VLIES

▲▲**Burg Square**—The opulent square called Burg is Bruges' civic center, historically the birthplace of Bruges and the site of the ninth-century castle of the first Count of Flanders. Today it's the scene of outdoor concerts and home of the TI (with a pay WC, 10BF). It's surrounded by six centuries of architecture. Sweeping counterclockwise 360 degrees, you'll go from Romanesque (the round arches and thick walls of the brick basilica in the corner, best seen inside the lower chapel), to the pointed Gothic arches of the Town Hall (with its "Gothic Room"), to the well-proportioned Renaissance windows of the Old Recorder's House (next door, under the gilded statues), and past the TI and the park to the elaborate 17th-century Baroque of the Provost's House.

▲**Basilica of the Holy Blood**—Originally the Chapel of Saint Basil, it is famous for its relic of the blood of Christ, which, according to tradition, was brought to Bruges in 1150 after the Second Crusade. The lower chapel (through door labeled *Basiliek*) is dark and solid—a fine example of Romanesque style (with some beautiful statues). The upper chapel (separate entrance, climb the stairs) is decorated Gothic and is often filled with appropriately contemplative music. An English flier tells about the relic, art, and history. The small but sumptuous Basilica Museum contains the gem-studded hexagonal reliquary that carries the relic on its yearly Ascension Day trip through the streets of Bruges (museum is next to upper chapel, 40BF, daily 9:30–11:50 and 14:00–17:50; shorter hours and closed Wednesday afternoon off-season).

▲**City Hall's Gothic Room**—Built around 1400, this is the oldest room in the Low Countries. Your ticket gives you a room full of old town maps and paintings, and a grand, beautifully restored "Gothic Hall." Its painted and carved wooden ceiling features hanging arches (explained by an English flier). The free ground-level lobby is a picture gallery of Belgium's colonial history, from the Spanish Bourbon king to Napoleon (100BF, includes admission to Renaissance Hall, daily 9:30–16:30, closed 12:30–14:00 during off-season, Burg 12).

Renaissance Hall (Brugse Vrije)—This is just one ornate room with an impressive Renaissance chimney. If you're into heraldry, the symbolism, explained in the free English flier, makes this worth a five-minute stop. If you're not, you'll wonder where the rest of the museum is (100BF, includes admission to City Hall, daily 9:30–12:30 and 13:15–16:40, longer lunch until 14:00 in winter, entry in corner of square).

From Burg to Fish Market to View—From Burg, walk under the Goldfinger family down Blinde Ezelstraat. Just after you cross the bridge, the persistent little fish market (Vismarkt) is on your left. Take an immediate right to Huidevettersplein, a tiny, picturesque, and restaurant-filled square. Continue a few steps to Rozenhoed-kaai street, where you can get a great photo of the belfry reflected

in the canal. Can you see its tilt? It leans about four feet. Down the
canal (past a flea market on weekends) looms the huge brick spire
of the Church of Our Lady (tallest brick spire in the Low Countries). Between you and the church are the next three museums.
▲▲▲**Groeninge Museum**—This diverse and classy collection
shows off mostly Flemish art from Memling to Magritte. While it
has plenty of worthwhile modern art, the highlights are its vivid
and pristine Flemish Primitives. ("Primitive" here means before
the Renaissance.) Flemish art is shaped by its love of detail, its
merchant patrons' egos, and the power of the Church. Lose yourself in the halls of Groeninge: Gaze across 15th-century canals,
into the eyes of reassuring Marys, and through town squares littered with leotards, lace, and lopped-off heads (200BF, daily
9:30–17:00, closed 12:30–14:00 and Tuesday October–March,
Dijver 12). The **Brangwyn Museum** (Arentshuis), next door, is
only interesting if you are into lace or the early-20th-century art
of Brangwyn (80BF, daily 9:30–17:00, closed 12:30–14:00 and
Tuesday during off-season, Dijver 16).
▲**Gruuthuse Museum**—A wealthy brewer's home, this is a
sprawling smattering of everything from medieval bedpans to a
guillotine. There's no information inside, so to understand the
crossbows, dark old paintings, and what a beer merchant's doing
with box seats peeking down on the altar of the Church of Our
Lady next door, you'll have to buy or browse through the 600BF
guidebook (130BF, daily 9:30–17:00, shorter hours off-season,
Dijver 17).
▲▲**Church of Our Lady**—The church stands as a memorial to
the power and wealth of Bruges in its heyday. A delicate
Madonna and Child by Michelangelo is near the apse (to the
right, if you're facing the altar). It's said to be the only
Michelangelo statue to leave Italy in his lifetime (cloth money).
If you like tombs and church art, pay to wander through the
apse (60BF, Michelangelo free, art-filled apse Monday–Friday
10:00–11:30 and 14:30–16:30, closes at 16:00 on Saturday, Sun-
day 14:30–16:30, on Mariastraat).
▲▲**St. Jans Hospital/Memling Museum**—Beyond the Church
of Our Lady is a medieval hospital with six much-loved paintings
by the greatest of the Flemish Primitives, Hans Memling. His
Mystical Wedding of St. Catherine triptych deserves a close look.
Catherine and her "mystical groom," the baby Jesus, are flanked
by a headless John the Baptist and a pensive John the Evangelist.
The chairs are there so you can study it. If you understand the
Book of Revelations, you'll understand St. John's wild and intri-
cate vision. The Reliquary of St. Ursula, an ornate little mini-
church in the same room, is filled with impressive detail (100BF,
daily 9:30–17:00, off-season closed 12:30–14:00 and Wednesday,
Mariastraat 38).

▲▲**Straffe Hendrik Brewery Tour**—Belgians are Europe's beer connoisseurs. This fun and handy tour is a great way to pay your respects. The happy gang at this working family brewery gives entertaining and informative 45-minute/four-language tours (usually by friendly Inge, 140BF including a beer, piles of very steep steps, a great rooftop panorama, daily on the hour 11:00–17:00, occasionally skipping 14:00, October–March 11:00 and 15:00 only, one block past church and canal, take right down skinny Stoofstraat to #26 on Walplein square, tel. 050/332-697). Originally Henri Maes, this delicious brew is now known as Straffe Hendrik (strong Henry). They remind their drinkers: "The components of the beer are vitally necessary and contribute to a well-balanced life-pattern. Nerves, muscles, visual sentience, and a healthy skin are stimulated by these in a positive manner. For longevity and life-long equilibrium, drink Straffe Hendrik in moderation!"

Their bistro, where you'll be given your included-with-the-tour beer, serves a quick and hearty lunch plate (the 150BF "bread with paste and vegetables" is the best value, although the 250BF "meat selection and vegetables" is a beer-drinker's picnic for two). You can eat indoors with the smell of hops or outdoors with the smell of hops. This is a great place to wait for your tour or to linger afterward—just watch out for the medieval whoopee cushions on the tables.

▲▲**Beguinage**—For military (and various other) reasons, there were more women than men in the medieval Low Countries. Towns provided Beguinages, dignified places in which these "Beguines" could live a life of piety and service (without having to take the same vows a nun would). You'll find Beguinages all over Belgium and Holland. Bruges' Beguinage almost makes you want to don a habit and fold your hands as you walk under its wispy trees and whisper past its frugal little homes. For a thin slice of Beguinage life, walk through the simple museum (Beguine's House, 60BF with English flier, daily 10:00–12:00 and 13:45–17:00, shorter hours off-season).

Minnewater—Beyond the Beguinage is Minnewater, an idyllic, clip-clop world of flower boxes, canals, swans, and tour boats packed like happy egg cartons. Beyond that is the train station.

Almshouses—Walking from the Beguinage back to the center, you might detour along Nieuwe Gentweg to visit one of about 20 almshouses in the city. At #8, go through the door (free) into the peaceful courtyard. This was a medieval form of housing for the poor. The rich would pay for someone's tiny room here in return for lots of prayers.

Bruges' Experiences
Chocolate—Bruggians are connoisseurs of fine chocolate. You'll be tempted by chocolate-filled display windows all over town.

Godiva is the best big-factory/high-price/high-quality local brand, but for the finest small-family operation, drop by **Maitre Chocolatier Verbeke**. While Mr. Verbeke is busy downstairs making chocolates, Mrs. Verbeke makes sure customers in the shop get the chocolate of their dreams. Ask her to assemble a bag of your favorites. (The smallest amount sold is 100 grams—about seven pieces—for 82BF). Most are pralines, which means they're filled. While the "hedgehogs" are popular, be sure to get a "pharaoh's head." Pray for cool weather, since it's closed when it's very hot. (Open at least in the mornings on Tuesday, Wednesday, Friday, and Saturday; open cooler afternoons as well; a block off Market Square at Geldmuntstraat 25; can ship overseas except during hot summer months, tel. 050/334-198.)

Lace and Windmills by the Moat—A 10-minute walk from the center to the northeast end of town brings you to four windmills strung out along a pleasant grassy setting on the "big moat" canal (between Kruispoort and Dampoort, on the Bruges side of the moat). One of the windmills (St. Janshuismolen) is open for visitors (40BF, 9:30–12:30 and 13:15–17:00, closed October–March, at the end of Carmersstraat).

To actually see lace being made, drop by the nearby Lace Centre, where ladies toss bobbins madly while their eyes go bad (60BF includes afternoon demonstrations and a small lace museum called Kantcentrum, as well as the adjacent Jerusalem church; Monday–Friday 10:00–12:00 and 14:00–18:00, until 17:00 Saturday, closed Sunday, Peperstraat 3). The Folklore Museum, in the same neighborhood, is cute but forgettable (80BF, daily 9:30–17:00, less off-season, Rolweg 40). To find either place, ask for the Jerusalem church.

▲▲**Biking**—While the sights are close enough for easy walking, the town is a treat to bike through, and you'll be able to get away from the tourist center. Consider a peaceful evening ride through the backstreets and around the outer canal. Rental shops have maps and ideas. The TI sells a handy *5X On The Bike Around Bruges* map/guide for 20BF; it narrates five different bike routes (ranging from 18–30 kilometers) through the idyllic nearby countryside. The best basic trip is 30 minutes along the canal out to Damme and back. The Netherlands/Belgium border is a 40-minute pedal beyond Damme. Two shops rent bikes in the center of town: 70BF/one hour, 150BF/four hours, 250BF/day. Both offer free city maps and child seats. **Popelier Eric's** doesn't require any kind of deposit and sells a good-quality map of the countryside for 80BF (daily 9:00–21:00 in summer, 10:00–19:00 in winter, 50 meters from the Church of Our Lady at Mariastraat 26, tel. 050/343-262). **'T Koffie Boont Je** asks for a deposit of 1,000BF, your passport, or a credit-card imprint. They sell an annoying double-sided photocopy of the TI's biking brochure for

20BF; the map is on one side and the directions—inconveniently—are on the other (Hallestraat 4, closer to the belfry, tel. 050/338-027). The less central **De Ketting** rents bikes for less (150BF/day, Gentpoortstraat 23, tel. 050/344-196).

Bryggia, My Love **Multivision Show**—(This might close in 1999.) Shown in a former neo-Gothic church, this multiscreen film tells of Bruges' Golden Age under the Dukes of Burgundy (mid-1300s–mid-1400s). Dial your audiophone to English and sit near the back to see all of the screens. The 30-minute show, which is informative yet uneven, beats standing in the rain. Parents might find a medieval grope or two objectionable (190BF, daily 10:00–17:00 April–October, shows every hour on the hour, Vlamingstraat 86, tel. 050/347-572). The same company offers a medieval dinner show—skip it.

Dolfinarium—At Boudewijnpark, just outside of town, dolphins make a splash at 11:00, 14:00, and 16:00 (275BF, Debaeckestraat 12, call to confirm show times, tel. 050/383-838). The theme park's roller-skating rink is open in the afternoon (and turns into an ice-skating rink off-season). From Bruges, catch the "Sint Michiels" bus #7 or #17 from Kuipersstraat.

Tours of Bruges

Bruges by Bike—The Backroad Bike Company leads daily bike tours through the nearby countryside (550–650BF, 30 km, three hrs, tel. 050/370-470, fax 050/374-960). Shorter, longer, and evening tours are available.

Bruges by Boat—The most relaxing and scenic (if not informative) way to see this city of canals is by boat, with the captain narrating. Boats leave from all over town (170BF, 10:00–18:00, copycat 35-minute rides).

City Minibus Tours—"City Tour Bruges" gives 50-minute/380BF rolling overviews of the town in a 13-seat, three-skylight minibus, with dial-a-language headsets and earphones. The tour leaves hourly (on the hour, 10:00–19:00 in summer, until 18:00 in spring and fall) from Market Square. The audio is clean, and the narration gives a good history as you tour the town the lazy way.

Bus Tours of Countryside—**Quasimodo Tours** is a hip outfit offering those with extra time two all-day tours through the rarely visited Flemish countryside. The "Flanders Fields" tour on Sunday, Tuesday, and Thursday from 9:00 to 16:30 concentrates on WWI battlefields, trenches, memorials, and poppy-splattered fields. On Monday, Wednesday, and Friday from 9:00 to 16:00, it's "Triple Treat": the port of Damme, a castle, monastery, brewery, and chocolate factory; and sampling the treats—a waffle, chocolate, and beer. Tours are offered in English only (1,400BF, 1,100BF for people under 26, CC:VM, 29-seat nonsmoking bus, lunch included, lots of walking, pick-up at your hotel or the train station, tel. 050/370-470 to book, fax 050/374-960). **Sightseeing Line** offers a bus trip to Damme and a boat ride back (660BF, daily April–June at 14:00 and 16:00, two hours, leaves from Market Square).

Walking Tours—Local guides walk small groups through the core of town daily in July and August (150BF, depart from TI at 15:00, or 1,500BF with private guide by reservation at the TI). The tours, while earnest, are heavy on history and in two languages, so they may be less than peppy. Still, to propel you beyond the pretty gables and canal swans of Bruges, they are good medicine.

Sleeping in Bruges
(33BF = about $1, tel. code 050, zip code: 8000)
Sleep Code: **S** = Single, **D** = Double/Twin, **T** = Triple,
Q = Quad, **b** = bathroom, **t** = toilet only, **s** = shower only,
CC = Credit Card (**V**isa, **M**asterCard, **A**mex). Everyone speaks English.

Most places are located between the train station and the old center, with the most distant (and best) being a few blocks beyond Market Square to the north and east. B&Bs offer the best value (below). All include breakfast, are on quiet streets, and (with two exceptions) keep the same prices throughout the year. Assuming you'll arrive at Market Square by foot or bus, I'll give hotel directions using a 12-hour clock, as if you were standing with your back to the belfry.

Hotels
Hansa Hotel offers 20 rooms in a completely modernized old building. It's bright and tastefully decorated in elegant pastels, and has all the amenities. This is a great splurge, with best prices Sunday through Thursday nights (Sb-3,000–3,900BF, Db-3,500–4,200BF, extra bed-1,250BF, nonsmoking, CC:VMA, elevator, Niklaas Desparsstraat 11, a block north of Market Square, tel. 050/338-444, fax 050/334-205, e-mail: information @hansa.be, run by Johan and Isabelle). Head for Vlamingstraat at 1:00 and take the first left.

Hotel Oud-huis Amsterdam is a classy canalside splurge that seamlessly mixes antiques and chandeliers with modern comforts (Sb-4,750–6,750BF, Db-5,750–7,750BF, five-minute walk from Market Square at Spiegelrei 3, tel. 050/341-810, fax 050/338-891).

Hotel Hans Memling is newly remodeled. There's Mozart in the morning and Beethoven in the afternoon. The giant living/breakfast room is palatial, while the 17 huge upstairs bedrooms are decorated in a classy modern style (Sb-4,200BF, Db-4,900BF, Tb-5,900BF, Qb-6,600BF, CC:VMA, cheaper in winter, buffet breakfast, elevator, Kuipersstraat 18, two blocks north of

Market, easy phone reservations if arriving before 18:00, tel. 050/471-212 fax 050/471-210). At 11:00, take Sint Jakobsstraat for one block, then angle right through Eiermarkt Square to Kuipersstraat.

Hotel Cavalier, across the street from Hans Memling, has less character but serves a hearty buffet breakfast in a royal setting (Sb-1,800BF, Db-2,300BF, Tb-2,800BF, Qb-3,200BF, two lofty "backpackers' doubles" on the fourth floor for 1,600BF, CC:VMA, Kuipersstraat 25, tel. 050/330-207, fax 050/347-199, run by friendly Viviane De Clerck).

Hotel Aarendshuis, an old merchant's mansion, is well-worn but comfortable. It's family run with spacious rooms, dingy carpets, chandeliered public places, and a small garden (prices vary with size and luxury: Sb-2,200BF, Db-3,000–4,000BF, Tb-4,000BF, Qb-5,000BF, kids under 10 free, grand boil-your-own-eggs buffet breakfast included, dinner available, carpark-300BF, elevator, CC:VMA, two blocks off Burg Square at Hoogstraat 18, tel. 050/337-889, fax 050/330-816). Immediately to your right at 4:00, take Briedelstraat, which becomes Hoogstraat.

Hotel Karel de Stoute has pleasant rooms in a 15th-century house with carved railings and a huge chandelier (Sb-2,450BF, Db-2,950BF, Tb-3,600BF, Qb-4,500BF, CC:VMA, Moerstraat 23, tel. 050/343-317, fax 050/344-472). Take Sint Jakobsstraat at 11:00, first left on Geldmuntstraat, first right on Geerwiynstraat, then left on Moerstraat.

Hotel Botaniek has three stars, nine fine rooms, and a quiet location a block from Astrid Park. This hotel is basic, small, and comfy. Rooms have TVs and phones, and some have a fridge at no extra cost—ask (Sb-2,400BF, Db-2,800BF, Tb-3,400BF, CC:VMA, Waalsestraat 23, tel. 050/341-424, fax 050/345-939). Immediately to your right at 4:00, take Briedelstraat to Burg, then Blinde Ezelstraat (under Goldfinger family); continue straight (with fish market on your left) for two blocks to Waalsestraat.

Hotel Rembrandt-Rubens has 18 rooms in a creaky 500-year-old building, with tipsy floors, a mysterious floor plan, tacky rooms, elephant tusks, a gallery of creepy old paintings, and probably the holy grail in a drawer somewhere (S-1,000BF, Ss-1,400BF, one D-1,500BF, Ds-2,000BF, Db-2,300BF, Tb-2,900BF, Qb-3,800BF, locked up at 24:00, on a quiet square between the Memlings and the brewery at Walplein 38, tel. 050/336-439). The breakfast room (which must have been the knights' hall) overlooks a canal (while Rembrandt and Rubens overlook you from an ornately carved and tiled 1648 chimney). There's a little warmth behind Mrs. DeBuyser's crankiness. The hotel has been in her family for 50 years. At 8:00, take Steenstraat two blocks to the square, turn left on Mariastraat, then right on Walstraat.

Hotel De Pauw is family-run with straightforward rooms on a quiet street across from a church (two D-1,800BF, Db-2,100–2,350BF, CC:VMA, cable TV and phones, Sint Gilliskerk-hof 8, tel. 050/337-118, fax 050/345-140).

Hotel Adornes is a great value with 20 comfy new rooms in a 17th-century canalside house. They offer free parking and free loaner bikes and the rooms come with all the comforts (Sb-2,600–3,400BF, Db-2,800–3,600BF depending upon size, CC:VMA, near Van Nevel B&B, below, and Carmersstraat at St. Annarei 26, tel. 050/341-336, fax 050/342-085).

Hotel t'Keizershof is a dollhouse of a hotel that lives by its motto, "Spend a night, not a fortune." It's simple and tidy, with eight small, cheery rooms split between two floors, a shower and toilet on each (S-925BF, D-1,350BF, T-1,980BF, Q-2,380BF free and easy parking, laundry service-300BF, Oostmeers 126, a block in front of train station, tel. 050/338-728, run by Stefaan and Hilde).

Hotel Maison Printaniere, outside of Bruges, has seven doubles (D-from 1,350BF, Db-from 1,850BF, CC:VM, Kapelleweg 7, 8200 Brugge Sint Andries, 20-minute walk from station or take bus #25 "Olympia" to the stop "Vogelzang," tel. 050/385-067, fax 050/380-081).

Bed-and-Breakfasts

These places offer the best value. Each is central, is run by people who enjoy their work, and offers lots of stairs and three or four doubles you'd pay 2,000 to 2,200BF for in a hotel.

Koen and Annemie Dieltiens are a friendly couple who enjoy translating for the guests who eat a hearty breakfast around a big table in their bright, homey, comfortable house. They are a wealth of information on Bruges (S-1,200BF, Sb-1,500BF, D-1,500BF, Db-1,800BF, T-2,000BF, Tb-2,300BF, Qb-2,800BF, nonsmoking, free street parking, Sint-Walburgastraat 14, three blocks east of Market Square, reserve in advance for this popular place, tel. 050/334-294, fax 050/335-230, e-mail: koen.dieltiens @skynet.be). At 1:00, take Philipstockstraat, turn left on Wapen-makersstraat, then take first right. The Dieltiens also rent a cozy studio and apartment for two to six people in a nearby 17th-century house (two pay 10,500BF per week for studio, 12,000BF for apartment, prices higher for shorter stays and more people; cheaper off-season).

Paul and Roos Gheeraert, around the corner from the Dieltiens, live on the first floor while their guests take the second. With big, bright, comfy rooms, this is a fine value (Sb-1,400BF, larger Sb-1,600BF, Db-1,600BF, larger Db-1,800BF, Tb-2,300BF; rooms have coffee makers, some have fridge; Ridderstraat 9, four blocks east of Market, tel. 050/335-627, fax 050/345-201, e-mail: paul.gheeraert@skynet.be). The Gheeraerts also rent two modern apartments across the street (minimum three nights).

Chris Deloof's rooms are a good bet in the old center. The ones with showers are more elegant, but the upstairs A-frame lofty room is fun (Ss-1,300BF, D-1,800BF, Ds-2,000BF, pleasant breakfast room, Geerwiynstraat 14, tel. 050/340-544, fax 050/343-721, e-mail: chris.deloof@ping.be). The upstairs rooms, which share a kitchenette/microwave, are great for a family or group (Qb-3,500BF). At 11:00, take Sint Jakobsstraat to the first left on Geldmuntstraat, then first right on Geerwiynstraat.

The **Van Nevel family** rents two attractive top-floor rooms with built-in beds in a 16th-century house (S-1,200–1,500BF, D-1,500–1,800BF, Carmersstraat 13, 10-minute walk from Market Square, tel. 050/346-860, fax 050/347-616, e-mail: robert.vannevel@village.uunet.be). Robert enthusiastically shares the culture and history of Bruges with his guests. Take Vlamingstraat at 1:00, turn right on Academiestraat, continue on Spinolarei (runs along right side of canal), and turn right on Carmersstraat.

Yvonne De Vriese rents three tidy but neglected B&B rooms on a corner overlooking two canals (one S-1,000BF, D-1,500BF, Db-1,800BF, 500BF extra for third or fourth person; breakfast served in your room; canal views come with mosquitoes; CC:VMA, free parking, Predikherenstraat 40, four blocks east of Burg Square, take bus #6 or #16 from station and get off at the first stop on Predikheren Rei, tel. 050/334-224). At 4:00, take Breidelstraat to Burg Square, go through archway, pass fish market, and turn left on Braambergstraat, which becomes Predikherenstraat.

Jan Degeyter, a block away, rents two airy, spacious, wood-floored rooms on a quiet street (Db-1,800BF, Tb-2,300BF, Qb-2,800BF, CC:VMA, Waalsestraat 40, tel. 050/331-199, fax 050/347-857).

Arnold Dewolf's B&B is in a stately, quiet neighborhood on a dead-end street. To keep the peace, the rooms lack TVs and radios (S-900BF, D-1,300BF, one big family room-1,400–2,200BF depending on the number of people, free parking, Oostproostse 9, 20-minute walk from center, near the windmills, tel. 050/338-366). Follow directions to Van Nevel's (above), continue on Carmersstraat, turn left on Peterseliestraat, then right on Leestenburg to Oostprootse.

Hostels

Bruges has several good hostels offering beds for around 380BF in two- to eight-bed rooms (singles go for around 550BF). Pick up the hostel info sheet at the station TI. Smallest, loosest, and closest to the center are: the dull **Snuffel Travelers Inn** (Ezelstraat 47, tel. 050/333-133), the **Bauhaus International Party Hotel** (Langestraat 135, tel. 050/341-093), and the funky **Passage** (Dweerstraat 26, tel. 050/340-232; its hotel next door has 1,200BF doubles).

Bigger, more modern, and less central are: **International Youth Hostel Europa** (Baron Ruzettelaan 143, tel. 050/352-679), **IYH Herdersbrug** (Louis Coiseaukaai 46, tel. 050/599-321), and **Merkenveld Scout Center** (Merkenveldweg 15, tel. 050/277-698).

Eating in Bruges

Specialties include mussels cooked a variety of ways (one order can feed two people), fish dishes, grilled meats, and French fries. Touristy places on the square are affordable; candle-cool bistros flicker on backstreets.

Wittekop is very Flemish, specializing in the beer-soaked equivalent of beef bourguignon (18:00–24:00, closed Sunday and Monday, terrace in the back, Sint Jakobsstraat 14). **De Kluiver** offers great "seasnails in spiced bouillon" simmered in a whispering jazz ambience (19:00–1:00, closed Wednesday and Thursday, Hoogstraat 12). For jazz and hearty budget spaghetti (210BF), head for **Estaminet**, on the northern border of peaceful Astrid Park (open from 11:30 on, closed Monday afternoon and all day Thursday, Park 5). Another jazzy place to join locals for dinner is **De Versteende Nacht Jazzcafe** on Langestraat 11 (19:00–2:00, closed Sunday and Monday).

Locals like **La Dentelliere** for its good Flemish food, service, and prices (CC:VMA, Wijngaardstraat 33, tel. 050/331-898); and **Vlissinghe 1515**, a pub at Blekersstraat 2, for its friendly atmosphere (open from 11:30 on, closed Tuesday). Two restaurants popular for their high-quality lunch specials (345BF) are the classy **'t Heerenhuys** (12:00–14:30, closed Thursday and Sunday, Vlamingstraat 53, tel. 050/346-178) and **Brasserie Georges** (12:00–14:30, closed Sunday, Vlamingstraat 58, tel. 050/343-565).

Bistro 't Gezelleke (next door to the Van Nevel B&B and near Bauhaus hostel) offers fine fresh food at bring-'em-in prices (weekdays 12:00–24:00, Saturday from 18:00, closed Sunday, Carmersstraat 15, tel. 050/338-102). **Restaurant 't Gulden Vlies**, just off Burg, is also good (from 19:00 on, closed Monday and Tuesday, Mallebergplaats 17).

Picnics: Geldmuntstraat is a handy street when you're hungry. A block off Market Square on Geldmuntstraat, **Pickles Frituur** serves the best sit-down fries in town. A block farther, past the Verbeke chocolate shop, the **Nopri Supermarket** is great for picnics (push-button produce pricer lets you buy as little as one mushroom, open 9:00–18:00, closed Sunday). The small **Delhaize grocery** is on Market Square opposite the belfry (8:00–12:00 and 13:30–18:00, closed Sunday). **Selfi** has cheap sandwiches to go (Breidelstraat 16, between Burg and Market Square). For midnight munchies, head to the tiny **Nightshop grocery** just off Market Square (daily 14:00–2:00, Philipstockstraat 14).

Frietjes: These local French fries are a treat. Proud and traditional *frituurs* serve tubs of fries and various local-style shish kebabs. Belgians dip their *frietjes* in mayonnaise, but ketchup is there for the Yankees (along with spicier sauces). For a quick, cheap, and scenic meal, hit a *frituur* and sit on the steps or benches overlooking Market Square, about 50 yards past the post office.

Beer: Belgium boasts more than 350 types of beer. Straffe Hendrik (strong Henry), a potent local brew, is, even to a Bud Lite kind of guy, obviously great beer. Among the more unusual of the others to try: Kriek (a cherry-flavored beer), Dentergems (with coriander and orange peel), and Trappist (a dark, monk-made beer). Non–beer drinkers enjoy Kriek and Frambozen Bier (the cherry- and raspberry-flavored beers). Each beer is served in its own unique glass. Any pub carries the basic beers, but for a selection of more than 300 types, drink at **t'Brugs Beertje** (16:00–1:00, closed Wednesday, Kemelstraat 5). When you've finished those, step next door, where **Dreupel Huisje "1919"** serves more than 100 Belgian gins and liqueurs (closed Tuesday). Another good place to gain an appreciation of the Belgian beer culture is **de Garre**, off Breidelstraat (between Burg and Markt) on the tiny Garre alley (daily 12:00–24:00).

Transportation Connections—Bruges
From Brussels, all of Europe is at your fingertips (see Brussels Connections, next chapter). Train info: tel. 050/382-382.

By train to: Brussels (2/hrly, 1 hr), **Ghent** (3/hrly, 20 min), **Oostende** (3/hrly, 15 min), **Köln** (6/day, 4 hrs), **Paris** (3 direct highspeed Thalys trains/day, 2.5 hrs, 400BF supplement for Eurail), **Amsterdam** (hrly, 3.5 hrs).

Trains from England: Bruges is an ideal "welcome to Europe" stop after London. Take the Eurostar train from London to Brussels under the English Channel (6/day, 3 hrs), then transfer to Bruges (hrly, 1 hour). Or, if you'd prefer to cross the Channel by boat, catch the London–Dover train (2 hrs, from London's Victoria station), then the catamaran to Oostende (2 hrs; train station at Oostende catamaran terminal), then the Oostende–Bruges train (15 min). Five boats run daily (900BF one way, same price for the cheap five-day return ticket; call at least three days in advance to book with credit card, otherwise just call to reserve a seat and pay at the dock; CC:VMA, tel. 059/559-955).

BRUSSELS

Brussels, the capital of Belgium, is also the capital of Europe. This is where Europe comes together. Since WWII it has been the convenient home of both NATO and the "government of Europe," working busily to move things towards unity. It's the linguistic hinge as well (60 percent of all Belgians speak the Germanic Flemish and 40 percent speak the Romantic French). It's easy to miss Brussels as you zip from Amsterdam to Paris on the train, but those who stop are pleasantly surprised.

Brussels, like Belgium, is officially a bilingual country. Most maps and signs here list place names in French and Flemish (Dutch). Since 80 percent of the people in Brussels speak French, I normally list only the French names in this chapter.

Planning Your Time

Brussels is low on great sights and high on ambience. On a quick trip, a day and a night are enough for a good first taste. It could even be done as a day trip from Bruges (an hour away by train) or a stopover on the Amsterdam–Paris ride (nearly hourly trains). The main reason to stop—La Grand Place—takes only a few minutes to see. With very limited time, skip the indoor sights and enjoy a coffee or a beer on the square. Even travelers not "into art" can spend an enjoyable three hours at Brussels' ancient- and modern-art museums. If you do the auto and military museums (side by side), plan on a three-hour trip from the town center. Most important, this is a city to browse and wander.

Orientation (tel. code: 02)

Central Brussels is defined by a ring of roads (which replaced the old city wall) called the Pentagon. All hotels and nearly all the sights I mention are within this circle. The epicenter is the main square (La Grand Place), TI, and Central Station (three blocks away). To get to La Grand Place, walk downhill from Central Station (through the arch in Le Meridien Hotel across the street), turn right, and, after a block, you'll reach a small square with a fountain. For La Grand Place, turn left at the far end of the square; for the TI, continue straight past the square for one block. For the restaurant streets, take the first right (an alley) past the TI (see Eating, below).

Tourist Information: Although the office at rue du Marche-aux-Herbes 63 is for all of Belgium, it does Brussels just fine (downhill three blocks from the Central Station, Monday–Friday 9:00–19:00, Saturday–Sunday 9:00–13:00 and 14:00–19:00, closes off-season at 18:00, tel. 02/504-0390). There's also an office in the city hall in La Grand Place (daily 9:00–18:00, closed on Sundays off-season, tel. 02/513-8940). Among their countless fliers, pick up "Brussels, Yours to Discover," the weekly *What's On*, a city map, and a public transit map. The 70BF *Brussels Guide & Map* booklet is worthwhile if you want a series of neighborhood walks and a more complete explanation of the city's many museums. If your next destination is Bruges, get your Bruges map here.

Arrival in Brussels

By Train: Brussels can't decide which of its three stations is the main one. Ask on board if your train stops at Central. Most international trains leave and land at the Nord or Midi Stations. The Midi Station (also called Zuid or South) is the place to catch the speedy Eurostar train that gets you to London in three hours. The area around the Midi Station is a rough-and-tumble immigrant neighborhood (with a towering Ferris wheel); the area around the Nord Station is a seedy red-light district. The Central Station has handy services (grocery store, fast-food, luggage storage, waiting rooms, and so on) and is nearest to the sights.

Trains zip under the city, connecting all three stations every two minutes or so. It's a free and easy three-minute chore to connect from Nord or Midi. At the Nord or Midi Stations, ask at the info kiosk or Travel Centre for the next train to Central. As you wait on the platform for your train, look at the track notice board that tells which train is approaching. They zip in and out constantly. Anxious travelers often board the wrong train on the right track.

By Plane: Shuttle trains run between the three stations (Midi, Central, and Nord) and Brussels International Airport, 14 kilometers away (90BF, 3/hrly, 25 min). Airport info can connect you to your airline desk: tel. 02/753-3913.

Helpful Hints

Laundry: Laundromat "Washing 65" is handy to my recommended hotels and has plenty of machines (daily 7:00–21:00, good

Brussels

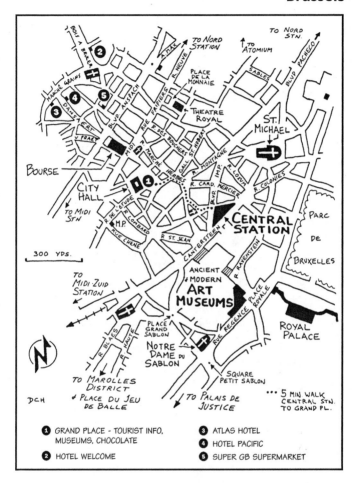

1. GRAND PLACE - TOURIST INFO, MUSEUMS, CHOCOLATE
2. HOTEL WELCOME
3. ATLAS HOTEL
4. HOTEL PACIFIC
5. SUPER GB SUPERMARKET

change machine, soap machine, clear English instructions, rue du Midi 65).

Sights: Museums usually close one hour earlier off-season. If you're in Brussels on a Monday, when most sights are closed, consider the City Museum, Auto World, Atomium, shopping, a walking tour, or a minibus tour.

Getting Around Brussels

Most of Brussels' sights are walkable. For a few of the sights, like the auto and military museums, take the Métro. Get the TI's excellent "Métro Tram Bus Plan"—it's free. The integrated system uses one 50BF ticket that is good for one hour (notice the time when you first stamp it, buy tickets on bus or at Métro stations). The deals (five tickets for 240BF, 10 tickets for 330BF) are available at newsstands and Métro stations, and TIs sell the one-day ticket for 130BF (cheaper than three rides).

Sights—Brussels

▲▲▲**La Grand Place**—Brussels' main square, aptly called La Grand Place, is the heart of the old town and the greatest sight Brussels has to offer. Any time of day it's worth swinging by to see what's going on. Concerts, flower markets, sound-and-light shows, endless people-watching—it entertains (as do the streets around it).

The museums on the square are pretty dull. You'll see them advertised and featured in the travel literature, but only because there's precious little else in town with a turnstile worth paying to use. The **Hôtel de Ville**, or city hall, with the tallest spire, is the square's centerpiece but no big deal to see (80BF, visits only by 30-minute tours, Tuesday 11:30 and 15:15, Wednesday 15:15, and Sunday 12:15). The **City Museum**, opposite the city hall, is in a neo-Gothic building (1875) called "the King's House" (in which no king ever lived). The top floor has an entertaining room full of costumes the Manneken statue has pissed through; the middle floor features maps and models of old Brussels; and the bottom floor has a few paltry pieces of art (80BF, Monday–Thursday 10:00–12:30 and 13:30–17:00, weekends 10:00–13:00, closed Friday). Opposite the King's House is the **Brewery Museum**, with one room of old brewing paraphernalia and one room of new (all explained in Flemish and French). It's really bad (100BF with a beer, daily 10:00–17:00). The **Lace and Costume Museum** has not a word of English and is worthwhile only to those who have devoted their lives to the making of lace (80BF, 10:00–12:30 and 13:30–17:00, weekends 14:00–16:30, closed Wednesday, Violette 6, a block off the square).

For many, the best thing about the Grand Place is **chocolate** at Godiva's or Leonidas. The Godiva shop offers the very best (123BF for 100 grams). But most locals sacrifice 10 percent in quality to double their take by getting their fix at Leonidas (46 BF for 100 grams). At Godiva the smallest amount sold is 100 grams (six to eight pieces), but Leonidas will sell by the piece.

Manneken-Pis—Brussels is a great city, but its mascot (apparently symbolizing the city's irreverence) is a statue of a little boy urinating. For the story about this little squirt, read a postcard stand. It's three short blocks off the Grand Place, but for exact directions, I'll let you ask a local, *"Où est le Manneken-Pis?"* He may be wearing some clever outfit. By tradition, costumes are sent to Brussels from around

La Grand Place

① HOTEL L'AUBERGE ST. MICHEL
 & T'KELDERKE RESTAURANT
② HOTEL LA MADELEINE
③ HOTEL OPERA
④ HOTEL SEMA
⑤ RESTAURANT AUX ARMES
 DE BRUXELLES
⑥ ROTISSERIE VINCENT
⑦ RESTAURANT DE L'OGENBLIK
⑧ FALSTAFF RESTAURANT
⑨ ZEBRA CAFE
⑩ P P CAFE
⑪ PANOS SANDWICHES
⑫ AD DELHAIZE SUPERMARKET
⑬ FOR OTHER HOTELS, SEE BRUSSELS
 MAP

the world. Cases full of these are on display in the City Museum
(described above).

▲▲▲**Museum of Ancient Art**—This museum, featuring Flemish and Belgian art of the 14th to 18th centuries, is packed with
a dazzling collection of masterpieces by Van der Weyden,
Breughel, Bosch, and Rubens (150BF, worthwhile 20BF map of
ancient- and modern-art museums complex, Tuesday–Sunday
10:00–17:00, some sections close for lunch from 12:00–13:00 or
13:00–14:00, closed Monday, rue de la Regence 3, tel. 02/508-
3211). Start your visit with the free 30-minute audiovisual lesson
in Flemish art appreciation. This show features a handful of
pieces, enabling you to go through the museum with an ability
to understand these as if you were an art historian. Or get headsets at the info desk and take a Walkman tour (100BF). For
more information and a good souvenir, consider the 100BF

Twenty Masterpieces of the Art of Painting—A Brief Guided Tour
guide booklet or the more complete *The Royal Museum of Fine
Arts of Belgium* guidebook. Tour the rooms of this museum in
numerical order.

▲**Museum of Modern Art**—Take a look at Belgium's contribu-
tion to the art of the 19th and 20th centuries (same admission
ticket and entrance as above, connected to the ancient-art museum
by underground escalator, Tuesday–Sunday 10:00–17:00, some
sections close for lunch 12:00–13:00 or 13:00–14:00, closed Monday). Each section is well-described in English. David's neoclassical work (e.g., *Death of Morat*) is a treat, as are the surreal fantasies
of René and Georgette Magritte. Enjoy riding the living room
from one floor to the next.

▲**Park of the Cinquantenaire**—This park sprawls out from
under a massive triumphal arch, which was built in 1880 to celebrate the 50th anniversary of Belgian independence. While there's
precious few of the governmental buildings of the European
Union (EU) to get visually excited about, you can emerge from
the Métro at the Schuman stop to be surrounded by the political
headquarters of a more or less united Europe. The huge, star-
shaped Berlaymont building (built in 1963 to house the Commission of the European Union) was polluted by asbestos insulation
and is now empty and awaiting renovation. From there, walk 10
minutes through the park to the AutoWorld and military museums (under the giant arch). The next Métro stop (Merode) is
much closer to the museums.

▲▲**AutoWorld**—This is a delight for any car enthusiast and even
worthwhile for people who think a Studebaker is some kind of
French cannibal dish (200BF, daily 10:00–18:00, until 17:00 off-
season; in the Palais Mondial, Parc du Cinquantenaire, Métro:
Merode, tel. 02/736-4165). Starting with Mr. Benz's motorized
tricycle of 1886, you'll walk through a giant hall filled with 400
historic cars. It's well-described in English. There is a one-hour/
100BF Walkman tour available.

▲**Royal Museum of the Army and Military History**—Wander
through a vast collection of 19th-century weaponry and uniforms
and a giant hall dedicated to airplanes of war (free, Tuesday–
Sunday 9:00–12:00 and 13:00–16:45, closed Monday, tel. 02/734-
2157). There's a good display from the Belgian struggle for independence (early 1800s).

Natural History Museum—Jazzed by the movie *Jurassic Park*,
the museum has added a "live" dinosaur to its world's largest collection of iguanadon skeletons (150BF, Tuesday–Saturday
9:30–16:45, Sunday 9:30–18:00, closed Monday, Chaussée de
Wavre 260, Métro: Merode, tel. 02/627-4233).

Belgian Centre of the Comic Strip—This strip joint is housed
in an industrial warehouse designed by Horta, the local Art Nou-

veau great. It's free to get inside to visit the brasserie and book-store. Upstairs the comics are interesting only to the Belgians (200BF, Tuesday–Sunday 10:00–18:00, closed Monday, rue des Sables 20, tel. 02/219-1980).

Royal Museum of Central Africa—Remember the Belgian Congo? Brussels has an excellent museum of the Congo and much more of Africa (ethnography, sculptures, jewelry, colonial history, flora, and fauna) an hour from the center. Take Métro 1A to Montgomery, then take tram #44 to its final stop, Tervuren. From there walk 200 meters through the park to a palace (80BF, Tuesday–Friday 10:00–17:00, weekends until 18:00, closed Monday, tel. 02/769-5211).

Antoine Wiertz Museum—This 19th-century artist painted some of the world's largest canvases, with themes from biblical to political (free, 10:00–12:00 and 13:00–17:00, closed Monday and every other weekend, rue Vautier 62, Métro: Troon, tel. 02/648-1718).

Atomium—This giant molecule, with escalators connecting the various "atoms" and a restaurant with a view in the top sphere, was the symbol of the 1958 Universal Exhibition held in Belgium (200BF, daily 9:00–20:00, open less off-season, Métro: Heizel, tel. 02/477-8977). Today it's the cheesy nucleus of a park on the edge of town that has the kid-pleasing **Mini-Europa**, with 1:25 scale models of 300 famous European buildings (395BF, discounts for kids, daily 9:30–18:00, tel. 02/478-0550).

Tours of Brussels

Chatter Tour offers the best organized insight into Brussels. This creative 2.5-hour tour, which mixes walking and public transport, makes hard-to-understand Brussels more than a collection of sights. The groups are small and the guides seem to care. The Chatterbus slogan is, "Our guides are not parrots, our groups are not crowds." Guides expertly explain the delicate balance between French and Flemish through the architecture and art of the city. Starting with medieval and moving through modern styles, this is a study in how a region in an almost perpetual state of flux until the last century somehow managed to find some cohesion and cre-ate a modern state. Of special interest is the late-19th-century Art Nouveau style, especially as pioneered by Belgian Victor Horta. You'll see several of his buildings on the tour (300BF, 250BF for hostelers who buy tickets at their hostel; daily at 10:00 mid-June–mid-September; meet your guide at Galeries Royales Saint-Hubert, rue Marche-aux-Herbes 90, near La Grand Place, tel. 02/673-1835). Ask about their other tours.

De Boeck's City Tours, a typical three-hour, tape-recorded bus tour, provides the handiest way to get the grand perspective on Brussels (790BF, starts with a walk around the Grand Place before jumping on a tour bus at rue de la Colline 8, daily in-season at 10:00, 11:00, 14:00, and 15:00; off-season at 10:00 and 14:00; tel. 02/513-7744). You'll see (and learn about) the Royal Palace, Atomium, and the European Union Headquarters.

Sleeping in Brussels
(33BF = about $1, tel. code: 02, zip code: 1000)
Sleep Code: **S** = Single, **D** = Double/Twin, **T** = Triple,
Q = Quad, **b** = bathroom, **t** = toilet only, **s** = shower only,
CC = Credit Card (Visa, MasterCard, Amex). Everyone speaks English. Prices include breakfast unless noted otherwise.

Like everything else, hotel prices are high in central Brussels. You have three budget options: modern hostels with double rooms, safe but dingy old places, and business hotels offering summer or weekend specials. September is very crowded, and finding a room without a reservation can be impossible.

Business Hotels with Summer Rates
The fancy (5,000–6,000BF) hotels of Brussels survive off the business and diplomatic trade. They are desperately empty in July and August (sometimes May and June, too), and on weekends (most Friday, Saturday, and Sunday nights). If you ask for a summer rate you'll save about a third. If you go through the tourist office, you'll save even more—up to two-thirds. Four-star hotels in the center abound with summer rates between 2,500BF and 3,000BF. If you persist and are willing to sink as low as three stars, you'll probably get a double with enough comforts to keep a diplomat happy, including a fancy breakfast, for as low as 2,000BF.

While the TI assured me that every day in July and August there are tons of business-class hotel rooms on the push list, you can book in advance by calling the BTR room-booking service (tel. 02/513-7484). You will, however, get an even bigger discount by just showing up at the TI. In July and August I would arrive without a reservation, walk from the Central Station down to the TI, and let them book me a room within a few blocks. These seasonal rates apply only to business-class hotels. Budget accommodations charge the same throughout the year.

Moderate Hotels on or near La Grand Place
Hôtel L'Auberge Saint Michel, overlooking Europe's greatest square, features a royal setting. Of its 15 rooms, some are old, some are new, either quiet in the back or grand with a view (recently renovated overlooking the square: Sb-4,250BF, Db-5,100BF; without view, two tiny Sb-2,400BF, Db-3,850BF; breakfast in room, view comes with noise on weekends, all rooms have TVs and telephones, elevator, CC:VMA, La Grand Place 15, tel. 02/511-0956, fax 02/511-4600).

Hôtel La Madeleine, on the small square between the station and La Grand Place, is comfortable and hotelesque with small rooms (S-1,495BF, no shower; Sb-2,695BF, Db-2,995–3,495BF, Tb-3,995BF, CC:VMA, elevator, rue de la Montagne 22, tel. 02/513-2973, fax 02/502-1350).

Hôtel Opera, on a great people-filled street near the Grand Place, is professional, dark, and classy, with all the comforts and an elevator (Sb-2,300BF, Db-2,700–2,800BF, Tb-3,450BF, CC:VMA, rue Gretry 53, tel. 02/219-4343, fax 02/219-1720).

Hotel Sema, with wood floors and some beamed ceilings, has 11 cozy rooms just off the Grand Place and right across from the TI (Sb-3,500BF, Db-4,000BF, Tb-4,500BF, CC:VMA, elevator, rooms have phones and cable TV, 24-hour desk, tel. 02/514-0760, fax 02/548-9039.

Hotel Welcome, run by a bundle of hospitality energy named Meester Smeester, offers small but business-class rooms. With just 10 rooms, it brags it's the smallest hotel in Brussels (small Sb/Db-2,300BF, Db-2,700–3,200BF, extra bed 500BF, breakfast-250BF, free parking, reserve a week in advance, CC:VM, at Ste. Catherine Métro stop on a characteristic old square, 23 Quai au Bois a Bruler, tel. 02/219-9546, fax 02/217-1887, Web site: www.hotelwelcome.com). Guests get a discount at the attached restaurant, La Truite d'Argent.

Atlas Hotel has bright, modern rooms with all the comforts, but is not worth its winter rates (weekend and summer prices: Sb-2,900BF, Db-3,600BF, extra person-1,100BF, CC:VMA, rue du Vieux Marche aux Grains 30, tel. 02/502-6006, fax 02/502-6935, e-mail: reception@atlas-hotel.be). Prices are 30-percent higher on off-season weekdays.

Hotel Pacific is gently run by Paul Powells, whose motto is "safe, clean, and cheap." While the charming breakfast room is 19th-century, the ramshackle upstairs feels like a thrift shop. If you don't mind wrinkly linoleum and well-worn furnishings, you'll find the location excellent. Paul gives the place an enjoyable calmness (S-1,050BF, D-1,800BF, Ds-2,300BF, includes a cheese-omelet breakfast, nonsmoking, showers-100BF, elevator, 24:00 curfew, easy phone reservations, rue Antoine Dansaert 57, tel. 02/511-8459).

Hostels

Three classy and modern hostels, in buildings that could double as small, state-of-the-art, minimum-security prisons, are within a 10-minute walk of the Central Station. Each accepts people of all ages and charges about the same: S-695BF, D-1,140BF, beds in quads-470BF, beds in bigger dorms-405BF, sheets-125BF; nonmembers pay up to 100BF extra. All rates include breakfast and showers down the hall. These places serve cheap meals, and rooms are locked up from 10:00 to 14:00. **Breughel Hostel**, a fortress of cleanliness, is handiest and most comfortable. Twenty-two of its rooms are bunk-bed doubles (open 7:30–10:00 and 14:00–1:00, CC:VM, midway between the Midi and Central Stations, behind Notre Dame de la Chapelle church, rue de St. Esprit 2, reserve ahead in summer, tel. 02/511-0436, fax 02/512-0711). The new **Sleepwell**, surrounded by highrise parking lots, is also comfortable (offers Internet access and walking tours every morning at 10:00 for 100BF per person, rue de Damier 23, tel. 02/218-5050). **Jacques Brel** is a little farther out but still a reasonable walk to everything (rue de la Sablonniere 30, tel. 02/218-0187).

Eating in Brussels

Eat mussels in Brussels. They're served everywhere. You get a bucket and a pile of fries. Use one empty shell to tweeze out the rest of the mussels. When the mollusks are in season, from about July 10 through April, you'll get the big Dutch mussels. Locals take a break in May and June, when only the puny Danish variety is available. For an atmospheric cellar just off the Grand Place, step into the **t'Kelderke** (daily 12:00–2:00, La Grand Place 15, tel. 02/513-7344). It serves local specialties, including mussels (a splitable two-kilo bucket of *moules* for 625BF).

The restaurant streets are touristy but fun (exit left from TI on rue Marche-aux-Herbes and take the first right). Some of these restaurants take advantage of tourists by tacking on extra charges, but locals agree that there are four solidly reputable restaurants among the bunch: **Aux Armes de Bruxelles** (rue des Bouchers 13, closed Monday), **Rotisserie Vincent** (known for its meat dishes), **Brasserie Scheltema**, and **Restaurant de l'Ogenblik** (the last three are clustered on rue Dominicains/Predikheren). These are pricey, but offer a good value—check their posted menu for lunch specials.

Breakfast in your hotel is expensive. Consider the 130BF breakfast deal at the art-deco **Falstaff** restaurant (daily 7:00–11:30, Rue Henri Maus 25, across from the Bourse, tel. 02/511-9877).

If Brussels puts you in an Art-Nouveau mood, have a meal or coffee at the city's most atmospheric hangout, **De Ultieme Hallucinatie** (exotic 275–500BF meals, Monday–Friday 11:00–3:00, Saturday–Sunday from 16:00, beautiful patio, rue Royale 316, tel. 02/217-0614). Just a block from the Bourse, the **Zebra** is popular with the younger crowd (daily 12:00–2:00, place Saint-Géry 33, tel. 02/511-0901), and the neighboring **PP** café specializes in jazz (daily 12:00–2:30, rue J. van Praetstraat 28, tel. 02/514-2562).

You'll find *frites* (French fries) and sandwich shops throughout Brussels. **Panos** has good, cheap sandwiches (on Grasmarkt, across from the entrance of Galleries Royales St. Hubert).

Two **supermarkets** are about a block from the Bourse (Stock

Exchange) and a few blocks from La Grand Place. The **AD Delhaize** is at the intersection of Anspachlan and Marche-aux-Poulets (Tuesday–Saturday 9:00–20:00, Monday from 13:00, Sunday 9:00–13:00), and the **Super GB** is a half block away at Halles and Marche-aux-Poulets (daily 9:00–20:00).

Transportation Connections—Brussels

By train to: Amsterdam (hrly, 3 hrs), **Paris** (8/day, 90 min), **Berlin** (7/day, 9 hrs), **Bern** (4/day, 8 hrs), **Frankfurt** (9/day, 5 hrs), **Munich** (9/day, 8 hrs), **Rome** (4/day, 17–20 hrs). Train info: tel. 02/555-2525 (long wait).

To London: Brussels and London are now just three 140-m.p.h. hours apart by Eurostar train (under the English Channel in 20 minutes; 8/day). In 1999, "full-fare" tickets cost $219 for first class, $149 for second class; these are exchangeable and fully refundable even after your departure date. The cheaper "Leisure" tickets cost $179 for first class, $109 for second class; these are nonexchangeable and 50-percent refundable up to two days before departure. Call 800/EUROSTAR in the United States for the latest fares and to book your reservation. You can also buy Eurostar tickets at any major train station in Europe. If you buy in Belgium, go to a major train station rather than a travel agency; you'll get your tickets immediately (travel agencies can't deliver until the next day). To order your ticket by phone in Belgium, call 0900-10177 (expensive toll line costs 20BF/min from pay phone and 60BF/min from hotel); you can either pay with a credit card or simply reserve a seat (if you reserve, you must pay at the station an hour before the train leaves).

Another option is the slooooow train and ferry combination (8/day, 4.5–7.5 hrs). Or save a little money by riding a Eurolines bus ($42 one-way, $54 round-trip, tel. 02/203-0707 in Brussels).

THE NETHERLANDS

- 13,000 square miles (the size of Maryland)
- 15 million people (1,150 people per square mile, 15 times the population density of the United States)
- 1 guilder = about 60 cents

The Netherlands, Europe's most densely populated country, is also one of its wealthiest and best-organized. A generation ago Belgium, the Netherlands, and Luxembourg formed the nucleus of a united Europe when they joined economically to form Benelux.

Efficiency is a local custom. Though only 8 percent of the labor force are farmers, they cultivate 70 percent of the land, and you'll travel through vast fields of barley, wheat, sugar beets, potatoes, and flowers.

"Holland" is just a nickname for the Netherlands. North Holland and South Holland are the largest of the 12 states that make up the Netherlands. The word "Netherlands" means "lowlands." Half the country is below sea level, reclaimed from the sea (or rivers). That's why the locals say, "God made the Earth, but the Dutch made Holland." Modern technology and plenty of Dutch elbow grease have turned much of the sea into fertile farmland. While a new 12th state—Flevoland, near Amsterdam—has recently been drained, dried, and populated, Dutch reclamation projects are essentially finished.

The Dutch generally speak English, pride themselves on their frankness, and like to split the bill. Traditionally, Dutch cities have been open-minded, loose, and liberal (to attract sailors in the days of Henry Hudson), but they are now paying the price of this easygoing style. Amsterdam has become a bit too seedy for many travelers' tastes. Enjoy more sedate Dutch evenings by sleeping in a small town nearby and side-tripping into the big city.

The Dutch guilder (f, for its older name, florin) is divided into 100 cents (c). There are about f1.9 in one U.S. dollar (f1.9 = $1). To roughly convert Dutch prices into dollars, simply divide the price in guilders by half (e.g., f60 = $30). The colorful Dutch money has Braille markings and classy watermarks.

The country is so small, level, and well-covered by trains and buses that transportation is a snap. Major cities are connected by speedy trains that come and go every 10 or 15 minutes. Connections are excellent, and you'll rarely wait more than a few minutes. Round-trip tickets are discounted. Buses take you where trains don't, and bicycles take you where buses don't. Bus stations and bike rental shops cluster around train stations. The national bus system, both within and between cities, runs on a uniform "strip card" system (though single-ride tickets are also available). You can buy various strip cards on the bus or more cheaply (15 strip cards, f11.50) at train stations, post offices, and some tobacco shops. If you're caught riding without a card, you have to take off your clothes.

Holland is a biker's dream. The Dutch, who average four bikes per family, have put small bike roads (with their own traffic lights) beside every big auto route. You can rent bikes at most train stations and drop them off at most others. (You can take bikes on trains, outside of rush hour, for f9.50.)

Smaller shops are open from 9:00 to 18:00, and until 21:00 on Thursday (closed Sunday). Larger stores and supermarkets are open weekdays from 8:00 to 20:00, and until 17:00 on Saturday (closed Sunday). The businesslike Dutch know no siesta, but many shopkeepers take Monday mornings off.

The best "Dutch" food is Indonesian (from the former colony). Find any Indisch restaurant and experience a rijsttafel (rice table). With as many as 30 spicy dishes, a rijsttafel can be split and still fill two hungry tourists. *Nasi rames* is a cheaper miniversion of a rijsttafel. Local taste treats are cheese, pancakes (*pannenkoeken*), Dutch gin (*jenever*, pronounced "ya nayver"), light Pilsner beer, and "syrup waffles" (*stroopwafel*). Yogurt in Holland (and throughout northern Europe) is delicious and drinkable right out of its plastic container. *Broodjes* are sandwiches of fresh bread and delicious cheese, and are cheap at snack bars, delis, and *broodje* restaurants. For cheap fast-food, try a Middle Eastern *shwarma*, roasted lamb in pita bread. Breakfasts are big by Continental standards. Lunch and dinner are served at American times.

There are several experiences you owe your tongue while you're in Holland: a raw herring (outdoor herring stands are all over), lingering over coffee in a "brown café," an old *jenever* (smooth, local gin) with a new friend, and a giant *rijsttafel*. Tipping is not expected, but locals round the bill up (never more than 5 percent) as thanks for good service.

AMSTERDAM

Amsterdam is a progressive way of life housed in Europe's most 17th-century city. It's a city built on good living, cozy cafés, great art, street-corner jazz, stately history, and a spirit of live and let live. It has 800,000 people and as many bikes, with more canals than Venice—and as many tourists. While Amsterdam may box your Puritan ears, this great, historic city is an experiment in freedom.

Planning Your Time

While I'd sleep in nearby Haarlem, Amsterdam is worth a full day of sightseeing on even the busiest itinerary. While the city has a couple of must-see museums, its best sight is its own breezy ambience. Here are the essential stops for a day in Amsterdam (while it's easily doable on foot with a few hops on tram #20, lacing these sightseeing highlights together by bike—as described below—affords a more vivid experience):

Start the day by touring the Anne Frank House. Finish your morning at the city's two great art museums: Rijksmuseum (cafeteria for lunch) and Van Gogh.

Spend mid-afternoon taking a relaxing hour-long canal cruise (from the dock at Spui). Near Spui consider seeing the idyllic Begijnhof, the Amsterdam Historical Museum, and the flower market.

In the late afternoon, walk from Spui down the busy Kalverstraat pedestrian street to Dam Square, the heart of Amsterdam (palace, church, monument). From Dam Square the Red Light District is several blocks northeast (see map), or walk down Damrak a few blocks to get back to the train station.

With extra time: With two days in Holland, I'd side-trip by bike, bus, or train to an open-air folk museum and visit

Edam or Haarlem. With a third day I'd do the other great Amsterdam museums. With four days I'd do the "historic triangle" or visit the Hague.

Orientation (tel. code: 020)
The central train station is your starting point (TI, bike rental, and trolleys and buses fanning out to all points). Damrak is the main street axis, connecting the station with Dam Square (people-watching and hangout center) and its Royal Palace. From this spine the city spreads out like a fan, with 90 islands, hundreds of bridges, and a series of concentric canals (named "Prince's," "Gentleman's," and "Emperor's") laid out in the 17th century, Holland's Golden Age. The city's major sights are within walking distance of Dam Square.

Tourist Information
Try to avoid Amsterdam's inefficient VVV office across from the train station. (VVV is Dutch for tourist information office; daily 9:00–17:00; TI in train station open Monday–Saturday 7:45–20:00, Sunday 8:00–17:00). Most people wait 30 minutes just to pick up the information brochures and get a room. Avoid this line by studying the wall display of publications for sale and going straight to the sales desk (where everyone ends up anyway, since any information of substance will cost you). Consider buying a city map (f4), *What's On* (f4, monthly entertainment calendar), *Amsterdam: Your Favorite Capital* (f5 for two booklets covering attractions, museums, restaurants, and bars), and any of the walking tour brochures (f4, "Discovery Tour Through the Center," "The Former Jewish Quarter," "Walks Through Jordaan"). The "Amsterdam Culture & Leisure Pass," offering free or discounted admissions to some sights and boat rides, isn't worth the clutter or cost (f36.75, doesn't include Anne Frank House). Nor does it make sense to stand in line at the VVV to buy prepaid same-cost admissions to various Amsterdam sights.

The TI on Leidsestraat is much less crowded (daily 9:00–20:00, closing at 19:00 on Saturday and 17:00 on Sunday). But for f1 a minute you can save yourself a trip by calling the tourist information toll-line at 06-3403-4066 (Monday–Saturday 9:00–17:00). If you're staying in nearby Haarlem, use the helpful Haarlem TI (see Haarlem section, below) to answer most of your Amsterdam questions and provide you with the brochures.

At Amsterdam's Central Station, GWK Change has two hotel reservations windows that sell phone cards and cheaper city maps (f3), and answer basic tourist questions. The lines are short and move quickly. They also change money, including coins, for a hefty f5 fee (near the lockers, at the right end of the station as you leave the platform).

Amsterdam Overview

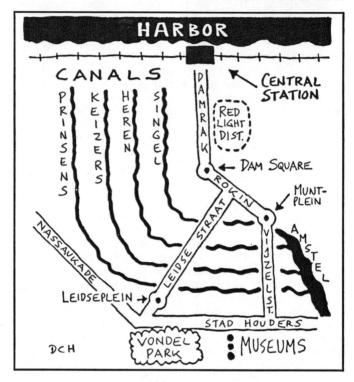

Don't use the TI (or GWK) to book a room. The phone system is easy, everyone speaks English, and the listings in this book are a better value than the potluck booking you'd be charged for at the TI.

Helpful Hints

Many shops close all day Sunday and Monday morning. A *plein* is a square, *gracht* means canal, and most canals are lined by streets with the same name. Handy telephone cards (f10, f25, or f50) are sold at the TI, the GVB public transit office, tobacco shops, the post office, and train stations. The Dutch go "*surfen*" at the Internet Center a couple blocks east of the Rijksmuseum (9:00–18:00, closed Sunday, Monday morning, and Saturday by 17:00, Weteringschans 165, tel. 0800-0403, Web site: www.eteringschans.com). Beware of the bogus telephone offices dressed up like government outlets but ready to rip you off. Tourists are considered green and rich, and the city has more than its share of hungry thieves.

Arrival in Amsterdam

By Train: Amsterdam swings, and the hinge that connects it to the world is its perfectly central Central Station. Walk out the door and you're in the heart of the city. You'll nearly trip over trams ready to take you anywhere your feet won't. Straight ahead is Damrak street, leading to Dam Square. With your back to the entrance of the station, the TI and GVB public transit office are to your left, just across the train tracks.

By Plane: From Schiphol Airport, take the train to Amsterdam (6/hrly, 20 min, f6). If you'll be staying in Haarlem, take a direct express bus from the airport to Haarlem (#236 or #362, 2/hrly, 30 min, f7).

Getting Around Amsterdam

The helpful transit-information office (GVB) is next to the TI (in front of the train station). Its free multilingual *Tourist Guide to Public Transport* includes a transit map and explains ticket options and tram connections to all the sights. Ask for the free "Circle Tram 20" brochure listing all of the stops (and nearby sights) of this handy tram that makes a loop around Amsterdam (#20A goes clockwise, #20B goes counterclockwise).

By Bus, Tram, and Metro: Individual tickets cost f3 and give you an hour on the buses, trams, and metro system (on trams and buses pay as you board; on the metro buy tickets from machines before boarding). **Strip cards** are cheaper than buying individual tickets. Any downtown ride costs two strips (good for an hour of transfers). A card with 15 strips costs f11.50 at the GVB public transit office, train stations, post offices, airport, or tobacco shops throughout the country (senior discount available); shorter strip tickets (two, three, and eight strips) are also sold on some buses and trams. Strip cards are good on buses all over Holland (e.g., six strips for Haarlem to the airport), and you can share them with your partner. An f12 **Day Card** gives you unlimited transportation on the buses and metro for a day in Amsterdam; you'll almost break even if you take three trips (valid until 6:00 the following morning; buy when you board or at the GVB public transit office, which also sells a two-day version for f15). If you get lost in Amsterdam, 10 of the city's 17 trams take you back to the central train station.

By Foot: The longest walk a tourist would take is 45 minutes from the station to the Rijksmuseum. Watch out for silent but potentially painful bikes, trams, and curb posts.

By Bike: One-speed bikes, with "brrringing" bells and two locks (use them both; bike thieves are bold and brazen here), rent for f9.5 per day at the central train station (daily 8:00–22:00; deposit of f200, $120, or your credit-card imprint required; entrance to the left down the ramp as you leave the station, tel. 020/624-8391). In the summer, arrive early or make an easy telephone reservation.

By Boat: While the city is great on foot or bike, there is a "Museum Boat" and a similar "Canal Bus," with an all-day ticket that permits tourists to shuttle from sight to sight. Tickets cost f22 (with discounts that will save you about f5 on admissions). The sales booths in front of the central train station (and the boats) offer handy free brochures with museum times and admission prices. The narrated ride takes 90 minutes if you don't get off (every 30 minutes in summer, every 45 minutes off-season, seven stops, live quadrilingual guide, departures 10:00–17:00, discounted after 13:00 to f15, tel. 020/622-2181).

Sights—Amsterdam's Museum Neighborhood

▲▲▲**Rijksmuseum**—Focus on the Dutch masters: Rembrandt, Hals, Vermeer, and Steen. For a list of the top 20 paintings, pick up the cheap f1 leaflet "A Tour of the Golden Age" and plan your attack (or follow the self-guided tour, one of 20, in my *Mona Winks* guidebook). Audiotaped tours are available (f7.50, more than 200 paintings described, shortcuts advisable).

Follow the museum's chronological layout to see painting evolve from narrative religious art, to religious art starring the Dutch love of good living and eating, to the Golden Age, when secular art dominates. With no local church or royalty to commission big canvases in the post-1648 Protestant Dutch republic, artists specialized in portraits of the wealthy city class (Hals), pretty still lifes (Claesz), and nonpreachy slice-of-life art (Steen). The museum has four quietly wonderful Vermeers. And, of course, a thoughtful brown soup of Rembrandt, including the *Night Watch*. Works by Rembrandt show his excellence as a portraitist for hire (*De Staalmeesters*) and offer some powerful psychological studies, such as *St. Peter's Denial*—with Jesus in the murky background (f15, daily 10:00–17:00, great bookshop, decent cafeteria; tram #2, #5, or #20 from the station; Stadhouderskade 42, tel. 020/673-2121).

▲▲▲**Van Gogh Museum**—Next to the Rijksmuseum, this outstanding and user-friendly museum is a stroll through a beautifully displayed garden of van Gogh's work and life (f12.50, daily 10:00–17:00, Paulus Potterstraat 7, tel. 020/570-5200). The museum also focuses on the late 19th-century art that influenced van Gogh (it happened to be in his brother Theo's collection). The f7 audioguides include insightful commentaries about van Gogh's paintings including related quotes from Vincent himself.

Note: This museum, which has been closed for renovation, will reopen in May '99. If you visit prior to May, look for van Gogh's art in the south wing of the Rijksmuseum.

Stedelijk Modern Art Museum—Next to the Van Gogh Museum, this place is fun, far-out, and refreshing. It has mostly

Amsterdam

post-1945 art, but also a sometimes-outstanding collection of Monet, van Gogh, Cézanne, Picasso, and Chagall, and a lot of special exhibitions (f9, daily 11:00–19:00, closes at 17:00 November–March, tel. 020/573-2737).

Sights—Near Dam Square

▲▲**Anne Frank House**—This house offers a fascinating look at the hideaway where young Anne hid when the Nazis occupied the Netherlands. Pick up the English pamphlet at the door. An expanded exhibit, new for 1999, offers more thorough coverage of the Frank family, the diary, the stories of others who hid out, and the Holocaust (f10, daily 9:00–21:00 April–August, closes daily at 17:00 September–March, 263 Prinsengracht, tel. 020/556-7100). For an interesting glimpse of Holland under the Nazis, rent the powerful movie *Soldier of Orange* before you leave home.

Westerkerk—Near Anne Frank's House, this landmark church, with a barren interior and Amsterdam's tallest steeple, is worth climbing for the view (f3, ascend only with a guide, departures on the hour, Monday–Saturday 10:00–16:00 April–September, closed Sunday, tel. 020/612-6856).

Royal Palace (Koninklijk Paleis)—The palace, right on Dam Square, was built when Amsterdam was feeling its global oats. It's worth a look (f5, daily 12:30–17:00 June–August, less off-season).

▲**Begijnhof**—Step into this tiny, idyllic courtyard in the city center to escape the crazy 1990s and feel the charm of old Amsterdam. Notice house #34, a 500-year-old wooden structure (rare since repeated fires taught city fathers a little trick called brick). Peek into the hidden Catholic church, opposite the English Reformed church, where the pilgrims worshiped while waiting for their voyage to the New World (marked by a plaque near door). Be considerate of the people who live here (free, on Begijnensteeg Lane, just off Kalverstraat between #130 and #132, pick up English info flier at office near entrance).

Amsterdam Historical Museum—Offering the town's best look into the age of the Dutch masters, this creative and hard-working museum features Rembrandt's paintings, fine English descriptions, and a carillon loft. The loft comes with push-button recordings of the town bell tower's greatest hits and a self-serve carillon "keyboard" to ring a few bells yourself. The museum is next to the Begijnhof, Kalverstraat 92 (f11, Monday–Friday 10:00–17:00, Saturday and Sunday 11:00–17:00, good-value restaurant, tel. 020/523-1822). Its free pedestrian corridor is a powerful teaser.

Sights—East Amsterdam

Rembrandt's House—This place is interesting only to Rembrandt's fans. There are 250 etchings (f7.5, Monday–Saturday 10:00–17:00, Sunday 13:00–17:00, 15-minute English audiovisual presentation upon request, Jodenbreestraat 4, tel. 020/638-4668).

Holland Experience—With the slogan "Experience Holland in 30 minutes," this show combines footage of Holland with multivisual effects (e.g., as you see a boat sailing, you feel wind on your face). It's fun but pricey, and focuses more on goofy tourists than on the wonders of Holland (f17.50, daily 10:00–18:30, Jodenbreestraat 8, near Rembrandt's House and Waterlooplein street market, metro: Waterlooplein, tel. 020/422-2233).

▲**Tropenmuseum (Tropical Museum)**—As close to the Third World as you'll get without lots of vaccinations, this imaginative museum offers wonderful re-creations of tropical-life scenes and explanations of Third-World problems (f10, Monday–Friday 10:00–17:00, Saturday and Sunday 12:00–17:00, tram #9 to Linnaeusstraat 2, tel. 020/568-8215).

Netherlands Maritime (Scheepvaart) Museum—This kid-friendly museum is fascinating if you're into Henry Hudson or *scheepvaarts* (f12.50, daily 10:00–17:00, closed Monday October–April, English explanations, bus #22 or #28 to Kattenburgerplein 1, tel. 020/523-2222).

Sights—Red Light District

Our Lord in the Attic (Amstelkring)—Near the station, in the Red Light District, you'll find a 17th-century merchant's house turned museum, with a fascinating hidden church. This dates from 1661, when post-Reformation Dutch Catholics were not allowed to worship in public. The church fills the attics of several homes (f7.50, Monday–Saturday 10:00–17:00, Sunday 13:00–17:00, O.Z. Voorburgwal 40, tel. 020/624-6604).

▲**Red Light District**—Europe's most high-profile ladies of the night shiver and shimmy in display-case windows between the Oude Zijds Achterburgwal and Oude Zijds Voorburgwal, surrounding the Oude Kerk (Old Church). It's dangerous late at night but a fascinating walk at any other time after noon.

According to CNN statistics, more than 60 percent of Amsterdam's prostitutes are HIV-positive (but a naive tourist might see them as just hardworking girls from Latin America or Africa trying their best to build up a bank account—f50 at a time).

Amsterdam has two sex museums, one in the Red Light district and one a block in front of the train station on Damrak. While visiting one can be called sightseeing, visiting both is a bit obsessive. Here's a comparison:

The Red Light district sex museum is less offensive, with five sparsely decorated rooms relying heavily on badly-dressed dummies acting out the roles that women of the neighborhood play. It also has videos, phone-sex phones, and a lot of uninspired paintings, old photos, and sculpture (f5, along the canal at Oude Zijds Achterburgwal 54).

The Damrak sex museum goes much deeper, with many more rooms. It tells the story of pornography from the 1860s through today, starting with early French pornographic photos. Every sexual deviation is uncovered in its various displays, and the nude and pornographic art is a cut above the other sex museum's. Also interesting is the international sex art and memorabilia from Europe, India, and Asia. You'll find a Marilyn Monroe tribute and some S&M displays, too (f4, Damrak 18, a block in front of the station).

More Sights—Amsterdam

▲**Herengracht Canal Mansion** (Willet Holthuysen Museum)—
This 1687 patrician house offers a fine look at the old rich of Amsterdam, with a good 15-minute English introductory film and a 17th-century garden in back (f7.50, Monday–Friday 10:00–17:00, Saturday and Sunday 11:00–17:00, tram #4 or #9 to Herengracht 605, tel. 020/523-1870).

Vondelpark—This huge and lively city park gives a fragrant look at today's Dutch youth, especially on sunny summer weekends.

Leidseplein—Brimming with cafés, this people- and pigeon-watching square is an impromptu stage for street artists, accordionists, jugglers, and unicylists. Sunny afternoons are the liveliest. Stroll nearby Lange Leidsedwarsstraat (one block north) for a taste-bud tour of ethnic eateries from Greece to Indonesia.

Shopping—Amsterdam brings out the browser even in those who were not born to shop. Ten general markets, open six days a week, keep folks who brake for garage sales pulling U-ies. Shopping highlights include Waterlooplein (flea market); the huge Albert Cuyp street market; various flower markets (daily along Singel Canal near the mint tower, or Munttoren); diamond dealers (free cutting and polishing demos at shops behind the Rijksmuseum and on Dam Square); and Kalverstraat, Amsterdam's teeming walking/shopping street (parallel to Damrak).

Tours of Amsterdam

▲▲**Canal-Boat Tour**—These long, low, tourist-laden boats leave continually from several docks around the town for a good, if uninspiring, one-hour quadrilingual introduction to the city (f13, 2/hrly, more frequent in summer). One very central company is at the corner of Spui and Rokin, about five minutes from Dam Square (9:30–22:00, tel. 020/623-3810). No fishing allowed, but bring your camera for this relaxing orientation. Some prefer to cruise at night when the bridges are illuminated.

Biking and Walking Tours—The Yellow Bike Tour company offers bike tours (f29 for three-hour city tour, f42.50 for 6.5-hour 35-kilometer countryside tour) as well as city walking tours for groups by arrangement (f15, 1.75 hours) daily April through November (Nieuwezijds Kolk 29, near train station, tel. 020/620-6940).

Do-It-Yourself Bike Tour of Amsterdam—A day enjoying the bridges, bike lanes, and sleepy off-the-beaten-path canals on your own one-speed is the essential Amsterdam experience. Do it Dutch-style: on two wheels. The real joys of Europe's best-preserved 17th-century city are the countless intimate glimpses it offers: the laid-back locals sunning on their porches under elegant gables, rusted bikes that look as if they've been lashed to the same lamppost since the '60s, wasted hedonists planted on canalside benches.

For a good day, rent a bike at the station. Head west down Haarlemmerstraat, working your wide-eyed way through the Prinsengracht (along the canal) and gentrified Jordaan area to Westerkerk, with the tallest spire in the city. Tour Anne Frank's House.

Pedal past the palace, through Dam Square, down Kalverstraat (the city's bustling pedestrian mall), and poke into the sleepy Begijnhof. Roll down tacky Leidsestraat. Lunch near Spui or at the Leidseplein (see Eating, below). Catch the hour-long cruise at Spui. Pedal to the Rijksmuseum and Van Gogh Museum, inhale art, then pedal back to the train station. For a detour through seedy, sexy, pot-smoking Amsterdam, roll down Damstraat, then down Oudezijds Voorburgwal through the land of Rastafarian "coffee shops," red lights over black tights, and sailors lost without the sea.

To escape to the countryside, hop on the free ferry for both pedestrians and bikes behind the Amsterdam station. In five minutes Amsterdam will be gone and you'll be rolling through your very own Dutch painting. (See Getting Around Amsterdam, above, for info on bike rental).

Brewery Tour—The infamous Heineken brewery tours are in full slosh Monday through Friday from 9:30 to 11:00 (f2; also open 13:00 and 14:30 mid-June–mid-September, and 11:00, 13:00, and 14:30 Saturdays July–August; Stadhouderskade 78, near the Rijksmuseum). Try to arrive a little early.

Sleeping in Amsterdam
(f1 = about 60 cents, tel. code: 020)
Sleep Code: S = Single, **D** = Double/Twin, **T** = Triple, **Q** = Quad, **b** = bathroom, **t** = toilet only, **s** = shower only, **CC** = Credit Card (**V**isa, **M**asterCard, **A**mex). Nearly everyone speaks English in the Netherlands, and prices include breakfast unless noted.

While I prefer sleeping in cozy Haarlem (see below), those into more urban charms will find that Amsterdam has plenty of beds. For a f5 fee, the VVV (tourist office) can find you a room in the price range of your choice.

Sleeping near the Station
Amstel Botel, the city's only remaining "boat hotel," is a ship-shape, bright, and clean floating hotel with 175 rooms (Sb-f125, Db-f143, Tb-f180, worth the extra f10 for canalside view, breakfast-f11, f30/day parking pass, CC:VMA, 400 yards from the station, on your left as you leave, you'll see the sign, Oosterdokskade 2-4, 1011 AE Amsterdam, tel. 020/626-4247, fax 020/639-1952).

Sleeping between Dam Square and Anne Frank's House
Hotel Toren is a chandeliered historic mansion in a pleasant, canalside setting in downtown Amsterdam. This splurge is classy,

Amsterdam Hotels

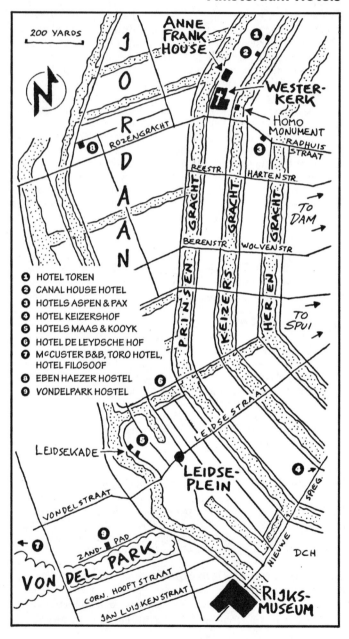

200 YARDS

JORDAAN

ANNE FRANK HOUSE

WESTER-KERK

HOMO MONUMENT

RADHUIS STRAAT

ROZENGRACHT

REESTR.   HARTEN STR.

PRINSEN GRACHT

KEIZERS GRACHT

HEREN GRACHT

TO DAM

BERENSTR.   WOLVEN STR.

TO SPUI

1 HOTEL TOREN
2 CANAL HOUSE HOTEL
3 HOTELS ASPEN & PAX
4 HOTEL KEIZERSHOF
5 HOTELS MAAS & KOOYK
6 HOTEL DE LEYDSCHE HOF
7 MᶜCUSTER B&B, TORO HOTEL, HOTEL FILOSOOF
8 EBEN HAEZER HOSTEL
9 VONDELPARK HOSTEL

LEIDSE STRAAT

LEIDSEKADE

LEIDSE-PLEIN

VONDEL STRAAT

ZAND· PAD

VON DEL PARK

CORN. HOOFT STRAAT

JAN LUIJKEN STRAAT

NIEUWE SPIEG.

DCH

RIJKS-MUSEUM

quiet, and two blocks northeast of Anne Frank's (S-f85, Sb-f185–200, three unadvertised D-f170, Db-f200–275, Tb-f240, pay for canalside rooms—it's worth it; bridal suites for f285–400 make you want to get married; prices vary according to season; CC:VMA, Keizersgracht 164, 1015 CZ Amsterdam, tel. 020/622-6352, fax 020/626-9705, e-mail: hotel.toren@tip.nl).

Well-heeled readers will prefer the pricier, fancier 17th-century **Canal House Hotel**, a few doors down, for its beautiful antique interiors, candlelit evenings, and soft music (Sb-from f215, Db-f235–280, CC:VMA, elevator, Keizersgracht 148, 1015 CX Amsterdam, tel. 020/622-5182, fax 020/624-1317, e-mail: canalhousehotel@compuserve.com).

Cheap hotels line the noisy main drag between the town hall and Anne Frank's House. Expect a long, steep, and depressing stairway, with quieter rooms in the back. **Hotel Aspen**, a good value for a budget hotel, is tidy, simple, and well-maintained, with firm beds (S-f55, D-f80, Db-f120, Tb-f130-150, Qb-f180, CC:MA, ideally reserve by fax using credit-card number, Raadhuisstraat 31, 1016 DC Amsterdam, tel. 020/626-6714, fax 020/620-0866). A few doors away, **Hotel Pax** has large, plain, but airy rooms, carefully managed by Mr. and Mrs. Veldhuiezen (tiny D-f75, large D-f90, T-f105, showers down the hall, Raadhuisstraat 37, tel. 020/624-9735).

Sleeping in the Leidseplein Area

The area around Amsterdam's museum square (Museumplein) and the rip-roaring nightlife center (Leidseplein) is colorful, comfortable, convenient, and affordable.

Hotel Keizershof is a wonderfully Dutch place, with six bright, airy rooms in a 17th-century canal house. You'll climb a steep spiral staircase to rooms named after old-time Hollywood stars. The friendly De Vries family has made this place a treat for 38 years and offers its guests plenty of fine eating advice (S-f75, D-f125, Ds-f135, Db-f150, T-f175, Tb-f200, nonsmoking, includes classy breakfast, nice garden, CC:VM, where Keizers canal crosses Spiegelstraat at Keizersgracht 618, 1017 ER Amsterdam, tel. 020/622-2855, fax 020/624-8412). It's a 10-minute walk from Leidseplein.

The next two hotels are on a quiet street, easy to reach from the central station (tram #1, #2, #5, or #20 to Leidseplein, then head west a block along the north side of canal), and within easy walking distance of the Rijksmuseum.

Hotel Maas, with a phone, TV, and coffeepot in every room, is a big, well-run, elegant, quiet, and hotelesque place (S-f110, one D-f125, Db-f225–275, prices vary with view and room size, extra person-f50, suite-f375, CC:VMA, hearty breakfast, air-conditioning, elevator, Leidsekade 91, 1017 PN Amsterdam, tel. 020/623-3868, fax 020/622-2613, e-mail: maas@worldaccess.nl).

Kooyk Hotel is a dumpy but cheap dive, with 17 rooms, four on the ground floor. Halls are narrow, some top rooms are disappointing, bedspreads and furnishings are faded, but the canalside rooms are bright (S-f75, D-f120, T-f165, Q-f200, Quint-f225, CC:VM, Leidsekade 82, 1017 PM Amsterdam, tel. 020/623-0295, fax 020/638-8337, run by Pierre).

Hotel Seven Bridges, decorated with antiques, is a lot nicer than my house. The 11 rooms feature fine draperies, woven carpets, and beautifully crafted furniture, though some may find the big mirrors above the beds on the walls a bit weird (Sb-f170–230, two D-f150, Db-f200–300, prices vary with quality, ask for room #5 for a splurge, CC:VMA, near Rembrandtplein, Reguliersgracht 31, 1017 LK Amsterdam, reserve three to four weeks in advance, tel. 020/623-1329). Take trams #16, #24, or #25 from the station and get off at "Keizersgracht."

Hotel De Leydsche Hof is canalside with simple, quiet rooms. Its peaceful demeanor almost helps you overlook the flimsy cots and old carpets (D-f85, Db-f95–110, Tb-f130, Qb-f170, no breakfast, Leidsegracht 14, 10-minute walk from Leidseplein, 1016 CK Amsterdam, tel. 020/623-2148, run by friendly Mr. Piller).

Sleeping near Vondelpark

These options connect you with the sights via an easy tram ride or a pleasant 15-minute walk or short bike ride through Vondelpark.

Karen McCuster, a friendly Englishwoman, rents cozy rooms in her home as a B&B without the breakfast. Rooms are clean, white, and bright with red carpeting and green plants; one room has a private rooftop patio. Advance reservations are necessary (D-f80–110 per night). Tram #2 from the station gets you to Zeilstraat 22 (third floor, 1075 SH Amsterdam, tel. 020/679-2753, fax 020/670-4578); get off at "Amstelveenseweg" and cross street in same direction that tram runs (every 10 minutes; buy ticket or day card on board).

Toro Hotel, in a peaceful residential area at the edge of Vondelpark, is your personal turn-of-the-century hotel/mansion, with an elegant dining hall and 22 rooms with TVs, safes, and phones. Rooms in the back overlook the park, canal, and terrace, which is yours for relaxing. Mr. Plooy fusses over his guests (Ss-f165, Sb-f200, Db-f250, Tb-f300, CC:VMA, elevator, easy parking, Koningslaan 64, 1075 AG Amsterdam, tel. 020/673-7223, fax 020/675-0031). Take tram #2 from the station; get off at "Koningslaan."

Hotel Filosoof greets you with Aristotle and Plato in the foyer and classical music in its lobby. Its 25 rooms are subtly decorated with themes; the Egyptian room has a frieze of hieroglyphics. Philosophers' sayings hang on walls, professors wander down the halls, and on Thursday evenings in fall, guests meet to discuss philosophy—in Dutch. The rooms are small (and split between two buildings), but the hotel is endearing and the terrace is made for pondering (Sb-f155, Db-f185, Tb-f235, Qb-f275, CC:VMA, cheaper off-season, all rooms with TV and phone, reserve three weeks in advance for summer weekends, Anna Vondelstraat 6, five-minute walk from tram #6 line, get off at "Constantyn Huygenstraat," tel. 020/683-3013, fax 020/685-3750).

Hostels

Christian Youth Hostel Eben Haezer is scruffy, with 20-bed women's dorms and a 40-bed men's dorm. Friendly, well-run, and in a great neighborhood, it has Amsterdam's best rock-bottom budget beds (f22.50 per bed with sheets and breakfast, maximum age 35, near Anne Frank's House, Bloemstraat 179, tel. 020/624-4717, e-mail: eben@globalxs.nl). It serves cheap, hot meals, runs a snack bar, offers lockers to all, leads nightly Bible studies, and closes the dorms from 10:00 to 14:00. The hostel will happily hold a room for a phone call (three to seven days in advance in the summer). Its sister Christian hostel, **The Shelter** (in the red-light district, open to any traveler, f22.50 for a bed, tel. 020/625-3230), is similar but definitely not preaching to the choir.

The city's two IYHF hostels are **Vondelpark**, Amsterdam's top hostel (f34.50 with breakfast, S-f72, D-f90, nonmembers pay f5 extra, lots of school groups, 6–22 beds per dorm, right on the park at Zandpad 5, tel. 020/683-1744, fax 020/589-8955); and Stadsdoelen YH (f25.25 with breakfast, f5 extra without YH card, f6.25 for sheets, just past Dam Square, closed January, Kloveniersburgwal 97, tel. 020/624-6832, fax 020/639-1035).

Eating in Amsterdam

Dutch food is basic and hearty. *Eetcafés* are local cafés serving budget sandwiches, soup, eggs, and so on. Cafeterias, *broodje* (sandwich shops), and automatic food shops are also good bets for budget eaters. Picnics are cheap and easy. A central supermarket is **Albert Heijn** near the flower market, at the corner of Koningsplein and Singel canal (Monday–Saturday 10:00–20:00, Sunday 12:00–18:00).

Eating near Spui in the Center

The city university's **Atrium** is a great, budget cafeteria (f9 meals, Monday–Friday 12:00–14:00 and 17:00–19:30; from Spui, walk west down Landebrug Steeg past the canalside Café 't Gasthuys three blocks to Oudezijds Achterburgwal 237, go through arched doorway on the right, tel. 020/525-3999). **Café 't Gasthuys**, one of Amsterdam's many "brown" cafés (named for their smoke-stained walls), makes good sandwiches and offers indoor or canal-side seating (daily 12:00–1:00, walk west down Landebrug Steeg to Grimburgwal 7).

La Place, a cafeteria on the ground floor of the Vroom Dreesmann department store, has islands of entrées, veggies, fruits, desserts, and beverages (Monday–Saturday 10:00–21:00, Thursday until 22:00, Sunday 11:00–21:00, near Mint Tower, corner of Rokin and Muntplein). The locals splurge for Dutch food at **Restaurant Haesje Claes** (f25 entrées, daily 12:00–22:00, Spuistraat 275, tel. 020/624-9998). **Blincker Theatercafé** is popular with the younger crowd (open from 19:00, St. Barberenstraat 7-9, tel. 020/627-1938).

Eating in or near the Train Station
Keuken van 1870 has been cooking basic, cheap cafeteria meals in a simple setting since, you guessed it, 1870 (Monday–Friday 12:30–20:00, weekends 16:00–21:00, Spuistraat 4, several blocks west of station, tel. 020/624-8965). The train station has a surprisingly classy budget self-service Stationsrestauratie on platform 1 (Monday–Saturday 7:00–22:00, Sunday from 8:00).

Eating near Anne Frank's House
For pancakes in a family atmosphere, try the **Pancake Bakery** (f11 pancakes, splitting is OK, offers an Indonesian pancake for those who want two experiences in one, daily 12:00–21:30, Prinsengracht 191, one block north of A.F. House, tel. 020/625-1333). Across the canal, DeBolhoed serves great vegetarian food (daily 12:00–22:00, Prinsengracht 60, tel. 020/626-1803).

Eating near the Rijksmuseum, on Leidseplein
The art deco **American Hotel** dining room serves an elegant all-you-can-eat f12 salad bar (available 12:00–14:30 and 18:00–20:30, where Leidseplein hits Singel Canal). **De Smoeshaan** offers classy and tasty f25 meals (next to Hotel Maas, 50 meters down Singel canal from the American Hotel). On the café-packed street called Lange Leidsedwarsstraat, **Bojo** is a reasonably-priced Indonesian restaurant at #51 (Monday–Wednesday 16:00–1:30, Thursday–Sunday 12:00–1:30, 020/622-7434). If hunger hits in the **Rijksmuseum**, head for the cafeteria in the west wing's ground floor.

Bars
Try a *jenever* (Dutch gin), the closest thing to an atomic bomb in a shot glass. While cheese gets harder and sharper with age, *jenever* grows smooth and soft. Old *jenever* is best.

Drugs
Amsterdam, Europe's counterculture mecca, thinks the concept of a "victimless crime" is a contradiction. While hard drugs are definitely out, marijuana causes about as much excitement as a bottle of beer. A "pot man" with a worldly menu of f25 baggies is a fix-

ture in many bars (walk east from Dam Square on Damstraat for a few blocks, then down to Nieuwmarkt). While several touristy Bulldog cafés are very popular with tourists, less-glitzy smaller places (farther from the tourists) offer a better value and a more comfortable atmosphere. Near the corner of Leidsestraat and Prinsengracht, the **Easy Times** rasta coffee shop dangles its menu from a string at the bar. At the brighter **Tops** coffee shop next door, you can use the internet to say high to your friends back home. **Homegrown Fantasy** coffee shop and gallery, about two blocks northwest of Dam Square, has a gentle Dutch atmosphere and cosmic restroom (daily 9:00–24:00, Nieuwe Zijds Voorburgwal 87a, tel. 020/627-5683). They also have a grow shop next door.

The tiny **Grey Area** coffee shop is a cool, welcoming, and smoky hole-in-the-wall appreciated among local aficionados as a seven-time winner of Amsterdam's Cannabis Cup award. Judging by the proud autographed photos on the wall, many of America's most famous heads have dropped in. You're welcome to just nurse a bottomless cup of coffee (open high noon to 22:00, closed Monday, between Dam Square and Anne Frank's House at Oude Leliestraat 2, tel. 020/420-4301, e-mail: greyarea@xs4all.nl).

▲**Marijuana and Hemp Museum**—This is a collection of dope facts, history, science, and memorabilia (f8, daily 11:00–22:00, Oudezijds Achterburgwal 148, tel. 020/623-5961). While quite small, it has a shocker finale: the high-tech grow room in which dozens of varieties of marijuana are cultivated in optimal hydroponic (among other) environments. Some plants stand five feet tall and shine under the intense grow lamps. The view is actually through glass walls into the neighboring "Sensi Seed Bank" Grow Shop (which sells carefully cultivated seeds and all the gear needed to grow them). Pot should never be bought on the street in Amsterdam. Well-established coffee shops are considered much safer. Up to five grams of marijuana can be sold in coffeeshops per person per day. Minimum age for purchase: 18 years.

Transportation Connections—Amsterdam

Amsterdam's train-information center requires a long wait. Save lots of time by getting train tickets and information in a small-town station or travel agency. For phone information, call 0900-9292 for local trains or 0900-9296 for international (75 cents/min, daily 7:00–24:00, wait through recording and hold . . . hold . . . hold . . .).

By train to: Schiphol Airport (6/hrly, 20 min, f6.25), **Haarlem** (6/hrly, 15 min, f10.50 round-trip), **The Hague** (4/hrly, 45 min), **Rotterdam** (4/hrly, 1 hr), **Brussels** (hrly, 3 hrs), **Oostende** (hrly, 4 hrs, change in Roosendaal), **Paris** (5/day, 5 hrs, required fast train from Brussels with f21 supplement), **London** (4/day,

10–12 hrs), **Copenhagen** (5/day, 11 hrs), **Frankfurt** (10/day, 5 hrs), **Munich** (8/day, 8 hrs, change in Mannheim), **Bonn** (10/day, 3 hrs), **Bern** (8/day, 9 hrs, change in Basel).

    Amsterdam's Schiphol Airport: The airport, like most of Holland, is English-speaking, user-friendly, and below sea level. Its banks offer fair rates (24 hours daily, in arrivals). Schiphol Airport has easy bus and train connections (seven miles) into Amsterdam or Haarlem. The airport also has a train station of its own. (You can validate your Eurailpass and hit the rails immediately or, to stretch your train pass, buy the short ticket today and start the pass later.) Schiphol flight information (tel. 06-350-34050 or 0900-503-0141) can give you flight times and your airline's Amsterdam number for reconfirmation before going home (f1 per minute to climb through its phone tree).

HAARLEM

Cute, cozy yet real, and handy to the airport, Haarlem is a fine home base, giving you small-town, overnight warmth with easy access (15 minutes by train) to wild and crazy Amsterdam.

Haarlem is a busy Dutch market town, buzzing with shoppers biking home with fresh bouquets. Enjoy Saturday (general) and Monday (clothing) market days, when the square bustles like a Brueghel painting with cheese, fish, flowers, and families. You'll feel comfortable here. Buy some flowers to brighten your hotel room.

Orientation (tel. code: 023)

Tourist Information: Haarlem's VVV, at the train station, is friendlier, more helpful, and less crowded than Amsterdam's. Ask your Amsterdam questions here (Monday–Friday 9:00–17:30, Saturday 10:00–14:00, closed Sunday, tel. 0900-616-1600, f1 a minute).

Arrival in Haarlem: As you walk out of the train station, the TI is on your right and the bus station is across the street. Two parallel streets flank the train station (Kruisweg and Jansweg). Head up either one and you'll reach the town square and church within 10 minutes. If uncertain of the way, ask a local person, "Grote Markt?" ("Main Square?"), and they'll point you in the right direction.

Helpful Hints: The handy GWK change office at the station offers decent exchange rates (Monday–Saturday 8:00–20:00, Thursday and Friday until 21:00, Sunday 9:00–17:00). The train station rents bikes cheaply and easily (f9.50/day, f100 deposit, Monday–Saturday 6:00–1:00, Sunday 7:30–24:30). Haarlem lacks a cyber café, but even nonguests are welcome to use Hotel Amadeus' computer (f7.50/30 minutes). My Beautiful Laundrette is handy, self-service, and cheap (f10 wash and dry, daily 8:30–20:30, near Vroom Dreesman department store at Boter Markt 20). The VVV and local hotels have a helpful parking brochure.

Sights—Haarlem

▲▲**Frans Hals Museum**—Haarlem is the hometown of Frans Hals, and this delightful museum displays many of his greatest paintings in a glorious old building (f8, Monday–Saturday 11:00–17:00, Sunday 13:00–17:00, tel. 023/516-4200). Enjoy take-me-back paintings of old-time Haarlem. Peter Brueghel the Younger's painting *Proverbs* (outside room 24) shows 72 old Dutch proverbs; the handy English-language key gives you a fascinating peek into the Dutch old days. The museum across the street features the architecture of old Haarlem.

Corrie Ten Boom House—As many Americans (but few Dutch) know, Haarlem is also home to Corrie Ten Boom (popularized by *The Hiding Place*, an inspirational book and movie about the Ten Boom family's experience hiding Jews from the Nazis). The Ten Boom House, at Barteljorisstraat 19, is open for 45-minute English tours (donation requested, Tuesday–Friday 10:00–16:00, Saturday until 15:30; open Tuesday–Saturday 11:00–15:00 November–April; only one tour/day off-season, tel. 023/531-0823). Some of the guides do more preaching than teaching.

Grote Kerk (Church)—You'll see (and maybe hear) Holland's greatest pipe organ (regular free concerts mid-May–mid-October on Tuesdays at 20:15; additional concerts in July and August on Thursdays at 15:00; confirm schedule at TI). The church is open and worth a look, if only to see its Oz-like organ (f2.50, Monday–Saturday 10:00–16:00; closes at 15:00 in winter). Note how the organ, which fills the west end, seems to steal the show from the altar. To enter the church, look for the small entrance marked "*Entree*" behind the church, kitty-corner from La Plume restaurant. (There is a handy public WC in the east end of the church.) The new church (Kathedrale Basiliek Sint Bavo at Leidsevaart 146) offers free concerts on Saturdays at 15:00 from April through September.

▲**Teylers Museum**—Famous as the oldest museum in Holland, it used to be interesting mainly as a look at a 200-year-old museum. New exhibition halls (with rotating exhibits) and a café have brought life to the dusty exhibits. Stop by if you enjoy mixing, say, Renaissance sketches with pickled coelacanths (f7.50, Tuesday–Saturday 10:00–17:00, Sunday 12:00–17:00, Spaarne 16, tel. 023/531-9010).

Red Lights—For a little red-light district precious as a Barbie doll, wander around the church in Haarlem's cutest Begijnhof (two blocks northeast of the big church, off Lange Begijnestraat, no

Haarlem

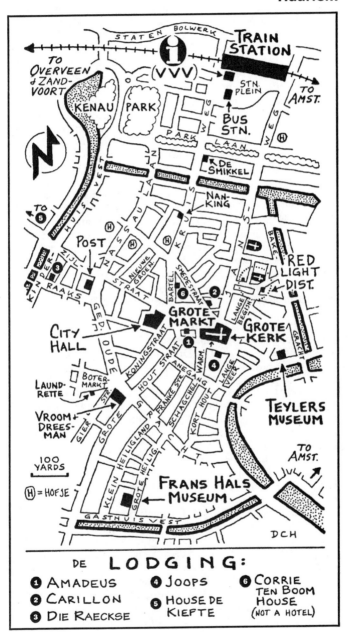

STATEN BOLWERK

TRAIN STATION

TO OVERVEEN & ZANDVOORT

KENAU PARK

STN. PLEIN

BUS STN.

TO AMST.

PARK LAAN

DE SMIKKEL

NAN-KING

TO ⑤

POST

RED LIGHT DIST.

GROTE MARKT

CITY HALL

GROTE KERK

LAUNDRETTE

BOTERMARKT

VROOM DREESMAN

100 YARDS

Ⓗ = HOFJE

TEYLERS MUSEUM

TO AMST.

FRANS HALS MUSEUM

GASTHUIS VEST

DCH

DE **LODGING:**
1 AMADEUS
2 CARILLON
3 DIE RAECKSE
4 JOOPS
5 HOUSE DE KIEFTE
6 CORRIE TEN BOOM HOUSE (NOT A HOTEL)

senior or student discounts). Don't miss the mall marked by the red neon sign, t'Steegje. The nearby t'Poortje ("office park") costs f7.50.

Nightlife in Haarlem

Haarlem's evening scene is great. The bars around the Grote Kerk and Lange Veerstraat are colorful, lively, and always full of music.

The **Studio**, jammed with Haarlem's 30-something crowd, has a pleasant ambience (on the square, next to Hotel Carillon). **Café Brinkman**, also on the square, is a good people-watching perch. **Café 1900** (across from the Corrie Ten Boom House) is classy by day and draws a young crowd with live music on Sunday nights. **Lange Veerstraat** (behind the church) is probably the best bar street in town. The **Crack** (Lange Veerstraat 32) is the wild and leathery place to go for loud music and smoking. Across the street at **High Times** (#47), smokers can choose from 16 varieties of joints in racks behind the bar (neatly prepacked in trademarked "Joint Packs", f2.50 to f7.50). The **Imperial Café and Bar** has live music every Monday, Wednesday, Thursday, and Friday (a few doors down from the Crack, at Korte Veerstraat 3).

Don't be shocked if locals drop into a bar, plunk down f25 for a baggie of marijuana, and casually roll a joint. (If you don't like the smell of pot, avoid "coffee shops" sporting Rastafarian yellow, red, and green colors; wildly painted walls; or plants in the windows.)

Sleeping in Haarlem
(f1 = about 60 cents, tel. code: 023)

Sleep Code: S = Single, **D** = Double/Twin, **T** = Triple, **Q** = Quad, **b** = bathroom, **t** = toilet only, **s** = shower only, **CC** = Credit Card (**V**isa, **M**asterCard, **A**mex).

The helpful Haarlem tourist office ("VVV" at the train station, Monday–Friday 9:00–17:30, Saturday 10:00–14:00, tel. 0900-616-1600, f1/minute) can nearly always find you a f32.50 bed in a nearby private home (for a f9-per-person fee plus a cut of the hotel's money).

Haarlem is most crowded in April, on Easter weekend, May, and August, but if you phone ahead, my recommended hotels will happily hold a room without a deposit (though they may ask for a credit-card number). Nearly every Dutch person you'll encounter speaks English. The listed prices include breakfast (unless otherwise noted) and usually include the f3.50 per-person-per-day tourist tax. To avoid this town's louder-than-normal street noises, forego views for a room in the back. Don't needlessly use the TI's room-finding service. Call direct.

Hotel Amadeus, on the town square, has 15 small, bright rooms, all with simple modern furnishings, TVs, private showers, and toilets. Some have views of the square. This characteristic hotel, ideally located above a turn-of-the-century dinner café, is relatively quiet and has an elevator. The lush old lobby is on the second floor in a "*pianola* bar" (Sb-f90, Db-f120, Tb-f165, nicer rooms go to earliest reservations, seconds-on-everything buffet breakfast, kid-friendly, a 12-minute walk from train station, CC:VMA, use credit card to secure reservations, Grote Markt 10, 2011 RD Haarlem, tel. 023/532-4530, fax 023/532-2328, e-mail: info@amadeus-hotel.com, Web site: www.amadeus.com, brothers Dave and Mike run the place for their family).

Hotel Carillon, also right on the town square, has an ideal location. Many of the well-worn rooms are small, the stairs are ste-e-e-p, and front rooms come with great town-square views, lots of street noise, and double-paned windows (22 rooms, tiny loft singles-f57.50, Db-f137, Tb-f180.50, Qb-f194, no elevator, 12-minute walk from train station, CC:VMA, Grote Markt 27, 2011 RC Haarlem, tel. 023/531-0591, fax 023/531-4909). The Carillon also runs the nearby **Die Raeckse Hotel**, which has fewer stairs, less character, more traffic noise, smoky halls, and decent rooms (Sb-f92.50–110, Db-f135–160, CC:VMA, attached restaurant, Raaks 1, 2011 VA Haarlem, tel. 023/532-6629, fax 023/531-7937).

Hotel Joops is an innovative concept. A well-organized central office, just behind the church in the town center, administers a corral of 80 rooms in different buildings (all within three blocks of the church). They have cheap, run-down, spacious rooms (S-f55, D-f95, T-f130); and new, elegant suites with kitchenettes (Db-f125–145, Tb-f165–195, CC:V, get one day free if you stay a week, office at Oude Groenmarkt 20, 2011 HL Haarlem, tel. 023/532-2008, fax 023/532-9549, e-mail: joops@hotelinformation.com).

Bed and Breakfast House de Kiefte, your get-into-a-local-home budget option, epitomizes the goodness of B&Bs. Marjet (mar-yet) and Hans, a young Dutch couple who speak fluent English, rent four bright, cheery, nonsmoking rooms (with good breakfast and travel advice) in their quiet, 100-year-old home (S-f50, Ds-f90, T-f130, Qs-f165, Quint/s-f190, cash only, minimum two nights, family loft sleeps up to five, very steep stairs, kid-friendly, Coornhertstraat 3, 2013 EV Haarlem, tel. 023/532-2980, cellular phone 06/5474-5272). It's a 15-minute walk or f12 taxi ride from the train station, and a five-minute walk from the center. From Grote Markt (main square) walk straight out Zijlstraat, over the bridge, and take a left on the fourth street.

Family Dekker B&B is in a fine, quiet neighborhood near the station. For 25 years Mrs. Dekker has given her guests a cheery welcome in her clean but well-worn place (small D-f60, D-f70, T-f105, Q-f140, three-night minimum, closed 12:00–18:00 and October–March, one block from the station at Ripperdastraat 9, 2011 KG Haarlem, tel. 023/532-0554).

Hotel Lion D'Or is a classy business hotel with all the professional comforts, an attached restaurant, and a handy location. Don't expect a warm welcome (Sb-f203, Db-f272, extra beds-f50, request a "weekend package" at least three days in advance to get substantial weekend discounts June–September and in winter months, some nonsmoking rooms, CC:VMA, across the street from the station at Kruisweg 34, 2011 LC Haarlem, tel. 023/532-1750, fax 023/532-9543).

The 300-room, very American **Hotel Haarlem Zuid** is sterile but a good value for those interested only in sleeping and eating (Db-f127, Tb-f150.50, breakfast-f13.50, elevator, easy parking, inexpensive hotel restaurant, in an industrial zone, a 20-minute walk from the center on the road to the airport, CC:VMA, Toekenweg 2, 2035 LC Haarlem, tel. 023/536-7500, fax 023/536-7980). Buses #70, #72, and #75 connect the hotel to the station and town square every 10 minutes.

Sleeping near Haarlem

Pension Koning, a 15-minute walk north of the station or quick hop on bus #71, has five simple rooms in a rowhouse in a residential area (S-f40, D-f80, T-f120, two-night minimum, includes breakfast, Kleverlaan 179, 2023 JC Haarlem, tel. 023/526-1456).

Hostel Jan Gijzen charges f24.75 for beds in six-bed dorms (f5 extra for nonmembers), f6.50 for sheets, and includes breakfast (daily 7:00–24:00, closed November–February, Jan Gijzenpad 3, two miles from the Haarlem station—take bus #2, or a five-minute walk from the Santpoort Zuid train station, tel. 023/537-3793, fax 023/537-1176).

Eating in Haarlem

Eating between Grote Markt (Main Square) and Train Station

Enjoy an Indonesian *rijsttafel* feast at the **Nanking Chinese-Indonesian Restaurant** (Kruisstraat 16, a few blocks off Grote Markt, tel. 023/532-0706, daily 12:30–22:00). Couples eat plenty, heartily, and more cheaply by splitting a f24.50 Indonesian rice table for one. (Each eater should order a drink.) Say hi to gracious Ai Ping and her daughter, Fan. Don't let them railroad you into a Chinese (their heritage) dinner. They also do cheap and tasty take-out.

Going Dutch? How about pancakes for dinner at **Pannekoekhuis "De Smikkel"**? Dinner and dessert pancakes cost f12 each; there's a f2.50-per-person cover charge, so splitting pancakes is OK (daily until 20:00, two blocks in front of station, Kruisweg 57, tel. 023/532-0631).

Eat well and surrounded by trains in the classy Station Restaurant (between tracks #3 and #4) in Old World atmosphere in the

Netherlands' oldest train station (kitchen 12:00–20:00, also serves continental breakfast from 6:30 weekdays and 8:00 on weekends).

Eating on or near Zijlstraat
Eko Eet Café is great for a cheery, tasty vegetarian meal (f18 menu, daily 17:30–21:30, Zijlstraat 39).

For a "bread line" experience with basic/bland food, well-worn company, and the cheapest price in town (f9), eat at **Eethuis St. Vincent** (Monday–Friday 12:00–13:30 and 17:00–19:00, Nieuwe Groenmarkt 22).

The friendly **De Buren** offers traditional Dutch food and handlebar mustache fun (such as *draadjesvlees*—beef stew with applesauce; and *oma's kippetje*—grandmother's chicken) to happy locals (daily 17:00–22:00, Brouwersvaart 146, near intersection with Zijlsingel, across the canal from Die Raeckse Hotel and close to House de Kiefte B&B, tel. 023/534-3364).

Eating between Church and Frans Hals Museum
For good food, classy atmosphere, and f30 dinners, try the **Bastiaan** (opens at 18:00, closed Monday, CC:VMA, Lange Veerstraat 8, off Grote Markt, behind the church). Nearby, **La Plume** is a less expensive steak house (open daily at 17:30, CC:VMA, Lange Veerstraat 1). Popular with locals, **Jacobus Pieck** offers a varied menu selection (daily 10:00–22:00, Sundays from 12:00, Warmoesstraat 18, tel. 023/532-6144). For a (f2) cone of old-fashioned local French fries, drop by **Friethuis de Vlaminck** on Warmoesstraat 3 (closed Sunday and Monday).

Dine at the Indonesian **De Lachende Javaan** ("The Laughing Javanese," opens at 17:00, closed Monday, Frankestraat 25, tel. 023/532-8792) or get Indonesian take-out from the **Toko Nina** deli (Koningstraat 48, just off Grote Markt).

For a candlelit dinner of cheese and wine, consider **In't Goede Uur** (opens at 17:30, closed Monday, Korte Houtstraat 1).

For a healthy budget lunch with Haarlem's best view, eat at **La Place**, on the top floor or roof garden of the Vroom Dreesman department store (Monday–Saturday 9:30–18:00, Thursday until 21:00, closed Sunday, on the corner of Grote Houtstraat and Gedempte Oude Gracht).

Picnic-shoppers head to the **DekaMarkt** supermarket (Monday–Saturday 8:30–20:00, closed Sunday, Gedemple Oude Gracht 54, between Vroom Dreesman department store and the post office).

Transportation Connections—Haarlem
By train to: Amsterdam (6/hrly, 15 min, f10.50 same-day return), **Delft** (2/hrly, 38 min), **Hoorn** (4/hrly, 1 hr), **The Hague** (4/hrly, 35 min), **Alkmaar** (2/hrly, 30 min), **Schiphol Airport** (2/hrly, 40 min, f10,

transfer at suburban Amsterdam-Sloterdijk); the direct buses #236 (use a strip card) and #362 (buy ticket at the train station ticket windows) to the airport are faster (2/hrly, 30 min, f6.25); by taxi it's a f70 ride.

Sights—Near Haarlem and Amsterdam

The Netherlands are tiny. The sights listed below are an easy day trip by bus or train from Haarlem or Amsterdam. Match your interest with the village's specialty: Choose from flower auctions, folk museums, cheese markets, delft porcelain, resort beaches, and modern art.

▲▲**Enkhuisen's Zuiderzee Museum**—As far as open-air folk museums go, this one in the salty old town of Enkhuizen is particularly lively, with a "Living on Urk" village populated by people who do a very convincing job of role-playing no-nonsense 1905 Dutch villagers. No one said "Have a nice day" back then. You can eat herring hot out of the old smoker, see barrels and rope made, and enjoy children enjoying the dress-up chest, the old-time game zone, and making sailing ships out of old wooden shoes (f17.50, daily 10:00–17:00 early April–late October, free tours at 14:00, private guide for f80, tel. 0228/351-111). Trains zip from Amsterdam directly to Enkhuisen, where a shuttle boat will take you to the museum, avoiding a pleasant 15-minute walk.

▲**Zaanse Schans**—At this 17th-century Dutch village turned open-air folk museum, you can see and learn about everything Dutch, from cheese-making to wooden-shoe carving. Take an inspiring climb to the top of a whirring windmill (get a group of people together and ask for a tour) and buy a small jar of fresh ground mustard for your next picnic. Located in the town of Zaandijk, this is your easiest one-stop look at traditional Dutch culture and the Netherlands' best collection of windmills (free, daily 8:30–18:00, until 17:00 in winter, parking-f7.50/1 hr, tel. 075/616-8218). Fifteen minutes by train north of Amsterdam: Take the Alkmaar-bound train to Station Koog-Zaandijk, then walk following signs—past a fragrant chocolate factory—for 10 minutes.

▲▲**Aalsmeer Flower Auction**—Get a bird's-eye view of the huge Dutch flower industry. Visitors are welcome to wander on elevated walkways (through what is claimed to be the biggest building on earth), over literally trainloads of fresh-cut flowers. About half of all the flowers exported from Holland are auctioned off here in six huge auditoriums (f7.5, Monday–Friday 7:30–11:00; the auction is pretty dead after 9:30 but the warehouse swarms; gift shop, cafeteria; bus #172 from Amsterdam's station, 2/hrly, 1 hr; from Haarlem, take bus #140, 2/hrly, 1 hr, tel. 0297/393-939). Aalsmeer is close to the airport and a handy last fling before catching a morning weekday flight.

Day Trips from Haarlem and Amsterdam

▲▲▲**Keukenhof**—This is the greatest bulb-flower garden on earth. Each spring 6 million flowers conspire to make even a total garden-hater enjoy them. In 1999 the Keukenhof gardens will celebrate their 50th birthday with a special exposition from August 19 to September 19. This 100-acre park is packed with tour groups daily from about March 25 to May 20 (f17.50, 8:00–19:30, last tickets sold at 18:00; if you bus from Haarlem, transfer at Lisse; tel. 0252/465-555). Go very late in the day for the best light and the fewest groups.

Zandvoort—For a quick and easy look at the windy coastline in a shell-lover's Shangri-La, visit the beach resort of Zandvoort, a breezy 45-minute bike ride or eight minutes by train or car west of Haarlem (from Haarlem, follow signs to Bloemendaal). South of the main beach, beach bathers work on all-around tans.

▲**Hoorn**—This is an elegant, quiet, and typical 17th-century Dutch town north of Amsterdam. Its TI can rent you a bike or give you a walking-tour brochure. Any TI offers the flier describing the "Historic Triangle," an all-day excursion from Amsterdam that connects Hoorn, Medemblik, and Enkhuizen by steam train and boat (f22.75 plus f6.25 for the train back to Haarlem, tel. 0229/214-862).

De Rijp—This fine, sleepy town is worth visiting if you're driving north of Amsterdam.

Volendam, Marken, and Monnikendam—These famous towns are quaint as can be (although Volendam is too touristy).

▲**Delft**—Peaceful as a Vermeer painting (he was born here) and lovely as its porcelain, Delft is a typically Dutch town with a special soul. Enjoy it best by simply wandering around, watching people, munching local syrup-waffles, or daydreaming from the canal bridges. The town bustles during its Saturday antiques market (9:00–17:00). Its colorful Thursday food and flower market (9:00–17:00) attracts many traditional villagers. The TI on the main square has a f3.50 brochure outlining Delft's sights, including a do-it-yourself "Historical Walk through Delft" (Monday–Friday 9:00–18:00, Saturday 9:00–17:30, Sunday 10:00–15:00, tel. 015/212-6100). The town is a museum in itself, but if you need a turnstile, it has an impressive Army Museum (f5, Monday–Saturday 10:00–17:00, Sunday 13:00–17:00). Or you can tour the Royal Porcelain Works to watch the famous 17th-century blue delftware turn from clay into art (f5, Monday–Saturday 9:00–17:00, Sunday 9:30–17:00, tel. 015/256-9214).

▲**Alkmaar**—Holland's cheese capital is especially fun (and touristy) during its weekly cheese market (Friday 10:00–12:00).

▲▲**Edam**—For the ultimate in cuteness and peace, make tiny Edam your home base. It's very sweet but palatable, and 30 minutes by bus from Amsterdam (2/hrly). Don't miss the Edam Museum, a small, quirky house offering a fun peek into a 400-year-old home and a floating cellar (Tuesday–Saturday 10:00–16:00, Sunday 14:00–16:00, on main square). Wednesday is the town's market day (9:00–13:00). In July and August market day includes a traditional cheese market (10:00–12:00).

Consider making Edam your home base. **Hotel De Fortuna,** an eccentric canalside mix of flowers, a cat of leisure, a pet turtle, and duck noises, offers steep stairs and low-ceilinged rooms in several ancient buildings in the old center of Edam (Db-f182, includes breakfast, garden patio, attached restaurant, CC:VMA, Spuistraat 3, 1135 AV Edam, tel. 0299/371-671, fax 0299/371-469). The centrally located **Damhotel** (on a canal around the corner from the TI) has attractive, comfortable rooms with a plush feel (Sb-f80, Db-f120, Tb-f180, includes breakfast, attached restaurant, CC:VMA, Keizersgracht 1, 1135 AZ Edam, tel. 0299/371-766, fax 0299/374-031). The TI (tel. 0299/371-727) has a list of cheaper rooms in private homes. **De Harmonie**, with simple small rooms above a bar, is a last resort (f40 per person, W.C. down the hall, Voorhaven 92, 1135 BT Edam, tel. 0299/371-664). For reasonably-priced Chinese/Indonesian food, **Tai Wah** has take-out (eat in the De Fortuna garden) and indoor seating (Monday–Saturday 13:00–21:45, closed Tuesday, Lingerzijde 62, tel. 0299/371-088).

▲**Rotterdam**—This city, the world's largest port, bounced back after being bombed flat in World War II. See its towering Euromast, take a harbor tour, and stroll its great pedestrian zone. It's an easy train connection to Amsterdam (TI tel. 0900/403-4065, toll call—f1 a minute).

▲▲**The Hague (Den Haag)**—Locals say the money is made in Rotterdam, divided in the Hague, and spent in Amsterdam. The Hague is the Netherlands' seat of government and the home of several engaging museums. The Mauritshuis' delightful, easy-to-tour art collection stars Vermeer and Rembrandt (f12.50, Tuesday–Sunday 11:00–17:00, Korte Vijverberg 8, tel. 070/302-3456). Across the pond, the Torture Museum (Gevangenpoort) shows the medieval mind at its worst (f6, Tuesday–Friday 10:00–16:00, weekends 12:00–16:00, closed Monday, required tours on the hour; confirm with ticket-taker if film and talk will be in English before committing, tel. 070/346-0861). For a look at the 19th century's attempt at virtual reality, tour Panorama Mesdag, a 360-degree painting of the nearby town of Scheveningen in the 1880s, with a 3-D sandy-beach foreground (f6, Monday–Saturday 10:00–17:00, Sunday 12:00–17:00, Zeestraat 65, tel. 070/310-6665). The nearby Peace Palace, a gift from Andrew Carnegie, houses the International Court of Justice (f5, Monday–Friday open only for required guided tours at 10:00, 11:00, 14:00, or 15:00; tram #7 or #8 from the station; tel. 070/302-4137; closes without warning, call ahead or check at TI). Scheveningen, the Dutch Coney Island, is liveliest on sunny summer afternoons (take tram #7); and Madurodam, a mini-Holland amusement park, is a kid-pleaser (f19.50, discounts for kids, daily 9:00–17:00, until 21:00 in June, until 22:00 in July and August, tram #1 or #9, tel. 070/355-3900). The Hague's TI is at the train station (Monday–Saturday 9:00–17:30, later in summer, Sunday 10:00–17:00, tel. 06/3403-5051, f1 a minute).

Utrecht—The Museum von Speelklok tot Pierement has free guided tours, musical clocks, calliopes, and street organs (f9, Tuesday–Saturday 10:00–17:00, Sunday 12:00–17:00, closed Monday).

▲▲**Arnhem's Open-Air Dutch Folk Museum**—An hour east of Amsterdam, Arnhem has a home show in a time tunnel: Holland's first and biggest folk museum. You'll enjoy a huge park of windmills, old farms, traditional crafts in action, and a pleasant education-by-immersion in Dutch culture. The English guidebook (f7.50) explains each historic building (f17, daily 10:00–17:00 April–October, tel. 026/357-6111). The park has several good budget restaurants and covered picnic areas. Its rustic **Pancake House** serves hearty (splittable) Dutch flapjacks.

Trains make the 70-minute trip from Amsterdam to Arnhem twice an hour (likely transfer in Utrecht). At Arnhem station, take bus #3 or #13 (faster, 4/hrly, 15 min) to the Openlucht Museum. By car from Haarlem, skirt Amsterdam to the south on E9, following signs to Utrecht, then take A12 east to Arnhem. Just before Arnhem, take the Arnhem Nord exit (you'll see the white "Openluchtmuseum" sign) and follow the signs to the nearby museum. For the Kröller-Müller Museum, follow the white signs to Hoge Veluwe.

▲▲**Kröller-Müller Museum and Hoge Veluwe National Park**—Also near Arnhem, the Hoge Veluwe National Park is Holland's largest (13,000 acres), and is famous for its Kröller-Müller Museum. This huge and impressive modern-art collection, including 55 paintings by van Gogh, is set deep in the wilderness. The park has lots more to offer, including hundreds of white bikes you're free to use to make your explorations more fun. After paying f8.50 at the park entrance, the museum is "free" (f8.50, Tuesday–Sunday 10:00–17:00, easy parking, tel. 055/378-1441). Pick up more information at the Amsterdam or Arnhem TI (tel. 026/442-6767). Bus #12 connects the Arnhem train station with the Kröller-Müller Museum (March–October). Consider combining a visit to the park and the open-air museum for a great day trip from Amsterdam.

APPENDIX

"La Marseillaise"
There's a movement in France to soften the lyrics of their national anthem. Sing it now . . . before it's too late.

Allons enfants de la Patrie, (Let's go, children of the fatherland,)
Le jour de gloire est arrivé. (The day of glory has arrived.)
Contre nous de la tyrannie (The blood-covered flagpole of tyranny)
L'étendard sanglant est levé, (Is raised against us,)
L'étendard sanglant est levé. (Is raised against us.)
Entendez-vous dans nos campagnes (Do you hear what's happening in our countryside?)
Mugir les féroces soldats? (The ferocious soldiers are groaning)
Qui viennent jusque dans nos bras (They're coming nearly into our grasp)
Egorger nos fils et nos compagnes. (They're slitting the throats of our sons and our women.)
Aux armes citoyens, (Grab your weapons, citizens,)
Formez vos bataillons, (Form your battalions,)
Marchons, marchons, (March on, march on,)
Qu'un sang impur (So that their impure blood)
Abreuve nos sillons. (Will fill our trenches.)

French History in an Escargot Shell
Around the time of Christ, Romans "Latinized" the land of the Gauls. With the fifth-century fall of Rome, the barbarian Franks and Burgundians invaded. From this unique mix of Latin and Celtic cultures evolved today's France.

While France wallowed with the rest of Europe in medieval darkness, it got a head start in its development as a nation-state. In 507, Clovis established Paris as the capital of his Christian, Merovingian dynasty. Clovis and the Franks would eventually become Louis and the French. Charles Martel stopped the spread of Islam by beating the Spanish Moors at the battle of Poitiers. And Charlemagne, the most important of the "Dark Age" Frankish kings, was crowned Holy Roman Emperor in 800 by the pope. Charles the Great presided over the "Carolingian Renaissance" and effectively ruled a vast-for-the-time empire.

The treaty, which in 843 divided Charlemagne's empire among his grandsons, marks what could be considered the birth of Europe. For the first time, a treaty was signed in vernacular languages (French and German) rather than in Latin. While this split established a Franco/Germanic divide, it also heralded an age of fragmentation. While petty princes took the reigns, the Frankish king ruled only Île-de-France, a small island of land around Paris.

Vikings, or Norsemen, settled in what became Normandy. Later, in 1066, these "Normans" invaded England. The Norman king, William the Conqueror, consolidated his English domain, accelerating the formation of modern England. But his rule also muddied the political waters between England and France, kicking off a centuries-long struggle between the two nations.

In the 12th century, Eleanor of Aquitaine (a separate country in southwest France) married Louis VII, king of France, bringing Aquitaine under French rule. They divorced and she married Henry of Normandy, soon-to-be Henry II of England. This marital union gave England control of a huge swath of land from the English Channel to the Pyrénées. For 300 years, France and England would struggle over control of Aquitaine. Any enemy of the French king would find a natural ally in the English king.

In 1328, a French king (Charles IV) died without a son. The English king was his nephew, and naturally was interested in the throne. The French resisted. This pitted France, the biggest and richest country in Europe, against England, with the biggest army. They fought from 1337 to 1453, in what was modestly called the Hundred Years' War.

Regional powers from within France sided with England. Burgundy actually took Paris, captured the royal family, and recognized the English king as heir to the French thrown. England controlled France from the Loire north, and things looked bleak for the French king.

Enter Joan of Arc, a 16-year-old peasant girl driven by religious voices. France's national heroine left home to support the dauphin Charles VII (boy prince, heir to the throne but too young to rule). Joan rallied the French, inspiring them to ultimately throw out the English. In 1430, Joan was captured by the Burgundians, who sold her to the English, who convicted her of heresy and burned her at the stake in Rouen. But the inspiration of Jeanne d'Arc lived on and by 1453, English holdings on the Continent had dwindled to the port of Calais.

By 1500, a strong centralized France had emerged with borders close to today's borders. Her kings (from the Renaissance François I, through the Henrys and all those Louises) were model divine monarchs, setting the standards for absolute rule in Europe.

Of course these excesses, coupled with the modern thinking of the Enlightenment—whose leaders were the French *philosophes*—led to the French Revolution (1789) and the end of the Old Regime and its notion that some are born to rule while others are born to be ruled.

But the excesses of the Revolution led to the rise of Napoleon, who ruled the French empire as a dictator until his excesses ushered him into a south Atlantic exile and a compromise king returned. The modern French king was himself ruled by a constitution. Rather than leotards and powdered wigs, he went to work in a suit with a briefcase.

The 20th century spelled the end of France's reign as a military and political superpower. Devastating wars with Germany in 1870, 1914, and 1940, and the loss of her colonial holdings have left France with not quite enough land, people, or production to be a top player on a global scale.

Still, France is the cultural capital of Europe and a leader in the push to integrate Europe into one unified economic power. When that happens, Paris will once again emerge as a superpower capital.

Camping

Here are some good campgrounds for the French destinations recommended in this book. All provide free hot showers and clean bathroom facilities, and average 60F for two per night. Campers should pack sleeping bags, tent, tarp, sleeping pads, thongs for the showers, a camping *gaz* stove (no Coleman fuel here), a light kettle, plastic plates, and silverware. Consider buying cheap fold-up camping chairs (40F), available at big French *supermarchés*.

Paris: Avoid camping here. It's too hard to reach the city center. Still, if you must, try Camp du Bois du Boulogne, allée du Bord de l'Eau in the Bois (woods) de Boulogne (tel. 01 45 24 30 00). It's the only campground "in" Paris, but it is not strong on security and is generally crowded. Open all year and fully equipped.

Rouen: Municipal Camping. Ten minutes by car or bus from Rouen, in Deauville, on the N-15 toward Le Havre (tel. 02 35 74 07 59). Nice but small area, immaculate bathrooms.

Honfleur: Camping du Phare. A scruffy facility with a great location—a few minutes' stroll from the heart of Honfleur. It's just outside the city as you head to Trouville. Open April–October 15. A far nicer facility, but a five-minute drive to town, is Camping Domaine Catinière, in Fiquefleur (tel. 02 32 57 63 51, open April–September).

Bayeux: Municipal Camping. Very friendly, small sites, but a terrific facility and a 10-minute walk to the city center (boulevard Eindhoven, tel. 02 31 92 08 43, open March–October 31).

D-Day Beaches: You'll see small campgrounds everywhere. The area between Arromanches and the Pointe du Hoc is best.

Mont St. Michel: Camping du Mont St. Michel (Pb. 8/50116 Le Mont St. Michel, tel. 02 33 60 09 33, check in at the Motel Vert). It's 1.5 miles from Le Mont and 50 yards from great views of it. Otherwise, nothing to write home about. Open year-round.

Amboise: Camping de L'Île d'Or. On the island across the bridge from the city center, you can't miss it. Scenic location and easy walk into Amboise. Mini-golf and pool (tel. 02 47 57 23 37).

Sarlat: Camping Les Perieres. A 15-minute walk downhill to Sarlat. This resort sports a pool, tennis courts, store, café, and lovely setting. Call ahead in the summer or forget it (Rd. 47, tel. 05 53 59 05 84, open April–September 30).

Albi: Parc de Caussels. One mile east of town. Crowded but friendly, with a huge supermarket across the street (tel. 05 63 60 37 06, open April–November).

Carcassonne: Camping de la Cité. Brand-new site and facility; 15-minute walk to la Cité. Inquire at TI for information or follow signs from the *ville basse*, the newer part of the city (tel. 04 68 25 11 77).

Arles: Camping City. The best and most convenient of several in the area. Fifteen-minute walk into the city center; a new pool, poolside café, and hairy umbrellas (on the road to Crau, tel. 04 90 93 08 86, open March–October 31).

Avignon: Camping Bagatelle. Right across the Pont (bridge) Daladier from Avignon. Great city views, popular, but lots of sites and a great café (tel. 04 90 86 30 39).

Cagnes-sur-Mer (Nice): Camping Panoramer. Meet the friendly owners and admire the best Riviera view around. It's a long walk to the Nice-bound bus stop, but buses run often (open Easter–September 20, chemin des Gros Buaux, follow chemin du Val Fleuri from the N-7 in Cagnes-sur-Mer, call ahead in summer, tel. 04 93 31 16 15).

Antibes: Camps are everywhere; you'll see signs. There's easy access to Nice via bus. Be sure to arrive by noon in the summer.

Annecy: Campgrounds line each side of the lake.

Chamonix: Camping les Rosières. Comfortable site, wonderful views, and a beautiful 20-minute walk to town—follow the stream. Funky trailers for rent one mile from Chamonix on route du Praz (open all year, tel. 04 50 53 10 42).

Beaune: Camping les Cent Vignes. This is my favorite campground in France, a 15-minute walk to the city center, fully equipped (great restaurant), individual sites, and campers from all over Europe (open March 15–October 31, 10 rue Dubois, follow signs toward Dijon and watch for camping signs, tel. 03 80 22 03 91).

Dijon: Camping Municipal du Lac. Streamside location and a short waddle to the lake. Fine facilities (open April–November 15, one mile from Dijon, follow signs from the station in the direction of Paris, tel. 03 80 43 54 72).

Colmar: Camping intercommunal de l'Île. A few miles from the city center, but a nice riverfront location and good facilities (Plage de L'Île, follow the N-415 toward Fribourg, open February–November 30, tel. 03 89 41 15 94).

Let's Talk Telephones

Dialing Direct

Calling between Countries: Dial the international access code (of the country you're calling from), the country code (of the country you're calling), the area code (if it starts with zero, drop the zero), and then the local number. See the chart below for international access codes and country codes.

    Calling Long Distance within a Country: First dial the area code (including its zero), then the local number.

    Europe's Exceptions: Some countries do not use area codes, such as France, Italy, Spain, Norway, and Denmark. To make an international call to these countries, dial the international access code (usually 00), the country code, then the local number in its entirety. Okay, so there's one exception: for France, drop the initial zero of the local number. To make long-distance calls within any of these countries simply dial the local number. (For example, within France, dial the 10-digit telephone number direct throughout the country.)

International Access Codes

When dialing direct, first dial the international access code of the country you're calling from. For most countries, it's "00." Only the exceptions are noted below.

Estonia—800	Finland—990	Latvia—800
Lithuania—810	Russia—810	Spain—07
Sweden—009	U.S.A./Canada—011	

Country Codes

After you've dialed the international access code, then dial the code of the country you're calling.

Austria—43	Belgium—32	Britain—44
Czech Republic—420	Denmark—45	Estonia—372
Finland—358	France—33	Germany—49
Greece—30	Ireland—353	Italy—39
Latvia—371	Lithuania—370	Netherlands—31
Norway—47	Portugal—351	Russia—7
Spain—34	Sweden—46	Switzerland—41
U.S.A./Canada—1		

Calling Card Operators

	AT&T	MCI	Sprint
France	0800 99 00 11	0800 99 00 19	0800 99 00 87
Belgium	0800-100-10	0800-100-12	0800-100-14
Netherlands	0800-022-9111	0800-022-9122	0800-022-9119

Telephone Directory

Useful Parisian Phone Numbers and Addresses
Emergency: Dial 17 for police, otherwise 01 42 60 33 22
Paris & France Directory Assistance (some English spoken): 12
English tourist information recording: 01 47 20 88 98
American Church: 01 47 05 07 99
American Express: 11 rue Scribe, Mo: Opéra, 01 47 70 77 07
American Hospital: 01 46 41 25 25
American Pharmacy: 01 47 42 49 40
Office of American Services (lost passports, etc.): 01 42 96 12 02
U.S. Embassy: 01 43 12 22 22
Sunday Banks: 115 and 154 avenue des Champs-Élysées

Airline Offices in Paris
Roissy-Charles de Gaulle Airport Information: 01 48 62 22 80
Orly Airport Information: 01 48 84 32 10 or 01 49 75 52 52
Air Canada: 01 44 50 20 20
Air France: 01 43 35 61 61 or 01 44 08 22 22
American: 01 42 89 05 22
British Air: 01 47 78 14 14
British Midland: 01 48 62 55 65
Continental: 01 42 99 09 09
Delta: 01 47 68 92 92
Iberia: 01 40 47 80 90
KLM: 01 44 56 18 18
Lufthansa: 01 42 65 37 35
Northwest: 01 42 66 90 00
Olympic: 01 42 65 92 42
SAS: 01 53 43 25 25
TWA: 01 49 19 20 00
United: 01 48 97 82 82

Numbers and Stumblers
•Europeans write a few of their numbers differently than we do.
1 = 1 , 4 = 4 , 7 = 7. Learn the difference or miss your train.
•In Europe, dates appear as day/month/year, so Christmas is
25/12/99.
•Commas are decimal points and decimals commas. A dollar and a
half is 1,50 and there are 5.280 feet in a mile.
•When pointing, use your whole hand, palm downward.
•When counting with fingers, start with your thumb. If you hold
up your first finger to request one item, you'll probably get two.
•What we Americans call the second floor of a building is the first
floor in Europe.
•Europeans keep the left "lane" open for passing on escalators and
moving sidewalks. Keep to the right.

Climate Chart

First line, average daily low; second line, average daily high; third line, days of no rain.

Paris

J	F	M	A	M	J	J	A	S	O	N	D
34°	34°	39°	43°	49°	55°	58°	58°	53°	46°	40°	36°
43°	45°	54°	60°	68°	73°	76°	75°	70°	60°	50°	44°
16	15	16	16	18	19	19	19	19	17	15	14

Nice

J	F	M	A	M	J	J	A	S	O	N	D
40°	41°	45°	49°	56°	62°	66°	66°	62°	55°	48°	43°
56°	56°	59°	64°	69°	76°	81°	81°	77°	70°	62°	58°
23	20	23	23	23	25	29	26	24	22	23	23

Amsterdam

J	F	M	A	M	J	J	A	S	O	N	D
31°	31°	34°	40°	46°	51°	55°	55°	50°	44°	38°	33°
40°	42°	49°	56°	64°	70°	72°	71°	67°	57°	48°	42°
8	11	14	14	16	16	13	12	11	10	9	9

The French Rail System

Basic French Survival Phrases

English	French	Pronunciation
Hello (good day).	**Bonjour.**	bohn-zhoor
Do you speak English?	**Parlez-vous anglais?**	par-lay-voo ahn-glay
Yes. / No.	**Oui. / Non.**	wee / nohn
I'm sorry.	**Désolé.**	day-zoh-lay
Please.	**S'il vous plaît.**	see voo play
Thank you.	**Merci.**	mehr-see
Goodbye.	**Au revoir.**	oh vwahr
Where is...?	**Où est...?**	oo ay
...a hotel	**...un hôtel**	uhn oh-tehl
...a youth hostel	**...une auberge de jeunesse**	ewn oh-behrzh duh zhuh-nehs
...a restaurant	**...un restaurant**	uhn rehs-toh-rahn
...a grocery store	**...une épicerie**	ewn ay-pee-suh-ree
...the train station	**...la gare**	lah gar
...the tourist info office	**...l'office du tourisme**	loh-fees dew too-reez-muh
Where are the toilets?	**Où sont les toilettes?**	oo sohn lay twah-leht
men / women	**hommes / dames**	ohm / dahm
How much is it?	**Combien?**	kohn-bee-an
Cheaper.	**Moins cher.**	mwan shehr
Included?	**Inclus?**	an-klew
Do you have...?	**Avez-vous...?**	ah-vay-voo
I would like...	**Je voudrais...**	zhuh voo-dray
...a ticket.	**...un billet.**	uhn bee-yay
...a room.	**...une chambre.**	ewn shahn-bruh
...the bill.	**...l'addition.**	lah-dee-see-ohn
one	**un**	uhn
two	**deux**	duh
three	**trois**	twah
four	**quatre**	kah-truh
five	**cinq**	sank
six	**six**	sees
seven	**sept**	seht
eight	**huit**	weet
nine	**neuf**	nuhf
ten	**dix**	dees
At what time?	**À quelle heure?**	ah kehl ur
Just a moment.	**Un moment.**	uhn moh-mahn
Now.	**Maintenant.**	man-tuh-nahn
today / tomorrow	**aujourd'hui / demain**	oh-zhoor-dwee / duh-man

For more user-friendly French phrases, check out *Rick Steves' French Phrase Book and Dictionary* or *Rick Steves' French, Italian & German Phrase Book and Dictionary.*

Road Scholar Feedback for
FRANCE, BELGIUM & THE NETHERLANDS 1999

We're all in the same travelers' school of hard knocks. Your feedback helps us improve this guidebook for future travelers. Please fill this out (attach more info or any tips/favorite discoveries if you like) and send it to us. As thanks for your help, we'll send you our quarterly travel newsletter free for one year. Thanks! **Rick**

Of the recommended accommodations/restaurants used, which was:

Best _____

    Why? _____

Worst _____

    Why? _____

Of the sights/experiences/destinations recommended by this book, which was:

Most overrated _____

    Why? _____

Most underrated _____

    Why? _____

Best ways to improve this book:

_____

I'd like a free newsletter subscription:

___ Yes   ___ No   ___ Already on list

_____

Name

_____

Address

_____

City, State, Zip

_____

E-mail Address

Please send to: ETBD, Box 2009, Edmonds, WA 98020

Jubilee 2000—Let's Celebrate the Millennium by Forgiving Third World Debt

Let's ring in the millennium by convincing our government to forgive the debt owed to us by the world's poorest countries. Imagine spending over half your income on interest payments alone. You and I are creditors and poor countries owe us more than they can pay.

Jubilee 2000 is a worldwide movement of concerned people and groups—religious and secular—working to cancel the international debts of the poorest countries by the year 2000.

Debt ruins people: In the poorest countries, money needed for health care, education, and other vital services is diverted to interest payments.

Mozambique, with a per capita income of $90 and life expectancy of 40, spends over half its national income on interest. This poverty brings social unrest, civil war, and often costly humanitarian intervention by the U.S.A. To chase export dollars, desperate countries ruin their environment. As deserts grow and rain forests shrink, the world suffers. Of course, the real suffering is among local people born long after some dictator borrowed (and squandered) that money. As interest is paid, entire populations go hungry.

Who owes what and why? Mozambique is one of 41 countries defined by the World Bank as "Heavily Indebted Poor Countries." In total, they owe $200 billion. Because these debts are unlikely to be paid, their market value is only a tenth of the face value (about $20 billion). The U.S.A.'s share is under $2 billion.

How can debt be canceled? This debt is owed mostly to the U.S.A., Japan, Germany, Britain, and France either directly or through the World Bank. We can forgive the debt owed directly to us and pay the market value (usually 10 percent) of the debts owed to the World Bank. We have the resources. (Norway, another wealthy creditor nation, just unilaterally forgave its Third World debt.) All America needs is the political will . . . people power.

While many of these poor nations are now democratic, corruption is still a concern. A key to Jubilee 2000 is making certain that debt relief reduces poverty in a way that benefits ordinary people: women, farmers, children, and so on.

Let's celebrate the new millennium by giving poor countries a break. For the sake of peace, fragile young democracies, the environment, and countless real people, forgiving this debt is the right thing for us in the rich world to do.

Tell Washington, DC: If our government knows this is what we want, it can happen. Learn more, write letters, lobby legislators, or even start a local Jubilee 2000 campaign. For details, contact Jubilee 2000 (tel. 202/783-3566, www.j2000usa.org). For information on lobbying Congress on J2000, contact Bread for the World (tel. 800/82-BREAD, www.bread.org).

Faxing Your Hotel Reservation

Most hotel managers know basic "hotel English." Faxing is the preferred method for reserving a room. It's more accurate and cheaper than telephoning and much faster than writing a letter. Use this handy form for your fax. Photocopy and fax away.

One-Page Fax

To: _____ @ _____
     hotel   *fax*

From: _____ @ _____
     name   *fax*

Today's date: ____ / ____ / ____
     day *month* *year*

Dear Hotel _____,

Please make this reservation for me:

Name: _____

Total # of people: _____ # of rooms: _____ # of nights: _____

Arriving: ____ / ____ / ____ My time of arrival (24-hr clock): _____
   day *month* *year* (I will telephone if I will be late)

Departing: ____ / ____ / ____
    day *month* *year*

Room(s): Single___ Double___ Twin___ Triple___ Quad___

With: Toilet___ Shower___ Bath___ Sink only___

Special needs: View___ Quiet___ Cheapest Room___

Credit card: Visa___ MasterCard___ American Express___

Card #: _____ _____

Name on card: _____

Expiration Date:_____

You may charge me for the first night as a deposit. Please fax or mail me confirmation of my reservation, along with the type of room reserved, the price, and whether the price includes breakfast. Thank you.

_____
Signature

_____
Name

_____
Address

_____
City   *State*   *Zip Code* *Country*

_____
E-mail Address

INDEX

A new book from Rick!

1978

1998

Rick Steves' Postcards from Europe
25 Years of Travel Tales from America's Favorite Guidebook Writer

Travel guru Rick Steves has been exploring Europe through the Back Door for 25 years, sharing his tricks and discoveries in guidebooks and on TV. Now, in *Rick Steves' Postcards from Europe*, Rick shares his favorite stories and his off-beat European friends.

Postcards takes you on the fantasy trip of a lifetime. While goofy and inspirational, it's informative, too—giving you a close-up look at contemporary Europeans.

You'll meet Marie-Alice, the Parisian restaurateur who sniffs a whiff of moldy cheese and says, "It smells like zee feet of angels." In an Alpine village, meet Olle, the schoolteacher who lets Rick pet his edelweiss, and Walter, the innkeeper who schemes with Rick to create a fake Swiss tradition. In Italy, cruise with Piero through his "alternative Venice" and learn why all Venetian men are mama's boys.

Postcards also tracks Rick's passion for wandering—from his first "Europe-through-the-gutter" trips, through his rocky early tours, to his career as a travel writer and host of a public television series.

These 272 pages of travel tales are told in that funny, down-to-earth style that makes Rick his Mom's favorite guidebook writer.